HISTORIC ANNALS OF THE
NATIONAL ACADEMY OF DESIGN

Library of American Art

HISTORIC ANNALS

of the

NATIONAL ACADEMY OF DESIGN

By Thomas S. Cummings

Kennedy Galleries, Inc. • *Da Capo Press*
New York • *1969*

This edition of *Historic Annals of the National Academy of Design* is an unabridged republication of the first edition published in Philadelphia in 1865.

Library of Congress Catalog Card Number 71-87503

Published by
Kennedy Galleries, Inc.
20 East 56th Street, New York, N.Y. 10022
and
Da Capo Press
A Division of Plenum Publishing Corporation
227 West 17th Street, New York, N.Y. 10011

Manufactured in the United States of America

HISTORIC ANNALS

OF THE

National Academy of Design

NEW-YORK DRAWING ASSOCIATION, ETC.,

WITH

OCCASIONAL DOTTINGS BY THE WAY-SIDE,

FROM

1825

TO THE PRESENT TIME.

BY

THOS. S. CUMMINGS, N. A.,

PROFESSOR OF THE ARTS OF DESIGN IN THE NEW YORK UNIVERSITY,

NATIONAL ACADEMY OF DESIGN, ETC.

PHILADELPHIA:

GEORGE W. CHILDS, PUBLISHER,

628 & 630 CHESTNUT STREET.

1865.

SACKETT & COBB, PRINTERS.

PREFACE.

————•◆•————

THE NATIONAL ACADEMY OF THE ARTS OF DESIGN is the
FIRST, and, as is believed, the ONLY, Art Academy on the
American Continent governed, as it was originally insti-
tuted, by professional Artists alone.

Its history, which well-nigh spans the half of a century,
necessarily forms a large portion of the Art history of New-
York; its preservation is therefore desirable.

Of the twenty-five primitive founders of the Institution,
three only remain, (personal depositaries of its early history); and of these, the writer has generally been looked
upon as the one most likely to be induced to become its
recorder.

The task has been undertaken partly from the fact above
stated—more so at the solicitations of the late CHARLES M.
LEUPP, JOHN W. FRANCIS, and F. W. EDMONDS, and other
old and indulgent personal friends—nevertheless, gentlemen whose sincerity could not be doubted—and against
whose wishes there was no desire to offer opposition.

The writer had no wish to appear as "an author." There has been, therefore, no endeavor to make "a book," but simply to leave a useful record. Nor was it supposed that such a record would be of very general interest; though of no less value to the profession.

If more is collated than is of present interest, or important to future and more general chroniclers of the rise and progress of Art, the excess is easily rejected—less might prove a serious inconvenience, perhaps an irremediable loss.

Such as it is, the work is given to the public, as requested. If compliance with that request prove an error, the fault is more with the advisers than the advised.

In conclusion, the author trusts to the indulgence of the critical world and public towards the work of one who professes indeed to be an Artist—but not a writer

THOS. S. CUMMINGS.

HISTORIC ANNALS

OF THE

NATIONAL ACADEMY OF DESIGN.

N the 19th day of January, 1826, was formed in the City of New-York, the NATIONAL ACADEMY OF DESIGN, the first institution in this city, and indeed in the country, established by, and under the exclusive control and management of, the professional Artists, in whom alone it was contended could Art, and its general dissemination, be properly placed.

To give the reader a knowledge of the causes that led to its formation, it will be necessary to notice an Art Institution that preceded it, the only one of which New-York City could boast prior to the establishment of the National Academy of Design.

In 1802 it was proposed to found an institution for the promotion of Art, under the title of the "New-York Academy of Fine Arts," and on the third of December of that year it was consummated by the election of a President and six Directors, Secretary and Treasurer.

It was resolved to form By-Laws, and to apply to the Legislature for an Act of Incorporation, under the title of the "New-York Academy of the Fine Arts." The shareholders to be five hundred in number, and the amount of subscription $100, payable by installments.

The Charter was not obtained until February 12th, 1808. The words "New-York" were exchanged for "American," and the word "Fine" was omitted. "We had then," says

Dunlap, "gentlemen of every profession, but that of an artist, constituted by law an Academy of Arts."

By the Charter, the income of this corporation was limited to 5,000 dollars per annum, the stockholders in number to one thousand, and the shares to 25 dollars each.

The first officers after the obtaining of the Charter were: Robert R. Livingston, President; Jno. Trumbull, Vice-President; De Witt Clinton, David Hosack, John R. Murray, William Cutting, and Charles Wilkes, Directors.

As Dunlap remarks, "there was now *one* artist in the direction."

Shortly before the obtaining of the Charter, "Robert R. Livingston, Esq., then Ambassador to France, purchased by order of these gentlemen, and sent to New-York, a number of casts from the antique."

"When these casts arrived in New York, a building on the east side of Greenwich, near Morris Street, which had been erected for a circus or riding-school, was hired, and the statuary opened for public exhibition."

This was probably in 1803, for on the 1st of February, 1804, the annual admission ticket was fixed at $5.

It attracted but little attention; and the funds of the Society (which had been furnished by Mr. John R. Murray) suffering, the casts were packed and stored. After the Charter was granted, the upper part of a building on Broadway, once intended as a house for the President of the United States, but then occupied as the Custom-House, was loaned to the Academy, and the casts removed thereto. Whatever use was made of them, it appears to have been unsuccessful, for they were again stored.

The collection was removed from the Custom-House, and in consequence of inability to procure any suitable place for their display, were carefully deposited in the store of Captain Farquhar, in Vesey Street; and they remained in this obscurity until they were removed to the rooms on the Park.

For the introduction of the above-mentioned casts, probably the first introduced, art is greatly indebted to these gentlemen; and for this, and their other efforts in the same sphere, they should, and it is hoped they will, receive the artists' lasting and grateful remembrance.

This Institution lay dormant for many years; even its existence was almost forgotten. "In the year 1816, De Witt Clinton, then its President, his friend Dr. Hosack, Cadwallader D. Colden, John R. Murray, Charles Wilkes, and William Cutting, made an effort to revive the Institution." "The time was in some respects propitious, and by the liberality of Dr. Hosack, and the influence of De Witt Clinton, the object was to a certain extent accomplished."

"Fortunately, a long building facing on Chambers Street,* which had been occupied as an alms-house, was at that time empty." Application was made to the Corporation, and the place was appropriated, in part, to the American Academy of the Fine Arts, and money was borrowed to fit up the granted portion of the building.

"Galleries for pictures and statuary were made ready. The casts were removed, repaired, and put up. Preparations were made for an EXHIBITION, in order to raise funds to repay the loan, and, as was hoped, to re-establish the Institution."

"De Witt Clinton having used his influence to give an impulse to the body, proposed that Mr. Trumbull should succeed him in office, and declared his determination to resign it."

In the Autumn of 1816 (October 25th) the first Exhibition of the revived American Academy of the Fine Arts was opened. "The receipts were far beyond expectation, and the Directors began to make expenditures as if they had opened a never-failing mine. On the 18th December, 1816, a revised code of By-Laws was adopted, and it was provided that the present Board of Directors should elect from the 'stockholders' a number, not exceeding twenty Academicians, artists by profession. That after the election in January the 7th, 1817, twenty Associates shall be elected, artists by profession. That there shall not be more than THREE Academicians in the Board of FIVE Directors." The duties of the officers were pointed out. The section of the law relative to EXHIBITORS, which says, "All artists of DISTINGUISHED merit shall be 'PERMITTED' to exhibit their works," while "Amateurs shall be INVITED to expose in the gallery of the Academy any of their performances," proved highly offensive to the profession.

In 1817 the laws were again altered, and it was enacted that eleven Directors, instead of five, should govern the Academy, but no increase was made in the proportion of the professional artists in this more numerous Board of government. The profession was in the minority.

October 23, 1816, Governor Clinton delivered an address, and resigned.

This was probably the first address delivered before any Academy of Arts in the United States. It was delivered before the citizens of the first city in the first State of the

* On the site now occupied by the New City Hall.

8 HISTORIC ANNALS OF THE

Union, and it will not be objected to, that it should be said it was by the *first* man in the State.

It is an historical record, and deserves a high place. It will doubtless be read with as much pleasure by the reader as it has been by the writer. The work is out of print, and extremely rare; and for months the writer searched for it in vain. Kind friendship brought forth at last what other means could not—" good old Dr. Francis " —now no more—hearing of the writer's efforts, searched his library, and was successful in finding it, and generously loaned it for introduction.

GENTLEMEN OF THE AMERICAN ACADEMY OF THE ARTS :

I have complied with your request to open the Academy on this interesting occasion, with great pleasure, but not without unaffected diffidence.

You must be sensible that this Institution has struggled against a succession of serious difficulties from the origin to the present time : that at different periods it has indeed cheered us with a glimmering light; but, at most times, it has appeared like an expiring taper.

The causes are various : the absence of vigorous and systematic exertion— the want of funds—of suitable apartments—of public exhibitions—and of a complete co-operation with our artists, and a consequent indisposition in the public to countenance it. Under all these embarrassments, and when it was found almost impracticable to obtain even a meeting of the Directors, I did not consider it necessary to attend to their request, to pronounce an eulogium on our late President, until a more favorable condition should enable us to execute it in a manner the most respectful to the deceased, and the most creditable to the Academy. That auspicious period has now arrived. The liberality of our municipality has furnished us with spacious apartments; and the public spirit and taste of a few of our associates have prepared them for our reception. The collections of the Academy have been drawn from their obscure receptacles to adorn that edifice—and the rich and various contributions of genius will, it is hoped, give elevation to this city, and reflect honor on our country.

It is a subject of deep regret that the correcting interposition of reason is necessary to remove the strong prejudices which exist against this Institution : for it is believed by many that the state of society, and the form of our Government, are unfriendly to the encouragement of the Fine Arts ; and that they ought to be neglected or overlooked, until more important establishments are endowed by private and public liberality, and until the higher departments of human knowledge are improved to the utmost extent. If this subject were presented for consideration as a controversy of preference between the Fine Arts and the Sciences, or between the Polite and the Mechanic Arts, there would be no room for hesitation. The useful must always take precedence of the agreeable—the accommodations must always be preferred to the luxuries of life : the investigations of science, and the acquisitions of learning, must ever take the highest rank in intellectual estimation, but in this case there is fortunately no collision. The physical, the moral, the intellectual, and the political appearances of the world exhibit an extraordinary state of things. We have seen, within a few years, society torn from its foundations, and governments sanctioned by time, and fortified by prejudice, prostrated and hurled into ruin. We have seen the world in arms, and on a sudden, the olive-branch of peace extended to mankind. We are witnessing the silent and rapid progress of a great moral revolution, by the extension of the blessings of education and the lights of religion. We have beheld some of the most destructive diseases disarmed of their fury. We have seen endless sidereal worlds, which were hitherto impervious to human vision, fully opened to our contemplation. The sciences which relate to inorganic matter and to organized bodies have been cultivated with wonderful ardor: the depths of mathematical and physical knowledge have been sounded, and the most intricate recesses of the human mind have been explored; and yet, in the midst of all this intellectual activity—of this science of elevation—of these moral improvements, and political mutations, ample room has been found for the cultivation and encouragement of the Fine Arts. Genius has been cherished; taste has exercised its high endowments; the world has been explored for specimens of Art, and the costly and magnificent contributions of the present age have triumphed over all the enterprises of former times. It is impossible to restrain the operations of the human mind within the severe boundaries of science. The direction which nature gives must be pursued; and as in the economy of society it is essential that a division of labor should exist in the mechanic arts, so is it requisite in the arrangement of the intellectual world, that different minds should be impelled to different pursuits, in order that every science, and every art depending for its success upon mental exertion, should attain the greatest perfection. Hence it is that some will devote themselves to works of imagination, and others to the exercise of the reasoning power—some to the polite arts, and others to the abstract sciences.

In the progress of a civilized and enlightened community, all the professions, whether liberal or mechanical—whether depending upon the labor of the mind or the hands, the exercise of the fancy or the judgment, must be filled up; and it is the duty of a patriotic Government to encourage all, by dispensing its beneficence like the dew of heaven: preferring, however, whenever preference becomes necessary, such as are most conducive to general and permanent prosperity.

And indeed when we consider the origin, the history, and the uses of the Fine Arts, we must be persuaded that they ought to receive the encouraging smiles of public beneficence. They occupy an extensive field; they administer to the enjoyments and accommodations of mankind; they demand great mental labor, and produce high mental pleasure; and they mark with an unerring hand the boundary between barbarism and refinement.

Sculpture, Painting, Engraving, Architecture, Gardening, Music, and Poetry, compose the Fine Arts. At the earliest dawn of civilization they attracted the attention of the human race. The Sacred Scriptures inform us of the high estimation in which they were held. The institutions of Moses and the edifices of Solomon demonstrate great proficiency—and the garden of Alcinous and the shield of Achilles, as described by Homer, show that the Arts must have flourished before the composition of his immortal work. The history of Attica proclaims the high regard in which they were held by the ancient Grecians, and at the same time exhibits the most elevated and most degrading views of human nature. The whole territory covered but about 150,000 acres of land, and its greatest population did not exceed 300,000 souls. Athens has been described as the Metropolis of Learning, the School of Arts, and the centre of taste and Genius.*

Under all circumstances, and in all conditions, whether blessed with a free government, or oppressed by tyranny—whether overrun by the Persian, the Macedonian, the Roman, the Goth, or the Turk—whether enlightened by the effulgence of science, or bewildered in the night of ignorance, this little spot has attracted the attention, and has commanded the admiration of mankind for more than three thousand years. The Acropolis is perhaps the most interesting place on the globe. In the School of Phidias, and under the administration of Pericles, it was replenished with pictures, statues, pieces of sculpture, and the most finished models of architecture. In the time of Pliny, 3,000 statues remained; after sustaining the depredations of Roman conquerors, the ravages of barbarian invaders, and the dilapidations of Turkish tyrants, it still con'-ained the most precious monuments of Art, and the most noble objects

* Chandler's Travels.

of curiosity. It has always engrossed the attention of enlightened travelers; drawings, prints, and descriptions of its riches, have been given from time to time to an admiring world; and the most invaluable specimens of sublime skill have been transported to adorn the collections of taste and munificence. We thus see the immortal honor which a small Republic has acquired by cultivation of the Arts; and we also perceive the degrading effects of a bad Government upon its ill-fated inhabitants.

They still retain the form, the beauty, and the native wit of their ancestors, but they are covered with the gloom of ignorance: and a late traveler says, that the "state of the Arts in Greece is, as might be expected, most deplorable—it would be difficult to find an architect, a sculptor, or painter equal to the common workmen in the towns of Christendom."*

The ancient Grecians, highly favored by the Almighty with a benignant clime and a fertile soil; blessed with the choicest gifts of intellect and the freest institutions of government, were at the same time possessed of a generous thirst for praise, and a noble spirit of emulation, that carried to perfection all the works of art, and all the productions of genius. When the father of profane history read his immortal work to the men of Greece, assembled at the Olympian games, what more sublime spectacle could be exhibited of human nature?

The greatest genius submitting the greatest effort of the human mind to the judgment of the most enlightened people. And when even the herb women of Athens could criticise the phraseology of Demosthenese, and the meanest artisan could pronounce judgment on the works of Apelles and Phidias, what might not be expected from the well-directed efforts of that wonderful nation?

An enthusiasm, unequaled in its intensity, and unparalleled in its effects, pervaded Greece in favor of the arts and sciences, and sometimes it even arrested the hand of desolation, and averted the horrors of war. A beautiful story is told in the Attic Nights of Aulus Gellius, illustrative of the dominion of this noble spirit, which puts at a distance the most chivalric exhibitions of modern times.

Demetrius, the celebrated commander, attacked the Island of Rhodes, and laid siege to the principal and richest towns in it. That general had obtained the surname of Poliorcetes, for the skill which he manifested, and the machines he employed in the conduct of his sieges. In the course of his attack, he was preparing to destroy and consume, by fire, some public buildings, without the walls of the town, which were protected only by a slight guard. These buildings contained the famous picture of Ialysus, from the hand of that illustrious painter, Protogenes. Enraged against the Rhodians, he envied them the beauty and the excellence of this work; but they sent ambassadors to him with this message, "What is the reason that, setting fire to the buildings, you would destroy this picture? If you conquer us, you will possess the whole town, and by right of victory, the picture, unhurt, will be yours; but if you are unable to subdue us, we desire you to consider whether it is not dishonorable, because you cannot conquer the Rhodians, to make war upon the deceased Protogenes."

Having heard this message from the ambassadors, relinquishing the siege, he spared at once the picture and the city.

Plutarch has indeed represented this transaction in a different light, but highly creditable to Demetrius and the art.

It is also related of this celebrated picture, that Protogenes was seven years in finishing it; that he gave it four coats of colors, in order that, when one was effaced by time, another might supply its place; that when he had long labored in vain to paint the foam of a dog, he happily hit it off, by throwing the brush in anger at the dog's mouth, and that when Apelles first saw this production, he was so much astonished that he could not speak. It was conveyed to Rome by Cassius, and placed in the Temple of Peace, where it remained until the time of Commodus, when, together with the temple, it was consumed by fire.

* Hobhouse.

In course of time, the seat of the fine arts was transferred from Athens to the Eternal City; and the monsters who occupied the throne of Augustus endeavored, by encouraging them, to varnish over their own crimes, and to propitiate the affections of mankind.

After a long night of darkness, the restoration of letters was accompanied by the resurrection of the fine arts; and the Italian, the Flemish, the Dutch, and the French schools bear testimony to the high estimation in which they were held. Great Britain and the North of Europe have also cherished this benign propensity; and amidst the extraordinary calamities and overwelming desolations of modern times, it has been the pride and the glory of the great characters who have participated in these mighty events, to secure blessings to their country, and immortality to themselves, by collecting the costly and superb monuments of the arts, and by creating and diffusing the light of science. If, however, in the history of the world, it should sometimes appear that usurpers and tyrants have been the patrons of magnificent works, let not the praise be transferred from the individual to the government. The career of successful ambition has placed in his hands the power of dispensing good, and he endeavored to conciliate affection by accommodating his acts to the taste and science of the community.

But if, unfortunately, ignorance prevail, and a hatred of knowledge bear sway, then the despot will involve the country in the thickest gloom of chimerian darkness. The prolific power—the fertile soil that produces all good must reside in the body of the people, and where a free nation passes under the yoke of tyranny, some of the original stamina of greatness—some of the celestial fire of liberty will still survive the prostration, and may enable the usurper to spread the blessings of knowledge and refinement; but if there were at no time a pre-existent state of freedom, it will be difficult to trace, in the experience of the world, any successful cultivation of knowledge, until the lapse of ages or the benefits of extended intercourse shall have introduced some radiations of light from countries which are, or once have been, free.

Even modern Italy, degraded as she is by the loss of liberty, still feels the divine impulse which was communicated in the day of her freedom; and, although the sword of her heroes has been transformed into the stiletto of the assassin, and the sublime genius of her poets, her orators, her historians, and her artists, has evaporated in the refinements of Machiavelian policy, and in subtleties of polemic controversy, yet she has within our day produced illustrious men, who have enlarged the boundaries of knowledge, and extended the empire of virtue. A Republican government, instead of being unfriendly to the growth of the Fine Arts, is the appropriate soil for their cultivation. The ability to promote useful undertakings and beneficial institutions must exist, to a certain extent, in every community. And it certainly may be called into exertion with greater potency in a free state than under an arbitrary government, where the money expended for their encouragement is extorted from the people.

The privileged orders which prevail in civilized monarchies are hostile to the higher prerogatives of intellect. They create a barrier against the ascent of genius to the highest stations, and they cast the most distinguished talents and the most exalted endowments in the background of society; and, although they sometimes produce herbs of salubrious virtue and trees of noble growth, yet they in general originate and support those pestilent plants whose seeds, elevated by the winds, are scattered in every direction, and are propagated by the exhaustion of the most fertile soils, and the destruction of the most valuable productions.

The condition of our community, in relation to manners or education, cannot be urged as an objection against the cultivation of the Fine Arts. A nation highly agricultural, and the second commercial people in the world, improved by science, and abounding in institutions of education, must surely be contemplated as friendly to those arts which polish and refine society. Although the ancients were superior in sculpture, yet the moderns have in all probability excelled them in the graphic art. It is believed that the former had but

four pigments in coloring—that they were deficient in *chiaro scuro* and keep
ing—that they were ignorant of the art of painting in oil: and it is well
known that the art of engraving is a modern invention—and is a great patron of the painter, by multiplying and extending his productions.

The ancient artists had undoubtedly superior advantages. They were called upon to supply statues of the gods, and to adorn the temples of religion.
The statue of Jupiter by Phidias, and of Juno by Polycletus, were renowned
through all antiquity. The Archetypes. from which they delineated the human form, were the most beautiful of the human race.

The Greek artists were men of the first consideration, and of the most finished education. Socrates himself was a statuary.

The imitative arts must act upon the models furnished by nature or by
man. The images which constitute the materials on which the inventive or
plastic powers proceed, must be drawn from one or both of these sources.
The pictorial art embraces an extensive field—it includes historical painters,
painters of portraits, of landscape, of sea-pieces, and of natural history;
and in the higher orders of the Art, there are two distinct styles—the Grand
or Sublime, and the Ornamental or Beautiful. With respect to the comparative advantages or disadvantages of the ancient and modern artists, we stand
precisely on the same footing as our brethren of the Old World: but we are
unfortunately deficient in having but few distinguished models of art.

The Professors of the Fine Arts occupy the same ground with us as other
callings. There are some who adorn society by their talents, and are distinguished for their education and virtues. In these respects we are not inferior
to those of other times and other countries.

And it certainly cannot be alleged that there is an inaptitude in the American
genius for the Fine Arts—on the contrary, from the anecdotes which are related of some of our distinguished painters, it would appear that an irresistible impulse had devoted them to Art. And it is well known that, both abroad
and at home, our countrymen (whose names delicacy forbids me to mention
in this place) have exhibited powers of genius and taste which have commanded not only applause, but admiration.

It has been well observed:

— Mutum est pictura poema *

The inventive power in both cases acts upon those images which have been
collected by observation, and deposited in the storehouse of memory—and
which refer not only to the world of sense without us, but to the world of
thought within us. But as almost all our ideas are derived in the first instance
from sensation—and as the imitative arts rely for their field of operation
upon the material world, it must be obvious that the imagination of the artist
must derive its forms and receive its complexion from the country in which he
was born, and in which he resides.

And can there be a country in the world better calculated than ours to exercise and to exalt the imagination—to call into activity the creative powers of
the mind, and to afford just views of the beautiful, the wonderful, and the sublime? Here Nature has conducted her operations on a magnificent scale: extensive and elevated mountains—lakes of oceanic size—rivers of prodigious
magnitude—cataracts unequaled for volume of water—and boundless forests
filled with wild beasts and savage men, and covered with the towering oak
and the aspiring pine.

This wild, romantic, and awful scenery is calculated to produce a correspondent impression in the imagination—to elevate all the faculties of the
mind, and to exalt all the feelings of the heart. But when cultivation has
exerted its power—when the forest is converted into fertile fields, blooming
with beauty and smiling with plenty, then the mind of the artist derives a correspondent color from the scenes with which he is conversant: and the sublime,
the wonderful, the ornamental and the beautiful thus become, in turn, familiar to his imagination. America, notwithstanding its infancy, has witnessed

* Horace.

events as worthy of the delineation of genius as any that have occurred in the Old World. Even in our Colonial state, the richest themes exist for the pencil of the painter—but commencing with the Declaration of Independence, and coming down to the events of the present time, what more magnificent subjects could be selected for the graphic art? The painter of history has here an ample field for the display of his powers.

The deliberations of our statesmen—the exploits of our heroes may be revived, and perpetuated—deeds of mighty import, the offspring of ethereal minds, and the parents of immortal glory—and here the Portrait Painter, the Statuary, and the Engraver, may transmit to posterity the likenesses of those men who have acted and suffered in their country's cause.

The portrait collection of this city, by comprising many of the principal heroes of the country, is entitled to great praise in its tendency to stimulate to noble deeds, and to encourage the Fine Arts, by displaying to advantage the compositions of our best painters; and its merits would be greatly enhanced if it were extended so as to embrace illustrious men who have done honor to the Arts and Sciences, or who have distinguished themselves in other respects as men of extraordinary talents or virtues. The utmost care ought to be adopted in the selection, as one unworthy preference may disgrace the whole gallery; and any unmerited omission may recall to mind the observation of the historian respecting the images of illustrious men displayed in a magnificent procession at Rome : " Praefulgebant Cassius et Brutus, eo ipso quod effigies eorum non visebantur."* Although I am not prepared to go the whole length with a distinguished countryman,† and to say that the genius of Architecture seems to have shed his maledictions over our land, yet it must be admitted that too little attention and encouragement have been given to this important art. Many of our public buildings have a sombre and heavy appearance, and the interior arrangements show the absence of skill and taste. Within a few years, however, great improvements may be seen in our private as well as our public edifices. This revolution in our taste may be traced from the time when, with a spirit truly wise and munificent, the foundations of the edifice in which we are now assembled were laid—a building which, for magnificence of design and elegance of execution, transcends every public edifice in America. Let it be strongly impressed on our minds that the most beautiful and sublime works of Athens were erected during the administration of one great man—that during their execution, so many kinds of labor, and such a variety of instruments and materials were requisite, that every art was exerted, every hand employed, and the whole city was in pay—and at the same time, adorned and supported by itself; and that it was never in a more prosperous condition than when all its resources were expended in great public works.

The treasure thus applied was in a' state of incessant activity and circulation, enlivening all the avenues of industry, cheering the brow of labor, and rewarding the hand of skill. The magnificence of a free people ought always to be seen in their halls of justice, in their edifices of learning, and in their temples of religion.

As the streams and springs which nature has produced are, when collected into reservoirs, and regulated by skill, rendered subservient to subsistence, accommodation and pleasure, so will the rays of genius, concentrated in this Institution, create and diffuse a taste for the Fine Arts, and elevate our country in the estimate of the civilized world. Its apartments will contain the best models of ancient and modern Art, and the most distinguished specimens of all that can occupy the genius or perfect the taste of our country. To that place the artist will resort for study and improvement. There he will deposit the fruits of his genius—there he will enter the lists of fame, and there he will attain the palm of glory.

How many men are there, upon whom nature has shed her choicest gifts, who, restrained by diffidence, the companion of genius, or prevented by an ele-

* Tacitus.   † Jefferson.

vation of sentiment, which, like the celebrated flower of the East, disdains the support of the earth,* or bewildered by that ignorance of the world which attaches itself to the man of seclusion and contemplation, linger out an obscure existence without notice, without patronage, without one smile of comfort, or one word of encouragement!

And how many more are there, who feel the divine inspiration of genius, and who possess commanding, ductile, and transcendent minds, which might enable them to ascend to the highest, or stoop to the lowest flights of Art, but who, for the want of opportunities for cultivation, are either compelled to wander abroad, or to smother the nascent powers of intellect! This Academy will conquer all these difficulties, and surmount all these disadvantages. On these altars, dedicated to the Muses and the Graces, will be offered the choicest gifts of genius, and the most finished specimens of art. Here the temple will be reared—the sacrifice will be made—the fire will be kindled—and no longer shall the votary be compelled to seek under foreign skies and in distant lands the objects of his adoration.

In this place shall be deposited the portraits, the busts, and the statues of those illustrious men who have extended the fame of their country, brightened the path of glory, illuminated the regions of knowledge, and exemplified the blessings of religion. Here shall the future great men of America, the guides, the lights, and the shields of unborn generations, repair to view the monuments of Art—to behold the departed worthies of former times—to rouse the soul of generous emulation, and to catch the spirit of heroic virtue.

Here shall the virtues—here shall wisdom's train—their long-lost friends rejoicing, as of old, embrace the smiling family of Arts—the Muses and the Graces.†

And if our artists shall ever expect on eagle wings to penetrate into lofty and untried regions, and to ascend into the highest heaven of invention, let them cultivate that noble enthusiasm, that sublime sensative ability, without which exertion is useless: which animated Corregio, when he said: "And I also am a painter,"—and which fired the bosom of Zeuxis, when he exclaimed, "that he designed for eternity." Let them also respect the decencies of life, the charms of virtue, and the injunctions of morality.

The most inimitable powers of invention and execution cannot atone for that perversion of decorum which addresses the sensuality of the imagination, and which loosens the restraints of the moral sense. A great artist ought to be emphatically a good man, illustrating in his works the beauties of art, and in his life the beauties of virtue.

There are certain mighty pillars which support the complicated fabric of society, and there are distinguished ornaments which beautify and embellish it. Upon agriculture, manufactures and commerce; upon science, literature, morality and religion, all associations of the human race must rely for subsistence or support—but the Fine Arts superadd the graces of a Chesterfield to the gigantic mind of a Locke. They are the Acanthi which adorn the Corinthian column—the halos which surround the Sun of Knowledge: they excite labor, produce riches, enlarge the sphere of innocent amusements, increase the stock of harmless pleasure, expand our intellectual powers, improve our moral faculties, stimulate to illustrious deeds, enhance the charms of virtue, diffuse the glories of heroism, augment the public wealth, and extend the national reputation.

There are but two Institutions of this kind in America—one in Mexico, of an earlier, and one in Philadelphia, of a more recent origin. Seeing that they are calculated to produce so much good, and to reflect so much honor—that ours is the first establishment in the United States—that it has, after discouraging obstacles and severe struggles, attained a permanent and prosperous condition, it is no more than right and proper that its eminent benefactors and friends, who have preceded us to the grave, should receive the humble tribute of our applause. Among the most distinguished of these are Robert R. Livingston, once President, and Robert Fulton,‡ formerly a Director of this

---

* Epidendrum flos æris.   † Akenside.   ‡ R. Fulton was a portrait painter.

Academy. In the dispensations of the Almighty, it frequently happens that constellations of great men appear at the same period in the world. Great talents are elicited by great occasions, and produced by great exigencies. This was eminently the case at the commencement of the American Revolution.

An infant people were called upon to measure swords with a great nation, and Providence prepared us for the contest, by giving us men eminent in the cabinet and heroic in the field, to enlighten our councils and to direct our energies. Among those illustrious men was Mr. Livingston. He was descended from a distinguished family, was favored with an excellent education, and was endowed with great and original talents, possessing in an eminent degree *mens divinior*—the divinity of genius. His mind was improved by contemplation, by conversation, and by reading. His eloquence was the fruit of a fertile imagination, the offspring of a prolific mind, enriched by splendid diction, and embellished by a graceful delivery. Those that have heard him speak will recognize the character of his oratory in Denham's admirable description of the Thames :—

> Tho' deep, yet clear ; tho' gentle, yet not dull ;
> Strong without rage ; without o'erflowing full.

He was also an able writer, and had devoted himself to the study of the law, and to the acquisition of political knowledge. With these endowments, and with these talents, and with a zeal corresponding with the crisis, he was chosen a member of the first Congress: he was one of the Committee that prepared the Declaration of Independence, and he continued a distinguished actor in the great scenes of the Revolution: he was Minister of Foreign Affairs, a member of the Convention that formed the State Constitution, Chancellor of the State, and Delegate to Congress on extraordinary occasions. To him we are indebted for the Council of Revision in our State Constitution, which, by combining the Judiciary with the Executive, in the exercise of a qualified negative, creates a joint defence against the absorbing powers of the Legislative Department, and therefore more fully accords with the views of eminent political writers, than an arrangement which commits this power to the Executive authority alone.

After the conclusion of the Revolutionary War, he continued to fill the high office of Chancellor.

He was a member of the Convention that adopted the Federal Constitution, and he finally closed his political life, after serving several years as Minister Plenipotentiary in France.

Let us now contemplate Mr. Livingston in a more interesting attitude: as the friend of science, the patron of the arts, and the inventor and introducer of useful improvements. In the scale of excellence adopted by the ancients, founders of States, law-givers, and heroes, were graduated below the authors, and inventors of beneficial arts and institutions. The former, such as Hercules, Theseus, Minos, and Romulus, were considered demi-gods ; while the latter, such as Ceres, Apollo, Mercury, and Bacchus, were enrolled among the gods ; and, according to the opinion of the greatest philosophers, justly :

"For the merit of the former is confined within the circle of an age ; or a nation is like fruitful flowers, which, though they be profitable, and good, yet serve but for the season, and for a latitude of ground where they fall: but the other is, indeed, like the benefits of Heaven, which are permanent and universal. The former, again, is mixed with strife and perturbation ; but the latter hath the true character of Divine presence, coming in *aura leni*, without noise or agitation."*

At an early period Mr. L. had turned his attention to the improvement of our agriculture and manufactures. A Society was instituted in 1793 for the promotion of the useful arts, of which he was elected the first President, and which office he held during his life.

* Bacon.

The volumes published by this Society, under the patronage of the State, contain many valuable papers written by him.

The best soil, after a long process of cultivation, loses its prolific power. Some of our lands are of so slight a texture, that the vegetating principle is soon exhausted, and large tracts of country, without extraneous aid, are incapable of cultivation.

The application of manure was always laborious—generally expensive, and sometimes impracticable, until Mr. L. introduced the use of gypsum into this State. His essays on this subject contain many valuable remarks, and show a spirit of experimental observation highly creditable to his discernment. The western parts of this State contain this fossil of various kinds, of excellent qualities, and to an unbounded extent. Its benign effects are well known, although the mode of its application is still a subject of doubt. Like the hand of Midas, it has converted our soil into gold. His attention was also directed to the introduction of useful plants and animals from abroad, to the domestication of some of our animals, to the improvement of our fruits and grasses, to the diseases of cattle, and to the growth and nourishment of plants in general. The volumes of the Society furnish his observations at length on these subjects. But his efforts were more especially directed to the introduction of Merino, and the amelioration of common sheep.

He wrote an invaluable essay on this subject, which was printed by the direction of the Legislature, and which was republished in Europe with great applause. I am sensible that a contrariety of opinion exists in this country, as well as in England, respecting the advantage of the Merino sheep. It was easy to foresee that the exorbitant price would, in course of time, meet with a corresponding depression ; that the animal would fall into unskillful hands, and that the disappointments of cupidity would excite a vehement clamor against it. The well-regulated judgment of the public will, however, pronounce a favorable decision. An animal yielding such fine wool, so essential to the manufacture of fine cloths, and which will always command a high price, as long as a duty is laid on the exportation of it in Spain, must be considered a great acquisition. He had for a series of years, long before his acquaintance with Mr. Fulton, contemplated the power generated by steam, and considered the utility of its application to the propulsion of vessels and carriages. His acquaintance with the great mechanical genius introduced a new era into navigation.

During his foreign embassy, he devoted himself to the improvement of our agriculture. His letters on that occasion reflect equal credit on his intelligence and patriotism.

He also endeavored to improve our national taste ; to his exertions and influence we are indebted for a valuable portion of our collection. We have thus seen Mr. L. converting the lessons of his experience and observation into sources of practical and general utility.

He was not one of those remote suns whose light and heat have not yet reached our planetary system. His object, his ambition, his study, was to do the greatest good to the greatest number. There is no doubt but that he felt the extent of his own powers, and the plenitude of his own resources; but he bore his faculties meekly about him—never offending the pride or the delicacy of his associates by arrogance, or by intrusion, by neglect, or by slight, by acting the oracle or dictator. He was an elegant *arbiter elegantiarum*, or judge of propriety : his conversation was unpremeditated ; it abounded with brilliant wit, apposite illustrations, and with various and extended knowledge, always as gentle as "zephyrs blowing below the violet,"* and always exhibiting the overflowings of a fertile mind. His greatest qualities were attended with a due sense of his own imperfections, and of his limited powers.

He did not see in himself the tortoise of the Indian, or the Atlas of the heathen mythology sustaining the universe—nor did he keep himself at an awful distance, wrapped up in a gloomy abstraction, or veiled in mysterious or supercilious dignity.

* Shakespeare.

He knew that the fraternity of mankind is a vast assemblage of good and evil, of light and darkness—and that the whole chain of human beings is so connected by the charities of life, by the ties of mutual dependence, and reciprocal benevolence—such was Robert R. Livingston ; he was not one of those factitious characters who rise up, and disappear, like the mountains of sand which the wind raises in the deserts, nor did he pretend to possess a mind illuminating all the departments of knowledge, like that great elementary substance, which communicates the principle to all animated nature : but he will be ranked by the judgment of impartial posterity. Among the great men of the Revolution, and in the faithful pages of history, he will be classed with George Clinton, John Jay, Pierre Van Cortlandt, Philip Schuyler, William Floyd, Philip Livingston, Gouverneur Morris, James Duane, John Morin Scott, and other venerable and conscript fathers of the State. Fortunately for the interests of mankind, Mr. L. became acquainted with Robert Fulton, a self-created great man, who had risen into distinguished usefulness, and into exalted eminence, by the energies of his own genius, unsupported by extrinsic advantages. Mr. F. had directed the whole force of his mind to mathematical learning and to mechanical philosophy. Plans of defence against maritime invasion and of subaquatic navigation had occupied his reflections. During the late war, he was the Archimedes of his country. The poet was considered under the influence of a disordered imagination when he exclaimed :—

> " Soon shall thy arm, unconquer'd Steam ! afar
> Drag the slow barge, or drive the rapid car,
> Or on wide waving wings, expanded bear
> The flying chariot through the fields of air."*

The connection between Livingston and Fulton realized to a great degree the vision of the poet. All former experiments had failed, and the genius of Fulton, aided and fostered by the public spirit and discernment of Livingston, created one of the greatest accommodations for the benefit of mankind.

These illustrious men will be considered through all time as the benefactors of the world. They will be emphatically hailed as the Castor and Pollux of antiquity—*lucida sidera*—stars of excellent light and of most benign influence.

Mr. Fulton was personally well known to most who hear me. To those who were favored with the high communion of his superior mind, I need not expatiate on the wonderful vivacity, activity, comprehension, and clearness of his intellectual faculties : and while he was meditating plans of mighty import for his future fame and his country's good, he was cut down in the prime of his life, and in the midst of his usefulness.

Like the self-burning tree of Gambia, he was destroyed by the fire of his own genius, and the never-ceasing activity of a vigorous mind. And, O ! may we not humbly hope that his immortal spirit, disembodied from its material incumbrance, has taken its flight to the world of pure intellect—" where the wicked cease from troubling, and where the weary are at rest ?"
23rd October, 1816.

January 7, 1818, the elected were Jno. Trumbull, President ; John R. Murray, Vice-President ; Cadwallader D. Colden, William Cutting, John G. Bogert, David Hosack, Archibald Bruce, Archibald Robertson, Benjamin W. Rogers, William Dunlap, John McComb, Samuel L. Waldo, and James Renwick, Directors ; John Pintard, Treasurer ; Alexander Robertson, Secretary ; William Dunlap, Keeper and Librarian.

Of these, four, including the President, were artists ; seven were of other professions.

* Darwin.

About that time, two of Trumbull's paintings—"The Woman taken in Adultery," and "Suffer Little Children," &c.—were offered to the Academy, at 3,500 dollars each—and several of his other works at smaller sums. All were purchased, and a debt incurred, which could ultimately be paid only by returning the pictures—*to the artist*.

It was supposed to have been, in a great measure, one cause of the failure of the Institution. Another was: "That the President opposed the opening of schools."

The want of funds had doubtless much to do in the matter. Subscribers had to be solicited, and a person employed and paid to endeavor to obtain them.

They were honored with the title of "*Patrons*." During the Summer, the collection of antique casts was opened to students in the mornings from 6 to 8 o'clock; W. Dunlap, keeper. The hours were inconvenient—few attended, and in a very short time the first attempt at founding an Art School expired. What occurred during the few following years, is not accessible—probably not even on record. The Institution was in possession of ample accommodations, furnished gratuitously by the city, a fine collection of casts, and many paintings of high merit—a library, and a direction of influential men; yet it steadily declined.

The stockholders had become discouraged, and took so little interest in the Institution, as scarcely ever to attend the meetings to vote for officers. The President, Secretary, and Keeper most frequently discharged the functions of electors; and the same limited attendance in the Board directed its affairs. Within, it was dead—why so without? That is a matter worthy of inquiry. On its walls were West's "Lear," "Ophelia," "Orlando"—Trumbull's small Battle Pieces, and still more beautiful studies of the heads therefor—his larger works—those presented by Napoleon I.—Sir Thomas Lawrence's full-length of West—the works of the city artists, and many loaned by lovers of Art. These formed no insignificant exhibition for its date, or the existing taste for Art. Where, then, was its want of success to be looked for? It was to be found in the unchangeableness in its exhibitions, which was not suited to a novelty-seeking public. Its permanency of material was its death. A daily attendance of often not more than two or three persons, art vigilists, mourned over its expiring moments. At that time the writer was in the habit of spending many hours a day in the rooms, and frequently without being interrupted. The yearly receipts were insufficient to meet the door-keeper's salary—a very moderate item.

[*Evening Post, May 6th*, 1826.]

"WEST AND FULTON.—In our walks through the City Hall this morning, we observed stuck up on the Sheriff's board an advertisement, notifying all good people who should chance to pass that way that he, the said Sheriff, in virtue of an execution in that behalf directed, would sell on Saturday (to-day), at 11 o'clock, at the Academy of Arts, three splendid pictures, to wit:—King Lear, Ophelia and Orlando. These were the productions of *West*, and the property of Fulton; and yet, neither their authorship nor their proprietorship, although associated with the proudest recollections of our country, has been able, it seems, to rescue them from the common fate of bankruptcy and neglect.—*Sic transit gloria mundi*. West and Fulton brought to the hammer, in the polished, patriotic, public-spirited City of Gotham. We could hardly give credence to our senses, although fortified by a pair of Pike's best optics, when we gazed upon the advertisement. To remove our doubts, we traveled on to the Academy itself, and there found, but too truly, that there was no mistake in the matter. The strong arm of the law had been laid upon these specimens of genius, and with as little ceremony as though they had been so many pigs of iron. Justice, it seems, must be done, though the sky fall—the creations of fancy and of fact must bow alike to the mandate of the law. Such then being the case, and a sale being unavoidable, ought these monuments of American genius to be permitted to be sacrificed? The Lear, we understand from Mr. Robertson, of the Academy, cost originally five hundred guineas in London. The Ophelia, four hundred, and the Orlando, three hundred—making, together, upwards of five thousand dollars.

"Were they, in their design, of a national character, we should not hesitate to recommend them to the attention of the lords of our city. Might they not, however, with reference to their author merely, as the productions of Benjamin West, be proper ornaments of the Legislative Chamber of the first city of America?"

"PHILO EDITOR."

Is apathy to such exhibitions peculiar to New-York alone? The answer is, *No*. A petition of the Artists of Philadelphia to the Pennsylvania Academy recites as one of the causes of failure of the exhibitions held in that city, "That the Annual Exhibitions are *not attended*, because the Academy keeps works on exhibition all the year."

This is dwelt on rather more than its merits would appear to require, for the purpose of placing past experience before the profession, many members of which yet desire to have such an exhibition established in the City of New-York, a continuous mart for the sale of works of Art, and for their immediate reception when finished. Such an arrangement was found not to answer expectation in 1820, and time seems to have made no change in public opinion.

The business of the American Academy from 1816 to 1823 was the same as the preceding years. In 1824 or '5, students were again invited to study from the casts, provided they came between the hours of six and nine o'clock, A. M. The opportunity was eagerly sought, but it was soon found that the hope of advantage was illusory. The young men who attended at six, or even at seven o'clock, were sometimes admitted and sometimes excluded. They generally had to wait several hours for admittance, and then were

frequently insulted, *always* if they presumed to "*knock.*" At
length a scene occurred which seemed to put an end to the
pretence of the Academy being open to students. Of this
scene Dunlap happened, as he says, to be a witness:

"I had been accommodated by the Common Council of the City with a
painting-room in the building, and coming to the place generally before breakfast to prepare for the labors of the day, witnessed the treatment which those
who wished to instruct themselves received. On the occasion alluded to,
Messrs. Cummings and Agate, then artists, although young, came to the door,
and found that it was closed; they were turning away, when I advised them
to speak of the exclusion to the Directors. They replied, 'that it would be
useless,' and at that moment one of the Directors appeared coming from Broadway towards them. I urged the young gentlemen to speak to him, but they
declined, saying, 'they had so often been disappointed, that they gave it up.'
The Director came and sat down by the writer, who mentioned the subject of
the recent disappointment, pointing to the two young men, who were still in
sight. The conduct of the person whose duty it was to open the doors was
promptly condemned by that gentleman; and while speaking the President
appeared coming to his painting-room, which was one of the apartments of the
Academy. It was unusually early for him, although near eight o'clock. Before he reached the door, the Curator of the Academy opened it and remained.
"On Mr. Trumbull's arrival, the Director mentioned the disappointment of
the students: the Curator stoutly asserted, 'that he would open the doors
when it suited him.' The President observed, in reply to the Director:
'When I commenced the study of painting, there were no casts in the country. I was obliged to do as well as I could.'
"These young gentlemen should remember that *the gentlemen* have gone to a
great expense in importing casts, and that they (the students) have no property in them;" concluding with these memorable words, in the encouragement of the Curator's conduct, 'they must remember that BEGGARS are not to
be CHOOSERS.' WE MAY CONSIDER THIS THE CONDEMNATORY SENTENCE OF THE
AMERICAN ACADEMY OF FINE ARTS."

That Curator was Lewis Rogers, an old Revolutionary
soldier, who had crossed "on the ice from New-York to
Staten Island," in the "memorable winter." That was his
ruin—it being an excuse for insufferable insolence to every
one. He was a *Dictator.* To that man may not be given
the importance of causing the downfall of the American
Academy—but he certainly contrived to make it exceedingly disagreeable to any one who had anything to do
with it.

Dr. Francis coincides with the writer, and states that he
attended him gratuitously in sickness for years, even unto
his death; that he never heard him utter the first word of
thankfulness.

The scene described by Dunlap, as occurring to the writer and Mr. Agate, is strictly correct, so far as the writer has
personal knowledge. The language ascribed to the President, "he did not hear,"—but as it stood in print for many
years without contradiction, during the lives of the parties,
it is only reasonable to suppose, it is equally and strictly
correct with the report of the rest of the scene.

Dunlap is, however, slightly mistaken as to the submission of one of the young men referred to—Agate did submit, and advised so doing, but it was otherwise with the writer. On returning to the rooms of Mr. Henry Inman, with whom he was then completing his studies in Oil Painting, he drafted a complaint and remonstrance, and also a petition, asking that the students should be "SUSTAINED" in the privileges the Directors of the American Academy had granted them. Both the remonstrance and the petition were to be presented to the Board at their next meeting. Probably the complaint, drawn up under the sting of the moment, was stronger than necessary—at least so Inman thought, and he destroyed it. The petition he retained, promising to give it his influence and signature.

It was given by him to C. C. Wright—by Wright to Samuel F. B. Morse, who warmly seconded it. To give it influence, Morse called together a few of the artists at his rooms, and there the propriety of further endeavors to conciliate the Directors by petition was discussed, and for the time in part, or wholly, abandoned.

So circumstanced, Mr. Morse suggested that an association might be formed "for the Promotion of the Arts, and the Assistance of Students"—simply a union for improvement in drawing.

On the 8th of November, 1825, a meeting of the Artists, probably the first ever held in the city, took place in the rooms of the Historical Society, (generously loaned them on that occasion,) for the purpose of taking into consideration "the formation of a Society for Improvement in Drawing." Mr. Durand was called to the chair, and Mr. Morse was appointed Secretary.

The question of organization was put, and carried unanimously; and the so associated artists were from thenceforth to be known as the "NEW-YORK DRAWING ASSOCIATION." Samuel F. B. Morse was chosen to preside over its meetings.

The members were:

Samuel F. B. Morse, Henry Inman, A. B. Durand, Thos. S. Cummings, Ambrose Andrews, Frederick S. Agate, William G. Wall, Wm. Dunlap, James Coyle, Charles C. Wright, Mosley J. Danforth, Robert Norris, Edward C. Potter, Albert Durand, John W. Paradise, Gerlando Marsiglia, Ithiel Town, Thos. Grinnell, Geo. W. Hatch, John R. Murray, Jr., John Neilson, John L. Morton, Henry J. Morton, C. C. Ingham, Thomas Cole, Hugh Reinagle, Peter Maverick, D. W. Wilson, Alexander G. Davis, John Frazee.

By its few and simple Rules it was provided, "That its members should meet in the evenings, three times a week, for drawing. That each member furnish his own drawing materials. That the expense of light, fuel, &c., be paid by equal contributions. That new members should be admitted on a majority vote—paying five dollars entrance fee. That the lamp should be lighted at 6, and extinguished at 9 o'clock, P. M.*

Thus it will be seen that the Association paid its own expenses, furnished its own models, had its own officers, and were provided with a room loaned them by the Historical and Philosophical Societies. It was entirely distinct from the American Academy of Arts, and probably would ever have remained so without organizing a new Academy, had it not been for the interference of the President of the American, which, as the writer was a witness and party, he will relate:

After all the insult that had been heaped on the artists, who attempted to avail themselves of the privilege of drawing in the American Academy of Arts, the associated artists were no sooner organized than they were claimed as STUDENTS of the AMERICAN Academy.

On one of the drawing evenings in December, 1825, Colonel Trumbull, President, and Archibald Robertson, Secretary of the American Academy, entered the room in which the associated artists were drawing, and going directly to the President's seat, took possession of it, and looking authoritatively around, beckoned to the writer, who was in charge of the room, to go to him—producing the matriculation-book of the American Academy, he requested that it should be signed by all, as students of that Institution. That the writer, as one, declined, bowed to Mr. Trumbull, and left him, and reported to the members. The Colonel waited some time, but receiving neither compliance nor attention, left in the same stately manner he had entered; remarking aloud, that he had left the book for our signatures, with the additional request, that when signed, it should be left with the Secretary of the American Academy! The circumstance naturally led to a little excitement in the usually quiet Society. Groups gathered together and discussed the proceedings, and finally the Society was called to order, and the questions were presented: "Have we

---

* The lamp was a can, containing about ½ a gallon of oil, into which was inserted a wick of some 4 inches diameter—it was set upon an upright post, about 10 feet high. To give sufficient light, the wick was necessarily considerably out of the oil—and caused smoke. There was no chimney, and lamp-black was abundant; added to that, some forty draftsmen had an oil-lamp each. The reader may easily imagine the condition of the room.

any relation to the American Academy of Arts ?"—" Are we their students ?" It was promptly determined, " None whatever." " We are not." "They have cast us adrift, and we have started on our own resources,"—and the determination was unanimous, that the names should not be enrolled on the books of the Academy.

At the time there were a few, not exceeding half a dozen in number, of the smaller casts, from which the artists were drawing, which belonged to the American Academy of Fine Arts. That was the *only* connection, and that it was at once determined to sever. On the 14th of January, 1826, the following resolution was unanimously passed:

"*Resolved*, That the casts belonging to the American Academy be returned, and that the thanks of this Association be tendered to the gentlemen of the American Academy for their politeness in loaning them to us."

A Committee of two members was appointed to carry the measure into effect.

Other casts, to fill the vacancy thus occasioned, were immediately tendered by Messrs. Durand, Cummings, Frazee, and Ingham.

Dunlap describes the circumstances, though it will be seen, by the resolution quoted, that he is slightly mistaken as to the non-return of the casts to the American Academy. They were reported by the Committee as returned January 16, 1826.

" This proposition [to sign the matriculation-book] caused the suggestion of forming a new Academy. It was proposed by some immediately to return the casts borrowed from the old institution. It was thought THAT would indicate hostility. All were unwilling to be looked upon as dependent upon an institution which had neglected them, and was inefficient, in its present form, to the ends they desired. It was suggested that perhaps a plan could be arranged by which the artists might unite with the Academy, and that, by becoming parties to a revision and remodeling of its By-Laws, the practical knowledge and experience of the artists, and the valuable collection of the Academy, might be rendered reciprocally subservient to the promotion of art.

" This was cordially received, and it was the general wish that it might be found profitable.

" But before taking any measures to ascertain whether any plan of this nature could be carried into execution, it was thought advisable that some method should be resorted to of uniting the views, and concentrating the opinions, of all on the subject of the situation. It was therefore proposed that a Committee be appointed to draw up and lay before the Drawing Association a distinct statement of its views, and its position in relation to the American Academy of Fine Arts."

Dunlap was probably mistaken in the last point, for no such Committee, or report from any such Committee, are to be found on record. The minutes, though, are very imperfect.

It was the wish of the Associated Artists to have a union with the Academy, for though they felt themselves competent to form a new Academy, to be governed by themselves, they knew the advantages that would be derived from the use of the casts of the old institution, and the disadvantages of being, in appearance, hostile to the gentlemen who composed the body of stockholders of the American Academy. Therefore, "it was their wish that there should be but ONE institution; and they held themselves ready to join in building it up, so soon as it should be placed on such a footing that they could unite in it with confidence, and with well-founded hopes of such a management that the energies of all might be directed to the attainment of the noble ends of an Academy of Fine Arts."

The wish was communicated to the American Academy, and the hope expressed that means would be found to admit the artists to such a share in the direction as should be to the benefit of all. The wish was reciprocated by the Directors, and they transmitted a resolution, December 17, 1825, which appointed a Committee of three—Van Rensselaer, Coles, and Brevoort—to meet a similar Commitete of the Association, and to confer with them on the subject-matter of the report which had been laid before the Board.

Morse, Durand, and Dunlap were appointed the Committee on the part of the Drawing Association. The Committees met, conferred, and adjourned, "leaving the form of a report to be adjusted by the two Chairmen." That was apparently never done.

The result, however, was, that the Committee of Directors engaged or guaranteed to exert all their influence to effect the election of six artists into the Board of Directors of the American Academy, as representatives of the body of artists.

Six artists were unanimously chosen by the associated artists, and four of them not being *stockholders*, one hundred dollars was paid from the treasury of the Association for the shares necessary to qualify them.

The associated artists, and those elected to represent them, looked upon the affair as settled, (it may be well to repeat here, that so little interest had for years been taken by the stockholders in the affairs of the American Academy, that few or none attended the elections—two or three voters only were frequently determinators of the officers for the ensuing year,) and left the election to take its own course; but on the evening previous to the election they were informed, by an anonymous letter, that some of the names given in by them as candidates would, by the intrigues of certain Directors, be struck off the ticket." The mode of delivery of that letter is worthy of notice. Dunlap and the writer were walking in the Park, when an old woman, apparently a beggar, approached, and asked if their names were Dunlap and Cummings? On receiving an affirmative answer, she placed a letter in Mr. Dunlap's hands, and vanished.

The communication stated that the ticket would be defeated—that two only would be elected—that the rest would be rejected—naming them all particularly; and that the information might be relied on. The result was, that Dunlap published a card in the morning papers, announcing that none of the candidates would serve, unless all were chosen: they considered themselves as the judges of their representatives, and of those fit to govern and direct an Academy.

The election took place, and two only of the six candidates chosen by the artists *were elected.* They immediately resigned. There was not only a breach of faith—an injury inflicted by taking the money of the Association, (which was never returned,) but at the time of the election, the most contemptuous expressions were used by members of the Directory. The artists were declared unnecessary to the Institution; and one of the Directors, whose name is spared, proclaimed that "Artists were unfit to manage an Academy"—"that they were always *quarreling;*" and concluded with the words, "Colonel Trumbull says so."

It is worthy of remark, that the names of the six candidates were given in to the officers of the Academy seventeen days before the election took place: and so far from any official objections being made to the mode or purpose of presenting them, when a difficulty appeared which seemed likely to prevent the acquisition of the hundred dollars, which by agreement was to be paid to render them elegible, that difficulty was removed by a special vote of the Directors, which the artists were certainly justified in considering as a tacit assumption of the agreement entered into by their committee, and a pledge for its fulfillment—else why take the money of the Association? That it was so intended, there can be no doubt: nor is it believed that the intention was frustrated through the agency, or with the concurrence, of the Directors.

There was an agency within the government of the Academy hostile to the union; and that agency was successfully exerted. The artists now resolved to organize a new Academy, to be governed, as all Academies of Fine Arts should be, by artists.

At a meeting of the NEW-YORK DRAWING ASSOCIATION, held on the evening of the 14th of January, 1826, Mr. Morse, the President, stated, " That he had certain resolutions to offer the Association, which he would preface with the following remarks:—We have this evening assumed a new attitude in the community: our negotiations with the Academy are at an end; our union with it has been frustrated, after every proper effort on our part to accomplish it. The two who were elected as Directors from our ticket have signified their non-acceptance of the office. We are, therefore, left to organize ourselves on a plan that shall meet the wishes of us all. A plan of an Institution which shall be truly liberal, which shall be mutually beneficial, which shall really encourage our respective Arts, cannot be devised in a moment; it ought to be the work of great caution and deliberation, and as simple as possible in its machinery.

Time will be required for this purpose; we must hear from distant countries to obtain their experience, and it must necessarily be perhaps many months before it can be matured. In the mean time, however, a preparatory simple organization can be made, and should be made as soon as possible, to prevent dismemberment, which may be attempted by out-door influence. On this subject let us all be on our guard—let us point to our public documents to any who ask, what we have done, and why we have done it? while we go forward minding only our own concerns, leaving the Academy of Fine Arts as much out of our thoughts as they will permit us, and bending our attention to our own affairs, act as if no such institution existed.

One of our dangers at present is division and anarchy, from a want of organization suited to the present exigency. We are now composed of Artists in the four arts of design, viz. : Painting, Sculpture, Architecture and Engraving. Some of us are professional Artists, others Amateur, others Students. To the professed and practical Artist belongs the management of all things relating to schools, premiums and lectures—so that Amateur and Students may be most profited. The Amateurs and Students are those alone who can contend for the premiums, while the body of professional Artists exclusively judge of their rights to premiums, and award them.

How shall we first make the separation, has been a question which has been a little perplexing—there are none of us who can assume to be the body of artists, without giving offence to others, and still every one must perceive that to organize an Academy, there must be the distinction between professional artists, amateurs who are students, and professional students. The first great division should be, the body of professional artists, from the amateurs and students constituting the body, who are to manage the entire concerns of the new Institution, who shall be its officers, &c. There is a method which strikes me as obviating the difficulty—place it on the broad principle of the formation of any society—Universal Suffrage. We are now a mixed body—it is necessary for the benefit of all, that a separation into classes be made: who shall make it? why obviously the body itself. Let every member of this Association take home with him a list of all the members of it. Let each one select for himself from the whole list *fifteen*, whom he would call professional artists, to be the ticket which he will give in at the next meeting—these fifteen thus chosen, shall immediately elect not less than *ten*, nor more than *fifteen* professional artists, in or out of the Association, who shall (with the previously elected fifteen) constitute the body to be called the National Academy of the Arts of Design. To these shall be delegated the power to regulate its entire concerns, choose its members, select its students, &c. Thus will the germ be formed to grow up into an Institution, which we trust will be put on such principles as to encourage, not to depress the Arts. When this is done, our body will be no longer the Drawing Association, but the National Academy of the Arts of Design, still including all the present association, but in different capacities.

One word as to the name, National Academy of the Arts of Design. Any less name than National, would be taking one below the American Academy, and therefore is not desirable. If we were simply the Associated Artists, their name would swallow us up—therefore, National seems a proper one, as to the Arts of Design: These are Painting, Sculpture, Architecture and Engraving, while the Fine Arts include Poetry, Music, Landscape, Gardening, and the Histrionic Arts. Our name, therefore, expresses the entire character of our Institution, and that only."

This arrangement was unanimously adopted, and a list of the members of the Association was immediately furnished to each member—who from it was requested to select by the next meeting fifteen professional Artists to form his ticket. The fifteen having the highest number of votes to constitute a "Body of Artists," who shall before Wednesday evening next elect not less than ten, nor more than fifteen others, from professional artists, resident in the City of New-York. This whole body thus chosen, to be called the National Academy of the Arts of Design.

And by resolution, those remaining in the Association after such election, and wishing to belong to the new institution, were to be declared students of the new institution, and a certificate of membership to be given to them.

On the fifteenth of January, 1826, in conformity with the resolution, the Association proceeded to ballot.

Whereupon the following gentlemen were chosen:
S. F. B. Morse, Henry Inman, A. B. Durand, John Frazee, William Wall, Charles C. Ingham, William Dunlap, Peter Maverick, Ithiel Town, Thomas S. Cummings, Edward Potter, Charles C. Wright, Mosley J. Danforth, Hugh Reinagle, Gerlando Marsiglia.

And between the fifteenth and eighteenth of the month, the above-named artists assembled for the performance of their part of the task; for on the eighteenth of January, 1826, the President stated, that "the professional artists chosen at the last meeting of the Association had balloted for *ten* professional artists on one ticket, and five subsequently on separate tickets, and that the following gentlemen were those elected:" Samuel Waldo, William Jewitt, John W. Paradise, Frederick S. Agate, Rembrandt Peale, James Coyle, Nathaniel Rogers, J. Parisen, William Main, John Evers, Martin E. Thompson, Thomas Cole, John Vanderlyn, Alexander Anderson, D. W. Wilson. By this method was formed THE NATIONAL ACADEMY OF THE ARTS OF DESIGN. Samuel F. B. Morse and John L. Morton were chosen to act as President and Secretary until the adoption of a Constitution.

The National Academy of Design, thus ushered into the world, was publicly declared to be as follows—the members professional artists—and thus divided in the four Arts of Design:

In Painting.

Samuel F. B. Morse,	Frederick S. Agate,
Henry Inman,	Edward C. Potter,
Thomas S. Cummings,	Hugh Reinagle,
William Dunlap,	James Coyle,
Rembrandt Peale,	D. W. Wilson,
Charles C. Ingham,	J. Parisen,
Thomas Cole,	John W. Paradise,
John Evers,	Nathaniel Rogers.

In Sculpture.

John Frazee.

In Architecture.

Ithiel Town,	Martin E. Thompson.

In Engraving.

A. B. Durand,	Mosley J. Danforth,
William Main,	Peter Maverick,

Charles C. Wright.

The following students in the

Antique School of the 1st Grade.

John L. Morton, *Amateur,*

Henry J. Morton, "	Robert Morris,
John I. Neilson, "	Albert Durand,
George W. Hatch,	John W. Paradise,
Thomas Grinnell,	Alexander G. Davis,
Ambrose Andrews,	John R. Murray, Jr.

Dr. F. G. King was appointed Professor of Anatomy.

The Antique School was open every Monday, Wednesday, and Saturday evening.

There was no Life School.

The Anatomical Lectures were announced as in course of delivery on Monday evenings.

Mr. Morse was requested to prepare a short address to the public, setting forth the views and general intentions of the Institution, from which the following is an extract; a further portion will be found in the opening remarks to the First Exhibition:

NATIONAL ACADEMY OF THE ARTS OF DESIGN.

" An institution with this name has recently been organized by the Artists of this city, founded upon principles which, it is believed, will elevate the character and condition of the Arts of Design in our country.

" The want of such an institution has long been felt by those interestsd in the advancement of the liberal arts—especially by artists themselves; and to its establishment, accordingly, almost the whole body of the profession in this city have concentrated their efforts.

" The National Academy of the Arts of Design is founded on the common-sense principle, that *every profession in society knows best what measures are necessary for its own improvement.* Its success is no more problematical than the success of many societies that might be named, where the members are exclusively of one profession. *To others* shall be left the discussion of the question, WHETHER THE COMMON METHOD OF RAISING FUNDS FOR THE SUPPORT OF INSTITUTIONS FOR THE ENCOURAGEMENT OF LITERATURE and the arts by connecting a large body of stockholders with them, be on the whole advisable, or not. It may be observed, however, that the little experience had on this subject does not seem favorable to such a mode of procedure. IN THE PERMANENT FORMATION OF THIS INSTITUTION, a DIFFERENT COURSE WILL BE PURSUED: a course sanctioned by the experience of Academies of Arts in Europe—especially the Royal Academy of London."

In the American Academy, the formation of the new art institution was severely felt and dreaded, and harsh recriminations were passed in the Board of Direction. The American made strenuous efforts to invigorate itself, and to revise its proceedings, and adopted measures of counteraction to the progress of the infant National.

The Library was increased. They purchased copies of Hogarth, Sir J. Reynolds, and other works. Students were *again invited* to attend—free of charge. The rooms were to be *warmed*—a thing never before attempted. Instructors were to be furnished—lectures delivered. Effort beyond effort was made, and the venerable Dr. Francis, then equally known to fame with Bell and Hunter, was called to fill the chair of Demonstrative Anatomy, in opposition to Godman and King in the National.

It was in vain!

All the members first elected into the National consented to serve; of those subsequently chosen there were no acceptances, and some altogether declined; among the latter was Mr. Vanderlyn.

[*New-York American, May* 26, 1826.]

MESSRS. EDITORS—I observe that my name has been, *without my authority*, and in a very unceremonious manner, inserted in a list of persons composing a new association, pompously entitled "The National Academy of Design," at the same moment that this *soi-disant* Academy have thus *deigned* to rate me among the number of its associates—an honor I decline. They have, with equal modesty, intimated to the Corporation that the Rotunda, erected with great cost and exertions under my superintendence, upon ground leased from the Honorable the Common Council, expressly for the purpose of exhibiting panorama and other splendid paintings, may be transferred from my hands and appropriated to their use.

I have the honor to be your ob't serv't,

JNO. VANDERLYN.

[*New-York American, May* 29, 1826.

MESSRS. EDITORS—It is with some degree of surprise that I perused in your paper of Saturday the note of Mr. Vanderlyn, and I cannot but feel a deep regret that that gentleman should have deemed it necessary to give the first notice of his non-acceptance of membership of the National Academy in the manner he has thought proper to adopt. He had no friends who more cordially sympathized with him, or who were more disposed to aid him in every way in their power, than the members of this institution. In proof of this, soon after the formation of the National Academy of Design, a member brought to one of our meetings the pamphlet of Mr. Vanderlyn, in which he prefers his claims to the Rotunda, and petitions the Common Council for a renewal of his lease. No sooner was it read, than the following resolution was offered; the President remarking, that "perhaps we could not better begin our career than by an act of courtesy and kindness to a brother artist, whose genius commanded our respect, and in whose misfortunes we sincerely sympathized:"

"*Resolved*, That a Committee be appointed to wait on Mr. Vanderlyn to assure him of our sympathy, and to ask if any act of ours as a body can be of any service to him in procuring a renewal of his lease, and tendering our services for that purpose."

Mr. Vanderlyn was in Washington, which rendered useless the appointment of the Committee.

In the late petition to the Corporation, we distinctly *and expressly disclaimed all interference with the prior claim of Mr. Vanderlyn.* Our reason for applying at all for the Rotunda, at this time, was that other societies had made application, and as we had been informed that a renewal of it to Mr. Vanderlyn would not be made, we wished merely to be considered, in such case, *among* the applicants.

As to the unauthorized insertion of his name among the members of the Academy, I would observe, that Mr. Vanderlyn was elected on the 18th day of January last, more than four months ago, and was notified of his election as soon as it was ascertained he had returned to the city: his note in your paper of Saturday is the first intimation to the Academy, public or private, of his decision.

It is to be regretted that an act designed to be complimentary should not have received from Mr. Vanderlyn the attention which common politeness dictates.

As his election into the Academy seems to have produced an effect so unexpected, his public renunciation will doubtless be accepted at our next meeting, and Mr. Vanderlyn will be relieved from the distress of belonging to our number.

A MEMBER OF THE N. A. D.

The letter of Mr. Vanderlyn, and the reply, the writer trusts, will be a sufficient answer to all who ask: Why is Mr. Vanderlyn not a member of the N. A. D.?—He was so made, *and refused it.*

June 7th, Dunlap proposed the following resolution:

"*Whereas*, Mr. Jno. Vanderlyn has given public notice in the papers that he is dissatisfied with his election as a member of the National Academy of Design: therefore,

"*Resolved*, That the said election be annulled, and his name stricken off the list of members."

Which was carried unanimously.

The above clearly showed that Mr. Vanderlyn had a temper—who has not? There is, however, another and more acceptable view of Mr. Vanderlyn. To him is New-York indebted for the most beautiful panoramas that have ever graced the city.

In 1813 there existed a building in Broadway, between White and Franklin Streets, used for the exhibition of panoramic views. It was in the possession of Mr. Holland, the artist, who, assisted by his pupils, Reinagle and Evers, painted and had on exhibition a panorama of the City of New-York.

In 1817 Mr. Vanderlyn erected a building on the northeast corner of the Park, to which he gave the name of the "Rotunda." In that building he commenced the exhibition of a series of panoramic views, Versailles, Paris, Athens, Mexico, &c., &c. That may not be the order of their introduction. That of Versailles was painted by Vanderlyn, and was the first exhibited. That of Mexico not until 1828— it was a superb production, painted by Robert Burford. The whole series was one of an unusual degree of excellence.

Since that day there was a building on the corner of Broadway and Prince Street, called the "New Rotunda," in which Catherwood exhibited his Jerusalem, which was

burned, together with much of his valuable property. Since
that time there has been no building in the city devoted
to panoramic pictures. *Query.* Would not the Harlem
Railroad Engine Depot, on Fourth Avenue and 31st Street,
make an admirable place for such purposes ?

In the selection of members as previously named to constitute the National Academy of Design, one of the artists
of the city, John R. Smith, an eccentric Englishman—a
teacher of the highest order of excellence, and keeper of the
American Academy, was not, for cause, included. That
slight he never forgave—and from that time commenced his
untiring animosity and open hostility to the Academy of
Design and its members. Smith, unfortunately, was of a
violent temper and unaccountably quarrelsome disposition,
and the artists properly feared the introduction of such a
one among them, in so early and tender an age of their then
infant Institution. Hence his rejection. At a preliminary
and informal meeting held, his name had been considered,
and his admissibility or non-admissibility canvassed, and as
was supposed, in a strictly confidential manner, such as
should have properly belonged to so respectable a body.
That confidence, however, was abused. At the subsequent
and formal meeting, his name was by one pressed to a ballot. It required in all cases a unanimous vote to elect.
On counting the ballot for Smith, it was found that there
was but one in his favor. That fact was by one of the
number, long since deceased, communicated to the party,
and with the additional voluntary—that the writer had in
the midst of a "fierce debate," jumped on the table, and
with great emphasis and passion declared—"That so long
as he held a ball that could defeat him, HE NEVER SHOULD BE
ELECTED." Such was unqualifiedly false in every particular.
The writer never made such, or any other assertion on the
subject—the whole was a barefaced fabrication, and all otherwise at variance with the facts.

No such angry debate took place at all, anywhere. The
formal balloting was merely confirmatory of a previously
agreed selection. In Mr. Smith's case, it was almost a silent one—no one but his friend speaking. It was received
in silence—was silently balloted for, and in silence he was
dropped forever. The result was to each *blackballer* a written and peremptory demand for "satisfaction, public or private." The letters were by common consent inclosed in
one package, and returned to their author. That, perhaps
of all others, was a proceeding he was least able or prepared to bear.—There was no bloodshed. From that time the
newspapers of the day, and indeed for years after, bore am-

ple testimony to the activity of his pen, which was seldom at rest. The articles were of the most bitterly vindictive kind, personal and sarcastic. He was, however, never answered, which was to him the "cut unbearable." Everything has an END, and so had Smith's writings—not an *untimely one*. Some twenty years or more after the date of the matter referred to, Smith called upon the writer and other artists, and expressed his deepest regret that anything of the kind should ever have occurred; particularly so to the writer, his former pupil. Admitted its injustice—apologized, and asked that it should be forgiven; closing up the conversation by saying, "that he now found to his sorrow, that his own temper had been his worst enemy and ruin." The days of Mr. Smith's old age were clouded by necessity— which were in some degree alleviated by those who had suffered most from his pungent pen.

To return to the proper run of history. On the 18th of January, the night of organization, a committee was **1826.** appointed to procure rooms, and otherwise devise the ways and means for an Exhibition to be held in the Spring. Messrs. Durand, Ingham, Maverick, Frazee, Dunlap, and Marsiglia had the honor (little so thought then, probably,) to be *First Exhibition* Committee. Messrs. Morse, Cole, Dunlap, Cummings, Durand and Ingham, the first on the exposition of works. A committee was appointed to draft a Code of BY-LAWS.

Dr. F. G. King was appointed Professor of Anatomy, and Charles B. Shaw, Professor of Perspective. And it was directed, "that each member of the former Association should be furnished with a certificate, in conformity with the resolution passed." And it was resolved, "that any artist wishing to become a member of this Academy before the adoption of the Constitution, may be so admitted by a *unanimous vote of the Academy* at a monthly meeting."

It could not, I think, have been construed as written, viz.: requiring the unanimity of the thirty members. By a following resolution it was declared, "that not less than 10 should form a quorum." At a meeting held May 3d, Mr. Catlin, *previously proposed*, was elected. The names of the present are not given in the minutes, and it therefore does not fully determine the question—but, inasmuch as there is no probability every member of the Society was present, it was probably construed to mean, a unanimous vote of *those present*. (A very different matter.)

Dunlap remarks: "Immediately after the organization of the new Institution, measures were taken to open its first Exhibition, and notwithstanding the many difficulties under which they labored, the artists succeeded in collecting together such a display of talent, as surprised every visitor of their newly formed gallery, consisting of works of *living artists* only.

The Catalogue was prefaced by an appeal by Dunlap and Morse:

"THE NATIONAL ACADEMY OF THE ARTS OF DESIGN TO THE PUBLIC.

*   *   *   *   *   *   *   *   *

" The Artists of the City of New-York have associated under the above title, for the purpose of mutual improvement and the instruction of their pupils.

" They have no object in view but the advancement of the Arts and the benefit of the Artists.   *   *   *   *   *   *   *

" The name they have adopted is meant to express their wish to be associated with all Artists.   Although they have a name and a flourishing school, they have no ' local habitation.'   The constituted authorities of the State and of the City will judge how far it may be for their honor to grant them one. The Exhibition is for the purpose of showing the state of the Arts, and raising the funds necessary to defray the expenses.

" It is hoped that the establishment of an Institution directed and supported BY ARTISTS, will prove worthy of the patronage they ask of their fellow-citizens.

" Their good wisher,   D****P."

*   *   *   *   *   *   *   *   *

" For the support of this Institution the Artists look to the revenue derived from *Exhibitions and Lectures.*   These, without any other aid, they have the fullest confidence will be amply sufficient for all exigencies.   Public and private aid may advance its progress by donations, particularly by the grant of rooms. But with the resources derived from Exhibitions alone, they can supply all that is wanted in an Academy of Design.

" The only encouragement asked from the public at present, is their attendance on the Exhibitions and Lectures.   M***E."

The Exhibition took place in a room in the second story of a house on the southwest corner of Broadway and Reade Street; an ordinary dwelling, and not covering an area of more than twenty-five by fifty feet, with no other than the usual side windows.   That limited space served for the first Exhibition.   It was open from 9 A. M. to 10 P. M., and "lighted with gas."   The *gas* consisted of 3 two-light ordinary branch burners—6 lights in all, for the whole Exhibition.   Dunlap, in his remarks, should therefore be understood as speaking very comparatively of the infant effort.

Nevertheless, the Institution, or members, like many others, who have risen from humble "two stories to magnificent brown stone," were as happy, and felt as large as with their galleries six times multiplied.

That little effort was most ceremoniously heralded to the public by a "private opening" by invitation, and the Council formally received the visitors. His Excellency Governor Clinton and suite, his Honor the Mayor, the Common Council of the City, (then a respectable body,) the Judges of the Courts, the Faculty of Columbia College, the members of the American Academy of Fine Arts, and *persons of distinction* at "*present residing* in the city." The members of the Academy of Design in their new-fledged honors, *appearing with a white rosette in their button-holes.* So much for the opening—the ushering in of the first-born. On the day following, the 14th of May, it was presented to the public. It consisted of copies, originals—Oil Paintings, Water-Colors, Drawings for Machinery, Architecturals, Engravings, &c., &c., to the unprecedented number of 170 productions.

That was the first solely artistic effort at Exhibition in the country. The Catalogue is now a curiosity—out of print, with the single exception, perhaps, of a copy in the writer's possession. The Institution was an acorn then, not an oak.

What were the receipts of the Exhibition, or what its expenses, never appeared in figures. The accounts were artistically kept, and probably did not exceed, so far as can be gathered, the sum of three hundred dollars. It closed on or about the 1st July, and as Dunlap remarks, who then acted as Treasurer, failed to meet its expenses. The fact of deficiency is duly entered in the minutes, the account audited, and by a report made on the 11th July, declared to be $163, it was ordered to be made up by an assessment on the members of $7 each, which it is said was paid.—Why $210, which would have been the amount, was required to pay $163, does not appear—probably to cover contingencies.

The Institution had at that time not only to contend with the discouragement of want of pecuniary success, but likewise the full weight, powerful influence and hostility of the American Academy, which was brought to bear in every possible manner on the newly formed Academy and its members. That influence, it must be remembered, was exerted on a public already prejudiced in favor of the old Institution. The statements were heralded forth by persons holding high position and favor; and at a time when the very name of artist was looked upon with distrust—their actions and credit, if not even their sanity doubted, (it is fortunately otherwise now,) and in a great measure to the Academy do the younger artists owe so favorable a change of opinion.

During the Exhibition many availed themselves of the opportunity to assail the artists in severe and unjust personalities, and abusive criticism on the works on exhibition.

"Neutral Tints," one and two, were conspicuous champions in that warfare, annoying, it is true, and particularly so, when accompanied with the other and heavier metal at work.

The artists, in no way discouraged by the want of success of their first effort, determined unanimously on continuance.

Mr. Vanderlyn had a second time been ordered to vacate the Rotunda in the Park, and that it would, by non-compliance with the terms and expiration of contract, revert to the Corporation of the City. The committee appointed to procure a building for the Academy presented a memorial to the Common Council, asking for said building—again adding thereto, *provided it could be done without interfering with any arrangement the Corporation might make with Mr. Vanderlyn.* They received for answer, "That the Common Council had taken no order as yet on the subject, and had not determined what disposition they would make of the building.

That was the second application made by the Academy for assistance without success.

That it was a failure, the writer felt truly thankful. The Institution so far owed no debt of *gratitude*, and had not, therefore, become *ungrateful.*

On December 16th, a Code of Laws and Constitution was read by paragraphs—adopted, and 300 copies ordered to be printed for the use of the members: and on the 5th January following, the Committee on Printing reported the performance of their task, and the copies were that evening distributed—so say the minutes. That copy is out of print, (and record even has been denied,) and where the mistake as to date or reference occurs, cannot readily be seen. An asterisk and note appended to order to print of December 16, says: "See printed copy of Constitution and By-Laws at the end of this book." The copy is there, but it is of the date of 1829, and after the act of incorporation of 1828.—Of its existence there can be no doubt; a copy is in the writer's possession.

The schools of the season were opened in the rooms of the Philosophical Society three evenings in the week—Monday, Wednesday, and Friday. There being no funds in the Treasury, it was resolved, "that for the payment of expenses a voluntary subscription be made by the members;" and the Secretary was directed to forward to each the foregoing resolution. This appears to have been placed at $5. The school was of the most promising character, numbering some 40 students. Lectures on Anatomy were delivered by Dr. King, and on Perspective by Chas. Shaw, Esq. Premiums were offered for the best drawings—the decision thereon was made by the students' own ballots; though in the case of the first premium, the vote being a tie, it was referred to the Council.

Dr. King was requested to sit for his portrait. It was painted by Mr. Morse, is an excellent likeness, though never quite finished—one hand and chair not completed. It is now in the collection of the Academy portraits.

At the end of the academic season Mr. Morse delivered an address to the students in the Chapel of Columbia College—the venerable old building on Church Street, opposite Park Place—(now no more,) and also the premiums to the successful candidates—Geo. W. Hatch, William Page, J. W. Paradise, Samuel Wallin, Abner Whitlock.

GENTLEMEN OF THE ACADEMY:

The occasion of our first anniversary furnishes me with an opportunity, which I gladly improve, of explaining to you more at large the nature of those institutions among which we have lately ranked ourselves.

Almost every country of Europe possesses, among its essential institutions, an Academy of Arts; and even in Mexico, in Lima, and in Puebla, among our southern neighbors, similar institutions have long been established and appreciated. From their universal adoption in civilized countries, their beneficial influence can scarcely be doubted; and, although it has been a disputed point whether, on the whole, Academies of Arts have a favorable effect in eliciting genius of the first order, and whether genius is not rather shackled by their discipline, I am inclined to think that, where the latter effect is produced, it has been owing not so much to the institution itself, as to the influence of some erroneous principles in the economy of a particular academy. Too much may be attempted to be taught; rules founded in narrow views of intellectual philosophy may be enforced; but it does not therefore follow that we should teach nothing, nor that no system should be observed. Were we to educate a poet, by confining him chiefly to the study of measure and versification, and to the graces of style, and to insist that there could be no poetry without these desiderata, we should doubtless throw obstacles in the way of genius, and exert an unfavorable influence on its development; but should we, on this account, leave the poet to his wild sallies and unrestrained enthusiasm, and be content with the diamond in its rough coat, lest it be spoiled in the polishing? It has been urged against academies that, while they may encourage genius, they for the most part foster pretension and mediocrity. What should we think of the florist who should keep his flowers in total darkness, lest the same sun which invigorates the flower, should also warm into life the weeds which will spring up around it?

With proper care these difficulties may be avoided; and the experience of similar institutions, in other countries, may be advantageously consulted, to enable us to shun their errors, and adopt such of their principles and regulations as can be made subservient to the interests of the Arts of Design in our own country.

With this view I will engage your attention, in the first place, to a rapid glance at the origin and economy of some of the principal Academies of Arts in Europe.

Academies for the promotion of the Arts of Design are by no means of recent date: so early as the year 1345 an association was formed by the painters of *Venice*, under the protection of St. Luke, for the purpose of improvement in their own art; and in 1350 a similar institution was established in *Florence*, under the patronage of the illustrious House of Medici. The date of these establishments, coeval with the revival of the arts not many years after the death of Cimabue and Giotto, renders it probable, at least, that the celebrity of that age was, through their influence, essentially promoted.

In France, in the year 1648, *the Academy of St. Luke* was organized at Paris, by the painters and sculptors of that city, among whom were Le Brun, Sarazin, and Corneille. They received the royal sanction in the beginning of that year. Their principal object, in thus associating together, appears to have been their own improvement and that of their pupils: they met two hours every day for drawing and designing, and their schools were under the direction of twelve professors. Every three months three prizes for Design were distributed among the pupils, and two for Painting and two for Sculpture every year.

In Austria, the *Imperial Royal Academy of Arts, at Vienna,* was founded in 1704; and Baron Strudel, one of the most eminent painters of that day, was at its head. Many local causes prevented the Academy's progress, and at the death of Strudel it languished for many years. In 1726 it again revived, under the direction of a celebrated Flemish painter, James Van Schuppen. By the efforts of Van Schuppen the Arts flourished in Vienna until his death, when the direction was offered to Gran, the only painter then in Vienna possessing literary knowledge sufficient for the station. Gran declined the offer, and officers called Rectors, who were professional artists, were appointed to fill the place, by dividing the duties of the office: this arrangement continued for nine years, when Martin Von Meytens, a Swedish painter, was placed at the head. He is represented as a man of polished mind, liberal disposition, and possessing great love for his art, and sensibility to the exalted character of his profession. Under him the Arts consequently became respected, and artists arose who reflect honor on their country to the present day. The Academy continued to flourish, and at length the Emperor Joseph II. assigned to it a large building and spacious apartments; those for study alone occupying fifteen large rooms besides ante-chambers. It was divided into four schools: a School of Painting and Sculpture; of Engraving; of Architecture; and of Designs for Manufactures. Jewelers, gold and silversmiths, and all artificers in metals, practiced drawing in these schools, and had before them the most select models and designs to improve their taste; and every profession and trade to whom some skill in drawing is necessary, were admitted and taught gratuitously. All these schools were under the direction of artists of eminence in their respective arts, who endeavored to form their pupils on those philosophic principles which they had made the foundation of their own skill.

To encourage industry and emulation among the pupils, *premiums* were periodically bestowed, and fixed stipends or pensions given to the most distinguished.

In Spain, the *Royal Academy of St. Ferdinand* was established at Madrid, in the year 1752. As early as the year 1619, however, the Artists of the capital presented a memorial to Philip III., petitioning for the establishment of an Academy of Painting. The petition was unsuccessful; and during the reign of his successor another ineffectual attempt was made by them, which is said to have failed principally for want of unanimity among themselves. In the reign of Philip V., Olivieri, an artist of eminence, first established a public School of Design at his own house. His school attracted the attention of the government, and at length a proposition was made to the king by Olivieri, for the creation of a Public Academy, which, after many delays, obtained the royal sanction.

The Secretary of State is, in this country, *ex officio* President of the Academy. The Directors, however, are artists, who teach their pupils, from designs of their own, the elementary branches of the Arts. There are schools for the study of Mathematics and Perspective, and a library of authors on the Arts belongs to the Academy. Its expenses are paid by the king, who appoints to all the offices. Personal nobility is granted to the Academicians.

As an incentive to the students, eighteen premiums are ordered to be distributed, nine of gold, and nine of silver triennially. The premiums are delivered to the successful candidates in public with great pomp and ceremony, in presence of the principal nobility of the kingdom. The effects of this Academy on taste, and especially in Architecture, are exhibited to this day in the "temples, palaces, streets, walks, gates, and even private dwellings," of Madrid.

In Russia, *The Imperial Academy of the Fine Arts* was instituted at St. Petersburg, in the year 1758, by the Empress Elizabeth; but its regulations were not officially sanctioned until Catherine II. ascended the throne. It appears to be organized on a plan somewhat different from other European academies, and embracing a wider range of subjects. It comprehends a college of early education, commencing with instructing the student at five or six years of age. His studies are not confined to those branches of science which bear more immediately, but rather remotely, upon his future profession. He is taught Arithmetic, Geography, History, Civil Obligations, Physic, and Natural History. And among the duties of the Inspector, is that of instilling into the minds of his pupils "politeness, and every sentiment inseparable from probity and humanity." The term of college education is nine years, after which time those students who are approved are admitted to the first or lowest classes in the Academy, where they remain for a further term of six years. There is a public exhibition of the works of the artists once in two years. A system of premiums is also established. Two silver medals are distributed every four months; and two gold medals to the authors of the best sketches of subjects proposed by the Academy. Twelve artists who have obtained prizes are sent abroad every three years, and their expenses borne by the Academy, under certain regulations. Those mechanic trades are also cultivated which are in any way influenced by the Fine Arts. A Church, and even a Dispensary and Infirmary, are connected with the Institution.

So late as the year 1800, the *National Academy of Milan* was established, connected, as it would seem, with a similar academy in Paris, instituted at the same time. The Academic Body contains 30 academicians, artists of distinction, who have a settled residence in the city, and of an indefinite number of honorary associates, chosen by the academicians from among the artists and friends of the arts. Their premiums consist of two classes. The first of six gold medals of various value, from twenty to one hundred and twenty sequins, for original designs in the various branches of art. The second class consists of fourteen silver medals for academic drawings in the different schools. The premiums of the first class purchase the successful productions which are preserved in the academic collection.

The National Academy is supported from the national treasury.

It has seven schools, under the care of nine professors; and besides these schools, one for the living model, a hall of statues, a collection of pictures and a library. The various schools are furnished with models and other materials and instruments of use to the student. The Academy also possesses a collection of garments in the costume of every age; tunics, palliums, chlamides, togas, and models and drawings of every sort of ancient armor. The premiums are delivered in public before the local authorities. The Secretary delivers a discourse illustrating some branch of the Arts of Design, and an orator appointed by the academicians also addresses the audience, after which the premiums are distributed by the local authorities.

I come now to notice the English *Royal Academy of Arts*. Before touching on the economy of an institution which we profess to make the model of our own, a brief sketch of the rise and progress of the Arts in England will best elucidate the origin of the Royal Academy.

Previous to its establishment the Arts of Design in England had given but feeble signs of life; their early struggles promised nothing but a temporary and sickly existence. While they were in their full vigor in Italy and other continental countries, the political state of Britain was unfavorable to their growth. Henry VIII., indeed, invited Raphael, Titian, Holbein, and Torrigiano to his Court; the two latter accepted, but the two former declined the invitation. To Holbein may be ascribed the introduction of Portrait Painting in England. During the reigns of the first Mary, of Elizabeth, and of James the First, there was little or nothing that indicated the existence of the Arts of Design. Charles I. was better disposed to their encouragement than his predecessors, and had he lived, would without doubt have contributed to their more early development. He invited Rubens to England, who, while he practiced his profession assiduously, resided at court in the situation of Ambassador from the King of Spain. Vandyck, Inigo Jones, and Dobson, were also encouraged by this monarch. But the early death of Charles, and the political troubles of that period, again prostrated the rising arts; nor did they revive with anything of manly vigor during the foppish age of his successor. The attention of the nation, in the troublous times of James II. and William and Mary, was wholly engrossed with war and politics: the Arts of Design, so emphatically the arts of peace, were of course asleep; they momentarily awoke at the bidding of Queen Anne, when Sir Christopher Wren, in Architecture, and Sir James Thornhill, in painting, were employed in erecting and decorating the splendid cathedral of St. Paul's; but they were roused only to sink back again into a more profound slumber through the reigns of George I. and George II. The signs of vitality at this period are not to be sought for at the Court, but among the neglected professors of art. Even in the reign of Queen Anne, the artists formed private schools, and continued them with various modifications for more than fifty years. Having made several unsuccessful attempts to establish a Public Academy, undiscouraged, they zealously pursued their studies, supporting themselves by their own individual subscriptions. It was not until the reign of George III. that the Arts of Design rose in earnest from their lethargy in England; but, like one awaking from long sleep, their first steps were feeble and timid. Artists had now multiplied in London; their individual struggles for public notice seemed to be met only by *neglect* or *contempt*, and their early history shows much of the unhappy effect of that *native irritability* so often the concomitant of genius, and so interesting when it is evinced by a chastened sensibility; but so lamentable, when excited by such causes, it is perceived silently preying upon its possessor, and breaking his spirit, or uttering itself in splenetic and ungenerous remark against contemporary merit. But now commenced a new era. "Neglect," (says the Corresponding Secretary of the Royal Academy,) "although it might mortify, did not subdue the British artist. When the artists found that expectation offered no prospect, and patience drew forth no hope, they assembled in an almost unnoticed society for the renovation of the drooping arts. They endeavored to unite their individual forces, in order to give weight to their movements." Their first symptoms of success were visible in 1760, in the popularity of the first exhibition of their works, in a room loaned them by another society, and to which the public were admitted gratis. Some change was made the following year in the mode of admission; but in the next exhibition, evidently with much timidity, they ventured to ask an admission fee of one shilling from each visitor; and to prepare the public for this innovation, as it was then thought to be, they deemed it necessary to conciliate public opinion, in a preface to their catalogue, written by Dr. Johnson. In this manner was introduced an important feature which distinguishes the English from the Continental exhibitions.

These promising prospects, which seemed to be opening upon the arts, were soon overclouded by bitter contention among the artists. For three years they continued their disgraceful contests, which at length ended in a division into two parties. They separated. The smallest and weakest, and seemingly defeated party, composed, however, of the most distinguished artists, formed the plan of instituting a Royal Academy, under the protection of the sovereign; the plan was successful; and in the year 1768 the Royal Academy of Arts was established, and Sir Joshua Reynolds was elected their first President.

The plan of the Academy is very simple, embracing in its objects to be attained the two most important of all the continental academies. The artists, in their petition to the king, avow them to be: "1st. The establishment of a well-regulated *School*, or Academy of Design for the use of students in the arts; and, 2d. An *Annual Exhibition*, open to all artists of distinguished merit, where they may offer their performances to public inspection." Its internal regulations, in the early stages of its existence, were mostly borrowed from those of the Imperial Academy of St. Petersburg: they have since been modified according as circumstances and experience suggested. In connection with the schools, a system of premiums is established. A gold medal and fifty guineas are given every two years for original works, by the students in each of the three departments of Painting, Architecture, and Sculpture. The biennial premiums are delivered in public, when it is the custom (commenced by Sir Joshua Reynolds) for the President to address the Academy on some subject connected with the Arts of Design. Other premiums are distributed annually for the best drawings.

The Exhibition is annual, consisting of works by living artists never before exhibited in London. It opens in May to the public, and continues from six to eight weeks only, and is then closed. All the expenses of the Academy are paid from the receipts of the exhibitions.

The schools of the Academy are, a School of the Antique, a School of the Living Model, and more recently a School of Painting.

The whole government of the Academy is vested in a President, a Council, and General Assembly, all the individuals of whom are professional artists.

I have thus presented you with a brief sketch of some of the principal Academies of Europe. In reviewing the ground we have passed over, we find that all these Academies bear a strong resemblance to each other in their *origin* and in their *most prominent features.*

And First: With scarcely an exception, *Artists were the first movers in the establishment of the European Academies of Arts.* This was the case in Florence, in Venice, in Paris, in Madrid, and in London. In *all cases their entire government is intrusted to Artists.* If there is any instance where there is a seeming contradiction of this remark, as at Madrid and St. Petersburg, the deviation is one of form, and is sufficiently explained by adverting to the form of government under which it exists. In a despotic government, all offices of influence and patronage must be at the disposal of the monarch; and it is not to be supposed that the first offices of an institution of such importance, would be the only situations unoccupied with the favorites and supporters of a despotic court.

Second: Another prominent feature in all of them, is *Schools for the Students of the Arts,* where not only models and materials are collected for their use, but where they are instructed by the most distinguished artists of the country composing the Academic Body.

Thirdly: Intimately connected with this instruction, a system of *Premiums to incite the students to industry and emulation,* is another prominent feature. To this *all the Academies, without exception, have attached the greatest importance.*

Fourth: Another principal feature, common to all, is *an Exhibition of the works of living artists;* and although respectively modified in regard to time of exhibition, and to terms of admission, according to the peculiar circumstances by which each is surrounded, there is no evidence that they are composed of any other than the recent works of the artists of the day.

With these examples before us, we formed, more than a year since, our National Academy of Design, and on similar principles. We have incorporated into its constitution those features common to all Academies of Arts. It has been created by the union of most of the principal artists of the city. Our constitution provides for the establishment of the various schools. Our very limited means has allowed us, as yet, only to establish our School of the Antique; and thus far, unaided from without, (except by the generous, but temporary loan of a room for the school by the Literary and Philosophical Society,) we have sustained this school from the beginning to the present time; we have been enabled to give instruction, *gratuitous instruction,* to about 30 students. Two courses of Anatomical Lectures, illustrating with ability this science as connected with the Arts of Design, have been delivered by our Professor of Anatomy, and the students universally have made laudable progress in drawing, the common grammar, or basis of each of the Arts of Design. With respect to the third feature of Academies, viz.: *Premiums,* early in the season, we put into operation this essential part of our plan. The subjects for which they were offered, are adapted to the incipient state of the school, and consequently belong to the lower classes of premiums. We have reserved for a more mature state of our institution, and for works of a higher order of Art, the larger and more valuable prizes.

The plan of *Exhibitions*, as it exists in the English Royal Academy, is that which we have adopted, as better suited to our state of society than those of the Continental Academies. All the exhibitions of the latter, as far as I am able to learn, are *free* to the public: the funds of the several institutions derive no benefit from them. These Academies are consequently an annual tax to the national treasury; that at St. Petersburg at the expense of 156,000 rubles, and that at Milan of more than 1,500 pounds sterling per annum. On the contrary, the Royal Academy of London, since the few first years of its establishment, has not only been without cost to the government, but derives a vast and increasing income wholly from a species of tax never more equitably levied—a tax, the merest pittance in its amount, and asked from those alone who directly receive for it much more than an equivalent; a tax, however, which in the aggregate amounts to much more than is sufficient to defray the expenses of the Academy, and leaves an annual surplus in its treasury. This is a method of support to Academies without burthening the Government, which is peculiarly adapted to the state of our country, and to our situation. One which, with a little extrinsic aid in furnishing us with apartments only, for our Schools and Exhibitions, will insure our eventual success. We have taken the English Royal Academy for our model, as far as the different circumstances of form of government and state of taste will admit. It is the most flourishing of all foreign Academies; it has among its members a great variety of talent, embracing all the numerous departments of Art in their most minute subdivisions of subject, and the Annual Exhibitions display a rich and diversified feast to the refined portion of London society. It is deservedly popular, and its success is a happy illustration of a sound remark of d'Israeli, that "an Academy......can only succeed by the same means in which originated all such Academies—among *individuals* themselves; it will not be by the favor of the *many*," he observes, "but by the wisdom of the *few*. It is not even in the power of Royalty to create at a word, what can only be formed by the *co-operation of the workmen themselves*, and of the great task-master, Time."

The Royal Academy is a pre-eminent example of the effect of united effort among the Artists. "This establishment," says Mr. Shee, "which by foreigners is supposed to be a splendid example of public munificence, derives its income from the disinterested labors of artists; and, except the advantage of apartments at Somerset Place, has not for many years received the smallest assistance from the State." This honorable tribute to the Artists of England is not exclusively bestowed by one of their own number. A writer in the *Quarterly Review*, many years since, although not favorably disposed towards Academies, testifies to the same truth. "It should be remembered, however, to the honor of the artists of this country, that whatever progress they have made is principally owing to their own exertions." And why should not this be the result? That individuals of a particular profession should best know how to manage the concerns of that profession, is no unreasonable, it certainly is no new doctrine: Horace long since expressed the sentiment—

> ....Quod medicorum est
> Promittunt medici : tractant fabrilia fabri.

The Royal Academy system is diffusing itself in the formation of other Academies, in Britain, on its popular model. The Royal Hibernian Academy of Arts, recently established at Dublin, is an example; and within the present year we learn that "an Academy is about to be established at Edinburgh, on the plan of the Royal Academy of London, by the northern Artists."

From the facts laid before you, gentlemen, you perceive the course which we must pursue to attain the same noble ends. It is a truth which cannot be too often enforced, and one which each of us should constantly bear in mind, that our *individual prosperity depends on the prosperity of the whole body.* I need not descant to you on the necessity of union, as an indispensable requisite to success. Not only is all history admonitory on this point, but the history of the arts in Britain is especially full of warning to us: their progress seems to have been accelerated or retarded in exact proportion to the prevalence or absence of harmony among the artists themselves. We have felt the beneficial influence of this harmony; and I feel confident that the good which has already resulted will stimulate us all to preserve with care, and to increase this happy disposition. Let no selfish, narrow views interfere with those of a more enlarged and liberal character which we desire to accomplish. The prospect before us is on the whole encouraging: when we compare the condition of our young institution with that of the infant Royal Academy, (not yet sixty years old,) when we see it struggling for existence amidst neglect, and ignorance, and misconception, and quackery, and every species of false taste; bitterly ridiculed without, and distracted by dissensions within, who would have predicted that in a half a century it could attain to its present gigantic manhood? We also shall have difficulties to contend with, some peculiar to ourselves, others similar in character to those of our transatlantic brethren; they are the diseases to which infant Art is subject; they must be borne, and with as much patience as possible. But why do I speak to you of difficulties? They are the glory of genius, without which its energy and its brilliancy would pass unnoticed away, like the electric fluid which flows unobserved along the smooth conductor; but when its course is thwarted, then, and only then, it bursts forth with its splendor, and astonishes by its power. Difficulties will yield to perseverance. We must not look for sudden changes in the public mind. They are not to be desired; for they will be as transient as they are sudden. The natural progress of taste in Art is gradual: its advance is slow—urged onward by the constant action and reaction of the artists and the public upon each other, of the works of the former, and the demands of the latter. It is through our Academy, but more especially through our Exhibitions, that the concentrated labors of the artists of the country can be brought to bear upon the public mind: it is here can be seen, as in a mirror, the state of the general taste. Such works as artists are commissioned to execute, such will they exhibit. Every work of a higher class of Art, and of a character above the common standard, will exert an influence to increase such works. Comparisons will be made, and discussion will result in a more thorough understanding of the true principles of Art; and thus public opinion will be formed: just taste will not be matured in a year; no, nor in many years; the various evidences of bad taste, as in other countries, will precede it. Popularity will often be the meed of some gaudy error. Bold pretension will be successful, while more retiring merit will be neglected, for it will not be understood. Empiricism will gather its temporary laurels; and ignorant wonder will utter its interjections at the juvenile efforts of some tyro in Art, in whom is fancied the future Raphael or Angelo of his country. Alas! a short-lived fame, to be deserted as soon as some newer candidate presents his claims, or the vain dreams of his admirers, have failed to be *in a moment* realized. These things have occurred in other countries, and they will occur here.

In this connection I cannot forbear a remark on the question of the expediency of an Artist's studying his profession in Europe. However desirable this course may appear on many accounts, especially in its influence on his own real improvement, it is attended with many and peculiar trials to him who returns to practice his profession at home. Unless he possesses great firmness of nerve, great self-denial, and a share of public spirit that belongs to few individuals in any class of society, he will scarcely be saved from misanthropic seclusion and despair. If the artist improves by his increased advantages abroad, is it not natural that he should outstrip in knowledge the public he leaves behind? When he returns he finds a community unprepared, however they may be disposed, to appreciate him. He has unfolded his powers in a society where the artists, and those that encourage them, have proceeded onward together to a far advanced point in the march of taste; but he comes back to a society which has scarcely begun to move in the great procession; and he sees before him a long, long track over which he has once successfully passed, all to be traveled again, and the whole mass by which he is surrounded also move with him, ere he reaches again the spot he has left, ere the enchanting prospects which began to open upon him can again be enjoyed. The country may indeed be the gainer by his acquirements, but it will too often be at the expense of the happiness, perhaps of the life, of the artist. The soil must be prepared at home. Our own sun must warm into life the seeds of native talent; they must not be planted in a more genial climate until they spread out their blossoms, and promise their fruit, and then be plucked up and replanted in the cold and sterile desert; they will perish by neglect, or be deprived of the nourishment and warmth which is their right, by some pretending weed that springs up and overshadows them. No! the artist may go abroad, but he must not return. He will there show the fruit of American genius fair among the fairest productions of foreign culture, and he will adorn the page of his country's history with a name which future generations will delight to pronounce, when they boast of their country's genius; but he must not return!

One word, before closing, on our responsibilities to the public. We hold a station in which we cannot be neutral. Our Academy of Arts must have some influence upon public morals: we may be of essential aid to the cause of morality, or we may be an efficient instrument in destroying it; we may help to elevate and purify the public mind by the disseminatien of purity of taste, and raise our art to its natural dignity as the handmaid of Truth and Virtue, or we may assist to degrade it to the menial office of pandering for the sensualist. The authority of great names in art must not here be our guide, for, alas! we may cite great names among those who have debased themselves and their art in the service of licentious patrons. You will not deem these remarks foreign from this occasion. The public have a right to a pledge from us; and happy we are to give it, knowing as we do that Vice in all its forms is not more an enemy to religion and morality than it is to genuine taste. "There is an intimate connection," says a judicious writer, "between purity of morals, and a true and refined taste, which must be accompanied by purity of mind, dignity and elevation of sentiment, love of decorum, symmetry, grace, beauty, and good order."

> "Say, what is Taste, but the internal powers,
> Active and strong, and feelingly alive
> To each fine impulse? A discerning sense
> Of decent and sublime, with quick disgust
> From things deformed."

If our course is marked with prudence; if, with the desire in our sphere of promoting the general good of society, we preserve our art pure at the fountain in morals and in taste, we shall enlist the affections of our fellow-citizens. Our difficulties will disappear. We shall receive their support; and our Academy having outgrown the weakness of its infancy, and gained strength by the gradual accession of public favor, will eventually become an ornament to the city, and to the nation.

*   *   *   *   *

ADDRESS TO THE STUDENTS.

In congratulating you upon your success on the present occasion, let me briefly offer to you, and to the other students, a few hints that may be useful in your future studies. You have just commenced your course; for *Drawing* lies at the very foundation of all the Arts of Design; it is the language by which they all express their thoughts. Whether these thoughts be valuable or worthless, will depend on other cultivation. *Correctness* is the first great requisite in Drawing. Your great object should be to imitate the model before you precisely as it appears, with all its apparent blemishes, too, if any part of it should seem defective to you. It is a mistake which young artists are apt to commit, to suppose they must improve upon their model; they turn critic on language, before they have learned to speak. You must consider your models *perfect* while you are learners. As to *manner* of imitation, suit yourselves; there are many ways of producing the same effect: it is of little consequence *how* this is done, if it only be done. Many beginners, and I have observed it in our school, are more intent on the *mode* of representation, than *accuracy* of representation: they leave the substance to seize the shadow. Seek accuracy, and style will follow without your being conscious of it. In acquiring correctness, seek to obtain it in the whole, before you proceed to the parts.

All the drawings which have been *offered* for the premiums are highly creditable to their authors; those who have obtained the premiums are deserving of great praise for having acquired in a good degree the first requisite of drawing which I have mentioned, viz., *correctness*. In some of them, more care in the finishing of parts, particularly in the extremities, would have made them more perfect.

Those who have commenced in the school with a view of pursuing either of the Arts of Design as a profession, I would warn against a common error of supposing that they have chosen one of wealth, of ease, or of pleasure. They will be disappointed. The pursuits of an Artist have their pleasures, indeed, and of the highest refinement, but they have also their pains, felt most keenly by those most susceptible of these pleasures. They are not arts acquired in a year, or in many years, and with ordinary industry; they require unremitting attention during a whole life. "Ars longa, vita brevis," is indeed too true. Life is too short for Art. If you have not courage to sustain you against neglect and poverty; perseverance to struggle through indifference; good temper to bear with well-meaning ignorance and false taste; good sense to endure a momentary prosperity without giddiness, and principle to resist its temptations: if you have not that *amor artis*, that indestructible love for the art itself, which shall lead you, in spite of all these difficulties, to feel that some of your happiest moments are those employed in your profession; then, leave it while you may; leave it while any other employment invites you; it invites you to more wealth and ease than any artist ever enjoyed.

But if you are determined to proceed; if none of these difficulties alarm you, and they are not imaginary evils,) go forward; all our experience is at your service freely; all we require in return is, that you extend the same privileges as freely to others: we have no secrets of trade; we know of none, but industry and perseverance.

[*North American Review, No. LVIII.*]

ACADEMIES OF ARTS.

A Discourse delivered on Thursday, May 3, 1827, in the Chapel of Columbia College, before the National Academy of Design, on its First Anniversary, by SAMUEL F. B. MORSE, *President of the Academy.*

WE hope the name which this Society has assumed, may be found hereafter more appropriate than it appears now. A *National* Academy may be understood to mean a public institution, founded and supported by the nation, or a private association of the first artists of a country. This Academy is of neither of these kinds. It is simply a society of artists in the City of New-York, organized for the purposes of exhibition and instruction. As such it is a respectable and praiseworthy beginning; and as we heartily wish success to such an undertaking, we regret the more that they have made so great a mistake in the selection of their name. To call themselves *National Academicians*, is making a claim of distinction which, we must say, is out of proportion to their merits. Nor do we think it is quite time for them to adopt the initials of their institution as a standing title. The N. A. would do very well in the catalogue of their own exhibitions, to distinguish the works of its members, but we find it affixed to their names in that of a private collection, given in a note to this Discourse. This, though a trifle, seems to us very ill-judged. The practice has been tolerated only in Societies which have established some reputation ; and even in those cases, it is a vanity of which their members begin to be ashamed. What would be thought if Mr. Stuart should choose to call himself National Portrait Painter, or Mr. Allston should take the style of National Historical Painter, and write accordingly after their names, N. P. P. and N. H. P. ? Yet they would but be claiming the rank which others yield to them ; while the name of National Academician is as inappropriate to some of those, who have dignified themselves with it, as it is injudicious in its application to the best.

It is unjust, moreover, to the reputation of the country. A foreigner could not be much blamed for judging of the state of the arts in America by the National Academy established in the first city of the Union. Nor could he be expected to examine very carefully by what right such a name is borne by this Society. Yet the Academicians could not be willing that their works should be thought by strangers among the highest efforts of American art. They have given themselves a name, which means, in the common use of language, the great institution of the United States for the arts of design. What may happen hereafter in this particular, we pretend not to foretell ; but at present this new Academy comes somewhat short of deserving such a title.

Mr. Morse's Discourse is short and appropriate to the occasion. It consists of a very brief sketch of the origin and constitution of the principal academies of arts in Europe, with remarks, chiefly contained in the notes, on the state and prospects of the arts in this country. We cannot agree with the author in all these remarks. Some of them seem tinctured with a degree of dissatisfaction and jealousy, for which we think there is no occasion. He complains bitterly of the practice of buying old pictures, as tending to the neglect of living merit ; insists on the inexpediency of any but professed artists intermeddling with the government or direction of academies ; and deplores the hard fate of the American artist, who, after cultivating his art in foreign countries, returns to find his own so far behind him in taste, that he is doomed to starve in unmerited neglect.

This is all unreasonable and mischievous. We call upon facts to bear witness for us, when we say, that our artists suffer neither from the neglect nor the interference of others. Not one of them, who could maintain any reputation in Europe (we mean well-earned and tried reputation, and not that very precarious one of being a very promising young man), has lost it by a return to America. There is no undeserved preference for the works of old or foreign painters, and no want of patronage for those of our own. We do not pretend to know all the artists of the country, but we take such an interest in the arts, that we think we have heard of all the good ones ; and, as far as our information extends, we say, that they have nothing to complain of. The source of the mistake and disappointment of others is this : our artists do but begin their education in Europe ; they are sent there as soon as they discover the first symptoms of genius, and before it is well ascertained whether it is worth while for them to go. There they seem at first to be making prodigious advances (for in art it is not the *premier*, but the *dernier pas qui coute*), and, either from impatience or necessity, they hasten home to enjoy prematurely the fruits of their studies. In so doing they underrate the taste of the country, as it is natural enough they should, having left it before their own was formed. Besides, it is so much easier to learn to judge rightly than to paint well, that even with less opportunity, our judgment may at least have kept pace with the progress of their skill. A taste for the fine arts is but of recent, and has, therefore, been of very rapid growth among us. It is quite as likely, therefore, that the young artist, while learning his elements by a short stay in Europe, should fall behind, as surpass the taste of his countrymen ; and it is equally natural, that if there be any interval of separation between them, he will consider himself most in advance.

But let him be assured, that his works are not tried here by a judgment formed only on what has been seen in America. That judgment is founded chiefly on the opinion of those who have had opportunities of observation at least as good as his own. The number of those who have traveled in Europe, to see and study the great works of art, has been rapidly increasing, and is now large. Our taste in these things is not of national origin. We have hitherto learned, and must long be content to learn from older countries. A very few years, therefore, are sufficient to do away the difference between the taste of Europe and America. We have, in fact, made more progress in years, than other nations have in centuries, simply by adopting the fruits of their labors. It is very idle, then, for any one to think, that by a few years' residence in Europe he can so get the start of us, that his merit cannot be understood here. It would be much more likely, that, led away by our admiration of foreign models, we should neglect the original beauties of the home-taught pupil of nature. We could give Mr. Morse, in vindication of our taste, some illustrious examples among us of those, who have labored long and patiently abroad, undazzled by their first success, and not content with the admiration of the ignorant, and who have not been disappointed or neglected on their return. Greater wealth and more splendid distinctions would have rewarded them in Europe, but nowhere could they have been more honored or valued than they are here. Nowhere could their works have been more eagerly sought at honorable prices. If these examples are too rare to encourage the desponding, let them at least believe, that in their profession as well as in others, industry and perseverance will prevail ; let them believe this, until they can find some examples of neglected merit to authorize their complaints. We have heard of starving and heart-broken genius in other countries, but there never was such a thing in this. The most liberal encouragement is offered to every hope of excellence, and that very liberality has, in many cases, by taking away the sting of necessity, destroyed the promise it would have fostered.

No artist can expect here the highest rewards of his art. He must seek them if he is entitled to them, in the great capitals of Europe. We cannot make him a prince, or even a knight, nor endow him with 'personal nobility,' like those whom Mr. Morse mentions as examples of European munificence. But we can offer him all the country has to give ; reputation, respect and competency. If these will not satisfy him, he must take Mr. Morse's advice, and not return. 'The American artist,' says he 'may go abroad, but he must not return.' Before his foreign acquirements can be appreciated, he must go back to the point from which he started, take the public by the hand, and lead them on to the eminence he has attained. He may go abroad, and adorn other countries with his works, and the history of his own, with an imperishable name ; but if he returns, it will be at the peril of his happiness and his life! Does any one believe this ? Is there anything of fact that justifies it ? We never heard of any who pined and died after this manner.

We should give a different advice to the young artist ; we should counsel him, if he has the means, to go and faithfully study his art where it is most successfully practiced ; and not to be in haste to return for fear he should grow too wise to be understood. Let him not only study, but practice, in Europe. Merely drawing in an academy, and copying a few master-pieces, will not enable him to return with credit and success. Hundreds of students do these things, and do them well, who are never heard of as artists. He must labor long and hard, with the best means of improvement around him, if he hopes for distinction in his own country. And then he may return without fear of injustice. But one thing we repeat to him, and let him not forget it—no attainments which are not sufficient to support and raise him into notice in Europe, will save him from neglect at home. The mere student of foreign academies will not at once be hailed as a master on his return. If he were, it would more clearly prove that deficiency of taste of which Mr. Morse complains, than even the neglect of real merit.

Something in the same spirit, Mr. Morse deprecates the intervention of any but professed artists in the management of academies. We doubt whether he is right in this. We are inclined to look on this exclusion as one cause of those bad effects which he admits to have proceeded from ill-constituted academies. It tends to the formation of a school; which is little else than a system of errors and deviations from that imitation of a general nature, which cannot be too exact even for ideal beauty: there is but one nature, and there can be but one true way of painting. Artists may differ, indeed, in their choice of subjects and circumstances; but independently of these, their peculiar manners are chiefly their peculiar defects. Yet it is exceedingly difficult, in the examination of nature, to overcome the prejudices of a favorite system of art. In the same scene, one painter will see nothing but light and shade, while to another it will seem full of color. Fuseli, no doubt, thought he was painting naturally, when he imitated humanity so abominably; and his students, if they had been confined to his instructions, would have learned to see in nature the contortions and extravagances of their master's imagination. But the fact, that the defects of great masters are apt to mislead learners, is as obviously true in painting, as in everything else. And it can hardly be doubted, that, if academies exercise any influence, those under the sole direction of artists will be more likely to sanction and perpetuate their errors, than those which admit in their government connoisseurs, who may be, at least, more impartial judges of nature than her professed imitators. But even if this be not so, the exclusion is impolitic. Artists cannot establish themselves in defiance of that portion of the public best qualified to judge of their works; nor hold themselves entirely independent of those who support their exhibitions and buy their pictures. It is essential to their success, that they should inspire others with a love of their art, and diffuse as widely as possible the taste necessary to enjoy it. These associations are highly useful in this way, if they are freely opened to all who are desirous of promoting their objects. But if the direction of them is, by the jealousy of artists, confined to their own number, others will soon be weary of their share in establishments where taxation and representation are so little united. Where a taste for the arts is already widely diffused, such a system may have some advantages; but where the taste is to be created, a more liberal course would be more expedient. In this, as in other particulars, the difference of the two countries seems to have been overlooked when the Royal Academy is proposed as the proper model of such institutions in America.

There could be no danger here of the other directors interfering improperly with the peculiar province of the artists; and they might often be useful as mediators or umpires between contending parties. They would be the defence of the meritorious against any of their brethren, who might otherwise pervert the power and influence of the academy to selfish or party purposes. That such differences and oppression may exist in these institutions, is well enough proved by their history; particularly by that of the same Royal Academy, whose example is thought to sanction this exclusive system. There has been but very lately a revolt in this institution, which withdrew much talent from its exhibitions. What has been the result, we do not know; but it may be presumed to have been unfortunate for the seceders, however just might have been their complaints. Such occurrences might often be prevented by the intervention of disinterested directors; and when they happen, they lead to consequences much worse than an occasional deviation from correct taste, even if that were to be feared from the admission of such mediators.

Mr. Morse supports this exclusion by the example of other professions. But in this he confounds associations for the mere regulation of practice, with institutions for the promotion and improvement of art. Besides, the fine arts are things that we can live without, while unhappily law and physic are necessary evils. The arts, to flourish, or even to exist, must be made agreeable to others besides artists. Others must be taught to love and to judge of them, before they will afford a subsistence to those who practice them; whereas, it requires no combination between doctor and patient to induce the latter to be sick; nor do clients quarrel and go to law because they love to hear the eloquence of their advocates. If the infirmities of mind and body, which support these two learned professions, needed encouragement by the establishment of academies for their development, no doubt the practitioners would be too liberal to engross to themselves all their advantages. The clerical profession is a more analogous case; for its necessity, though great, is of a moral nature; and the clergy have always, where their power and influence were not secured by the strong arm of authority, called into their associations the pious and sober-minded of the laity.

As to the purchase of old paintings, which is another subject of long and vehement complaint in the Notes to this "Discourse," we must again differ from the author. "No disease," he says, "has infected infant art so inveterate, and so retarding to the progress of taste, as this." Many quotations are added to show the little chance there is of any genuine old pictures being procured now, and the bad effects of collecting them, even if they could be obtained. Mr. Morse does indeed, among his censures, introduce this cautious salvo: that he "would not by any means altogether condemn the collecting of pictures by the old masters;" but he clearly thinks it much better to employ living artists, and even without much regard to their merit. To this effect he cites twice with great applause, from Opie's "Lectures," one of the grossest absurdities that ever were uttered—namely, "that he who employs the humblest artist in the humblest way of his art, contributes more to the advancement of national genius, than he who imports a thousand chefs-d'œuvre, the produce of a foreign land." "The correctness of this assertion," adds Mr. Morse, "is abundantly proved by the practice of those noblemen and others who stand first among the encouragers of art in England." The examples given of this practice are the purchase by three noblemen of Allston's *Uriel* and *Jacob's Dream*, and of Leslie's *Saul and the Witch of Endor;* which, instead of being humble works of humble artists, are, two of them, at least, among the finest pictures of modern times, and by artists who stand at the very head of their profession. When such pictures are neglected, because they are not old, or foreign, Mr. Morse may well be indignant; but it is a very different question, whether it is expedient to buy the works of our own artists, simply because they are so. If good American paintings were left unsold because others of less merit were bought, or for any other cause, we would join heartily in censuring such illiberality. But the fact is not so. The real want in America is not so much of good patrons, as of good painters; and we doubt very much whether Mr. Morse could tell us of a single good, not comparatively, but absolutely good artist in the country, who does not, or might not, by industry, receive a compensation for his labors in full proportion to that gained by other professions. We know of no good pictures left unsold. And if it is supposed that we ought here to be content with a less degree of merit, and buy pictures which could not be sold elsewhere, we think it is a great mistake. Why should we do so? It would improve neither the taste of the public, nor the skill of the artists, but degrade the one, and retard the other. To spend money in "employing the humblest artist in the humblest way of his art," is encouraging national genius, just as much as paying an honest, painstaking tinker for spoiling his work, is encouraging national ingenuity. If the artists could do better elsewhere, they would not stay here for the pleasure of complaining; if they could not, they have no cause to complain.

As to the genuineness of the imported pictures, we should not differ much from Mr. Morse in his final results, though we think they depend but very slightly upon his long and grievous preamble of frauds and impostures. For he admits, after all, that there are many good pictures of old masters in the country, obtained in Europe from genuine sources, and that a fine picture still finds its way occasionally across the water, and is added to the collections of professed dealers. This is the true state of the case, and we put as little faith as he does in the undoubted originals, which are sent here by hundreds to be sold by auction. But Mr. Morse writes on this subject under a great excitement, of which he has not very well examined the causes. When he speaks in person, indeed, it is chiefly of his apprehensions of what may happen; but we think his fears are quite unfounded. Let him look at the horrible lamentations and prophesyings of Barry, Opie, Shee, and Hoare, which he has quoted, and then consider that, so far from having become the receptacle of trash and counterfeits, England is hardly surpassed by any country in her treasures of ancient art.   We are not much alarmed by the stories told in the notes of Mr. Astley, and the "officer of more wealth than judgment, that paid a fortune to a London dealer for a gallery of the works of the most reputed masters;" nor do we in the least believe the episode, contained in the same extract, of a starving English painter, who was taken up by a modern-antique factory at Amsterdam, and accidentally found by them to be such a genius, that they were obliged to seek inferior artists to paint Teniers and Wouvermans, while he was employed on pictures in his own manner, to be kept on hand for a future period.   Such wholesale imposture cannot be carried on here; and as to the little misnomers that actually take place, they are not of consequence enough to make it worth while for any one to disturb his own tranquillity, or the innocent complacency of the purchasers.

The course of this business in our own city has been this.   We have, in the first place, a few small collections of good, and, we believe, genuine old paintings.   Many of these were procured in Europe, at a time when such acquisitions were more easy than they are now.   A few years ago we had two or three importations, and among them some good pictures (whether originals or not is of less consequence), which were bought at prices, probably not greater than they were intrinsically worth.   The modern English paintings sold about as well as those which were called old.   Both kinds were bought because they were thought good, without any great regard to their names.   Perhaps there were some mistakes made in that particular; but not more than there would have been in buying as many works of our own artists.   Since that time, there has been a flood of trash sent here for sale, too miserable to deceive any one; and it has been sold for prices as miserable, or carried away to a better market.   All this time the works of our own artists have been taken up at their fair value; while, on the other hand, several fine old paintings, well authenticated as the works of masters, have, for want of purchasers here, been sent to England for sale.   We know of but one native production of great merit being lost to the country, because its value was not understood.   The loss of these really fine pictures we regret, more than we should, that a whole generation of half-taught pretenders should be starved into some more useful employment.

Some of our remarks may seem harsh, but we make them from a sincere love of the arts.   We would by no means be illiberal to our own artists, who give any promise of excellence; but there is no propriety in encouraging them in false taste or mediocrity.   We would hold high the standard of taste; as high as it is in any place.   We would not have the arts degraded even in favor of the artists.   And so far are we from approving of anything which is said to discourage the importation of old and foreign paintings, that we wish still greater facilities were afforded for it.   If the old masters were, as we believe, better than the painters of our day, their works should be the models on which to form the public taste; and we would have as many of them as possible.   And the same may be said of the modern paintings of foreign countries, so far as they are better than our own.   We are not prepared to see the American system, as it is called, extended to literature or the arts.   It would be the worst possible policy for the artists.   Painting and sculpture are not among the necessaries of life.   Much as they improve and adorn society, a taste for them is not even the necessary accompaniment of a high degree of civilization.   That from the earliest recorded time, and in almost every nation, rude or refined, it should have been the occupation of a portion of the community to imitate the forms and colors of nature, shows some native propensity in the human mind favorable to the cultivation of these arts.   But whether they shall flourish or decay by the intellectual and moral improvement of society, depends, as far as we know, on no fixed law of our nature.   They are powerful means of such improvement, and not the necessary consequences of it.   A taste for them must not be expected to grow without care and cultivation.   And undoubtedly the best means of promoting such a taste, is the exhibition of those works which show of how much these arts are capable.   The better the specimens we see of what has been done, the more desirous we shall be to encourage their progress; and the greater interest we shall feel in the labors of our own artists.

The love of the arts is, moreover, greatly dependent on remote associations. No man can be thoroughly imbued with it in our times, who has not seen the wonders they have wrought in times past. For ourselves, at least, we confess that we should feel comparatively little enthusiasm for sculpture and painting, if we had seen none but their modern productions. They would lose much of the poetical influence which they exert over our minds. We attribute this, not so much to their inferiority in modern times, as to their associations with the history of the past. All painting and sculpture remind us, in some way, of those older works of which we can never think without delight. If Claude, Salvator, and Poussin were forgotten, landscape painting would be much degraded from the high place it now holds; and even historical composition owes much of its elevation to similar associations. Still more do sculpture, necessarily so simple in its forms and uniform in color and architecture, the principles of which seem so little founded on nature, depend for their interest on the wonderful works that have come down to us from a yet remote period.

Without these secondary attractions, we fear that the fine arts would languish and die in these busy and practical days. We have lost many of those sources of excitement which produced the master-pieces we admire and imitate. Nothing but the contests of the arena could have called out such counterparts of nature as the Fighting and Dying Gladiators, or clothed in such perfect human forms the ideal beauty of the Apollo and Antinous. It was not merely the opportunity of seeing the naked figure in all its variety of action; though that enabled the ancients, ignorant as they probably were of anatomy, to attain in their statues a correctness, which all the science of the moderns has failed to reach; but it was their perfect enthusiasm for athletic exercises, and for the full development of the physical powers, which made their sculpture the wonder and despair of succeeding ages. So to the enthusiasm of a pompous religion, which no longer exercises its dominion over the imagination, we owe the master-pieces of historical composition in painting. Inanimate nature is still unchanged; and therefore landscape painting has failed less than any other, except portrait, which is the natural growth of busy and selfish society. But even landscape painting requires for its perfection, like descriptive poetry, a secluded and contemplative life, which becomes every day more rare and difficult.

We cannot, therefore, join Mr. Morse in his confident anticipations of the triumph of American artists over the most transcendent efforts of European genius, ancient or modern. That our country will equal the contemporaneous works of others, we are well inclined to believe; though we cannot but see, in our peculiar situation, peculiar disadvantages. But we can hardly hope that the master-pieces of ancient art are ever to be surpassed here or in Europe. The forms and occupations of society are growing every day less favorable to the highest efforts of the imagination. We live in an age of utility. Everything which tends directly to improve the physical condition of man, and develop his reasoning and active powers, is cultivated with zeal and success. The most stubborn obstacles of nature are yielding to new and tremendous enginery. What were her impassable barriers, have become highways; and the fabled works of the giants are surpassed by the power of knowledge. Education is sent abroad into all classes of men, to make them feel their strength and use their reason. All this renders the world populous, prosperous and happy; but it is at the expense of much that we love, and much that elevates and refines the feelings. In this cultivation of the reason, the imagination loses its power. Eloquence, poetry, painting and sculpture, do not belong to such an age; they are already declining, and they must give way before the progress of popular education, science, and the useful arts. It may be, that when the great work about which the world is now occupied is accomplished, a new school of art of proportionate grandeur may arise; but we fear that its best days are past. We cannot but rejoice at this progress of society; still we must wish that the good it brings might be purchased without so great a sacrifice. We would not withhold the light of knowledge, for fear it should dissipate the most poetical phantoms of the imagination; but we may be allowed to look back on their old haunts, laid open to the vulgar day, with some feelings of regret.

This influence of the age may be doubted, because the disposition to encourage the arts seems still to remain unimpaired in the public. But its earliest effects must not be looked for there; the mind of the artist is its first victim. It chills his enthusiasm, and discourages him from attempting what, perhaps, he might still perform. He works under the fear of a cold-blooded judgment, which represses that confidence, without which genius cannot work its wonders. To what else can it be attributed, that the princely prices which the works of the old schools still command, have not brought into competition with them modern productions of equal merit? When sums are paid for single and small pictures, which would be an independence to an artist, why is there not in all Europe; nay, why has there not been for more than a hundred years past, a single one whom we can place on a level with the old masters ? The decay of eloquence is, perhaps, an even more striking example. Argument is almost all the oratory of our times. Premeditated appeals to feeling and passion have lost their power. Even the most popular assemblies must be convinced before they can be moved. We have grown cautious and suspicious, and are apt to distrust the orator, when he would win us to his side by any exhibition of emotion. We take pride in subduing our feelings to our reason. Every public speaker must feel this, and the consequence is, that our best public speaking is but a cold sort of argumentation. Accidental opportunities for great excitement still occur, but no one can now rely for success on the susceptibility of his audience. It is the same with poetry; it has almost ceased to be produced, and its popularity has sensibly declined even in our short day. The last that has held any dominion over the public mind, owed much of its interest to the personal character of its author, with which all his works were colored. The practical and historical details of the Scotch novels have already eclipsed it.

There are, however, other causes which have had their influence in degrading modern art. While the whole *costume* of the actual world has become less adapted to the arts, dramatic acting has been carried almost to perfection. The stage has been made so fascinating by its wonderful exhibitions of talent, that artists have either voluntarily chosen their models from it, or have by habit insensibly lost the power of distinguishing between true nature and these brilliant imitations. This effect is less observable here and in England, than in France and Italy, where it has sunk the art of painting into a gaudy puerility and affectation, of which we hardly know how to express our contempt. This cause has probably operated in fact less on English art, because the people are not so much attached and habituated to the theatre as the French. But the English schools of tragedy and acting, seem to us so much more natural than the French, that the fault is not so striking there, when it exists. That it is a fatal fault, is obvious; for it is copying a caricature instead of the original. Even the best acting can never be a true transcript of nature. The character and sentiments of the drama are poetical and exaggerated. It is in that, as in painting, necessary to color beyond nature to resemble her; and when that exaggerated copy is made the model for another, the departure from the original becomes too wide for the imagination to reconcile. It has been said, that the whole business of French society is *représenter;* it is the same with their historical painting; they aim to show, not how their characters would look and act, but how they should be *représentés.* That the Italians, surrounded by the master-pieces of the arts, which their own country has produced, should have followed in the same course, shows how difficult it is to resist the influence of the actual state of society; and that it degrades the mind of the artist, long before it quite corrupts the public taste, is proved by the fact that the old Italian school is as much as ever admired, even in those countries where modern art is in the most deplorable state of degeneracy.

If these views are correct, there is more in them to stimulate than to discourage artists. They exhibit no insurmountable obstacles to their progress. The peculiar difficulties that beset them are in themselves, and therefore within their control. They live in an age unpropitious to the development of that high enthusiasm which produces the greatest works of art; but, nevertheless, "the fault is not in their stars, but in themselves, if they are underlings." Great minds may resist even the pressure of the age; nay, to resist it, requires only a steady pursuit of acknowledged principles. If the artist will not be seduced by examples which he cannot approve; if he will disregard the fashion of the day and the practice of his contemporaries; if he will confine himself to his profession, and so avoid the seductions of society, which would lead him away from the contemplation of nature, he may still redeem the reputation of his age and country, and place himself on as high an eminence as he could have reached if he had lived in the most favorable period. That this can be done, we think is about to be shown; as much talent and enthusiasm as can be brought to the work have now been employed, in our own community, in one noble effort, for years of patient and persevering labor. That it should fail is impossible; but how much can be effected by such appliances in these degenerate days, is a question of deep interest to all among us who love the arts. We pretend not to guess how far this work is to rival those which have been so long the standards of excellence: but of all the productions of art in the present age, we have no fear in predicting that the greatest is behind, and not far off.

The subject on which our artists most need to be admonished is the cultivation of the mind. Their great deficiency is a want of vigorous and poetical conception. The mechanical process of drawing and coloring is often well done, but the mind seems not to contribute its share to the work. It is owing to this that so many have failed to redeem the promise of their youth. From the number who have made good beginnings without instruction, it has been thought that there was a peculiar talent for the arts in the Americans; but most of these were but examples of that mechanical ingenuity, which certainly is a general characteristic of the people. It may be difficult to convince the artist of this deficiency of mind; but let him place a landscape, for example, of almost any of the living painters by the side of one of the old masters. He may find the drawing, coloring, and perspective as good, and perhaps better; but the difference between them is, that one is the work of the hand only, the other of the imagination; one shows, perhaps even with less skill in the execution, and often in spite of injury and decay, a fine creation of the mind; the other is a dull copy of what happened to be before the artist, or a composition of commonplace and unmeaning objects. The parts of one seem selected to fill the canvas with picturesque forms and colors; those of the other chosen for the ideas and feelings they are adapted to convey. The difference is like that between poetry and mere musical verse.

It is natural that as excellence in composition declines, it should be replaced by mere ingenuity; but the attention that is now paid to execution in painting seems to us to have acted also as a cause in degrading the art. Success in that is comparatively so easy, and satisfies so many minds, that the attention of the artist is drawn from the more laborious task of invention. The common course of study, too, gives an undue importance to mere skill of hand. It is all that can be taught by a master, and those who study under distinguished artists are apt to be content with what they learn of them. This is one bad effect, which we may attribute to all academies. They can but teach the form and manner of the art, and they attach so much importance to them, and reward excellence in them with so much distinction, that the student forgets there is anything else to be acquired. The facilities for such acquisitions have become very great, but these will not make an artist. The fine arts are works of the imagination; and the skill of the hand and the eye is but the means of communicating to others those thoughts and feelings which distinguish the artist from the artisan. The mere picture-maker is not above any other nice workman. Even in branches of the art which seem hardly to admit of much invention or exercise of mind, their power is still enough to make all the difference between good and bad. No uncultivated man, whatever be his manual dexterity, can paint a good portrait, or even make a good likeness. The mind of the artist shines out even through his copy of another's features.

Great artists have sometimes begun their labors without intellectual cultivation, but they have never produced their great works until they had overcome the disadvantage. Their paintings were not the results of knack, or of
mere practice, but of study, observation, and reflection. Claude began to
paint late, without education, and in the lowest rank of life; but we read afterwards of his habit of walking in the fields, not merely to observe,
but to explain philosophically to his friends, the beautiful appearances
of nature, which he has preserved in his landscapes. Leonardo passed
months in studying his unfinished picture of the *Supper*, without touching it.

While we speak thus cautiously about the present claims of our artists, we
would by no means be thought indifferent to their success. We should be
sorry if anything we have said should in the least abate the liberality of the
public towards them. They must be supported and encouraged now, or we
can expect no improvement from them. All we mean in the way of caution
is, that this encouragement be governed by discretion; and that it be understood as a stimulus to future efforts, and not the reward of present excellence. We have endeavored to repress what seems to us a repining disposition, founded on an overestimate of their actual claims; but we would not be
understood to say that their rewards are beyond their merits. We have felt
the more urged to the remarks we have made, because we thought that complaints like those contained in this "Discourse," coming from an artist of so
much reputation and merit as Mr. Morse, at the head of an institution which
must exert a considerable influence on those within its immediate neighborhood, might have, if uncontradicted, a most discouraging effect on the
younger artists. And we confess, too, that, as part of the public, we feel
aggrieved at what we consider the injustice as well as the inexpediency of
some of the remarks. Even since we began this article, we have seen new
proofs that the American artist has no cause to complain of a want of patronage, in the liberal prices paid in Boston for several works of a favorite artist
of Philadelphia, immediately on their arrival. Still, we would urge on the
public the necessity of a liberal and untiring encouragement of the arts.
They are eminently useful to the community. They are an ornament at
home and an honor abroad. They elevate and refine the national character,
and may even in turn protect the country that has fostered them. They have
saved cities from fire and pillage, and given a character of sacredness to the
countries that honored them. Greece owes to her ancient arts, more than to
any other cause, her still cherished hopes of independence. The strength of
her citadel lies more in its architecture than in its fortifications; and her lost
gods have done better for her than her generals.

But we hope it is superfluous to reason about the usefulness of the fine
arts. We all feel and acknowledge the importance of a literature of our own,
and the good influence of the arts is no less certain. Their effect on the reputation of a country is extensive, because they speak a common language
equally intelligible to all nations. And though much more circumscribed in
their operation than letters, they act more immediately on the character of a
people. Painting, sculpture, and architecture are addressed to the whole
mass of society; and being presented directly to the senses, the ideas which
they are capable of conveying lose nothing of their power in the transmis-
sion; while written language, at the best, can but excite in the imagination
prepared by education to receive it, emotions resembling those of the author.
Literature operates on the few who seek its power, while the arts mingle their
influences with the objects and pursuits of daily life.

But as sources of pleasure, which, instead of degrading, elevate the mind,
they make large demands on our gratitude and care. They occupy, in this
way, a place so necessary to be filled, that the nation which can exist without
them must be, as the philosopher said of the man of solitude, much above or
much below the common standard of humanity.

REPLY TO THE FOREGOING CRITICISM OF THE NORTH AMERICAN
REVIEW.

In the last number of the *North American Review*, the article No. X. pur-
ports to be a critique on my discourse delivered before the National Academy
of Design. In that article, written with much ability, and for the most part
with courtesy, there are some strictures on the Institution with which I am connected, and on subjects relating to the Fine Arts generally, that I have thought
it my duty to notice. At a time when these Arts are beginning to attract the
public attention, every discussion which has for its object the extension of correct opinions respecting them, must be of public interest. It is for this reason,
and also from a very natural desire to see the art which I profess, as well as
the other Arts of Design, more generally appreciated, that I have ventured to
ask a portion of public attention to the following remarks.

The principal object of the discourse which I delivered before the National
Academy of Design, (as its title indicates,) was to show what constituted an
Academy of Arts, and thus to dispel the prevailing erroneous impression of
their nature. For this purpose I supposed that the surest method of arriving
at a right result, would be to set before the Artists, and through them the pub-
lic, the economy of the various Academies of Arts in the world ; and by comparing them together, to deduce from them the fundamental principles of these
Institutions. I accordingly considered more or less copiously the Academies
of Italy, France, Austria, Spain, Russia and England : from a review of these
I drew the following conclusions :—First. *In all cases the entire government of
Academies of Arts is intrusted to Artists.* Second. *Schools for Students in the
Arts are a prominent feature in them.* Third. *A system of premiums to incite the
students to industry and emulation is deemed of the greatest importance.* And
Fourth. *An exhibition of the works of living artists, is another prominent feature
in them.* In other words, an Academy of Arts is *an Association of Artists for
the purposes of Instruction and Exhibition.* This is the *first and chief point* of
the discourse, established by *precedent*, viz. : the example of all the distinguished Academies in the world, and further demonstrated to be according to the
dictates of reason and common sense, inasmuch as "individuals of a particular profession should best know how to manage what relates to that profession."

I next endeavored to incite the artists to union and perseverance, preparing
them to expect difficulties and discouragement from the infancy of taste in the
country, and the incipient state of our institution ; and in this connection, in
a note to the discourse, I collected a mass of evidence to show that the danger
of imposture, in the indiscriminate purchase of those old pictures, which were
so profusely poured into the country, was so great as to need much circum-
spection ; and that here, as in Europe, this passion for the purchase of what
is old, would operate to retard the progress of modern art. This may be considered the *second* point of the discourse. Towards the close, I touched upon
some peculiar discouragements which an Artist who studies in Europe must expect on his return, from the difference of taste in the two countries. This is
the *third* point of the discourse. To all these the Reviewer objects in the following language :

"We cannot agree with the author in all these remarks. He complains bitterly of the practice of buying old pictures, as tending to the neglect of living
merit ; insists on the inexpediency of any but professed Artists intermeddling
with the government or direction of Academies ; and deplores the hard fate of
the American Artist, who, after cultivating his art in foreign countries, returns
to find his own so far behind him in taste, that he is doomed to starve in unmerited neglect. This is all unreasonable and mischievous."

Thus we are at issue on all the principal points of the Discourse ; and with
those to whom the subject is of sufficient interest to induce them to examine

into the merits of the controversy, must be left the decision. But before proceeding to the discussion of the main points, there are some trifling matters that meet the eye of the reader at the threshold of the *Review*, which may as well be brushed away. The Reviewer commences by an attack on the *name* of the National Academy of Design.

"A National Academy," he says, "may be understood to mean a public institution founded and supported by the nation, or a private association of the first artists of a country. This Academy is neither of these kinds."

In this last remark he is mistaken, for, according to his own definition, it is a *National Academy;* it is an *Association of the first Artists of the country;* the Catalogue of the 64 members of the Academy will show nearly all the most eminent names of the Artists in the United States, not from New-York alone, but from Philadelphia, Boston, Washington and Charleston.

"It is simply a Society of Artists," he observes, "in the City of New-York, organized for the purposes of Exhibition and Instruction;" that is to say, it is *an Academy of Arts.*

Unacquainted with the duties pertaining to the class of Academicians, the Reviewer presumes to tell them rather unceremoniously, that to call themselves "National Academicians is making a claim to distinction which we must say is out of proportion to their merits. Nor do we think it is quite time for them to adopt the initials of their Institution as a standing title."

As to the propriety or expediency of putting the initials N. A. after their names, signifying, as they do, merely a *holder of the property,* and *responsible member* of the Academy, the gentlemen of the Academy are doubtless the better judges of their claim to the title. The folly of the practice, however, is thus curiously illustrated by the Reviewer:

"What would be thought if Mr. Stuart should choose to call himself National Portrait Painter, or Mr. Allston should take the style of National Historical Painter, and write accordingly after their names, N. P. P. and N. H. P. ?"

I should pay but a poor compliment to the understandings of the readers of the *Review*, were I seriously to attempt to show the entire want of parallelism between the assumption by an individual of initials proclaiming himself superior to all his class, and initials adopted by individuals of a society, simply signifying that they belong to that society. The Reviewer proceeds:

"It is unjust, moreover, to the reputation of the country. A foreigner could not be much blamed for judging of the state of the arts in America, by the National Academy established in the first city in the Union."

Where is the injustice of such a judgment? The Exhibitions have contained specimens of the productions of all the principal artists in the country; and it is a chief intention of these Exhibitions to enable the public "to form an accurate judgment of the state of the arts in America," by furnishing an opportunity for all artists in the United States to display, once a year, their various productions. "They have given themselves a name," continues the Reviewer, "which means, in the common use of language, the great institution of the United States for the Arts of Design."

Yes, this is the meaning, and it was the original intention, and continues to be the intention, thus to make it. "Established," as he observes, "in the first city in the Union." Why should it not be so?

"What may happen hereafter, in this particular," says the Reviewer, "we pretend not to foretell; but at present this new Academy comes somewhat short of deserving such a title."

In other words, the *child* is not yet a *man.*

Before leaving this part of the subject, (which is really too trifling to have occupied so much time,) I would ask the Reviewer in turn, merely to show him how easily his own weapons may be turned against him, "by what right" does the *Review* to which he has contributed, bear the name of *North American ?* "It means, in the common use of language, the great *Review of North America;*" not of the United States only, but of *Canada* and *Mexico* too; yet who objects to its name, or thinks it worth while to write a page to prove that, because it is published in Boston, it should have a more limited title?*

But enough of this. I now proceed to the main points of dispute.

What has the Reviewer advanced against the position that *Artists alone should have the management of an Academy of Arts?* for he says, "it is unreasonable and mischievous;" and again, "Mr. Morse deprecates the intervention of any but professed artists in the management of Academies. We doubt whether he is right in this." I have cited the example of every principal Academy of Arts in Europe as a precedent in support of my position. Does the Reviewer rebut it by a single example to the contrary? No! He does not rely, then, on *precedent* to support him. Neither does he propose any other definite plan in lieu of that which the National Academy of Design have adopted. We are left to gather, from a few insulated remarks, that he would have a sort of mixed institution, composed of Artists and gentlemen from other professions. Such a society perhaps might be formed, and be useful as an Institution for the general encouragement of the Arts, but it would not be an *Academy.* As an Academy is for the special purpose of *Instruction* and *Exhibition,* what part could the gentlemen associated perform in *instruction?* Some of them would feel, we imagine, somewhat awkward with the *crayon* or *pencil.* But this part of the business would perhaps come under what the Reviewer calls "the peculiar province of the artists," with which the "directors would not interfere." Will they, then, be of service in the other department of an Academy—*Exhibition?* But the artists are the only part of the coalition who make pictures and exhibit them; here, therefore, the gentlemen in the association would be useless. But there is one use to which the Reviewer thinks they could be put:

"They might be useful as mediators and umpires between contending parties. They would be the defence of the meritorious against any of their brethren, who might otherwise pervert the power and influence of the Academy to selfish or party purposes."

That is, they would form a kind of Court before whom the aggrieved artists should plead their causes. There is an objection or two to this. If the artists are such a quarrelsome, jealous class of men as many would persuade us, so much so as to need umpires and protectors against each other's violence, I fear that not many gentlemen could spare the time from their own professions necessary to hear and adjudge all the cases of grievance that must come before them. Moreover, as such an experiment has never been made, we should be loth to deviate from a tried model, until we had some grounds for belief that so novel a measure would produce the good effects intended. But we will be reasonable, and as there are other professions to whom we think we can with propriety yield precedence in the title of *genus irritabile,* if the Reviewer's method of producing social harmony should prove successful with them in subduing asperities, &c., and then, if we have any disagreements among ourselves which we cannot adjust, we will consider the plan; but even then it is by no means so obvious that this Court should be a *constituent part of the Academy.* These mistakes of the Reviewer arise from his having misconceived the nature of the Institution against which he writes; he has deceived himself by a phantom of the imagination, which stands in the place of the reality—an anomalous institution to which he has given the name of an *Academy,* but which, in truth, has no legitimate claim to the title. That this is the cause of the mistakes in his subsequent remarks, I think will be evident in noticing a few of them.

"Artists," he says, "cannot establish themselves in defiance of that portion of the public best qualified to judge of their works; nor hold themselves entirely independent of those who support their exhibitions and buy their pictures."

In what part of our plan does there appear anything like "*defiance*" to the

---

* Since writing this paragraph I perceive that the same thought, carried out into a more extended parody, has also occurred to a writer in the *College Miscellany,* (a promising periodical conducted by the students of Columbia College.) It is a happy exemplification of the danger of violating the common proverb concerning "*glass houses.*"

public? Is it in that part which relates to *instruction?* We claim, indeed, to know the best mode of instruction for students in our own profession. But by what law of right, or even courtesy, can others than artists demand to interfere in the management of our schools; or how, by refusing their interference, do we try to establish ourselves in defiance of such? But "they support our exhibitions and buy our pictures."

How support our exhibitions? We support them ourselves, by our productions *loaned to us,* indeed, *for a few weeks,* by those for whom they are executed, and who would be the last to demand, from that circumstance, a right to instruct our students, or control the arrangements of our exhibitions.

The language of the Reviewer on this subject, however unreasonable in itself, and offensive to the artist, is not new, nor uncommon, even in our own country. There has ever been an unfortunate difference on the subject of obligations and rights between the artists, and the purchasers of their works; it is not for me to say on which side the blame lies; probably on both sides. But there is frequently a disposition on the part of the purchaser to prefer claims to gratitude from the artist, which, as they are undefined, are very liable to exaggeration; and among these has often been. a claim to direct the studies and thoughts of the artist—in such a way, too, as to make him *feel* his absolute dependence on wealth. That this should be repulsive to that high feeling of independence which belongs to the *native nobility of genius,* (if I may be allowed the expression,) is not surprising; nor is it impossible that the *spirit* which brooks not control, (the parent of those lofty conceptions, which, whether fixed on stone or canvas, or on the poetic page, have commanded the admiration of mankind,) should sometimes be fretted into acts of imprudence, by contact with the pedantry of shallow critics, or the mere whims of a wealthy purchaser of its productions. That in a certain sense, and to a certain extent, the artist is dependent on the individuals who purchase his works, is unquestionably true; and in that sense, and to that extent, he is bound by the common laws of gratitude. It is only when those obligations are unreasonably or ungraciously pressed, that the artist, like every other man of independent feelings, will deny his obligation, and break from the trammels by which they would bind him.

The Reviewer has merely embodied in a more tangible form the every-day opinions with which every artist in the country is more or less conversant. If such notions were extensively to prevail in society, unmet, they would most effectually depress the artist. For by depriving him of his independence, you sink him down from his loftiness of purpose, and put him, not even on a par with the commonest barterer of goods. He is not to think for a moment that he has given to the purchaser of his works an equivalent in talent, or in property, for a sum of money often barely sufficient for his necessities; but, forsooth, because "Painting and sculpture are not among the necessaries of life," and "the Fine Arts are things we can live without," the artist must be put on the footing of a beggar; and having received his pittance in charity, is under an obligation which can never be repaid, but by ever after sacrificing his independence of judgment to that of his *patron,* as the name goes. The Reviewer may talk of "holding high the standard of taste," but let such views be predominant, and art will fall forever with the degradation of the artist. Better is it to bear with the eccentricities and waywardness of genius, than thus to tame it down, on this *composing* system.

"But," the Reviewer proceeds, "if the direction of Academies is by the jealousy of artists confined to their own number, others will soon be weary of their share in establishments where taxation and representation are so little united."

What taxation? and what representation? We have no taxation of those out of the profession, unless it be the 25 cents from those who visit the Exhibition; and surely the Reviewer does not think a taxation of this kind can lay claim to representation in the government of the Academy!

I have not time to pursue other errors, all which may be traced to misconception of the nature of an Academy of Arts. I will notice only a plausible objection to Academies raised by the Reviewer; he seems to fear that artists associated in an Academy will so control the general taste, as to force a false system of art upon the public.

"It tends," he says, "to the formation of a school, which is little else than a system of errors and deviations from that imitation of general nature," &c.

The *plan* of our Academy, formed, as it is, on the English model, renders any such fears groundless. Whatever danger from this cause might be apprehended from any ill-managed Academies on the Continent of Europe, the objection does not lie against the Royal Academy of London. The English school is not the school of Reynolds, or West, or Lawrence, or any other painter; it is a school pre-eminently diversified in talent and styles; and it may, perhaps, be attributed to that more perfect exemption from foreign interference, which in some respects distinguishes it from the Continental Academies, that English art is so replete with various beauty. Is it not most reasonable to suppose that the styles of the different artists, which are annually assembled in one Exhibition, and submitted to popular judgment, should rather produce a diversity of styles, according to the diversity of popular tastes, than foster the errors of any single master? But the error of *manner* does not lie with Academies. Popular and distinguished artists have always had, and ever will have, their imitators, whether connected with Academies or not. But I must not here enlarge; it is sufficient for my purpose now to show that, if Academies were the source of the error, the remedy of the Reviewer is useless. He thinks the "admission of connoisseurs into the government" of the Academy would cure the evil. But his criticism strikes equally at the root of *all* Academies, whether constructed on his *ideal*, or on the common model. How are the connoisseurs to act upon the evil?

"They may be," says the Reviewer, "at least more impartial judges of nature than her professed imitators." Granting the truth of this very paradoxical sentiment; we are then to understand that the judgment and advice of the connoisseurs expressed to the artists, will tend to the correction of those errors to which these latter are blind. But is the advice and judgment of such connoisseur changed by his belonging to the Academy? Will not his advice be as valuable out of the Academy as in it?

I must leave to the good sense of the reader, who takes any interest in this discussion, the pursuit of the errors of the Reviewer, having the same unfortunate source with those already considered.

I should regret if anything I have said, in defence of our Academy against an attack from so respectable a quarter, should be construed into the slightest disrespect towards the genuine connoisseur; he is a character as highly to be respected, as he is rarely to be found. Neither do I attack any other institution; if there are any which have, by a misnomer, been called Academies of Arts, it is unfortunate. The Artists have called their Society by the name which has ever been applied to the purposes for which they are associated, and if deceived, by a mere similarity of name, the Reviewer has found the Artists by themselves, in a separate society, and believes, from that circumstance, that they are opposed to associations of gentlemen for the encouragement of Arts, I will venture to say he has mistaken their views. For my own part, I wish all success to every well-directed effort to encourage the Arts; but I do profess to claim for my brother Artists the ability to manage an Institution which, like all other institutions of the name and character in the civilized world, is exclusively under the direction of Artists.

Having discussed the nature of an Academy of Arts, I will now consider the *second* point to which the Reviewer objects—viz., my sentiments on the subject of purchasing *old pictures*.

In the note appended to the Discourse, (and which contains all that I say on this subject,) I warn the public against the danger of a species of fraud to which, from their general inexperience in subjects of this nature, they were evidently exposed; and by quotations from distinguished writers on the Arts, in a country having the most experience in this matter, I showed what were the effects of this system upon the encouragement of modern art in England. I made this exposure for the double purpose of preventing the genuine connoisseur from being the dupe of imposture, and of directing his attention to a more patriotic, as well as more effectual method of promoting the growth of *native Art.* That these are the chief objects manifested throughout that note, I cheerfully leave to the judgment of those who will take the trouble to read it. The Reviewer has misconceived me. He would make his readers believe that I am an enemy to the introduction into the country of any pictures of the old masters, however excellent. He says, "Many quotations are added to show the little chance there is of any genuine old pictures being procured now, and *the bad effects of collecting them, even if they could be obtained.*"

As to the first part of this quotation, that there is little chance of any good genuine pictures, by the old masters, being procured in this country, I still maintain it to be true. The Reviewer will grant me the position, that the greatest quantity, and best of any article in demand, for sale, is to be found in that market which gives the highest prices for it. England, it is well known, has for many years been the best market in the world for genuine works in the fine arts. If it can, then, be proved that such works are now rarely to be met with, for sale, even in England, the inference is clear that the difficulty must be greatly increased in this country. The *London Quarterly Review,* [for October, 1826, No. 67, p. 189,] speaking of the formation of a National Gallery, says: "The opportunities of making such acquisitions," (good genuine pictures,) "are now but *seldom* presented, and we believe that those under whose recommendation they are likely to be made are fully sensible of the necessity of proceeding *cautiously* and *slowly* in offering their advice." If caution, then, is necessary in England, which, the Reviewer admits, "is hardly surpassed by any country in her treasures of ancient art," was it ill-timed, or altogether unnecessary, to throw a little distrust over the pretensions to *undoubted originality* which are invariably made for everything like a picture that is offered for sale in our own country, provided it is old, and deformed enough to belong to the dark ages?

As to the latter clause of his remark, intimating that I equally condemned good pictures if they could be obtained, I deny that anything I have written will bear this construction. The Reviewer himself seems aware that he has here not done me justice, for he immediately adds, "Mr. Morse does, indeed, introduce this cautious salvo, that he would by no means altogether condemn the collecting of pictures by the old masters." Now why, if he admits that I qualified my censures by this *salvo,* does he not give it its due weight in my favor, in his subsequent remarks? If I should say to a neighbor, "There is a great deal of counterfeit money offered, look narrowly at all moneys you receive"—"I would by no means altogether condemn your collecting that which is genuine," *if by accident you should find it,* but *there is great danger of deception;* (this continuation of the salvo the Reviewer should have done me the justice also to have quoted,) I say, would it be fair in that neighbor to accuse me of being an enemy to the *genuine currency;* especially, too, if in my cautions I had said, by way of further *salvo,* in speaking of good genuine pictures, "At such accessions to the mass of really meritorious productions, whether *originals or copies,* no one rejoices more than myself?" As it regards the general character of picture-dealing, a residence of four years in London enables me to speak not from the opinions of others only, but from personal observation. Scarcely a day passed that new deceptions were not practiced in the purchase and sale of old pictures; they were a common topic of conversation among the amateurs and artists. I hazard nothing in saying that the history of picture-dealing in London is, for the most part, a history of *trick* and *fraud.* That there are honorable exceptions to this charge, I do not deny; but they are rare, and the exceptions prove the rule. But it was not merely the waste of those means, in the encouragement of imposture, that, if flowing in right channels, would encourage native talent, that I deprecated; it was to the spirit of false and illiberal criticism on modern arts, which it occasions, and which is the worst evil of the two, that I also adverted. Show me a man who is smitten with this mania for picture-dealing, and I will generally show you one who looks with contempt on modern art; who decries the works of the living artists, and applies to their efforts degrading epithets;

who sees their faults, and is blind to their beauties; who makes no allowance for infancy of genius, nor looks with kindness on the first tottering steps of its course; and who can produce the exploded dogmas of the schools with an air of authority to silence any who maintain for the modern school any rank but that of the lowest. If authority is demanded for so bold a delineation, I will refer to the history of the rise and progress of Art in England, as furnishing full materials for the likeness; and to every distinguished artist in our country for confirmation in his own experience of such effects.

Do not let me be misunderstood; I am not speaking of the *real connoisseur* who may honestly prefer a small and genuine collection of works of the old masters, to a larger collection by modern artists; but of the flippant, half-taught pretender to taste, such as Sir Joshua Reynolds aptly designates as one, of whose opinions alone, of all mankind, "no use can be made,"—"*a half-learned connoisseur who has quitted nature, and not acquired art.*" It is a character of this description that I would expose, often united in the person of a vender of old pictures, and who turns his pedantry to account by imposing, on those whom he can make his dupes, first, his crude but plausible opinions, and then their worthy accompaniment, his precious ancient merchandise. It is against such that I endeavored betimes to put the public on their guard, and not against those who would introduce into the country the real masterpieces of Ancient Art. Whether my caution was unnecessary or premature, and whether the evils to be apprehended to taste are too highly colored, every one must form his own opinion. But if our country is to be saved from that scourge to taste in other countries, the *plausible dealer in vertú*, it will not be by lulling the connoisseur into a false security, or flattering his self-complacency on the fancied possession of the work of a master.

I cannot pass without notice a *misquotation* by the reviewer, which, after having altered the sense, he pronounces absurd, and then spends a page in combating the mistakes he himself has produced.

"He cites *twice*," says the reviewer, "with great applause from Opie's Lectures, one of the grossest absurdities that ever were uttered, viz., 'that he who employs the humblest artist in the humblest way of *his art*, contributes more to the advancement of national genius than he who imports a thousand *chefs-d'œuvre*, the produce of a foreign land." This passage I do cite *twice*, and in the first citation, (which is not the one used by the reviewer,) it reads "*his art*," by a very obvious typographical error for "*history.*" In the second citation, (and this is the one used by the reviewer, as the context proves,) it is printed correctly, "*history ;*" and why he should have gone out of his way to quote the erroneous passage, when the correct and rational one was before him, I cannot say. No one could be so misled as to suppose for a moment, that Mr. Opie here meant that the *humblest artist* in the *humblest way of history*, was to be sought out, and specially encouraged, or that I quoted him in support of such a sentiment. The spirit of the passage is plainly this: "the encouragement of national genius is more directly promoted by giving *practice* to our own artists in the highest department of painting, than by any efforts to place before them the best *models.*" This sentiment I would extend to the other departments of the art, and then let the reviewer have it as he has misquoted it, and I think it could be proved not so absurd as he pronounces it.

A construction might be put upon what immediately follows by those who are strangers to the long and most intimate friendship that has existed between the two distinguished artists spoken of, and myself, which would make me appear as designedly wishing to degrade them; this construction, I am persuaded, is not intended by the reviewer.

"The examples given of this practice," says the Reviewer, "are the purchase by three noblemen of ALLSTON's *Uriel* and *Jacob's Dream*, and of LESLIE's *Saul and the Witch of Endor :* which, instead of being humble works of humble artists, are two of them at least among the finest pictures of modern times, and by artists who stand at the very head of their profession." Some might very naturally infer from this passage, that moved by jealousy, or envy, or something of the kind, I had endeavored to detract from the fame and merit of these distinguished men, by classing them among the *humblest artists*, and their works among the *humblest works* of such artists. Now what is the real state of the case? I do not quote them at all as examples of the practice he mentions. Just before naming them I speak of the galleries of *native* productions formed by the Marquis of Stafford, the Earl of Egremont, Sir John Leicester, &c.; and then, to show that their patronage was not confined to works of *natives* of Britain only, I add, "The three former noblemen have several pictures by *Americans*," and I then give the names of these artists and their works.

I might proceed to expose other errors of the Reviewer, scattered through his remarks, but error often exists to such an amount in a single sentence, as requires pages to expose and refute; I must therefore notice but one.

"When such pictures," says the reviewer, (as those of Mr. Allston and Leslie,) "are neglected because they are not old nor foreign, Mr. Morse may well be indignant. If good American paintings were left unsold because others of less merit were bought, or for any other cause, we would join heartily in censuring such illiberality. But the fact is not so. We know of no good pictures left unsold."

In reply to this, I will ask the reviewer how long the splendid picture of *Elijah in the Desert*, by *Allston*, one of his most original and sublime conceptions, was submitted to the judgment of the public in his vicinity, and solicited a purchaser in vain? Was it not at least *six years?* Was it appreciated during this time? Was it not, on the contrary, unpopular, and was it before, or only since the distinguished foreign traveler saw it, and purchased it, and carried it to England, that its merit has been acknowledged, and unavailing regrets at its loss expressed? The Reviewer will say, perhaps, this is a solitary instance, and he probably alludes to this when he says, "We know of but one native production of great merit being lost to the country because its value was not understood." Be it so; the same blindness may still exist to the merits of other works of genius in the country, and may require, to satisfy the fastidious taste of some, the same proof of merit before they will see or acknowledge it.

Does not the Reviewer himself exemplify in his own case the effect naturally produced on the encouragement of modern art by this exclusive passion for old pictures—and *merely because they are old, too?*

"The love of the arts," he observes, "is, moreover, greatly dependent on remote associations. For ourselves, at least, we confess that we should feel comparatively little enthusiasm for sculpture and painting, if we had seen none but their modern productions. They would lose much of their poetical influence which they exert over our minds. We attribute this not so much to their inferiority in modern times, as to their associations with the history of the past. All painting and sculpture remind us in some way of those older works of which we can never think without delight," &c.

I have no doubt the Reviewer here speaks from the heart; modern pictures to him cannot possibly possess much interest, for while the artist is alive, his works, of course, can never be encircled by those associations which are, it seems, indispensable to their excellence; he must, therefore, paint with no expectation of admirers, or purchasers, until the time in which he lives has so far been lost in the lapse of years, that its associations shall be sufficiently ancient for the admiration of such lovers of the arts as the Reviewer; in the mean time, however, the artist has the consoling reflection that, by the neglect and starvation consequent from such a course, the happy time for his encouragement will at least be hastened by some few years.

I conclude what I have to say on this head by repeating, that "at any accessions to the mass of really meritorious works in the country, whether ancient or modern, no one rejoices more than myself." All my remarks are intended now, as they were in the Discourse, merely to guard the connoisseur against imposition, and to direct him to what I must still think a surer method of encouraging art in the country, than the importation of any quantity of good models in painting that is likely to be procured, viz., *the purchase of the works of our own artists.*

I now proceed to examine the *third* and last point of the Discourse to which the Reviewer objects, viz., "the discouragements I throw in the way of younger artists by my representations of the state of taste in our country." The sentiment advanced on this subject was this: that it was natural for the artist who studied his profession abroad, to outstrip in taste the mass of the community he left at home, and consequently when he returned his spirits would suffer depression. Is there anything wrong in this sentiment? Apply it to other professions. Is it not natural that a scholar pursuing his studies in foreign universities, with the increased advantages afforded by their accumulated treasures of literature, should, *ceteris paribus*, outstrip in knowledge the mass of the community at home? Or, on the contrary, is a man's competency to judge of excellence in literature and art in an inverse proportion to the advantages he has had for acquiring knowledge in them? The sentiment of the Reviewer that "connoisseurs may be at least more impartial judges of nature than her professed imitators," would seem to be in accordance with such a proposition, the mere statement of which alone, one would think, is sufficient to expose its absurdity. If Europe, then, possesses more and better means for the study of the Arts than our own country, which I think will be admitted, and an artist improves these means to acquire knowledge in his art, and then returns to his own country, the effects upon his spirits, which I have described as likely to occur, in passing from a region of more taste, to one of less taste, is perfectly rational; he must feel *disheartened;* and this, in reality, is the case with every artist with whom I am acquainted, on his first return from Europe.

There is not one such artist, I am confident, in the country, who will not give many proofs of the sinking effect produced upon his own spirits, by his frequent experience of the want of that discrimination which he values more than the price paid for his pictures, that judicious censure, too, as well as praise, that interest in what he is doing, that generous enthusiasm for works of art, which in Europe he finds pervading the well-educated and refined portion of society, equally with those in his own profession.

But the Reviewer's sentiments in different parts of his remarks on the state of taste in the country are somewhat contradictory. At one time he maintains that there is little or no difference between the state of taste here and in Europe; and at another, that taste is yet to be created in the country. He says, "A very few years, therefore, are sufficient to do away the difference between the taste of Europe and America. We have, in fact, made more progress in years, than other nations have in centuries, simply by adopting the fruits of their labors. It is very idle, then, for any one to think that by a few years' residence in Europe, he can so get the start of us, that his merit cannot be understood here." And again, "No attainments which are not sufficient to support and raise him into notice in Europe, will save him from neglect at home." But when he speaks against the propriety of artists' exclusively governing Academies, and pleads for the admission of connoisseurs to a share in their direction, he says, "Where a taste for the arts is already widely diffused such a system may have some advantages, but where the *taste is to be created*, a more liberal course would be more expedient." Both these views cannot be correct: either our own country is as far advanced in taste as European countries, or it is not; if the former, then taste is not to be created, and consequently this objection to our Academy system is removed; but, if the latter, then an artist, by studying where taste is more advanced, must feel the difference when transplanted to a country in which it is less advanced.

The truth of the matter is, that the country at large is very little advanced in taste for the Fine Arts; nor is there anything in this charge that should cause any one "as part of the public to feel aggrieved." I say it not in a spirit of dissatisfaction. It is according to the natural order of things, and therefore to be expected, that the *useful arts* should be encouraged before the *elegant;* and to the former, the predominant energies of our country have been, and are, to a great extent, still applied. It is from having observed the uncommon progress made in these useful arts, and the exuberance of talent displayed in them, that among other causes I was led to predict for our coun-

try the most elevated station, at some future period, in the *elegant arts* also.
I see no cause, from anything the Reviewer has advanced, to change my anticipations. He observes, that "The forms and occupations of society are
growing every day less favorable to the highest efforts of the imagination.
We live in an age of utility. Everything which tends directly to improve the
physical condition of man, and develop his reasoning and active powers, is
cultivated with zeal and success." These, and the subsequent remarks in
proof of this tendency of the age to mere utility, while they are enlarged and
generally correct as applied to the United States, appear to me, viewed on the
more comprehensive scale of the world's progress, *partial* and *incorrect*. The
Reviewer is misled by confining his attention too exclusively to the state of
things now existing in our own country, which is in that very point of progress to perfection in civilization, which is indicated by the encouragement of
the *useful* arts, and then, by a very common error of drawing general conclusions from particular cases, he applies his conclusions to the whole civilized
world. At any rate, facts are at war with his theory. What does he mean by
saying that "Eloquence, poetry, painting and sculpture do not belong to such
an age; they are already declining, and they must give way before the progress
of popular education, science, and the useful arts?" This is not true in reference to these arts in Europe. But a complete refutation of this sweeping
assertion would lead me into a longer disquisition than either my own time or
the patience of my readers will permit. I can only briefly repel the charge that
painting, and its sister arts of design, are on the decline, and refer to the present state of these arts in England, for an answer to the dogma of the Reviewer.
Sixty years circumscribe the age of the Arts of Design in that country. Within the memory of some of her living artists, such writers as Du Bos, Montes-
quieu, and Winkelman, supported the notion that painting and sculpture were
never to rise in Great Britain; and the climate, the prevalence of damps, &c.,
were asserted to be insurmountable obstacles to their encouragement; and
yet, what does the English school of design now present? It is already the
first in the world. The Architectural improvements everywhere projected in
London do not show decline. The Sculptural decorations of a triumphal
monument do not show it. The building of two noble piles for the Royal
Academy and National Gallery (with many other improvements, all indicat-
ing a popular feeling in favor of the arts,) do not show decline. The language of late English periodicals do not support the opinion, when they say,
"We see with pleasure the increasing interest with which all ranks, who ever
pretend to taste, are discussing and projecting improvements." And another,
in remarking on the fashion of traveling abroad, says, "Another, and a better result," (of foreign traveling,) "is the increasing taste for *music* and
painting; and in the *latter*, a juster taste and finer feeling than has ever yet
prevailed in this country." He proceeds: "The National Gallery and the
King's pictures have been this year a fashionable lounge; it was gratifying to
see the numbers of elegant women who crowded the rooms from morning till
night," &c. This does not look like decline. But take a familiar example
within the reach of every one. Let any one look into the decorated books
published in England some sixty years since, and observe their style of embellishment, and then compare them with the style of any of the embellished
annuals from that country, now so fashionable, and let him say whether
painting and *engraving* are on the decline. I do not cite this example in proof
of the *highest* state of cultivation, but only to show that the arts in England
have made great progress in the last century; and it is rather a reason for
believing that they will continue to advance, because at the present moment of observation they are not *highest*, than that they will for this reason
decline.

Painting and its sister arts of design, then, are not declining. Their place
in the march of civilization is in the train of the *useful* arts, and these, their
avant couriers, have long and eminently occupied a distinguished place in our
country. The *elegant* arts have already landed on our shores, and when their
beneficial influence in elevating the character of a nation is more fully appreciated; when the absurd notion shall be rejected that they are inimical to lib-

erty, while the atmosphere of a free government is that only in which they have ever freely breathed; when the truth is felt that our own country, from its very freedom, is the natural habitation of these arts, I do not believe that the opinions of any splenetic or rude legislator, or the forebodings of the polished Reviewer, will so far influence public opinion, that the nation will not receive the strangers with its characteristic hospitality. No! the nation will not frown them back; nor compel them to seek a shelter in the less genial atmosphere of despotic courts.

But, how is this? The Reviewer has objected to my opinions on the ground that the tone which I assumed in relation to taste in the country will have, "*if uncontradicted, a most discouraging effect on the younger artists;*" and in replying to him, I am found repelling some of his opinions, which strike at the root of all encouragement, and which, if believed to be true, and "uncontradicted," would certainly have a "most discouraging effect," not only on the younger, but older artists too. The discouragements, to which I alluded before the younger artists, were in their nature temporary and local, arising out of the infancy of the arts in the country; and whilst warning them of the difficulties they must expect, I still encouraged those who possessed the real *amor artis* to persevere in their course, from the intrinsic pleasure to be derived in the pursuit of their art. The Reviewer, on the other hand, by arraying before the artist the spirit of the age as hostile to all attempts at great excellence in the Fine Arts, and so likely to continue, strikes a fatal blow (if he can prove his positions) at the very heart of all future encouragement.

The artist, indeed, seems not to be very well provided for by the Reviewer, at least so far as regards his bodily wants; he fears to have the artist rich, lest, "by taking away the *sting of necessity*, the promise it would have fostered should be destroyed." This is very much like throwing a man into the water, for the pleasure of seeing him exert that vigor of muscle in saving himself from drowning, which might otherwise be used in benefiting his fellowmen. It was some other stimulus to great exertion than the "*sting of necessity*," which excited the best Greeks in the best ages of the arts. Polygnotus painted the Pœcile for nothing, and Zeuxis gave his pictures away; and Phidias, for all his works, received a smaller sum than Gorgias for his declamations. These, of course, must have been independent of their art for subsistence; Raphael and Michael Angelo, and Rubens, and most of the great painters of antiquity, were above want in their pecuniary circumstances; consequently, in all these cases the "*sting of necessity*" was not the operating cause of their excellence. None of our artists can boast of any such independence, so that although I believe, with the Reviewer, that "great minds may resist even the pressure of the age," and I fully approve of the course which he would have the artist adopt, of "disregarding the fashion of the day," and "the practice of his contemporaries;" and I assent that it would be delightful to indulge in that seclusion, "in the contemplation of nature," which would enable him to "redeem the reputation of his age and country, and place himself on as high an eminence as he could have reached, if he had lived in the most favored period;" yet one difficulty will prevent his following this course. How is the artist who takes so independent a stand to subsist? He cannot, like the hero of romance, live without those vulgar accompaniments of life, eating, drinking, and apparel. The artist with us is generally dependent on his profession for his support, and he will be forced, therefore, often to subdue his independence to the whims of fashion, however grating to his feelings; and fall in with the errors of contemporaries if they are popular, however repulsive to his sober judgment: and his beautiful reveries while contemplating nature, and picturing scenes for his canvas, will be very liable to interruption from the cry of dependents for food, or from those most unromantic associations connected with quarter-day. The artist, if he is expected to exert his genius to the best advantage, must be independent in some way. As he cannot be pensioned in our country, I know of no better way than that I proposed—viz., *to purchase his works.* And if but one in a hundred thus encouraged should possess that more excellent genius which permanently contributes to the honor of his country, the chance is better worth the risk of the expense, than one-fifth part of the sum expended to encourage the foreign manufactories of *originals.*

The Reviewer asks, "Why is there not in all Europe, nay, why has there not been for more than a hundred years past, a single one whom we can place on a level with the old masters?" It would have been well to have determined the fact before asking the question. *Hogarth* invented and carried to perfection a new department of art, unknown to the old masters. *Wilkie* and *Turner,* of the present English school, are unrivaled in their respective departments by any ancient master. *Sir Joshua Reynolds* of the former, and *Sir Thomas Lawrence* of the present English school, and *Stuart* of our own, have never had their superiors in portrait, Vandyke alone possibly excepted; and startling as it may seem to the Reviewer, I challenge him to point to any old master who possessed more originality and sublimity of conception, more chaste and polished imagination, greater powers of design, more exquisite feeling for color, and greater versatility of talent combined in one individual, than is possessed by *Allston.*

With regard to what the Reviewer alleges, that artists throughout the country have no cause of complaint of want of encouragement, I must think he has again drawn general conclusions from a particular case. He has supposed that the liberality which is so conspicuous in the region about him, in generally appreciating and rewarding merit in the arts, is more widely extended than facts will warrant. In this part of the country, with the exception of a few individuals whose names could be told in a very few minutes, there are none that buy pictures.

Of these few, I know of no one who has a modern picture (portraits excepted) which cost more than five or six hundred dollars; while in Boston it is well known that thousands, in many instances, and in two cases even 10,000 dollars each, have been given for single examples of modern art. The Reviewer, therefore, if he takes his own city as a standard of encouragement for the rest of the country, will be apt to draw a very unjust conclusion in *favor* of the public taste. On the other hand, I am also aware that too *unfavorable* an opinion of the general state of the Arts might be inferred, if this city were taken as the standard. The truth must be told. While Boston and Baltimore, and even Raleigh, all, especially the last, inconsiderable cities, compared with our great commercial metropolis, have each a statue erected to the memory of the "Father of his Country," all measures hitherto proposed for the purpose, in this city, have evaporated in a few feeble and ineffectual efforts to raise the adequate means. Besides these cities, Philadelphia, Washington, and Charleston have, to a greater or less extent, in their public buildings, historical pictures, commemorative of events either in the history of the country, or appropriate to the institutions in which they are placed; while in our own city, with the exception of the public collection of portraits in the City Hall, (a praiseworthy beginning,) I know not of a solitary instance (portraits excepted) of a picture or statue belonging to any public institution in this city. Can this be said, with truth, of any other city in the civilized world, of the same extent, population, and intelligence as the City of New-York?

In conclusion, I will say, that with many of the sentiments of the Reviewer, in the latter part of his article relating to the importance of encouraging the arts, I most cordially agree; and although differing from him so materially in the general tenor of his remarks, I must express my obligations to him for having written with so much sprightliness upon a subject which has in every civilized country attracted a great portion of the public regard; and which I have not a doubt will receive, in its proper time, the same attention in our own.

SAMUEL F. B. MORSE.

[As the NATIONAL ACADEMY OF DESIGN is of recent formation, and is the only Institution of the kind in the country, it has been thought that the History of its Origin and Progress would be acceptable to those who take an interest in the progress of the Fine Arts. On this account, the letters of a writer in the *Morning Courier*, under the signature of BOYDELL, as giving the fullest and apparently most authentic account of its formation which has appeared in print, is appended to Mr. Morse's reply to the *North American* Reviewer.]

LETTER I.

Certain statements and observations have been for some months in circulation in this city, tending to injure the Academy recently established by the artists, under the name of the "National Academy of Design;" their proceedings have been misstated; their motives misrepresented, and their prospects exhibited unfavorably and incorrectly; and the 58th number of the *North American Review*, just published, contains, in a critique upon the Discourse of Mr. Morse, the President of this Academy, the same false views and unfavorable representations of the Institution; it is time, therefore, that the friends of the Arts, who know the real state of things, and the injustice which has been dealt out to the founders of the New Academy, and how much of misconception they have submitted to for the sake of avoiding a public controversy, should no longer be silent as to the causes, hitherto not made public, which led to its formation.

The answer to the *Review* I do not undertake; it may be safely left to Mr. Morse, who holds a pen as well as a pencil, and who, I am confident, will not shrink from the defence of his professional brethren, thus wantonly and publicly attacked. I am not an artist, nor have I any interest in the success of the Academy, other than the natural desire for the encouragement and prosperity of the art; and it is this desire alone, and the possession of some facilities for the investigation, which have induced me to take upon myself the task of ascertaining and making known the truth in relation to the circumstances under which the National Academy was established, the reasons why that measure was resorted to by the associated artists, and the advantages which already have resulted, and will result from it, to the cultivation and improvement of the Fine Arts in America.

From the time of its first establishment, *the American Academy of Fine Arts* had been productive of little or no advantage to the artists of this city, *as a body;* and from the very nature of its government, it was next to impossible that any important benefit should have flowed from it to *them.* There were defects in its very inception, most of which, indeed, were the unavoidable consequences of the existing state of things, and therefore could not then be remedied. The principal difficulty with which the enlightened and public-spirited gentlemen by whom that Academy was established had to strive, was the want of a body of artists to whom might be committed the principal direction of the Institution; and by whom the pictures necessary for the formation of a respectable and attractive annual exhibition might be furnished. In the absence of such a source, it was supposed to be necessary that pictures should be purchased; and to raise a fund for that purpose, it was found expedient that the Institution should be formed upon the plan of a joint stock association, into which any person might be admitted, who should deem the honor of his membership, and the privilege of visiting the exhibitions, as an equivalent for a certain sum of money. Even this was found insufficient, and a debt was consequently contracted, the interest of which, and, if practicable, the principal, were of course to be paid from the proceeds of the exhibition. Lectures upon the various branches of science connected with the art of painting were not included in the plan of the proposed Academy, or, if included, were not instituted; and although it was at first intended that a school should be formed, and facilities afforded to students, it was soon found inconvenient and impracticable to carry this intention effectually into operation.

Artists, *as such*, were not entitled to vote at the election of President and Directors; this privilege they could only acquire by the payment of the price of a share in the stock of the Academy; and although by the 3d section of the By-Laws, it was expressly provided that three of the five Directors should be Academicians, and, of consequence, artists, this regulation was seldom complied with, and was virtually repealed by an amendment of the charter in 1817, extending the number of Directors to twelve, but making no provision for a proportionate increase in the number of Academicians, and the affairs of the Institution were in fact entirely governed by men not professional, and who could not, therefore, be possessed of either the zeal or knowledge requisite for the office, in an equal degree with artists, who must necessarily feel the deepest interest in its prosperity, and were surely the most likely to be acquainted with the best method for its management. It may be said that a strict compliance with that regulation was at first impossible, for the simple reason that there were not in the city a sufficient number of artists of eminence enough to be considered capable of performing the duties attached to the office. But even if this were true, in process of time that impossibility ceased to exist; the art began to meet with attention and encouragement, and, as a necessary consequence, artists of talent and reputation appeared among us, whose exertions seemed to promise that the day was not far distant when America, too, might claim an honorable place among the nations, as the abode of genius and munificence. Soon the artists became a numerous and distinguished body; their productions were sought after and admired, and a taste for the arts sprung up, and was encouraged in the minds of the community. Artists returned from Europe, who had devoted years to the study of their profession, amid the splendid galleries and collections of England and the Continent, where their minds had become filled with devotion to their art, and earnest and anxious wishes for its advancement in their own country; with them they also brought experience, and an intimate acquaintance with the principles and systems on which the flourishing institutions of the Old World are conducted. They saw, with regret, the deficiencies of the Academy; the total inaptitude of the system upon which it was conducted; the want of energy in its management; and the little probability that, burdened as it was with debts, and governed by men who knew nothing practically of the art for whose encouragement it professed to be established, the Institution would ever prove a source of good to them, or the community. They saw that in fact the Institution was not an Academy of Arts; that it was merely a company formed for the purchase and exhibition of pictures; that even this purpose was not fulfilled, for there were no funds wherewith to purchase, and the exhibitions were notoriously of the same pictures every year; and that in reality it was, to them, as if no Academy existed.

It was the opinion of the profession generally, that were artists associated in the management, as originally provided in the By-Laws, the face of things might be changed, and that the Academy might be erected into an establishment worthy the name, and made to fulfill the purposes of such an institution. But there seemed to be a determined hostility to this measure, in the minds of some few *acting* stockholders; for but a small proportion of the number appeared to take any lively interest in the concerns of the Academy; few attended or voted at the elections; and those few seemed to be governed in their votes by the wishes of a minority of their own number.

Why it should have been deemed an object of importance thus to exclude the artists from all participation in the management of the Academy, I do not know; but such was the fact, and for several years the artists of the City of New-York were thus forbidden to exert any influence over an institution, which yet looked to them for support and co-operation—and not in vain; and they submitted patiently, and in silence, for years, to a misfortune which they severely felt, and would have ended, had they been permitted.

In my next will be given the history of the establishment of the New Academy.

BOYDELL.

LETTER II.

I now proceed to the investigation of the steps which, though at first not taken with a view to the formation of a new Academy, by a combination of concurring causes, at length resulted in that measure.

In the month of November, 1825, it occurred to one of the most eminent of the body, that something might be done for the promotion of the art, and the assistance of students. The idea was suggested to a few of his professional brethren, and by them at once adopted. His plan was merely to form an Association for Improvement in Drawing; that those artists and students who might feel disposed to join the Association should meet a certain number of evenings in each week, during the winter, for the purpose of copying from casts; and the principal advantages which were aimed at in this proposition, were the increase of harmony among the artists by these occasional meetings, the benefit of mutual instruction and advice, and the promotion of a spirit of emulation and zeal for the art, among the members of the profession. A small sum was contributed by each to defray the necessary expenses; a Treasurer was appointed to manage their slender funds, and a Secretary to record the few regulations which it was found expedient to adopt, for the better prosecution of the objects of the Association. A President and Vice-President were elected; and thus these artists and students became an organized body.

In a short time it was found that, with a very few exceptions, all the artists of the city, and many amateurs, had joined the Association; and for some weeks affairs went on prosperously and smoothly, every one being zealously and willingly engaged in improving himself and his fellow-members, and all rejoicing in the efficacy of the school thus established, as it were, by accident; for, as yet, it was considered only as a school.

The establishment of the Association had by this time become generally known; some believed and reported that the Artists had founded an Academy in opposition to the American Academy; but the most widely-received opinion was, that the recently-formed Institution was connected with, and dependent on, the Academy of Fine Arts; and at length, it was mentioned at one of the meetings, that a Director of the American Academy had suggested to some of the members of the Association that they should sign the matriculation-book, and thus identify themselves with the Institution which had so long neglected them and their interests; and, now that they seemed to be rising into importance, manifested a willingness to extend to them its protecting patronage.

Until this period, the probability of a union with the Academy had never occurred to the members of the Association; nor, in fact, had they ever adverted to the question which now arose, "In what relation does this Association stand to the American Academy?" It was distinctly and separately organized, with its own exclusive officers, paid its own expenses, and was governed by regulations of its own adoption, and with reference to its own peculiar objects; but the casts and models of the Academy were, by the permission of the Directors, used at the meetings of the Association.

By some, the idea was suggested of forming, in reality, a new Academy; but the prevailing sentiment was unfavorable to the proposition. Others wished the casts and models to be returned, and that, in their stead, those only should be used which belonged to, or could be procured by, individual members of the Association; but this measure, it was considered, would be construed as indicative of hostility, and therefore was abandoned; still, there was a universal unwillingness in the minds of the artists to be looked upon, in the present state of things, as dependents on, or connected with, the Academy. At length, it was suggested that perhaps a plan might be adopted which would remove the objections of the artists to a union with the Academy; and that, by becoming parties to a revision and remodeling of its Constitution and By-Laws, the practical knowledge and experience of the artists, and the valuable collection of the Academy, might be rendered reciprocally subservient to the promotion of the art for whose cultivation they were associated. This was cordially received, and it was the general wish that it might be found practicable.

But before taking any measures to ascertain whether any plan of this nature could be devised and carried into execution, it was thought advisable by several of the members of the Association that some method should be resorted to of uniting the views and concentrating the opinions of all upon the subject of their actual situation. It was therefore proposed that a Committee should be appointed, to draw up and lay before the Association a distinct statement of its views, and of the exact relation in which it stood to the American Academy of Fine Arts. The proposition was approved of, and immediately adopted, and the Committee met. The substance, and consequences of their report, will be given in my next letter.

BOYDELL.

LETTER III.

In my last letter it was stated that a Committee was appointed to draw up and present to the Association a distinct statement of its objects, and of the actual situation in which it stood in relation to the American Academy of Fine Arts. The following is the substance of their report :

That the necessity of some measures to be resorted to by the artists for their own improvement, and that of their art, was obvious, and that the formation of the Drawing Association was the result of that necessity. That the principal object of their thus uniting was, as their name implied, improvement in drawing ; and that, in addition to this, it was hoped that a harmonious feeling, a feeling of interest in each other, might also grow from their union, which should destroy the seeds of dissension, and implant in the minds of all a disposition to kindliness and good-will, by the interchange of mutual good offices and civilities. That there existed no connection between the Association and the Academy, inasmuch as the former was a distinct and separate body, possessing its own rights and privileges, and governed by its own laws, but still in perfect harmony with that Institution.

So much of the report of the Committee I have thought it necessary for my purpose to present. Other subjects were touched upon, and many suggestions made which were applicable to the matters under consideration, and appropriate to the objects of their meeting, but do not strictly fall within the limits of my design, and which I shall therefore pass over without notice.

After the report was given in, questions again began to be started and canvassed respecting the future conduct of the Association, and the probabilities of some arrangement between it and the Academy. It was obvious to all, that there were difficulties in the way of a union with that Institution ; and so long as those difficulties continued to exist, it was, for many reasons, desirable that the Association should remain a separate body until the time arrived when some fortunate arrangement should give to the artists that portion of power to which, from their numbers, respectability and services, they thought themselves entitled. Had they been disposed, they certainly had the right to found a new and rival institution, and some advantages, and some disadvantages, also, would doubtless have resulted from that measure. The Academy was burdened with a debt, which *they* certainly were under no obligation to liquidate, and its government was encumbered with difficulties, with which it was not their interest to meddle. True, the advantages of its casts, and prints, and pictures, were an inducement to them to look favorably upon the prospect of a union, but the want of that valuable collection would not have been to them irreparable: the private collections of individuals belonging to the Association would have furnished a basis for the foundation of a new establishment, and the rapid and constant intercourse between this city and the depositories of art in Europe would speedily have enabled them to supply the place of what they should thus for a time relinquish. It might have been said, that the rooms of the Academy were desirable; and so they were—but what is the value of such an accommodation for a single year? For soon its lease was to expire, and then it would be dependent upon the will of the public for renewal. An admission into the Academy upon equal terms was not, therefore, an object of so great value to the artists; and the willingness which they expressed and felt for the adoption of that plan was evidence of a disposition, on their part, to measures of mutual accommodation. But it was apprehended by some, that the creation of a New Academy would alienate from them the minds of many of the most enlightened and influential of the community, interested as stockholders in the old. This would, indeed, have been a serious evil, had it been likely to befall them; but would any candid and reasonable man have censured them for asking an equivalent for the services which they alone could render? Was it equitable that their productions should be a source of revenue to an institution in which they were allowed no voice, and no interest? And would gentlemen of liberality condemn them for demanding such a share in its government as should restore confidence to their body, and enable them to bring their whole energies to the task of building up and supporting the establishment in which they were all alike interested?

In examining the government of the American Academy of Fine Arts, it will be perceived that there are two distinct and palpable interests—that of the artists on the one hand, and that of the stockholders on the other. The latter of these is the interest of those who hold the property of the Institution, and who have therefore an obvious right to a voice in the management of its fiscal department. The first is the interest of its contributors, whose works must form the principal attractions to its exhibitions, and consequently prove the permanent source from whence its revenue is derived. On the excellence and attractive power of these depends the character of the Academy, and on the proper management of the schools, the premiums, the exhibitions, and the lectures, must depend the improvement and cultivation of taste, both in the artist and the public. To the direction of these matters artists alone are competent, as being within the province of their own profession.

Such were the ideas of the Associated Artists, and it was with such views that they considered the probability of a union with the Academy as an event which, if not desirable, was at least not to be prevented by any illiberality or want of moderation on their part; inasmuch as it was preferable to the establishment of a new and separate institution; an undertaking to which they felt themselves competent, but yet would not be understood as desiring. It was their wish that there should be but one institution; and they held themselves ready to join, heart and hand, in building it up, so soon as it should be placed on such a footing that they could unite in it with confidence and with well-founded hopes of such a management, that the energies of all might be directed to the attainment of the noble ends of an Academy of Fine Arts. Their subsequent proceedings, and those of the Academy, will form the subject of my next letter.

BOYDELL.

LETTER IV.

At a subsequent meeting of the Drawing Association, it was resolved that a copy of the Report submitted by the Committee should be presented to the American Academy. The object of this measure was to remove any suspicions that might exist as to the intentions of the artists in this writing, and to make known to the Directors that the artists were in a state of union, and were friendly to that Institution, and not only willing, but desirous, of giving to it their services, provided something could be done towards removing the disadvantages which, in the existing state of things, would have been attendant upon that proceeding. They also wished the Directors to understand that they were conscious of possessing both the right and the power to found a new Academy; but that their respect for one already established by gentlemen of the first character, notwithstanding its deficiencies, prompted them to make some overtures which might have the effect of rendering that measure needless. That they were not ignorant of the nature or magnitude of the difficulties which existed in the organization of the American Academy, but did not desire then to agitate them, and were willing to discuss the whole subject coolly and amicably, and, if possible, agree upon some plan which should tend to the mutual benefit of all. In the event of a similar disposition on the part of the Academy, it was necessary that two points should be settled, previous to any consultation as to the subsequent management of the united interests. These were, first, the proportional number of artists to be received into the direction; and, secondly, the means of making them eligible to the office of Director; for by the charter of the Academy, this eligibility could only be acquired by the purchase of a share, and the donation of a picture; a requisition from which the artists thought they ought to be exonerated.

In the course of a conversation with some of the officers of the Academy, the members of the Association were informed that there was an equal willingness on the part of the Directors to come into some arrangement with them; and it was proposed that the two preliminary articles of adjustment should be examined into, and settled by a Committee of Conference. This proposition being agreed to, a resolution of the Board of Directors of the Academy was transmitted to the Association, which "appointed a Committee of three to meet a similar Committee of the Association, and to confer with them upon the subject-matter of the Report which had been laid before the Board." A Committee was immediately appointed by the Association to confer with that of the Academy; and the six gentlemen met, considered the matters submitted to them, and adjourned, leaving the form of their report to be adjusted by the two Chairmen. The following is the substance of that report, as it was drawn up by the Chairman of the Committee on the part of the Association, and with one exception, which will be hereafter noticed, approved by the Chairman of the other Committee:

As to the payment of the price of a share in order to render an artist eligible to the office of Director, it was stated on the part of the Academy that the regulation having been created by the charter, it could not be controlled or dispensed with by the Directors, and could only be repealed by the Legislature; and the ensuing election (at which, whatever should be agreed upon, must be done,) would take place at too early a period to admit of that remedy; which it was conceded by the gentlemen of the Academy was desirable, and would not be opposed by that Institution.

In consideration of this, the gentlemen offered to guarantee the election of six artists into the next Board of Directors, (being one-half of the number,) if the artists on their part would qualify themselves in the required manner. The Committee, therefore, recommended the adoption of this measure by the Association—namely, the election of six artists from all those in the city (not confining their views solely to such as were members of the Association) who, if not already qualified, should qualify themselves by the purchase of a share, and be recommended to the electors as representing the whole body of artists.

The exception which I have mentioned related to the word *guarantee*, and it was finally qualified by the mutual understanding that the gentlemen from the Academy engaged or guaranteed to exert all their influence to effect the election of the six artists into the next Board of Directors.

In pursuance of this recommendation of the Committee, six artists were chosen by the Association, by a unanimous vote; and two only of the six being stockholders of the Academy, a resolution was offered and agreed to, that the sum of one hundred dollars necessary to qualify the remaining four for election, and render the whole ticket eligible according to the agreement, should be paid from the Treasury of the Association. The names of the six candidates were handed to the Directors, and the Treasurer of the Association tendered the money. But he was told that by the laws of the Academy, it was necessary that members should be proposed at one stated meeting, and balloted for at the next (the interval being a month), .which would have deferred their admission until *after* the election, and of course defeat the purpose of the agreement.

How this difficulty was obviated, I propose to show in my next letter.

BOYDELL.

LETTER V.

My last letter concluded with an explanation of the unexpected obstacle to the accomplishment of the proposed arrangement, started when the Treasurer of the Association attended in pursuance of a resolution to that effect, to pay the required sum of one hundred dollars, as the admission fee of the four ineligible artists. Upon receiving information of this fact, the President of the Association addressed a letter to the President of the Academy, acquainting him with the selection of the six artists, and the arrangement in consequence of which this selection had been made, and also with the threatened defeat of that arrangement, and suggesting to him the expediency of adopting some measure to remove the obstacle which had intervened to prevent the desired and expected union. In reply, a copy of a resolution of the Board of Directors was received from the Secretary of the Academy, by which it was declared that the four candidates, having been more than a year before elected Academicians of that institution, were by that act entitled to become members on the payment of twenty-five dollars each, and that they would therefore be considered as stockholders, and eligible, whenever such payment should be made. This was of course perfectly satisfactory, so far; the difficulty was happily obviated, and now nothing appeared to be wanting to the success of the proposed arrangement, but the transfer of one hundred dollars from the Treasury of the Association to that of the Academy. The artists, relying implicitly upon the faith and honor of the Committee, with whom they had communicated, this transfer was immediately effected, and the four whom they had selected being now indisputably stockholders, the whole ticket offered by them became eligible. Unaccustomed to electioneering management, and little imagining that some of the officers of the Academy were determined, if possible, to prevent their admission, the artists conceived the pledge they had received to be all-sufficient, and that indeed they were neither called upon, nor ought to ask for this or that man's vote. The question whether it was, or was not, of importance to secure the co-operation of the body of artists, was for the Electors, and not for them to decide, and they awaited patiently, but confidently, the period which, as they thought, was to place in their power the means of exerting themselves earnestly and successfully for the advancement of their art. Their surprise, therefore, may be imagined, when, on the evening previous to the election, they were apprised, by an anonymous letter from one evidently friendly to the union, that a plan was in operation to divide their ticket, and that those, (whose names were given) and perhaps others of their nomination, would be excluded. There was but a moment for consideration—in a few hours the morning papers would be closed, and no other means were left to acquaint the Committee or the Electors of the design, in season to counteract it. As the only available resource, the following paragraph was hastily penned, and distributed to the morning papers:

"*To the Stockholders of the American Academy of Fine Arts.*—Many contradictory reports being abroad touching the election of officers for the ensuing year, which takes place this day, it has been thought advisable to apprise you, in a few words, of the more than ordinary importance of the present election, involving no less than the *union of the body of Artists with the Academy, or their separation from it.* There is only time for the statement of the following facts. Negotiations have been carried on for some weeks past, between the gentlemen composing the present Direction of the Academy and the Associated Artists, to bring about a cordial union of interests. At a meeting of the Committees .of Conference, it was agreed that the next Board of Directors should comprise at least six artists. The artists accordingly balloted for six of their number, to be submitted to the Electors—who, being the chosen *representatives* of the artists, it is to be understood that all or none will serve."

In this publication the artists unquestionably manifested an anxiety for the election of their ticket. Feeling that upon this point turned the question of their union with, or separation from the Academy, they did feel anxious that the previous negotiations, and the plan devised in those negotiations, should not be defeated through ignorance of the measure on the part of the Electors, or the intrigues of a few who might have private ends to gain. Be that as it may, the information given by the anonymous correspondent proved to be correct; the election took place, and but *two* of the six artists were admitted into the Direction of the Academy.

Some observations on this incident will be given in my next letter.

BOYDELL.

————

LETTER VI.

My last letter concluded by stating that four of the six artists nominated by the Association were not elected; the fact thus furnishing the most decisive evidence of the truth of the warning given by the anonymous correspondent, that there was a party regularly organized, and determinately opposed to the views of the artists, and to the successful issue of the negotiators. The result was, that the two who were elected instantly resigned their seats; and the whole body of the Associated Artists, in consequence, ceased to have any participation in the concerns of the American Academy of Fine Arts. It is worthy of remark, that the names of the six candidates were given in to the officers of the Academy *seventeen days* before the election took place; and so far from any official objection being made to the *mode* or *purpose* of presenting them, that when a difficulty appeared which seemed likely to prevent the acquisition of the hundred dollars which, by agreement, were to be paid to render them eligible, that difficulty was removed by a special vote of the Directors, which the artists were certainly justified in considering as a tacit assumption of the agreement entered into by their Committee, and a pledge for its fulfillment—else, why take the money of the Association? That it was so intended, in my opinion, there can be no doubt; nor do I believe that the intention was frustrated through the agency or with the concurrence of the Directors; but that there was an agency within the government of the Academy hostile to the union; and that this agency was successfully exerted, is established by the facts.

Such being the case, the Associated Artists conceived themselves to be now fully justified in giving up at once all idea of a union with the Academy, and forming a *new one* more in conformity with their views of what such an Institution should be; and they applied themselves, therefore, to the task with the same zeal and energy which they would have exerted in behalf of the American Academy, had those who prevented the union perceived and properly appreciated what was offered them, or had they not suffered themselves to be deceived or influenced by the representations of a few interested individuals.

One thing only was complained of by the artists: that they had not been given to understand that the offer of their services would be rejected, before the payment of their hundred dollars; for if they had known it sixteen days sooner than they did, their treasury would have been so much the richer.

In my next and last letter I propose giving a brief outline of the present situation of the National Academy, and its prospects, as well as of the plan on which it is conducted; but before I close this correspondence, I wish to express the pleasure I have felt in reading the first part of Mr. Morse's triumphant answer to the mistaken notions and fallacious reasoning of the writer in the *North American Review*, whose unfriendly criticism, but for his defence, might have deeply injured the young and vigorous Institution over which he presides.

BOYDELL.

LETTER VII.

In my preceding letters the circumstances which led to the establishment of the "National Academy of the Arts of Design" have been briefly related. I now proceed to give a short account of its present state and future prospects.

Immediately after the organization of the New Institution, measures were taken to open its *First Exhibition*, and notwithstanding the many difficulties under which they labored in this commencement of their undertaking, such as the want of a convenient and properly lighted room, &c., the artists succeeded in collecting together such a display of talent as surprised every visitor of their just-formed Gallery, consisting of works of *living artists* only; which had never before been exhibited, and which, by the rule of the Institution, can never be included in any future exhibition ; a plan which insures *novelty*, at least. The expenses of this, their first year of existence as an Academy, were somewhat greater than the proceeds of their exhibition, and the deficit was provided for by a small assessment upon the members, which was promptly and cheerfully paid. Not discouraged by this result, they immediately determined on another effort in the ensuing year; and to defray the expenses of the school, they concluded to receive from every student a small sum, sufficient to meet the expenses of lights and fuel. In their *Second Annual Exhibition* (in which was found a more splendid display of living talent than had ever before been presented in this city) they were more successful ; their receipts not only defrayed their expenses, but left them something in their treasury. Now, however, their greatest difficulty arose—the room in which the students assembled to prosecute their studies had been, till this time, loaned to them ; but now the Society which had so generously befriended the Academy could spare the room no longer. No alternative, therefore, was left to them, but to hire a room, or break up their school. An application for assistance to the Common Council was not listened to ; they therefore resolved to incur the risk of hiring for the year the room in which they made their exhibition, over the Arcade Baths in Chambers Street, and here they have their school at present. Thirty-five students have entered, who, with the members of the Academy, are found filling the seats three evenings in each week, occupied in drawing from the fine models belonging to the Academy, and the students profiting by the instructions and examples of the older artists. They have four professorships already filled : that of *Painting* by the President ; that of *Anatomy* by Dr. King and Dr. Godman ; of *Perspective*, by Dr. Neilson, and Charles Shaw, Esq. ; and of *Mythology* and *Ancient History* by W. C. Bryant, Esq. Lectures for the coming season are in preparation, and their Library has the promise of valuable accessions, as soon as they shall have acquired convenient rooms for their purposes.

Is not an institution like this, struggling with such difficulties, deserving of some notice and assistance from the public ? Is not the existence of a school like theirs an object worthy of the first city in the United States ? And can such a school be placed in better hands than those which have created it ?

My task is now ended ; and if I have succeeded in directing the attention of the public to an inquiry into the real merits of an undertaking which has been so much misconceived, or in awaking a friendly disposition towards an institution which is deserving of favor and assistance, and which is even now struggling against difficulties which would have conquered ordinary minds, I have accomplished my object, and shall feel myself rewarded for my labor.

BOYDELL.

In the latter part of 1826, or the beginning of 1827, (the precise date unknown,) died Edward C. Potter, Academician, an artist of more than ordinary promise. Few, if any, probably, of his works are remembered. As a draftsman he had few superiors, and that quality in his portraits generally insured him a strong likeness, a correspondent encouragement, and a pecuniary recompense. He was a successful portrait painter.

The minutes are not very explicit on the arrangements for the second exhibition. Ingham and Morton were to prepare the gallery. Dunlap, Cummings, Wall, Wright, Durand and Cole, to hang the pictures. When, or where it was to be held, sayeth not.

It was held in the upper story of the Arcade Baths, in Chambers Street, in a room about 25 by 50 feet, "*sky-lighted*," which Daniel E. Tylee, the liberal owner, had leased to the Academy at $300 per annum. *The building*, since, Palmo's Opera House, Burton's Theatre, and lastly District Court offices of the United States Courts.

On the 2d of May was held the first regular ANNUAL election under the new Constitution for officers in **1827.** the National Academy of Design. Twelve Academicians present.

SAMUEL F. B. MORSE was elected   *President.*
HENRY INMAN   "   "   *Vice-President.*
JOHN L. MORTON   "   "   *Secretary.*
THOMAS S. CUMMINGS   "   "   *Treasurer.*
CHARLES C. INGHAM, } *Members of*
A. B. DURAND,   }   *Council.*

On the 17th of May the second exhibition opened, with a *private view*. An entertainment was spread during the day, and a Committee of Academicians detailed to receive the invited guests. It continued until the 5th of July. The receipts $532.46 ; 57 days; averaging $9.34 per day; 117 productions.

It was assailed by severe criticism. "Middle-Tint" *the second* distributed his *handbills*, from which an extract is given.

"MACREADY AS WILLIAM TELL."

In various parts of our city, at almost every corner and pump, a large placard, entitled "*Macready as William Tell, by Inman*," meets the eye, and causes a thrilling sensation of pity and contempt, at the barefaced effrontery that has presumed to palm upon the public, as a *chef-d'œuvre* of Graphic composition, a specimen of Art which would disgrace a *tyro in Anatomical Drawing ;*—a picture incorrect in every feature, form and expression, as delineated by the great Tragic Histrio, William Macready.

As one of the Graphic Censors of this City, the undersigned feels it an imperious duty which he owes to the liberal profession and to the American

Public, to thwart the growing evil of "Graphic Puffing"—in order to establish the Fine Arts on a future firm and lasting basis.

The subscriber is aware of the arduous and highly responsible station he has assumed, as a public Graphic Censor, and the ill-will that may, at first, result from his undertaking. Enthusiastically fond of, and a practitioner in all departments of the Liberal Arts—he *will not shrink from* his task of exposing imposition and detraction, be the issue what it may.

Therefore, to evidence his determination, he now gives to the public his own ideas or critique on the merits of the above-named painting, which is to be disposed of on Friday ensuing. If the public be enlightened, his end is attained—if the proprietor be not a gainer, he regrets the infatuation which caused him to pay $500 for his picture.

Determined "*nothing to extenuate, or aught set down in malice,*" let us come immediately to our critique. Mr. Macready sat to Mr. Inman for the *Head*—the head *alone* of said portrait—the neck, trunk and lower extremities are not those of Mr. Macready. If we rightly understand, the Secretary of the National Academy of Design, and not Mr. Macready, stood for the completion of the whole figure, with the exception of the head. If, then, this be true, how can any man presume to assert that it is Macready as Tell, when the major part is * * * * * ? As well might it be averred that the great sea-serpent with his horse-like head is a horse, or that Peter Pindar was Julius Cæsar, each having a similarity of features, but diametrically opposite persons. Julius Cæsar was long-necked and raw-boned—Peter Pindar short-necked, and died of corpulency.

To convince the public that Mr. Inman is not a master of anatomical drawing, we refer to the painting. To ourself he has acknowledged his ignorance of the names, proportions, and uses of the bones and muscles of the human body. That he does not understand historic composition and the animal passions, is apparent by an examination of this picture. Whoever is acquainted with the manners, customs, and passions of the heroic Swiss, will attest them to be cool, deliberate, slow to anger, but mighty in vengeance. The name *cowardice* is not to be found in their vocabulary of records. According to Inman's ideas, Tell is in chains, and alone, without the pale of Gesler's jurisdiction. Is he grasping his chains as though he would make a weapon of them, to lay the smiter dead? Nay—he, apparently, stands shivering in the wind—frightened at his own shadow!!! In the painting, which is to be sold on Friday next, at the Exchange, the whole attitude and expression of countenance is utterly devoid of ennobling ideas, of enthusiastic patriotism; pusillanimity, the *vice versa* of the character of him who, sitting in his boat at night, could "eye the thunder breaking from his cloud, and smiled to see him shake his lightnings o'er his head," is the predominating trait in INMAN'S TELL.

Had Mr. Inman's picture remained in Boston, or been exhibited there, or in any other place, for profit or sale, we had not now entered into any description or exposition of its merits or demerits; leaving to each city in the Union the right of conducting its own fiscal concerns. But, to have it palmed on us a second time as a *chef'd'œuvre*, the *ne plus ultra* of Graphic composition—'tis too much for flesh and blood to bear; too much for free Americans patiently to endure. The painting, if we are rightly informed, sold for $500 to a gentleman in Boston, and by him was exhibited to the public for a period. All who have read the Boston critique on this picture, must say that it was therein handled more roughly than we do at this day. If, then, the people of Boston were unwilling to purchase it, why should *we* be again *insulted* by a second exposure, and attempt at sale? If "wisdom standing on the top of high places, by the way, in the places of the paths, at the entry of the city, at the coming in of the doors," cry, shall not *we*, the sons and daughters of man, pupils of wisdom, be permitted to cry also, and exalt our voices for the benefit of our species?

"He that spareth the rod hateth his son; he that loveth his kind chastiseth him betimes." Thus do we; not forgetting, however, "He that reproveth a scorner or braggart, getteth to himself [*now-a-days*] shame." And "he that rebuketh the wicked, getteth a blot."

Believing that "By giving instruction to a wise man, he will become yet wiser, and teaching a just man he will increase in knowledge," we have written this.

                                          MIDDLE-TINT.

The future reputation of Inman showed how false the critic's conclusions, or how greatly mistaken public opinion.

The second year's receipts rather more than equaled expenses, and left a small balance in the Treasury. The exhibition contained the works of "LIVING" artists "ONLY," not before exhibited by the Academy, and was considered a favorable exposition of the then existing standard of city art. Hostility was unabated. An arrangement had been made to *light* the exhibition gallery with *gas* in the evenings. A frame the shape of the room, but somewhat smaller, containing over one hundred burners, was suspended from the ceiling, and an equal and agreeable light was thrown on all the paintings.

The first exhibition was open in the evening and lighted with gas, but with three only of the common double-branch burners, six lights in all.

It was a convenience to those who were engaged in commerce or otherwise during the day. It proved as remunerative to the Institution as agreeable to the public, and soon became a " *special feature;*" the receipts in the evening frequently doubling, and even trebling those of the day. It was severely condemned by some ; it was unlike what had been done abroad, and was therefore wrong.

It, however, conquered all prejudice, and retained its supremacy. The practice has been copied in the English exhibitions, but whether they acknowledge the obligation or not is unknown.

In the early fall the school of the antique commenced, three evenings in the week, and in their own room, the one in which the exhibition had been held, and for the first time under the advantages of *gas-light* on the statues.

Cummings and Morton were directed to make application to the *Corporation* for the rooms occupied, but to be vacated by the Deaf and Dumb Institution. The request was not presented by the Committee, for what cause is not remembered ; their report to that effect to the Council was approved.

On the 28th of January it was resolved, that at all exhibitions of the Academy hereafter, " *None but Original* works shall be exhibited."

1828.

The exhibitions were thus restricted to "ORIGINAL

WORKS by LIVING ARTISTS, NEVER before EXHIBITED by the ACADEMY."

The rule was adopted for the purpose of placing all exhibiters on an equal footing. It had been found that young artists returning from abroad and exhibiting copies of works of established eminence had frequently been placed, by the want of discrimination in the public, far in advance of the more meritorious artist at home, exhibiting his own originations; an injustice it was thought the duty of the Academy to remedy. The restriction was a proper one, and ever very justly received favor.

On the 1st of April the schools closed for the season, and the *students* assembled for the purpose of rendering a decision on the drawings presented for the premiums; which resulted

1st Premium, 3d Class, to				J. W. WHITEHORNE.
2nd	"	"	"	——— WHEELER.
1st	"	4th	"	——— TIFFANY.
2nd	"	"	"	J. M. WARD.

They were delivered by the Council on the 7th June.

April 5th, the National Academy of Design was formally recognized by the State, and Samuel F. B. Morse, Henry Inman, Thomas S. Cummings, John L. Morton, Asher B. Durand, Charles Ingham, Frederick S. Agate, Thomas Cole, and such other persons as now are, or hereafter shall become members of said Society, are hereby constituted a body corporate, by the name aforesaid; and shall continue to be so incorporated, until the first day of January, in the year one thousand eight hundred and fifty-eight.

The minutes record that the President presented to the Council an address which he proposed should be printed, and delivered to future members when notified of their election, which was approved. That was never put in print or carried into effect, neither is the original to be found.

May 5th, was opened the THIRD Annual Exhibition, with a private reception. A committee was in attendance to receive the company, and a collation on the table during the whole day.

The first and most necessary wants of the Institution supplied, "LUXURY" soon crept in; the exhibition-room was ordered "CARPETED."

The number of works displayed did not materially differ from the preceding year, though limited, as before stated, to originals.

It was conceded to be by far the finest "home-made exposition" that had been given.

It was open 57 working days and received $812.83, an

average of $14.26 per day. It contained 178 works, and closed on the 10th of July.

May 7th, THE ANNUAL meeting. The following were elected officers for the ensuing year: Samuel F. B. Morse, President; Henry Inman, Vice-President; John L. Morton, Secretary; Thos. S. Cummings, Treasurer; Charles C. Ingham and William Dunlap, Members of Council.

Dr. Godman, John Neilson, Jr., Samuel F. B. Morse, and W. C. Bryant were elected Professors; Godman and Neilson delivered a course each. The first on Anatomy, the last on Perspective. For the first time a difficulty arose in consequence of the arrangement of the works on exhibition. Mr. Catlin, N. A., was dissatisfied with the places awarded to his productions, and serious and unpleasant words passed. A letter was received requesting the return of the pictures, and also resigning his post as an Academician. The President informed the Board that the pictures had been returned, and on the question of his resignation, it was " Resolved unanimously that the same be accepted."

The first year's exhibition of the National Academy of Design received but little attention on the part of its enemies.

It was generally conceived by them to be a mere " spasmodic effort" that would begin and end the days of the National, and the more particularly so as it proved a pecuniary loss.

The opening of the Second Exhibition, and the activity in the body at the period, was a surprise.

The opening of the third dispelled whatever hope they had entertained of the speedy dissolution of the body, and won their detestation; hostility was at its culminating point; " *Middle-Tint the Second*" opened the ball—from which extracts are given. The attacks were numerous and severe:

No. 3. Portrait of a Lady, by H. Inman, a native artist. Owing to the very pompous description, in the *Merchants' Telegraph*, of the works of this young gentleman, we were induced to visit the exhibition of the National Academy, in order to judge for ourself. When, lo and behold, our high-wrought expectations were withered in their bud, by a display of No. 3, the first of the exhibiting specimens of this *unrivaled artist;* or, as our mentorial Colonel will have it, " *very meritorious artist.*" Who that has ever viewed the spirited works of John W. Jarvis, could have believed that a pupil of his for many years his favored protégé apprentice, would have dared to exhibit such a specimen, as the product of his unwearied attention and instruction? A cold, phlegmatic, idiotic female face, without color or form, arrayed in the uncouth habit and style of a lay sister. If such drawing of features, form and dress be the product of fifteen years' steady application and practice, God keep our children from assimilating genius. In our humble opinion, Mr. Inman can rank but as secondary in the graphic arts. We wonder at the infatuation which has pervaded this community, in relation to this *young and illiterate aspirant!*

According to the plan laid down to, and pursued by the learned critics of our day, every artist of merit to be kept in the back-ground, like stool pigeons in a field to gull the public, and thereby fill the pockets of Messrs. Morse, Ingham, Inman, Cole, and Cummings. But *Deo et patria jubantibus,* these things shall not be—for wherever Vice shall dare to display her visage, we will mar it ; or, having caught her, will hold her up to public detestation. By particularizing the names of Quidor, Jocelyn, Agate, Inslee, Mount, Bennet, and Cogdell, we intimate our firm belief, that each of them have more real genius, than either Morse, Ingham, or Inman. In proof of the correctness of our belief, instances will be quoted, and left to the decision of an imperial public. As regards Mr. Cole, we believe him to be at this day, an unassuming and highly meritorious artist, uneqaled in the line of his profession, (landscape.) Mr. Cummings has evidenced to all the most rapid progress in Art ever heard of in this or any other country.

Mr. Quidor was a fellow-apprentice with Mr. Inman, to the justly celebrated Jarvis of this City ; but was maltreated by his master, while on the contrary, Mr. Inman was indulged to excess. Yet, under this disadvantage, we feel no hesitation to assert that as a general painter, as an original genius, Mr. Quidor is vastly superior to Mr. Inman. We challenge Mr. Inman or any one of the National Academicians, to produce specimens equal to several of his works as displayed on banners and fire-engine backs. But in speaking of his Ichabod Crane, it must be admitted his horse is not a horse, but such a horse it is as is the horse and horses of President Morse in No. 10—Una and the Dwarf—being unlike to anything in the heavens above, the earth beneath, or the waters under the earth.

" Palmas ferant." ! ! !

The fear of displeasing friends or acquaintances, induces critics, generally, to disguise their real sentiments, and to appear to approve what, in their hearts, they really condemn. Not so shall be our rule of conduct ; as we began, so shall we end ; knowing neither friend nor foe in the Arts ; and therefore, as advocates to the Liberal profession, we shall conclude our critique on No. 3, by advising Mr. Inman to cease from the pride of vanity, keep his own secrets, depend for fame on the work of his hand, and not on effusions of a——'s brain—*au fait.* And finally, to read, and if possible, commit to memory, the 27th chapter of Ecclesisaticus. *" Si fait." ! !*

Very few will be likely to accuse " Middle-Tint the Second" of disguising his sentiments. The affairs of the institution were indeed managed by the gentlemen referred to—and very well managed they were, too. They may have kept out some—they doubtless did, and exercised the privilege of *voting according to their conscience*, as probably Mr. Browere would have done, had he been in a place to exercise that privilege. They certainly kept him out—hence his anger—few who knew the gentleman will ask the reason why.

17th of May, a writer appeared in the *Evening Post* under the signature of *Denon*, who excited the wrath of the President of the American Academy to an unparalleled degree. All the known writers disclaimed any knowledge of who *Denon* was.

Trumbull having set his mind on the idea that there could be but *one* in the field, closed it against any other belief than that it was by Morse—and fell at once upon him; the wrong man.

The author of Denon was personally known to the writer, which, as he preferred an incognito, it is also equally unnecessary to disclose.

Suffice it to say, that, from the writer's PERSONAL KNOWLEDGE, it was NOT Morse, nor did Morse know even of the matter until it appeared in print.

"DENON."

[Evening Post, May 17th, 1828.]

THE TWO ACADEMIES.

Messrs. Editors—The Fine Arts, at the present moment, seem to have more than common attention paid them in the principal cities of the Union, and it, therefore, becomes a subject of much importance to observe a little the singular aspect which they now assume in this city. We have two Institutions—both called the Academies, both incorporated by the State, and both professing to be formed for the encouragement of the Fine Arts. One is managed exclusively by artists, the other almost as exclusively by gentlemen of other professions. If they are in reality alike in principle, the question naturally occurs, what necessity is the ·e for two? If they are unlike, then it is proper that the general principles on which each is founded, should be known, that the public may judge understandingly of the probably beneficial consequences which may result to the arts and to the community from each. Of the nature of an Academy of the Fine Arts, there has been of late much public discussion. The formation of the *National Academy of Design* gave rise to this discussion. The conflict of opinions between Mr. Morse, the President of the Academy, and the *North American Review*, has placed the whole subject very clearly before the public. With the principles, then, on which the *National Academy of Design* is founded, we are all well acquainted: it is (according to the account given by the artists themselves) "an Association of Artists for the purposes of instruction and exhibition." They maintain that artists alone should have the management of an Academy of Arts, and they assert that annual exhibitions, composed of the works of living artists only, will best show the state of taste in the country, while they will be the source of the permanent revenue to support the establishment. These are certainly important points, and I shall in the sequel examine whether thus far experience has proved them correct in their anticipations.

The *American Academy of Fine Arts* is the oldest Institution of the two; it was formed many years ago, when there were but few artists in the city; and by gentlemen who were liberally disposed towards the arts. The best of motives is conceded to them, the honest desire to promote the interests of the Fine Arts. The question, however, which I now mean to discuss, is not whether the founders of this Academy intended right, or whether it has been of any use; the question is, *are the principles on which the American Academy of Fine Arts is founded correct?* Is there not some error in the very foundation of the Institution, which will forever prevent it being of any benefit to the arts? The American Academy of Fine Arts consists of nearly 300 stockholders of various professions, Lawyers, Physicians, Merchants, &c., &c., who have each paid $25, and who have each a vote in the choice of officers for directing the Institution. Merged in this body of the stockholders, were some of the few artists who belonged to the Academy before the formation of the National Academy, a meagre minority, and who must from the principles of the Institution always have remained a minority. Here then were to be seen the members of a liberal profession, (a profession which, in countries in any degree advanced in the refinements of life, has held a rank among the highest,) degraded in the very outset into a set of dependents, from which dependence they could never expect to escape, through any provision in the Charter or Constitution of the Academy; and thus were they doomed to see the interest of their profession forever yielded to the disposal of men of other and diverse professions. In the American Academy then, the artist is in leading strings; men of other professions tell him that they are to judge for him, that he cannot be trusted with office, that the weakness of his judgment, and the *jealousy* to which he is prone because he is an artist, render him unfit to do justice to his contemporaries. In apportioning the influence of the Academy, therefore, on these principles, care must be taken that the artist never has more than a minority in office; such *has always been*, and *is now* the fact. The artist of independent feeling, especially if he has anything of our National spirit of freedom within him, must perceive at a glance the shackles by which he is bound in such an Institution, and will retire from it in disgust, or remain an unconcerned, inactive spectator of measures in which he has no voice, and against which he has no remedy, and on which perhaps his opinion is considered obtrusive, and gratuitous. And the shallow pretender in his profession, the half-souled artist, puffed up with sophomorical consequence, who can play the sycophant, and fawn upon the rich in hope of patronage, he is most likely to be the *pretégé* of such an Academy; here he will find just the place to play off his quackery upon superficial and therefore vain connoisseurs. Besure, he will not associate with the genuine artists, he knows full well that the borrowed plumes with which he is bunglingly decorated, will not bear the scrutiny of those who can see the jackdaw beneath them.

From this inaction and unconcern of artists of real talent will follow another evil. The exhibitions (which are the life-blood of an Academy,) will receive no support from the best artists, they will not contribute their productions; and why should they? The real artist has too much independence of spirit, too high a sense of the dignity of his profession to stoop to bear on his shoulders, any who would wish to ride to fame merely as *Directors of an Academy of Arts;* and, it may be, whose only claim to *direct him* is the payment of 25 dollars. Hence there must soon be a dearth of *new pictures* from the *best artists,* and the new works of the exhibition must consist principally of the ungainly daubs of such pretenders as we have described, or there will be a dull repetition, year after year, until public curiosity will be sated, and the exhibition room will gradually be deserted. What, now, has been the case in the American Academy of Fine Arts? Does not fact testify to the truth of this reasoning? Is it not notorious that for many years the principal novelty has consisted in a new arrangement of the same materials? A picture that hung on one side last year, hangs on the opposite side this year; so that a gentleman who had for many years observed these annual metamorphoses, suggested, upon examining the catalogue, that as invention seemed to be exhausted in giving new places to old works, the next change had better consist in turning pictures upside down, or with their faces to the wall, and then proposed that the *catalogue should be stereotyped* as a literary curiosity!! And in what does the present exhibition differ from the former ones? The room is again newly arranged, old acquaintances in new lights, are everywhere recognized on the sparsely covered walls; and some lamentable specimens of spoiled canvas, supply the principal novelties in the class of new productions. And how are the exhibitions in respect to popular attraction? Is it not also notorious that popular curiosity has from year to year regularly and gradually subsided, until the common answer to the question, "*Have you seen the exhibition this year?*" is "*No, I saw it last year.*"

Turn now to the operation of the principles of the National Academy. Being an Association of Artists for the purpose of promoting the advancement of their common profession, they have the excitement of a common interest to find out the best means of attaining their end, and to place the best officers in the management of their concerns. These officers holding their places at the will of the whole body of the principal artists, any *maladministration* or *favoritism* is at once checked being under the control of that body. Hence all the measures devised must have the concurrence of at least the majority of the profession, and when once determined upon, they will have the confidence of all. The result of this confidence, with the consciousness of power to remedy any evils that may occur in the government of the Academy to suit their own views, leaves upon the minds of the artists a feeling of *security*, as a feeling of independence highly favorable to the exercise of his art, and will inspire him with a generous and becoming emulation to outstrip contemporaries, not by the low arts of intrigue and defamation, (for his judges are his peers,) but by endeavoring to produce more excellent works. This is not mere speculation. The unparalleled progress of the National Academy proves this reasoning correct. Artists formed this Academy about three years ago, unaided by any loan of funds; they commenced their school, and opened their *first* exhibition consisting of works of living artists only, in a hired room. The expenses exceeded their receipts; but not discouraged, it seems they taxed themselves to liquidate the debt, which was cheerfully paid; the next year they opened their *second* exhibition, restricting themselves to works *never before exhibited*, and notwithstanding this restriction, so opposite to the custom of the American Academy, they filled their room with pictures, and the result was highly encouraging; their receipts paid their expenses, and left them something in their treasury. The present year they have opened their *third* exhibition with the same restrictions to works of *living artists* and to *new pictures* as before, and the additional one of receiving no *copies;* all it appears are now *original* works of *living artists, and never before exhibited by the Academy.* And yet with all these exclusions, they have the wall of their room literally packed with pictures, and we learn, that could they have found places to display them, at least 30 more would have been received. And if the crowd of visitors from morning till night to their exhibition is any proof of popularity and of excited public curiosity, they have also this proof. And now turn once more to the American Academy. Look at the present exhibition. It contains *ninety* pictures, *thirty* of which have been seen on the walls for years, (but altogether *old* and *new*, making just *half the number* of those in the National Academy,) and these are by all manner of artists, *known* and *unknown*, *ancient* and *modern*, from Salvator Rosa down to Archibald Robertson, and of all degrees of merit from the rich and glowing pencils of Sir T. Lawrence and Trumbull, down to the leaden caricatures of Parisen and Catlin. And there are *huge* copies, and *little* copies, and *whole* copies, and *half* copies, and *good* copies, and *baa* copies; indeed, it is a sort of Noah's Ark, in which were things of every kind, *clean* and *unclean, noble animals*, and *creeping things.*

And now let us glance a moment at the difference in natural advantages of the two Institutions. The American Academy of Fine Arts, with 264 patrons giving the sum of 6600 dollars, to which add the receipts of at least 12 years of exhibitions, forms an amount which should make a full treasury, or show in its property the manner in which these funds have been expended. It pays no rent, has rooms furnished by the city, rooms well adapted for *schools*, rooms for *exhibitions*, rooms for *officers*, all rent free; and why is it in debt? What has become of all these funds? Where are its schools? Where its lectures? Where indeed is there any evidence of prosperity and of energetic and discreet government, at all answerable to the means given by its patrons, or to the reasonable expectations of the public who have been so bountiful to it?

The National Academy, on the contrary, maintains a school of 30 pupils, pays a heavy rent for its accommodations, asks no money from rich patrons, has no city patronage, has no rooms or even common conveniences for its officers, and yet keeps free from debt, and is rapidly rising into reputation and wealth. With these facts before them, who can doubt under what administration an Academy of Arts most flourishes? The wish has been expressed in the public journals, and very often in common conversation, that there should be *a union of the two Academies.* This is an interesting subject, which, with your leave, Messrs. Editors, I will discuss in another number of your valuable paper.

DENON.

[*Evening Post, May*, 1828]

ON A UNION OF THE TWO ACADEMIES.

MESSRS. EDITORS—I showed in a former communication the difference in principle of the two Academies of Arts (the *American Academy of Fine Arts*, and the *National Academy of Design*,) and also the effects on the Arts which experience has shown to proceed from each. As the opinion has been *publicly* broached, as well as privately expressed, that a *Union of the Two Academies* would be a very desirable event, I propose briefly to consider its practicability, and its expediency. I should not trouble you at such length, did I not perceive misconception to exist to a very considerable extent respecting the actuating motives of the members of the National Academy, and the wish for the Union of the two Academies, expressed, in such a way as to imply, that their original movements were the result of freak or passion, and that in order to return from their *secession*, as it is sometimes called, it would only be to make the sacrifice of a little pride, such as truant boys are wont to make who have run away from school, and are solicited to return. They are supposed by many to have been actuated in the first instance by a spirit of petty cavil at some temporary slight; and in the continuation of their plans by a spirit of hostility and rivalry to the American Academy. This is as great a mistake as to suppose that our Revolution was undertaken only to revenge the imposition of the Stamp Act, and that our country might return to its former state of colonial dependence. From all I can gather in conversation with their most intelligent members, the New Academy took its rise as much from principle as our Republican Government. I will, therefore, as a preparatory step, direct a little attention to the immediate causes which led the Artists to form the National Academy of Design. The evils to which I alluded in my former article, particularly the hopelessly dependent state of the Artist in the American Academy, made the principal members of the profession in the city, anxious for some remedy. An accidental assemblage of them for mental benefit in a drawing association, while it showed them their strength, also suggested the plan of negotiations with the American Academy, on the subject of these evils; which it was hoped might lead to just such a union as seems now to be desired. I have read the account of their proceedings as they are given by a writer under the signature of *Boydell*, upon whose statements, as there has been no contradiction of them, I have presumed to rely for my facts; and I see nothing in any of their proceedings which has not the character of manly and respectful remonstrance against the existing evils, and a modest willingness to allow to the founders of the American Academy a full proportion of influence and control, in consideration of any sacrifice they were called upon to make. Negotiations were officially carried on between the artists and the Academy, and the terms of union amicably settled, in manner and on principles that seemed to promise the happiest effects. The event was to be decided by the result of the ensuing election. The Artists negotiated, more immediately, for such a proportion of the new Board of Directors, as should give a fair representation of the Body of Artists, and their object, (it should be borne in mind,) in seeking this representation, was not the paltry office of a *temporary Directorship*, but it was to "discuss the whole subject coolly and amicably, (in the new Board thus constituted,) and if possible agree upon some plan which should tend to the mutual benefit of all, Stockholders and Artists." A new organization of the Academy to suit a a new state of the Arts was their avowed object. The sincerity of their designs could not be doubted. The payment of *one hundred dollars* to make their ticket eligible, in compliance with a law of the American Academy, which was acknowledged at the time, on all sides, to be unjust, proved at least that they were in earnest in seeking a union. Here there was a golden opportunity for consummating the union. Why was it not improved? Whose fault was it that it did not take place? The truth should be known. *Intrigue* was at work, and two or three hundred voters scattered through the city, who never as a body took more interest in the Institution than to assemble at the polls to the number of eighteen or twenty, were excellent instruments to deceive, and the cry that *"the Artists were attempting violently to seize the Academy and thus might sell their property at auction,"* was a very good *"cry of arms"* to summon the deceived to the polls. More did assemble at this election than were ever known to come before, and they came to *defeat* the union. Will it be said, the voters were ignorant of the negotiations, and were not aware of the consequences of their votes? What means the *notice* which we are told was in all the morning papers on the day of the election, in which it is said to the Stockholders, "it has been thought advisable to apprise you, in a few words, of *the more than ordinary importance*, of the present election, involving no less than the UNION OF THE BODY OF ARTISTS WITH THE ACADEMY, OR THEIR SEPARATION FROM IT," &c., and then they are informed of the *negotiations* and *arrangements.* No! they were not ignorant. They voted with the warning before them, and they *defeated the union.* The *one hundred dollars,* (a pledge it may be called of good faith on the part of the Artists,) is taken, and then their own faith towards the Artists is violated, and they defend themselves from the accusation by a quibble.* I have looked minutely into the doings of these negotiations, I have wondered that such circumstances as these, marked as they seem to me to be with traits of at least very ungenerous character, should on the part of the public have been overlooked, and viewed by men of such high honor as the Stockholders of the American Academy, with perfect apathy, as though the *injustice* which is acted under the protection of their names reflected no disgrace upon them. But I am still more astonished at the *magnanimity* and *forbearance* of the Artists, under such treatment. What did they do? Did they spread their complaints before the public? Did they fill the newspapers with the story of unkept faith? No! *"There are two Academies,"* was a sentence that we are told was heard in the room of the election, the moment the result of the election was known, and sure enough *that very evening witnessed the formation of the National Academy of Design.* And how have they since conducted themselves? Have they proclaimed hostility to the other Academy? No! Their conduct has been uniformly marked towards them with courtesy and respect. They have themselves, indeed, been attacked, and they have shown that they neither wanted promptness nor spirit to defend themselves. They have applied all their efforts to the building up of the genuine Academy of Arts; such as they doubtless would have made the other, had the *union* been accomplished. But, now unshackled by the difficulties and debts by which they would then have been perplexed, they have been free to form their own plans, regardless of the sneers of some, the misrepresentations of others, and the general misconception of their intentions. They felt that they were *right*, and they felt *strong* in *right;* it is this that has been the soul of their exertions, the secret of their prosperity. They have surmounted the principal difficulties of their infancy; are firmly and discreetly organized. They have gained a name among the incorporated liberal Institutions of our State and country. They have made the name of *Artist* respected, and they are exerting an influence already perceptible on the character of the Arts. Quackery is fleeing from their gaze into deserved obscurity, while the genuine artist conscious that now his works are to be submitted to the judgment of his brethren who can appreciate them, and to be viewed by the side of those of his peers, is stimulated to greater industry, and care, and perseverance. Who that has seen their present exhibition that will not acknowledge the evidence of these effects?

And now let me ask who are to be the gainers by a union of the two Academies? Would the Artists? What would they gain? The *rooms* of the American Academy rent free. These at best are very bad. They would gain the property of the Academy, some of which is doubtless valuable; but all of it is capable of valuation in money, and its value stated in a definite sum; and all that is most important to them, or *really necessary*, such as the casts from

---

* When some of the gentlemen concerned were accused of violating these stipulations, the reply was, "The Artists have what they asked for, viz.: six Artists in the new Board," while two only of those who were their *representatives* were chosen.

the antique statues, can at a very moderate expense and in a much better condition be imported from Europe, and added to their own already respectable collection. This then is a matter of calculation whether they had better use their surplus funds to purchase them *new*, or make an arrangement to use the old ones. But are there no incumbrances to all this property? Yes, *debts;* to what amount I am not informed, but there are *debts*, and there is a still more serious incumbrance, there are the free admissions of 2 or 300 stockholders and *their families* to be provided for in a new organization. I say, *new organization*, for it is entirely out of the question, I should think, to suppose that the Artists would take up with the present feeble constitution on any terms; as well might you expect the spirit of a young man voluntarily to leave its tenement and take up with the consumptive frame of old age. What is the amount of gain then that would accrue to the *Artists* by a union? A certain amount of property, to the purchase of which their own funds will in a short time be adequate, and even this amount incumbered with such difficulties as no one of them, I should think, would care to meddle with. Is there any other advantage? Oh! yes; I think I hear in a whisper, (for it should not be spoken loud *to republican* ears,) there is the *patronage* of the Academy; see what a splendid list of *patrons* they would gain, the most respectable names in the city and country, (among which by the by I find my own humble name,) and read too the list of *honorary members;* there is Bonaparte, and Mr. Ames of Albany, and George the 4th of England, and a great many more respectable gentlemen. Are these of no value? But I forbear, I leave these advantages to be settled by every one according to his own taste.

And, now, what would the American Academy gain by a union? They would admit a rebellious set of independent Artists, who have lived so long in a free atmosphere, that they verily think they have a right to all the honors which their own profession produces; who have the presumption to assert that they know how to manage their own concerns without foreign interference; and the impudence, too, to manage them without asking the patronage of any. Such a headstrong set would certainly not harmonize with those who would graciously save them the trouble of legislating for themselves, and who would also as willingly relieve them from the burden of honor, and require of them but that trifling and easy part of the whole business, *working for the concern*. Until the Artists are more tractable, and are rid of those wild notions of liberty, and feel their dependence a little more on 25 dollar patrons, they would be very uncomfortable associates. As well might you expect harmony in the Divan at Constantinople, by composing it in part of rebellious Greeks.

I hasten to a more important point. *Would the public be the gainers by the union?* Just so far as the arts are of public importance—just so far as it is proper that their direction should be under the control of those who best understand them. Courts of justice are not placed under the control of physicians; medical degrees are not conferred by lawyers, nor the Chamber of Commerce composed of Artists. Why, then, should the concerns of the Artists be thought in better hands than in their own? Common sense dictates the answer—"*Tractant fabrilia fabri*." The Artists have shown their ability to conduct their own Institution, and it is not, therefore, for the interest of the public that their hands should be tied, and their energies repressed by any union with an Institution proved by reason and experience to be unsound in its very principles. If, then, I am to form my opinions from the visible success of one set of principles over those of another, I must say for myself, that I wish to see *no union*—at any rate, no such union as shall not leave the Artists *entire control* of an Academy of Arts.

DENON.

"DENON" contemplated a third letter, which he withheld in consequence of the Presidential contest. The following was published on the commencement of that passage at arms. As it completes "DENON'S" remarks, it is inserted:—

[*For the Evening Post.*]

THE CONTROVERSY ON THE TWO ACADEMIES.

MESSRS. EDITORS—I will trouble you but a moment. I intended giving you another letter, showing how completely uncontradicted are all the facts which I laid before the public, in regard to the principles and condition of the two Academies. I did expect, if these facts were disputed at all, that there would be attempts to falsify them by other facts, and that some arrangements would be brought forward to show the unsoundness of the principles which I advanced. Nothing of this kind, however, has appeared. Futile conjectures, indeed, have been made as to the author of certain anonymous pieces, and I have been considerably amused to see with what a hue and cry the whole pack have gone off on a false scent. Let me give a single piece of advice to those who are so eager to find an author for every anonymous article they see. It is not so easy to guess right, as they may think. As proof in point, let me adduce the late admirable satire of the *Letter from Joe Strickland to S. F. B. Morse*, in which the sins of maladministration are hit off to the life. It has been attributed to at least *five* different gentlemen among the wits of our good city; and let any one place before him in imagination either of these gentlemen, while he is reading it, and he will assert of each, with confidence, that the one then present to his mind is the writer. Don't fix, then, upon one suspected, too suddenly or too positively, lest, as in the present case, you get into a sad dilemma. It is, in reality, of no consequence to the public who are the authors of anonymous publications, while they confine themselves to the discussion of principles, and of public character. The present controversy is not of a personal nature, and I hope will not be suffered to degenerate into mere personal altercation. Who cares a fig whether Mr. Morse is ambitious, or Mr. Trumbull unpopular among his brother artists? As far as they are public men, their public character may freely be discussed. And as it respects public incorporated institutions, surely the principles on which they are based, their good or bad tendency, and the manner of their administration, are a legitimate subject of popular discussion. A truce, then, with personalities! The present aspect of the Academic controversy is particularly interesting. Philadelphia is an interested spectator; the controversy on both sides I find in the journals of our sister city. The contest has happily got into the hands of the two Presidents, and has assumed an official shape. I will hope the combatants will keep their temper, and divest the subject as much as possible of any irrelevant matter. Let us have the pith and marrow of the affair, and the public will no doubt pass a candid and correct judgment. In the mean time, it is but courtesy for me to withdraw.

DENON.

The controversy waxed warm. Known and unknown partisans entered the field in defence of their favorite leaders.

[*Evening Post*, May 31, 1828.]

ANSWER TO DENON.

MESSRS. EDITORS—Observing that you have opened your columns for the discussion of the comparative merits of the two Academies of Arts in this city, I feel as if I had a just claim upon your attention to the following remarks, which have been elicited by a communication from an individual to the public which appeared in your paper of the 17th inst. :

If the press has become already too frequently the scene of action and the instrument of warfare between individuals and institutions, yet will you not, I trust, deny an individual or an institution the means of defending themselves, upon the same ground, upon which you have suffered them to be assaulted and with the same weapons which you have placed in the hands of their assailants. It is not from any personal or private interest of my own, that I come forward at this time, but from my warm and friendly admiration of the rising arts in our country, and a wish that the public may not be deceived in their estimation of them. Nor is it my object, in this appeal, to contrast the comparative merits of the two Institutions, or inquire into the comparative soundness of the principles on which they are founded; but to invite back public attention to a careful perusal of the communication above alluded to, that they may clearly understand the object for which it was written, and the *true source* from which it sprung. That communication had not the merit of a criticism, but was the mere putrid effusion of the most deadly feelings of an individual against the *very Institution in which he was hatched.* I have too much faith in the wisdom and good sense of our enlightened citizens to believe that an attempt at so palpable an imposition upon their opinions will not meet its own refutation. I trust that the public are not so easily prejudiced in their opinions, and that the author of that venomous communication will learn, to his great mortification, that the public opinion will at last regulate and cleanse itself like the pool whose smooth surface is liable to be disturbed and poisoned by the foulest reptile.

As a disinterested spectator, I have beheld with great satisfaction the rising condition of the arts in our country; and with *peculiar interest* have I watched and cherished the rapid progress of the newly-created Academy. With it I had enlisted my warmest feelings, and in its success I had anticipated that rapid elevation of the arts in our country, which can only be obtained by that degree of emulation which fair and honorable competition is calculated to excite. However little I may be disappointed in the final result, yet I cannot help but express my fears for its ultimate success; and, at the same time, my mortification at the indiscreteness of some of their measures, whereby they are seeking that elevation which is due only to *just and honorable competition.*

From the fair and definite explanation which the public have long since heard of the different character of these two institutions—the different principles on which they are founded—and the different ends which they are calculated to answer—it appears evident, to my judgment, (as I think it must to every one,) that both the Institutions ought to be nourished and supported, as an honor to our country.

Were I myself an artist, jealous of my fame, and wishing for some new machine other than my brush to raise me to the astonished admiration of the world, I might likewise endeavor to create some new three-legged animal to stride upon, and goad it on with a goose's quill, before the admiring multitude, to be gazed at. I might, perhaps, become the champion of one Institution, and, like a snake that is hidden, or a disease, spread my poison over the other. I wish it to be understood, however, that I speak as the friend of both Institutions—as one who is ardently wishing for the final success of both. I am ready at any time to stand forth as the champion of both; but at this time I present myself from the impulse that would always rouse me to action —when I see foul play.

I step forth to arrest the hand of an assassin, *knowing*, as I *do*, the cloak from under which the dagger sprung. I should deem myself accessory to the deed, were I to suppress from the public eye the source from which it came, and the malicious motive which put it into action.

I will, then, refuse to strike a blow, or to deliver the weapon into the hands of the party assailed.

I will endeavor to stand between—to exhibit the weapon—and draw from the fellow the cloak from under which the dagger came. As to the ascendency that one Institution may have over the other, or the elevation that one artist may deserve over his fellow-artist in point of excellence, or whose are works of merit, and whose are caricatures, is not now my object to inquire; on that subject the public are best enabled to determine, and, without partiality, will assuredly decide for themselves.

I only wish at present to inquire which Institution and what artists are pursuing the most honorable means for that elevation which they all seek in public estimation. Whether it is that Institution which has stood for many years founded upon the most liberal principles, and calculated, from the wisdom of its laws, continually to increase its valuable collection of models and works of art for the benefit of its students, and the honor and ornament of the country—conducted by men of liberal views and dignified character—or is it that Institution which has just come into existence on the shoulders of a few disaffected young men, and has no existence except a name but for one month in the year. From its very nature unable even to accumulate a permanent collection of works of art to guide and direct the taste of our country, and conducted by *two* or *three* young men, ambitious of their own aggrandizement, even at the expense of everything that is about them; and not content with the rapid success which has deservedly attended their first efforts, and the meed of praise which the world was ready to bestow upon them, have hastened to palm upon the world, in the name of criticism, a panegyric upon their own works, and then turn with their venom upon that venerable Institution in which they were nursed, and spurn upon it, as if it was unworthy of a place in existence. I ask, then, which Institution is pursuing the most honorable course, and which is to be most applauded by the world?

And what artists—those who are silently pursuing the labors of their profession, or those who, swelled with the pompous title of President, &c., can stand behind the screen trumpeting forth their own fame to the world, and from that invisible source direct their deadly shafts against their parent Institution—and, what is most *illiberal* and *contemptible* of *all*, to aim them at the breasts of their fellow-artists? I appeal to every fair and honest man, who has read the eulogy on the works in the New Academy which appeared in the *Morning Courier*, immediately after the opening of the Exhibition, and before the world were able to estimate, or critic to decide; and answer me whether such unbounded, fulsome praise, ascends like the language of the critic, or like the sounds of a man speaking his own fame to the world.

And I need not ask whether that malignant communication, which came through the *Evening Post* of the 17th inst., was the language of an unbiased or disinterested critic, or whether such poison must have come from a more unfriendly source. What critic, or what partisan in the ranks of society, could have stepped forth, unprovoked, and endeavored to poison the atmosphere around that venerable Institution; or what individual is so base and unfeeling as to endeavor to blast the reputation of two or three of his fellow-artists, by holding up their names to society as quacks and impostors, unless he was influenced by feelings of jealousy or envy?

It is unnatural for man to stab his fellow-man in the dark, unless he fears to meet him on equal and honorable grounds, or has some secret ends to answer—either his own aggrandizement, or some feeling of revenge.

These are motives which can never enter into the breasts of disinterested spectators, but can only come from the heart that is debased and chilled by the deadly feelings of envy or jealousy—or is bent on its own aggrandizement by the aid of foul and dishonorable means.

To that share of the public who have read those communications, and do not know the source from which they come, it is only necessary to refer back to them again, which I invite them to do, and a moment's consideration will convince them beyond all doubt of their origin, and that disgrace will attach to the very person in the public estimation, who so richly deserves it, for his endeavors to direct the public prejudices to his own exaltation. The smooth and silkened language of their author has become too familiar in the public ear ever to be mistaken, and his heart too well known by his fellow-artists and amateurs, not to be recognized in every line of those communications.

I would not endeavor to turn the public ear from the dulcet sounds of his smooth-tongued eloquence; but I would remind them, while they look in his smiling face, and listen to his plausible sounds, that the charm comes from a thing that creeps in the grass.

A PATRON.

To the Editors of the " New-York American."

We have lately seen several articles on the subject of the discord which has arisen among the artists of this city, and from which has originated the new Institution, known by the name of the National Academy of Design. During the course of last winter there appeared in the *Journal of Commerce* " A Reply to Art. 10, No. 58, in the *North American Review*, entitled Academies of Arts, &c., by Samuel F. B. Morse, President of the National Academy of Design." And subsequently appeared seven letters signed "Boydell." These have since been published in pamphlet form, and circulated, and are understood to be the acknowledged productions of Mr. Morse. (*Oh no, Colonel.*)

Recently, since the opening of the spring Exhibition, several pieces have also appeared in the *Evening Post,* written in the same spirit and *style, possibly by the same hand*—particularly one of Friday the 23d inst., signed " Denon," on the union of the two Academies. (*Dreadfully mistaken, Col.*)

My attention has been arrested by these vicious articles, the object of all of which appears to be, to throw the blame of schism upon the Directors of the parent Academy, which has long been known by the title of the American Academy of Fine Arts.

And although I have little disposition or leisure for newspaper discussions, yet I have been irresistibly impelled to attempt this reply to these publications.

I am one of the early members of the original Academy—*lay-members*, I understand we who are not artists by profession are facetiously called, and thought that we performed a meritorious action in serving the arts by our subscription when the arts were too feeble, and the Artists too few to protect themselves effectually. But times are altered—these " Jeshuruns have waxed fat, and kicked." Artists—*the Artists* have become great in their own opinions, and spurn the hands which in fact ministered the very means and aliment of their improvement.

Abhorring *ingratitude*, and unwilling to submit to censure where I fancied I deserved thanks, yet anxious to know the truth, I have felt it my duty to ask for information on this subject from the President and Directors of the Academy. I have obtained what is perfectly satisfactory to my own mind ; and I beg leave to submit to the public through your paper the result of the inquiries I have made, because, after careful examination, it does appear to me that in the various statements to which I have alluded there has been some want of candor, and of kindness of disposition, to say the least, on the part of the *leaders of the Artists.*

I have learnt from conversations that not long after the establishment of Mr. President Morse in this city, some time in the Autumn preceding the memorable election of January, 1826, from which the complete separation has its date, there suddenly appeared a strong disposition among the Artists to meet during the approaching winter evenings for the very laudable purpose of studying drawing from the plaster casts, and as the Academy, although rich in a noble collection of casts from the antique, yet were poor in funds, and did not at the time possess any room properly fitted up (with fire-place, &c.,) for the purposes. The gentlemen first met in the room of the Historical Society, and the President of the Academy (who was at the same time one of the Vice-Presidents of the Historical Society,) was applied to and requested to use his influence in obtaining regular permission from the proper officers to hold those drawing meetings in that room.—(*Untrue.*)

The President, delighted to see this first symptom of a desire to commence the study of the Arts at the foundation, lost no time in making the proper application to Doctor Hosack, then President of the Historical Society— boasted to them of the zeal which had thus suddenly appeared, and of the progress which was now likely to be derived from a right plan of study, and obtained from the Doctor, who granted it with that hearty good-will which he has always shown for the advancement of the Fine Arts, a ready and prompt permission to use the room. Meetings were accordingly held in this room for some time—several evenings in the week. Mr. Morse, who was at that time an Associate of the Academy, apparently taking the lead. But soon the number of the students increased, so that the room was too small for their accommodation, and again the President of the Academy was solicited to use his influence in obtaining the room of the Philosophical Society, which was larger. This was readily and cordially done—permission was obtained, and the drawing meetings were continued to be held there during the rest of the winter. Figures from which the students made their drawings were furnished from the collection of the Academy whenever they were asked for. The President and Directors of the Academy, understanding that the gentlemen thus laudably pursuing their studies, were students of the Academy—and with good reason —for among them were several Academicians, Associates and members of the Academy—whose *mutiny* and *desertion* could not have been anticipated.

No suspicion of any ulterior design was entertained until some time early in December, when Mr. Morse called upon the President ; and after some previous conversation, stated that the object of his visit was to inform him, that a degree of dissatisfaction existed among the artists, as to the manner in which the affairs of the Academy were conducted. When urged to be specific as to the grounds of offence, he, after some hesitation, avowed explicitly that the great objection was to the fundamental principle of the Institution, by which gentlemen not of the professions were admitted as members on the paying of twenty-five dollars ; and that these "lay-members," as he was pleased to call them, were not only entitled to vote at elections for officers, but even to become Directors, and thus to control the Society, which ought rather to be regulated by professional men acquainted with the subject. It was in vain that the President represented that such was the Chartered Constitution of the Society, in which no alteration could be made by the Directors, or by any other authority than that from which the Charter emanated. That after all, these conditions had been important means of procuring public patronage, and funds to a certain extent, without which the objects could never have been obtained which had been arrived at. That the means, and materials for study thus obtained, had already produced a very rapid and important improvement in the artists, and that, perhaps, it was fair to regard the Institution as a sort of Benefit Club, where two hundred members had subscribed to a joint fund intended to advance a particular branch of knowledge, in which only fifty of the subscribers had any professional interest, and it would appear strange that objections should arise among the fifty to paying their subscription equally to a joint stock, and from which they alone were to derive any direct benefit.

Several meetings subsequently took place at the President's apartments, in which Mr. Morse came accompanied with other gentlemen, now leading members of the new Institution, and the subject was amply and amicably discussed ; but as neither Messrs. Morse, Boydell, or Denon have made any allusion to these meetings and conversations, it is unnecessary here to enter into further detail.

The result will be seen from the following extract from a report made by the President to the Board of Directors of the American Academy of Fine Arts on the 17th day of December, 1825, in which the whole subject seems to be happily and clearly condensed, and which I have been permitted to copy and publish it as follows :

The President of the Academy of Fine Arts begs leave to lay before the Board of Directors the following suggestions, which appear to him to deserve their serious and immediate attention, as being essentially connected with the prosperity of the Institution, the paramount object of which was originally, and ought always to remain—the cultivation of those arts—namely, Architecture, Sculpture, Painting and Engraving.

The founders of this Institution were not aritsts ; we, on the contrary, are indebted for the existence of this Academy to the liberality and zeal of a few gentlemen of taste and fortune, who, at the time when the arts were in their early infancy in this city, being strongly impressed with the persuasion that the Fine Arts contributed essentially to the refinement of civilized society, purchased in Europe, and imported at considerable expense, those casts from the Antique Statues now in the possession of the Society, which form the proper basis of an Artist's education. This was done in the hope (which has already been realized to some extent) that young men would gradually rise up in this city, with a disposition to devote themselves to the regular and systematic study of these subjects, and whose progress would be essentially aided by the opportunity of copying in their native country those sublime works of the ancient Greeks which early students could only avail themselves of by an expensive residence in some of the great capitals of Europe.

In the year 1808, the same gentlemen, associated with some others, among whom was *only one artist*, applied for an act of incorporation, under the style and title of the American Academy of Fine Arts.

This is the original legal basis of the Institution, and was acted upon with feeble success until the year 1817; when a second act of incorporation was solicited, and granted, by the style and title of the American Academy of Fine Arts.

The first act of incorporation required that the affairs should be managed by a President, Vice-President and five Directors; in the revised By-Laws, passed in 1816, in conformity with this act it was ordained, "That *three* of the five Directors shall be elected from among the Academicians, who by the same By-Laws are required to be artists by profession;" thus giving to the artists an important share in the government of the Institution.

The second act of incorporation, passed in 1817, increases the number of Directors to *eleven*, but no corresponding change has been made in the By-Laws, and the number of artists legally eligible to the direction remains, as at first, *three;* and, indeed, in the direction of the present year, there is but one artist by profession, to ten gentlemen who are not professional. It appears to the President that here is a departure of the most fatal tendency from the principle originally adopted of giving to the artists by profession a majority in the direction; for the effect of this departure must naturally be to damp the ardor of the rising artists, and to render them indifferent, if not hostile, to the prosperity of an Institution ostensibly devoted to the improvement of the Fine Arts, but from an efficient share in the administration of whose affairs they find the artists in a great measure excluded.

It is true that the Academy owes itse stablishment, and much of the prosperity which it has hitherto enjoyed, to gentlemen not professional. It is also true that, at the time of its foundation, there were not in this city artists sufficiently numerous, RICH, or skillful, to have formed or sustained such a system. But it is also true that circumstances are now essentially changed, and it must give great pleasure to those gentlemen who *patronized* the arts in their infancy, to see that their fostering care has already brought forward a number of young gentlemen who promise to become the future ornaments of their country, and some of whom are eminently qualified to take part in the direction of those studies in which they have made such decided progress. The President, therefore, asks leave to suggest to the Board the propriety of recurring to the principle originally adopted; and, for that purpose, of passing a by-law by "which it shall be ordained," that hereafter, of the *eleven* Directors authorized to be annually chosen, *six* at least shall always be taken from among the Academicians, artists by profession.

In compliance with this suggestion of the President, the Directors resolved that, at the approaching election, six of the Directors should be taken from among the artists who are artists by profession. By this step, the Directors gave the strongest possible pledge of their wish for the prosperity of the arts, and their sincere desire for union and good understanding; for it was evident that several among themselves must be displaced, to make room for the newly-elected Academicians. This resolution was made known to, and was perfectly understood by, members entitled to vote at the election, as well as to the artists; and by this measure, which was intended to give to artists by profession *a majority* in the Board of Directors, it was hoped that the spirit of misunderstanding and *discord* would have been silenced. But *no.*

The artists having so far succeeded in their views, took the further unfortunate step of *nominating* the six new Directors, with the expectation, it appears, that their will would here also prevail; and much was said at the time (and it has been frequently repeated) of a pledge or guarantee given by a Committee of Conference appointed by the Academy, that the persons thus nominated should be elected, and of the evidence of bad faith on the part of the Directors in their non-election.   But this accusation is puerile; for every *child* in America knows that a committee cannot pledge its principals, much less an independent body of electors, to any measure.   A committee can only pledge or guarantee the future conduct of its own members personally.   And after the accusation had been circulated in conversation and in squibs sufficiently to produce on the public mind that unfavorable impression, which the imputation of bad faith never fails, and never ought to fail, of producing.

Boydell, in his fourth letter, section 2, at length admits that the "gentlemen of the Academy engaged or guaranteed to exert all their influence to effect the election of the six artists into the next Board of Directors;" and I have no doubt the gentlemen kept their word.

At length arrived the 7th January, the day of the election; and on the morning of that day the *demon of vanity* and discord, instigated, we are told, by "an anonymous letter from one evidently friendly to the union," dictated the publication of the following notice in the morning papers.   The fifth letter of *Boydell* gives on the part of the artists, or I presume, rather, on the part of their leaders and advisers, "*their* history of this transaction," but omits to give the name of the writer of the following paragraph:

"*To the Stockholders of the American Academy of Fine Arts.*—Many contradictory reports being abroad touching the election of officers for the ensuing year, which takes place this day, it has been thought advisable to apprise you in a few words of the more than ordinary importance of the present election, involving no less than the union of the body of artists with the Academy, or of their separation from it, there is only time for the statement of the following facts: Negotiations have been carried on for some weeks past between the gentlemen composing the present direction of the Academy, and the Associated Artists, to bring about a cordial union of interests.   At a meeting of the Committees of Conference, it was agreed that the next Board of Directors should comprise at least *six* artists.   The artists, accordingly, balloted for six of their members to be submitted to the electors, who, being the chosen *representatives* of the artists, it is to be understood that all, or none, will serve."

Of this unexampled production, I find it difficult to decide, which is most to be admired, or rather most to be wondered at—its arrogance, or its indiscretion.   Is it conceivable that any man of common understanding could doubt for a moment what would be its result?

I should be sorry to cast upon its author, whoever he may have been, the imputation of such weakness.   Yet I must do it, or the alternative must be admitted, which is not honorable—that *the result was foreseen and intended.*

It could not, surely, have been expected that the body of the electors, the *lay members,* would submit quietly to such proud dictation from a small body of *seceders*—men who had not the spirit to qualify themselves generally as electors, by contributing the paltry sum of twenty-five dollars each to the common fund, by which they chiefly, if not solely, were to be benefited.   It may well be doubted whether, in the present days of Christianity, there can be found an example so pure, of the exalted influence of its divine principles on any established society of Christians, as to have induced the majority to yield their opinions, and the elections of their officers, to the dictation of a small minority of dissenters; and could it have been expected here?

Denon assigns as the cause which operated so unfavorably, and defeated the pretensions of the artists at this election—intrigue—intrigue operating upon two or three hundred voters scattered throughout the city.

Mr. Editor, I, for one, knew of no intrigue—heard of none; but I saw this preposterous advertisement, and felt, and acted, as I presume other *lay mem-*

bers did, indignant at the presumptuous folly of the leaders of the opposition.

I resisted it by my vote.

Still, the requisition of the Board was subtsantially complied with, and six Academicians, artists by profession, were elected Directors for the ensuing year; not all, indeed, of the nomination of the Society of Artists, but six artists; by which means, had there been in the leaders of the opposition but the ordinary share of modesty and common sense, their legitimate object would have been completely gained. The affairs of the Academy would have been entirely in the hands, and under the control, of artists; and one united, powerful association of talent would have existed at this day, worthy of the patronage of the nation, in place of two, who have been disgraced, and debilitated by discord.

From this statement, the public will be enabled to judge where the imputation of intrigue is most properly to be made, and to perceive with what accuracy the leaders of the Opposition have chosen for the style and title of the new Institution—"The National Academy of Design."

A LAY MEMBER.

———

MORSE.

[*For the Evening Post.*]

MESSRS. EDITORS:—On my return to the city this morning, after an absence of about a fortnight, I was not a little surprised to find that during my absence my name had been very freely and unwarrantably used in the public papers, in connection with certain pieces that have at intervals made their appearance, under the signatures of *Boydell, Denon, &c.* A writer in the *New-York American* of the 31st, signing himself "*A Lay Member,*" in no ambiguous terms charges me with being the author of them. After speaking of my Reply to the *North American Review,* which appears with my name, he says "several pieces have also appeared in the *Evening Post,* written in the same style, and spirit, possibly by the same hand signed *Denon.*" He also says, "And subsequently appeared in the *Morning Courier* seven letters signed *Boydell,* these have since been published in a pamphlet form and circulated, and are *understood to be the acknowledged productions of Mr. Morse.*"

Waiving for the present the consideration of the indecency of publicly charging upon any individual what has been published anonymously, especially where principles, and not private character seem to have been the object of discussion, I will in the present case condescend, (whilst I protest against the right of any one to interrogate me on the subject,) to inform the *Lay-Member* that he is *entirely mistaken.* A perusal of the pieces in question, will satisfy any fair-minded man that I could not be their author, and especially their *acknowledged* author, without subjecting myself deservedly to the imputation of *praising my own works;* an offence against common propriety, of which I have never yet been guilty.

I have not now time, nor is my mind in a state, to expose the *falsely colored* account of the origin of the National Academy of Design by the *Lay-Member.* This I propose hereafter to do, especially as it appears in at least a *semi-official* shape. "I have felt it my duty," says the *Lay-Member,* "to ask for information on this subject from the *President and Directors of the Academy.* I have obtained what is perfectly satisfactory to my own mind; and I beg leave to submit to the public, through your paper, *the result of the inquiries which I have made.*" From this, therefore, it seems that the information is derived directly from Col. Trumbull, the President of the American Academy, and the Directors of the Academy. And the general truth of the whole communication, with some additions, is acknowledged in a subsequent paper, under the name of Col. Trumbull himself. This communication shall, therefore, have early attention.

One word, however, on the term "*Lay-members.*" The writer says: "*Lay-members*, I understand, we who are not of the profession, are facetiously called:" and again, "these *Lay-members*, as he, (Mr. Morse) was pleased to call them." Now I resign all my claims to the *authorship*, and consequently to the *facetiousness* of this term: I not only never used it, but I do not recollect ever to have seen or heard the name before this morning applied to those who are not of the profession.

I have hesitated whether to notice at all the *tirade of inuendo* in your paper of the 2d inst., under the signature of "*A Patron*," in which after insinuating in terms which cannot be mistaken, that I am the author of a piece which I did not write, and which I have never, until the present moment, even read, *A Patron* singles me out for a pretty full measure of very delicate abuse. I have not known whether most to pity the passion into which the gentleman has wrought himself, or to be surprised at finding such an arary of "*daggers*," and "*deadly shafts*," and "*snakes*," "*reptiles*," and "*poison*," and "*venom*," and much more tragic furniture, from the dungeon of his uncomfortable spirit, marshaled out with such flourish of trumpets and such boasts of dreadful deeds, and then finding nothing but *about* it and *about* it—not a single point of public interest touched upon, and leaving but one dark mass of unmeaning, idle, harmless inuendo. The thing may safely be left to itself.

If any principle in the arts shall be at any time thought worthy of public discussion, (which is of more public interest than whether I or any one else wrote this or that anonymous article,) I shall be happy, when necessary, to discuss the subject as far as my humble knowledge extends, nor shall I be ashamed to put *my name* to my *creed*: but as for engaging in personalities, or in defences of myself against anonymous vituperation, I beg leave to say once for all, that I have too much respect for the tribunal before whom I may occasionally plead, to believe myself of so much consequence as to make it worth while to disabuse the public from the misconceptions of any scribbler, who may choose to fancy me the author of any anonymous article that happens to disturb the equanimity of his temper.

With respect, gentlemen, your most obed't servant,

SAM'L F. B. MORSE.

————

[*For the Evening Post.*]

EXPOSE OF THE TRANSACTIONS BETWEEN THE DRAWING ASSOCIATION AND THE
AMERICAN ACADEMY OF FINE ARTS, PREVIOUS TO THE FORMATION
OF THE NATIONAL ACADEMY OF DESIGN.

Messrs. Editors:—To the article signed Lay-Member, in the *N. Y. American*, of the 31st ult., containing information derived directly from the *President and Directors of the American Academy of Fine Arts*, and calculated to make a very injurious impression against the National Academy of Design, I promised you an early reply. The first part of that article appears to be composed principally of conjectures about the authorship of certain anonymous pieces—of insinuations of *discord, schism*, and *ingratitude* on the part of the artists—and of contemptuous expressions against the artists generally. To this succeeds a garbled and incorrect history of the early proceedings of the artists, associated in a society called the *Drawing Association*, and of certain negotiations between that body and the American Academy of Fine Arts. To this part of the statement of the *Lay-Member of the American Academy*, I invite particular attention, as I pledge myself to prove it *untrue in its most important assertions*, and to show that by these and by his omissions in the history, the writer of that article has thrown a *false coloring* over all the subsequent negotiations between the two bodies. The next part, occupying about half of the whole piece, is a long report of the President of the American Academy to the Directors, recommending some reform in the internal affairs of the Academy, which as it has but little to do with the material points of the case, calls for but little attention. The remaining part seems to be composed of some severe reflections upon an *anonymous notice* to the Stockholders of the Academy, upon which notice is charged the blame of the defeat of a *union* of the two bodies, the terms of which had been under negotiation. The main points lie in the History of the negotiations. The Lay-Member's account of the matter is briefly this : "That soon after Mr. Morse came to this city, the Artists suddenly showed a disposition to meet and study drawing, that as the American Academy had no rooms with a fire-place in it, they (the American Academy) procured for the students other rooms from the Societies in the N. Y. Institution, that the figures from which the students drew were furnished by the Academy—" *The President and Directors of the Academy understanding that the gentlemen thus laudably pursuing their studies were students of the Academy*"—whose *mutiny* and *desertion* could not have been anticipated. "That there was no suspicion of any other design until *sometime early in December,* when Mr. Morse called on the President to inform him that a degree of dissatisfaction existed among the Artists " *as to the manner in which the affairs of the Academy were conducted.*" That Mr. M. " after some hesitation explicitly avowed that the great objection was to the fundamental principle of the Institution, *by which, gentlemen not of the professions were admitted as members on the payment of* 25 *dollars ;* and that these *Lay-Members, as he was pleased to call them, were entitled to vote, &c.* That to this it was replied, by the President in vain, that no alteration could be made in the Chartered Constitution of the Academy, and that the Institution was a sort of *benefit club,* &c. ; and that it was strange that Artists should object to pay their subscription with the rest. In consequence of this and other conversations it seems the Report of the President was made, recommending to the Directors to pass a by-law, ordaining that in future there should be six Artists in the Board of Directors, which measure was adopted ; and *that the Artists having so far succeeded in their views took the further unfortunate step of* NOMINATING *the six new Directors, with the expectation, it appears, that their will would here also prevail.* That they made much talk about a *pledge* or *guarantee.* That they published an *arrogant, presumptuous,* notice, dictating to the Stockholders whom they should choose, that the Stockholders were indignant at the arrogance, and defeated the ticket. And it is then charged upon the Artists that " *this result was foreseen and intended.*"

Such then is the statement that has received the sanction of the President and Directors of the American Academy of Fine Arts. Such a tissue of improbable results could not gain a moment's credence, had it appeared without sanction. I will endeavor to show how little of truth there is in this whole relation.

Having been connected from the commencement with all the transactions of the Artists composing the Drawing Association, and more recently since they formed the National Academy, I feel that my advantages for knowing their history, are at least equal to those of the *Lay-Member* of the American Academy, who could not from his situation have more than a very partial knowledge of it. I ask particular attention to the following narrative ; the minuteness of detail will be excused since it is necessary to a clear development of the transactions.

The *Drawing Association* was thus formed. In the autumn of 1825, there were found to be a considerable number of Artists in this city. They had but little social intercourse. There was no common place of meeting. The Artists, therefore, were for the most part unknown to each other. In October in that year, a few of them assembled at the house of one of their number in Broadway, for conversation on the state of the Arts. Their low condition was lamented, and the plan suggested, that if a few of us would associate for drawing, in the evenings of the approaching winter, it would be a pleasant mode of passing the time, combining improvement with pleasure. The plan suggested for a *Drawing Association* was at once acceded to, and the number consisting of but *seven,* at first determined to meet in a private room in Canal Street and use the models belonging to the individuals of the Association. The private room proving inconvenient, it was thought if we could obtain permission to use one of the rooms of some of the societies in the New-York Institution, we could be better accommodated, we accordingly obtained permission to use the room of the Agricultural Society. Here we met and organized ourselves by the name of the DRAWING ASSOCIATION. A President, Vice-President, Secretary, and Treasurer were chosen, and a few laws passed to regulate the meetings, and the terms of admission into the Association. I wish here to remark, that no one will deny the right of Artists to form a *Drawing Association*—when thus formed and organized with their own officers and laws, and paying their own expenses too, were they not as *distinct* from the *American Academy of Fine Arts*, as *that Institution* is from the *Historical*, or *any other Society?* Being now under the same roof with the American Academy, and two of our Association being members of the Academy, we obtained through them, the loan of a few of the casts of the Academy, (it being inconvenient to transport our own models,) these were brought into our room. The Association increased rapidly until most of the principal Artists of the city were of our number, amounting in all to 31, and we successively as our numbers increased, occupied the rooms of the Agricultural, Historical and Philosophical Societies, through the generous indulgence of the gentlemen of these several Associations. From the share of credit due to the President of the American Academy for his influence in procuring us these accommodations, I have no disposition in the least to detract. To these several Societies and to the American Academy, the Association at various times passed unanimous votes of thanks. We continued for several weeks pursuing our studies; on the one hand having neither the most distant idea of forming a new Academy, nor on the other, supposing that any one could imagine that the principal Artists of the city had entered themselves *students* of the American Academy, especially when they were seen to be separately organized, with officers and laws of their own. An event now occurred which created some excitement— The officers of the Association were informed, (by one of the younger members who applied to know the meaning of the measure,) that one of the *Directors* of the American Academy, had been round among the younger members and informed them that it was necessary for them to sign the matriculation book of the Academy, thus endeavoring to enrol them as *students* of the Academy. The *manner* of proceeding by this Director, but especially the novel nature of his errand, created some disturbance. There was not one of the Association who did not instantly repel the idea of his being a student of the American Academy; and in the conversations and discussions that grew out of this excitement, the unequal and unjust operation of the principles and laws of the Academy upon the Artists as a class, were a natural subject. It was deemed a proper measure at this moment, by a vote of the Association, in order to allay this excitement, to appoint a Committee of six to draw up a report stating definitely to the Association their relationship to the American Academy, (the borrowing and using the models of the Academy seeming at first view to connect them in some way with it.) This report was made at some length. A duplicate was sent at the time, Dec. 14th, 1825, to the Directors of the American Academy, as the best means of refuting reports that were in circulation that the Artists had formed a new Academy. In that report the Artists stated explicitly that they were a "separate Association," unconnected with the American Academy, but at the same time clearly avowed their cordial good feelings towards it. "We are," say the Artists in their report, "at present a distinct body with rights and privileges of our own, but in perfect harmony with the Academy." With this document before them, on file, in the American Academy, I leave it to the President and Directors of that Academy and the Lay Member, to reconcile their declaration that "*the President and Directors understood that the gentlemen thus laudably pursuing their studies were students of the Academy, and with good reason!*"

The disposition manifested by the Artists in this report may be inferred from a few extracts. "In the Academy of Fine Arts we behold an institution founded by *men among the first in our city and country.* The difficulties they encountered in originating it were many and are duly appreciated, &c."

"How much soever we may lament the evils [in the Academy] it is proper that we (the Association) should view them with much indulgence, as having arisen out of the circumstances of the times." Is there anything of *opposition* or *mutiny*, in this advice? Again; "we wish there may be but *one* institution, and we hold ourselves ready to join heart and hand in building it up so soon as we can see it placed on such a basis that we can come into it with confidence." Once more; "we are ready to believe they (measures of injurious operation,) were intended for the best good of the arts, and have failed not through any fault of theirs, [the Directors,] but from circumstances beyond their control. But while we concede thus much, we cannot shut our eyes to evils which manifestly exist, and which a little prudence and dispassionate consultation may easily remove." This report, as before stated, is on file in the American Academy, as well as in the National Academy, where any one can examine it. That document speaks this language, "that although the Artists did not now belong to the American Academy, as the offensive conduct of the before-mentioned Director would have made it appear, yet they were willing to unite with that body, if it was desired, whenever they could safely and honorably do it." For this purpose they hinted at mutual *consultation*, and invited a *conference* on the subject; this was acceded to by the Academy in the following resolution, viz:

"*American Academy of Fine Arts*, }
"Dec. 17th, 1825. }

"On motion, it was resolved that a Committee of three be appointed to meet a similar Committee of the Drawing Association, and confer with them on the subject matter of the Report of that body laid before the Board at this meeting,"

"Extract from the minutes.

"ALEX. RORERTSON, Secretary."

As the terms *seceders, mutineers, deserters, &c*, are applied by the Lay-Member to the Artists, and they are charged with *separating* from the *parent* Academy, &c., it may be well here to remark that the American Academy themselves in this official act acknowledge the *Drawing Association* to be a *distinct body*, with whom they are about to hold a *treaty* for certain purposes; the object of this treaty further shows the relation between the *two bodies;* it was to devise means of *uniting the two;* if they were already united, what necessity was there for negotiating terms of *union?* and if the Artists were not *then* united to the Academy, *at what time previous*, were they ever united? It will thus be seen how much ground there is for the accusation of *separation, secession, &c.*

But to return to the narrative. The points in immediate discussion between the two Committees were, as a matter of course, the general principles of the American Academy to which we made our objections; we showed their unequal bearing upon Artists as a class, and proved to them that from the nature of the system the Artists could never compose more than a very small part of the whole body, that thus situated they could exert but a partial influence, that unless some prospect was held out to us of a total change in the system we must *remain distinct*. A disposition to accommodate this point to our satisfaction was manifested by the opposite Committee. But how was this to be brought about? They had, of course, no authority to change the *Constitution* of the Academy, this was a nice point, and required much deliberation. It was thus accommodated.

A new election of officers of the American Academy was soon to take place, and it was agreed, on all hands, that this whole subject could be better discussed and arranged in a *new board of Directors*. The main topic was, therefore, dismissed, and the whole attention of the Committees directed to the manner of composing this new board, so that both parties, the *Association* and the *American Academy* should feel confidence in the result of the important discussions in the new board. To make the representation perfectly fair, it was agreed that six (*one-half* the next board) should be Artists, and the other half ordinary Stockholders. The point as to *numbers* was therefore settled. What Artists should compose the *six*, was the next point. Under the peculiar circumstances of the case, it will be admitted that a *nomination* by the Artists themselves of *their own representatives* in a mixed board, in which they were one of two parties, to discuss matters of vital interest to *themselves*, was not only proper, but necessary. It was so viewed *at that time* by the Committee of the Academy, as events will show. The next point to be settled was, how were these *representatives* thus nominated by the Artists to be made *eligible* to *Directorship* on this occasion? The case was this: *Directors* must be *Stockholders*. The sum of twenty-five dollars was required of *Artists*, as well as others, to make them Stockholders of the Academy. Of this requisition they had complained as being unjust, and one of the evils to be remedied. That it was not unnecessarily complained of will be seen on looking into the operation of it upon Artists. According to the charter of the Academy, a Stockholder must pay twenty-five dollars for his share, which entitles him to certain privileges, among others to vote at the election of officers. An *Artist*, before he can have any share in the government of the Academy—before he can be *Director*, *Academician* or *Associate*, must become a Stockholder in the same way as others; he is then precisely on the same ground with two hundred Stockholders, except that he alone is eligible as *Associate* or *Academician;* but, for this honor, the Artist must make an addition to the property of the Academy of *some production of his own*, in many instances at least more valuable than the price of a share. If in consequence of this he had any additional influence in the government of the Academy, there would be some propriety in the requirement: but it is an *empty title*, without any *privileges* or *duties*. This is not all. The Artist, by the exhibition of his works, must procure the principal *revenue* of the Institution, and for this he has *no equivalent*. Will it be thought surprising, that the Artists were unanimously averse to make themselves Stockholders according to the requirements of such a law? Here, therefore, was a serious difficulty in the way of the new arrangements. To remove this difficulty, it was proposed that the Association having *nominated* their *six representatives*, the Artists should on this occasion secure the eligibility of the *six*, by seeing that they became *Stockholders* of the Academy.

The faith of the gentlemen of the Committee of the American Academy was then *pledged;* they *guaranteed* to use their influence among the Stockholders to promote the election of these *six representatives*, by explaining the *peculiar nature* and *object* of this transaction. The Committee of the Association assented to this arrangement. The Association temporarily waived their objections to the offensive law, that no fastidiousness on their part might impede the *union*. They elected unanimously their *six representatives*, and made the whole ticket eligible by paying out of the *treasury of the Association*, into the hands of the *Treasurer of the American Academy of Fine Arts*, ONE HUNDRED DOLLARS, to make four upon that ticket (the other two being already Stockholders) Stockholders of the American Academy. The names of the *six* thus qualified by the *Association*, and for the express objects I have mentioned, were presented to the Directors of the American Academy *seventeen days* before the election. Not only was there no official objection made to this whole transaction at that time, but it was impliedly sanctioned officially by the Directors of the Academy in a resolution, dated December 30th, 1825, by which a technical difficulty about the election was removed, so that *one hundred dollars* might be received. The election took place, and but TWO out of the SIX REPRESENTATIVES were chosen. Thus were all the measures which had been mutually devised for the *union* of the Association with the American Academy defeated. The Drawing Association lost their time, and their *one hundred dollars*, and were left as at first to pursue their own plans.

I might with perfect propriety here leave it to the President and Directors of the American Academy to settle the causes of the defeat of the union among themselves. Whether the influence pledged by the Committee was not used at all, or was used but without effect, it matters not. The blame of the result in either case is in the Academy. But the insinuation that the *Artists defeated it themselves, and "never seriously intended the union,"* (absurd as it is on the very face of it, when they had paid *one hundred dollars* to secure it,) demands a moment's notice.

The result of the election is attributed by the officers of the Academy, to a *notice to the Stockholders* which appeared in the papers on the morning of the election, and which (without any authority for such a charge) they insinuate was sent to the papers by the Artists, with the design of defeating the union. This notice, styled *arrogant, presumptuous*, weak, &c., it is said caused the *"insulted body of Stockholders"* to come out and *"resist proud dictation,"* &c. The Lay Member acknowledges that *he* voted against the union in consequence of this *"preposterous advertisement."* What is this notice? Here it is.

"To the Stockholders of the American Academy of Fine Arts: Many contradictory reports being abroad touching the election of officers for the ensuing year, which takes place this day, it has been thought advisable to apprise you in a few words of the *more than ordinary importance* of the present election; involving no less than *the union of the body of Artists with the Academy, or their separation from it.* There is time only for the statement of the following facts: *Negotiations* have been carried on for some weeks past, *between the gentlemen* comprising the present direction of the Academy, and the *Associated Artists*, to bring about a *cordial union* of interests. At a meeting of the Committees of Conference, it was agreed that the next board of Directors should comprise at least *six* Artists. The Artists accordingly balloted for six of their members to be *submitted* to the electors, who being the chosen *representatives* of the Artists, it is to be understood that all or none will serve."

Now, in the first place, *who* vouches for this notice? It is an *anonymous* paragraph! Why may it not have been written by the *Directors* of the Academy, or their *Committee of Conference*, or some other *Stockholders?* There is nothing in it which gives any clue to its source; nothing which (all circumstances considered) does not render it highly probable that it came from some member or members of the Academy. If written by any of them, every one can see, that the charge of *arrogance* and *presumption*, reverts with tenfold force on those that have made it. The information contained in the notice was important to the welfare of the Academy, and it was right that the Directors, or Committee, or other members should communicate it to those ignorant of it.

But suppose for a moment that this notice is exactly the reverse of what it is seen to be; suppose, instead of being a *brief, temperate, respectful* recapitulation of recent transactions, of vital interest to the Academy, and explicitly stating the *point*, on which the whole of the late negotiations turned; (a POINT *easily explained* by their *Committee of Conference!*) suppose, I say, instead of this, it was just what the Lay Member would wish to make it appear; an *arrogant, dictating, presumptuous* piece. It is still *anonymous!* Nobody vouched for it! Nor do I think the Stockholders of the Academy, the great majority of whom are men *dispassionate, sensible* and *reflecting*, will feel themselves much complimented by the Lay Member, when he represents them as coming to the polls *indignant*, and *thoughtlessly* voting under *high excitement* produced by an *anonymous* notice; he ought to have known that a charge of such *weakness* could never attach to them.*

And now, what will be thought of these charges of *arrogance*, &c., when the public are informed that this *dreadful notice was composed and sent to the papers by* THREE STOCKHOLDERS OF THE AMERICAN ACADEMY OF FINE ARTS! to caution their fellow Stockholders against any intrigue which might be used to defeat a union, of such vital importance to their common Institution!

I return one moment to the *Drawing Association.* Cut off from all prospect of *union* with the American Academy by the conduct of a few of the members of the latter body, they believed they had now good evidence, that the Academy of Fine Arts was an Academy in *name* only, else why should the Artists as a body, *so essential to an Academy*, be shut out from it. They took it for granted that they had been mistaken, that the American Academy was in reality what its President has called it, merely *" a sort of* BENEFIT CLUB," and of course not an Academy. The necessity for a *real Academy* was felt by the profession,

* Lest any one should suppose, from the Lay Member's representations, that the indignation was so universal among the Stockholders that they *crowded* to the polls to *"resist proud dictation,"* it may be well just to state the fact, that about *thirty*, in all, voted at the election, out of nearly 300 Stockholders !!

and the Artists, composing the Drawing Association, immediately resolved themselves into the NATIONAL ACADEMY OF DESIGN.

With the sincerest respect, gentlemen, your most obedient servant,

SAMUEL F. B. MORSE.

TRUMBULL'S ANSWER.

[For the Evening Post.]

MR. EDITOR :—Mr. Morse, in his *Exposé*, having pronounced the publication signed *A Lay Member*, on the subject of the two Academies, to be " a " tissue of improbable. results, which would not have gained a moment's " credence had it appeared without sanction, (of the President and Directors " of the Academy,) and having endeavored to show how little of truth there " is in the whole relation," I feel myself called upon to repel the imputation of having been accessary to the publication of a false statement.

I beg leave to make the following quotation, to prevent any misconception of the subject :

" To this part of the statement of the Lay Member of the American Acad- " emy I invite particular attention, as I pledge myself to prove it *untrue in* " *its most important assertions*, and to show that by these, and by his, omis- " sions in the history, the writer of that article has thrown *a false coloring* " over the subsequent negotiations of the two bodies. The next part, occu- " pying about half of the whole piece, is a long report of the President of " the American Academy to the Directors, recommending some reform in the " internal affairs of the Academy, *which, as it has but little to do with the* " *material points of the case, calls for but little attention*."

In contrast with this quotation, I beg to submit a very concise one from that Report of the President of the American Academy.

" The President, therefore, asks leave to suggest to the Board the propri- " ety of recurring to the principle originally adopted, and, for that purpose, of " passing a by-law, by which it shall be ordained, *that, hereafter, of the* " *ELEVEN Directors authorized to be annually elected, SIX*, at least, shall " *always be taken from among the Academicians, artists by profession*."

Mr. Morse knows well that this Report was drawn up by me, with the direct aud sole intention of putting an end to all discontent, by procuring the admission of a majority of artists into the Board of Directors. He cannot have forgotten that he, in company with Mr. Henry Inman and Mr. Peter Maverick, supped with me, and discussed the subject amicably, (I thought, satisfactorily and finally,) an evening or two prior to the date of the Report.

He knows well that, in consequence of this Report, the Committee of Conference, which (notwithstanding the recent publication by their Chairman) he persists in abusing for bad faith, was appointed.

He knows well that, in compliance with the suggestion above quoted, a law was passed having respect to the approaching election, that the election was conducted in conformity to that law, and that six artists, of whom he was one, were elected.

And yet Mr. Morse, knowing all these things, has the audacity to say, " that this Report has little to do with the material points of the case, and " calls for but little attention !"

The reader will pardon my making one more quotation.

" A new election of officers for the American Academy was soon to take " place, and it was agreed on all hands, that the whole subject could be bet- " ter discussed and arranged in a new Board of Directors, &c. To make the " representation perfectly fair, it was agreed that six (*one half* of the next " Board) should be artists, and the other half ordinary stockholders."

Is it possible that Mr. Morse can have signed his name to such a bare-faced misrepresentation as this without a blush? His friends must blush for him, when they are assured that he knew, as well as I, that the Board of Directors of the American Academy was and is composed of ELEVEN members. He knew, as well as I, that the Directors had acted *understandingly*, when they determined that, at the next election, SIX out of ELEVEN Directors should be chosen from among artists by profession. He knew, as well as I, that whenever the election should have taken place under this act, *all the legitimate and avowed objects of THE ARTISTS would be gained, and that artists would, in fact, be complete and absolute masters of the Institution.*

And yet this man, capable of and practising such gross perversion and suppression of truth, dares to accuse others of false coloring!

What is meant, in the last foregoing quotation, by "the whole subject be-" ing better discussed and arranged in a new Board of Directors," I do not presume to say—the ulterior object of the great reformer, veiled under these words, can only be explained by himself; but I may conjecture that the ultimate aim was, to obtain from the Legislature the revocation of the Charter of the American Academy, and an act to strip the obnoxious stockholders of their property, and to vest it in the President and Council of *the* Artists. *The* Artists!—modest gentlemen!—as if there were none besides themselves in the city! They forget there are such men as Waldo, Jewett, Frothingham, &c., &c., &c.; and I beg permission of my right honest, impartial, and funny friend, Jo. Strickland, to borrow for the occasion, and apply to my own case, his beautiful motto—"Cospetto di Baccho—e che sono io in questa casa?"

I pass over the long secret history of the origin and progress of the Drawing Association; all the honor unquestionably belongs to Mr. Morse. I will only observe that, by his own showing, the payment of twenty-five dollars was the great stumbling-block and rock of offence; the insuperable bar which those high-minded gentlemen could not pass over.

If the Lay-member has fallen into any errors in his history of this Drawing Association, it is not to be wondered at—he avowed that he was not in the secret. Mr. Morse, on the contrary, has demonstrated that he was; that he has been the author and finisher of the entire plan—and has amply proved his clear and unquestionable title to the whole honor of having excited and fomented dissatisfaction, until it ripened into separation.

When gentlemen become members of an Association for the advancement of science, literature, or the fine arts; when they have received honors from their brother members; and when they have acknowledged in writing, in the strongest language, their gratitude for such honors, it is not common to see them abandon such Association, and unite with others in forming a new one. The Lay Member, speaking of the conduct of some Academicians and Associates of the American Academy on this occasion, calls it mutiny and desertion. He had some reason derived from analogy, for, in military and naval service, such is the language, and the penalty is death. In political life, the same principle prevails, so far, at least, as to brand with infamy and contempt those who abandon the party which has supported and advanced them, and the term usually applied in such cases is traitor, deserter, or apostate; and it is generally understood that the same principle binds all associations of gentlemen.

Next comes the triumphant assertion by which it is intended to astound and silence forever the Lay Member, President, and all: "That the offensive no-" tice published on the morning of the election was, in fact, written by three "stockholders of the American Academy." This scene-shifting may be very pretty, but it is not very profound. It can surprise no one to learn that, in the composition of this kindly and modest notice, Mr. Morse should have had the assistance of two or three of the nominated aspirants to the directorship, who, of course, are stockholders. The character of the notice is not at all affected by the number or the names of the writers. The only question of importance is the intention—the *quo animo*, as the lawyers have it; and the answer is found in the letters of Messrs. Morse and Durand, declining the election: *their adjuncts in the Dictatorship might not have co-operated well in the ulterior measures of contemplated reform — it was essential to HAVE ALL.*

It is needless to wander longer in the intricate snares of this *Exposé.* We have exposed sufficient aberrations from candor and truth, to stamp its character, in the mind of every honorable man, as being little better than the quibbling defence of a bad cause by a wretched pettifogger, who keeps out of sight the main questions, and buries truth and sense in a mass of sounding words. Indeed, it does little honor to the talents or the rectitude of the writer, and evinces throughout as little respect for the intellect of the citizens of New-York—as *the* Artists, in the whole course of their conduct, have shown of gratitude, for the liberality with which the stockholders have aided the progress of the Arts *and of the Artists,* in furnishing the splendid materials for study which fill the Gallery of the American Academy of the Fine Arts.

A few words more, and I shall have done. It has been studiously represented, until some, perhaps, may have been tempted to believe, that the affairs of the American Academy of the Fine Arts have been badly managed. That it has been involved in debt by bad management: and that this bad management is to be ascribed to the improper formation of the Board of Directors.

Whoever has seen the Galleries, and the Collection of Sculpture, &c., must be sensible that all which surrounds him cannot have been accomplished without Money—the alterations and repairs in the Building, the Sculpture, and the exquisite portrait of Mr. West, by Sir Thomas Lawrence, have all been expensive, and Money has necessarily been borrowed at times. But both principal and interest of the Debt are now very nearly extinguished.

The Exhibitions have at times been unproductive, and the causes are obvious. At first, there were but very few Artists living in the City, whose Talents were so far cultivated as to render their works attractive; and of late years, since Talent has been ripened by the contemplation and study of those works, for which Money has been liberally expended by the Stockholders, and a small debt incurred by the Directors, a spirit of dissatisfaction has prevented many Artists from sending their works to this Exhibition; and has led to the establishment of the new one.

It is also said, that the American Academy furnishes no means of instruction to the rising Artists, and this also is ascribed to the bad management, and the improper formation of the Board of Directors. To this I answer, that on the 16th of December, 1817, the Directors passed a By-Law, of which the following is a copy, and which has ever been and is now in force:

"*Any Person* presenting to the Keeper of the Academy a Drawing or Model "from a Plaster Cast executed by himself, shall be permitted to make a draw-"ing from one of the Casts in the Academy under the view and direction of "the Keeper; which drawing shall be by the Keeper submitted to the Presi-"dent and Directors, who, if they regard it as possessing sufficient indication "of Talent, shall give to the person by whom it is executed a Student's Ticket, "which shall entitle him to pursue his Studies in the Academy, subject to its "rules."

In addition to the Gallery (which must be closed during exhibitions) there is now a Room 20 feet square, properly fitted up as a Study, with a grate and fuel, seats and lights, and a beautiful collection of small Copies from the best of the Antique Statues—*where Students are invited to pursue their object Gratis— by Day or in the Evening—Summer or Winter.* If Artists choose to withdraw and hold themselves separate from such an Institution, from such gratuitous offers of the means of improvement, let them not ascribe blame to the Board of Directors. Artists are free—the Directors can only *invite*—they cannot compel them to come in and partake of the rich Feast which has been provided for them by the liberality of our fellow-citizens the Stockholders.

Mr. Editor, I have lived seventy-two years in this vain world, more than ten of which have been passed in situations of high responsibility, in the military or political service of my country, and this is the first time that any man has dared to impute to me the baseness of having been accessary to the publication of a falsehood. I have seen, for a long time, with disgust, the smiling and insidious course of misrepresentation which has been pursued, and by which Junior Artists have been deluded and the community misled—and have remained silent. But it has become my duty, at last, to speak, and to speak plainly—in the spirit of the olden time, I have called a Cat a Cat, and not a pretty pussy. I have written deliberately—and I beg my Fellow-Citizens to read critically and deliberately, what I have written—to their impartial judgment I leave the result, and quit the painful subject, I hope forever.

I am, Mr. Editor, your faithful servant,

JNO. TRUMBULL,

President of the American Academy of the Fine Arts,
during the last nine or ten years.

———

[*From the Evening Post.*]

REPLY TO COL. TRUMBULL.

MR. EDITOR:—In his reply to my Expose, Col. Trumbull chooses to consider me as charging him with falsehood. I cannot perceive, sir, that any language which I have used, fairly interpreted, admits of this construction. I did indeed say, (and I think I have proved,) that the statements of the "Lay Member," which were sanctioned by Col. Trumbull, were "untrue," but that the misrepresentation was *wilful* I have never said; and as it was sufficient for my purpose simply to deny the *truth* of the statement, I conceive it was unnecessary, and therefore would have been uncourteous, to impeach the *motives* of those who made it. Such a charge would be utterly at variance with my sense of gentlemanly propriety. I regret however to perceive, that Col. Trumbull has been restrained by no such sense from charging me with "gross perversion and suppression of the truth." I certainly have too much self-respect to spend many words in answering such a charge, and, were it not for the station of my accuser, should pass it by with silent contempt. As it is, my friends will excuse me for bestowing upon it so much attention as is necessary to expose its *entire baselessness and futility.*

Col. Trumbull grounds his attack on the following quotation from my Expose:—"A new election of officers of the American Academy was soon to take "place, and it was agreed on all hands that the whole subject could be better "discussed and arranged in a new Board of Directors, &c. To make the repre-"sentation perfectly fair, it was agreed that *six (one-half* of the next Board) "should be Artists, and the other half ordinary stockholders." To this he appends the following remarks:

"Is it possible that Mr. Morse can have signed his name to such a barefaced "misrepresentation as this without a blush? His friends must blush for him, "when they are assured that he knew, as well as I, that the Board of Directors "of the American Academy was and is composed of ELEVEN members. He "knew, as well as I, that the Directors had acted *understandingly,* when they "determined that at the next election SIX out of ELEVEN Directors should "be chosen from among Artists by profession. He knew, as well as I, that "whenever the election should take place under this act, *all the legitimate and* "*avowed objects of THE ARTISTS would be gained, and that Artists would, in* "*fact, be complete and absolute masters of the Institution.* And yet this man, "capable of practising such gross perversion and suppression of the truth, "dares to accuse others of false coloring!"

Admit, sir, for one moment, that Col. Trumbull is correct—that "the Board of Directors is composed of ELEVEN members—and that SIX Artists would have constituted a majority of the Board: what motive could I have for disguising or suppressing this fact? what position have I assumed that would be strengthened or in the least affected by it? What relevancy has it to any one point which has been brought into this discussion? Do I anywhere complain that *six* Artists would not have been a fair representation of the body? Do I not, in the very sentence which is quoted by Colonel Trumbull, pronounce it "perfectly fair?" I defy Col. Trumbull to assign a probable motive for prevarication; and, as I know he cannot do it, I pronounce his charge of falsehood a wanton attack upon my character. I know, sir, that there is a respect due to age and station, and I know that Col. Trumbull ostentatiously connects with his name associations which his countrymen will ever cherish as sacred. But I know also, sir, that private character is a sacred thing, and that even age, station and revolutionary associations will not screen from public indignation the man who assails it wantonly, especially when he himself makes an open parade of them for the purpose.

But, sir, I have stronger ground. It is *not true* that "the Board of Directors of the American Academy is composed of ELEVEN members." Col. Trumbull ought to know that the *Board* is composed of THIRTEEN members. He ought to know that the act of incorporation of the Academy entrusts the management of its concerns to a President, Vice-President and eleven Directors. He ought to know that the *President* and *Vice-President* are members of the *Board*, that they are annually elected with the other members, and that there is no law or by-law which requires that they should be Artists. And he ought to know, therefore, that if a by-law had been passed, requiring that six of the eleven Directors should be Artists by profession, these Artists would still have been a *minority*, and not a *majority* of the *Board*.

I do not dwell upon this point of majority and minority, sir, because *I* deem it of importance. It was of little moment to *me*, and *those associated* with me, whether the number of Artists in the Board was one more or one less than a majority. Members of a liberal profession, and seeking to advance the interests of that profession only in a liberal and honorable way, we did not, like narrow-minded politicians, calculate to carry our measures by majorities of *one*. It was sufficient for us, in this crisis, that we had a *fair representation ;* and in point of fact, as I have shown, *six* (the number which was offered, and to which we acceded) was actually a *minority* of the whole. In the paragraph quoted by Col. Trumbull I called six "*half the Board*" for the sake of convenience, and every one must perceive it was not of the least consequence to be precisely fractionally accurate.* The error (if it can be called such—and who but the merest quibbler would notice it?) was made to incline to *their* favor, and not in my own ; and yet this point, this microscopic point, has been seized upon by Col. Trumbull, and made the foundation of a charge against me of "gross perversion and suppression of the truth !"

But, sir, although it is of no moment to *me*, or to *my* argument, whether *six* makes a *minority* or a *majority* of the Board, Col. Trumbull has made it of great importance to *himself*. His reply to my Expose is built almost exclusively on the assertion, which he takes care to emblazon everywhere in capitals, that the *six* Artists would have made a *majority* of the Board. This foundation is destroyed. His whole edifice, therefore, falls to the ground. There are a number of isolated fallacies which I had intended to notice, but I will not do it. I have said enough. Why should I expose all the blunders of a man who is too careless to count?

None of the material points, sir, in my Expose have been touched by Col. Trumbull. He "*passes them over.*" They are "*intricate snares*" to him. He pretends not to meddle with them. "He has exposed," he thinks, "sufficient aberrations from candor and "truth," in the pitiful quibble I have just answered, "to stamp" all I have said as nothing worth ; and he substitutes for argument the calling of hard names and declamatory abuse. He takes no notice of the *distinct* character of the Drawing Association ; no notice of its Report,

* If it had been necessary, I might have said *six-thirteenths of the Board.*

which led to negotiations for union with the American Academy; no notice of the matters arranged in the Committees of Conference; no notice of the *terms* of union. He gives no explanation of the payment of the *one hundred dollars;* no explanation of the defeat of the measures for union. Not one of my statements are controverted; not a single important point discussed.

But I gladly turn from mere personal controversy, to the original subject of discussion; the only subject in which the public can feel much interest.

The National Academy, sir, is a real Academy for the promotion of the Arts of Design. Its plan was formed by Artists on sound and proper principles; the only principles on which Academies have been successfully established in other countries. It is now nearly three years since it was instituted. The experiment has been fairly tried; and the Artists are satisfied with its success, The Institution has prospered beyond their most sanguine expectations. The receipts from their *first* exhibition were about $300; from the second, $500; and from that of the present year, more than $800; and they cannot doubt that in a little time this amount will be trebled, if not quadrupled. This success they ascribe entirely to the correct principles on which their Institution is founded.

The American Academy of Fine Arts, sir, is *not* an Academy. It is only, (as its President has termed it,) " a sort of Benefit Club."* The fundamental principle of its constitution is wrong; and the body of Artists never could have united with it, while they had a proper sense of their own character and rights, unless with the expectation of obtaining the consent of the Stockholders to a total transformation, and *re*-formation of the Institution. But it is asked, why was it necessary for the Artists to form a separate Institution? Why did they not unite with the American Academy, and attempt to obtain the consent of the Stockholders to the change which they considered so desirable and so essential to the prosperity of the Institution? To this I reply, that the attempt was made, and that it was not the fault of the Artists that it failed. Before they formed their Academy, while they were yet merely a Drawing Association, they entered into negotiations with the Directors of the American Academy with a view to union, and to a remodelling of that Institution. As *the result* of this negotiation, and as a first step towards reform, it was agreed, that at the next annual meeting of the Stockholders, all proper effort should be used to secure the election to the Board of Directors of six Artists, who had been *specially* selected by the Association as *representatives* of their interests and views. The Stockholders met. They elected *two* only of these representatives, and by this act blasted the hope of union, and compelled the Artists to form a new Academy. For what else under these circumstances could they have done? To have sought again to unite themselves to an Institution which they verily believed, nay, which they clearly saw and knew was founded on such principles that it could never flourish, and this too when they, and their desires for reform, were treated by *those who had the control* of the Institution with such marked contempt, would have shown a want of spirit and common sense. They of course chose the latter, and they have seen no reason to regret their choice. The men who had the folly to drive them away have indeed set up a cry of "rebellion," "desertion," "schism," "apostacy," "mutiny," "treason," &c., but so did the Lords of England, (as Col. Trumbull must remember, for he was with them at the time,) when his countrymen refused to form a part of the British empire, and for the very reason too that they could have no voice in its councils; and so do all lordlings when they find too late that they have mistaken a spirit of accommodation for a willingness to bear abuse.

In thus alluding to the circumstances which prevented a union with the American Academy, I wish it to be distinctly understood that the Artists feel

---

* In using this term, no one will accuse me of disrespect to the gentlemen who founded the Institution. It was formed more than twenty years ago, and was perhaps on the plan best suited to the state of the country at that period; a period when there were no Artists, and when even information respecting the Arts was in its infancy. Any person acquainted with the nature and history of Academies of Arts would have prophesied, at the outset, that the American Academy would live only till the Artists became sufficiently respectable in number and character to form an Institution for themselves.

no ill-will towards that Institution, or towards its Stockholders. They know, indeed, that for many years the Institution had been regarded with so much apathy that not one in ten of the Stockholders attended its annual meetings, and that, at the very meeting in which the plan of union was defeated, only about thirty out of nearly three hundred were present. The Artists certainly have no disposition to attribute to the very respectable gentlemen who compose that body, what was in truth the act of a few individuals, who, perhaps, having a private interest opposed to the change, availed themselves of the general apathy to rally friends enough to accomplish their purpose.

They have the satisfaction to believe that the great body of the Stockholders of the old Institution are pleased with the success which has attended the new Academy, and they know that many of them have taken the pains to express their gratification. In truth, the Artists can see but little cause of dissatisfaction with anything in their history, their present situation, or their prospects. They are satisfied with the reasons which induced them to establish their Academy; they are satisfied with its success; they are satisfied with the prosperity of the Arts, which is the main object they have in view, has been greatly promoted by the course which they have pursued. They are satisfied that every day, and every discussion of the subject, are adding to the number and attachment of their friends: and although in their infancy, and yet struggling with peculiar difficulties, they feel animated to persevere in their course, confident that the more the plan and objects of the National Academy of Design are understood, the more it will be found to deserve the fostering care of the public.

I remain, sir, your most obedient humble servant,
SAMUEL F. B. MORSE,
President of the National Academy of Design.

[*American, June* 7.]

Sir :—In several communications that have been made in this journal, and in the *Evening Post*, on the existing difficulties between the American Academy of Fine Arts and the National Academy of Design, reference has been made to a certain Committee of the American Academy of Fine Arts; and in your paper of last evening, "A Member of the Council of the National Academy of Design" has ventured the following assertion:

"But, sir, if the Committee only promised to exert their influence to effect the election of the six artists into the next Board of Directors, and did not exert their influence—is it not plain that they acted in bad faith?"

I will show how little foundation there is in truth for this, since the data are false.

The Committee from the American Academy of the Fine Arts, after their conference, made to the Board the following report:

"The Committee appointed to confer with a Committee of Artists, of which Mr. ——— was Chairman, beg leave to report:*

"That at a full meeting of the two Committees, your Committee, after some discussion, succeeded in convincing the gentlemen who met them, that it was not in the power of the Board of Directors to alter any part of the Constitution of this Academy, in which it is ordered by an act of the Legislature, that the Directors should be chosen from the body of the stockholders, and that none but stockholders were entitled to vote. Your Committee endeavored to persuade the other Committee that the most effectual manner in which the artists could assert the views of the Academy, and promote the interests of the Fine Arts, as well as themselves, would be to qualify as stockholders in our Academy, and thus render themselves eligible to the direction.

[* No such report is to be found in the minutes of the American Academy.—ED.]

Your Committee regard this point the more, inasmuch as the sale of 20 or 30 shares would in a great measure extricate the Academy from its present trifling pecuniary embarrassments, and the harmony which is said to exist among the artists would secure to them an influence to which they would be entitled, for that their own votes would give them the control of every election, and the Academy would be absolutely in their own hands, as it seldom happens that more than 30 votes are taken at an election.

"Here follow two sections on the alteration of the By-Laws.   *   *   "

This report was accepted. Sir, I ask, "*Where is the evidence of bad faith?*"

Does the member of the Council of the National Academy of Design, or does any reasonable man, suppose that the Committees were to canvass the votes of all the stockholders? The Committee did their *duty, and six artists were chosen—nay, seven, including the President—*the assertion of "A Member of the Council," notwithstanding.

"*Where* is the evidence of bad faith?"

But it is said that the *seven artists chosen* were not the six whom the opposite party desired to have elected. Now, sir, from that day to this, no one has as yet had the effrontery to say that during the conference of these two Committees, any ticket was agreed upon.

The Committee of the American Academy agreed to use their influence that six artists might be chosen, but they *never agreed* that the opposition party had the right to dictate whom the stockholders should vote for. The Committee made their report, and six artists—nay, seven were chosen.

"*Where is the evidence of bad faith?*"

But a member of the Council of the National Academy of Design says that the *seven artists* chosen *were not artists*, and objects to one who, it is true, never made his living by any of the Fine Arts, but who, nevertheless, is much consulted by artists, has *a more correct judgment, and a nicer taste, and has been engaged in more permanent works of art, than most artists in our city.* It is objected to another, that he has ceased to be an artist by profession.

But if his skill and knowledge enabled him by his profession to realize a handsome fortune, and he has now "left off work," his experience and observation certainly qualify him for a seat at the Board. In voting for two such gentlemen, there can certainly *be no evidence* of bad faith!

But, sir, your correspondent of last evening asserts, or insinuates, that the Committee, "on the contrary, voted for another ticket, to the exclusion of four of the six." No ticket was ever agreed upon. But what evidence does he bring that the Committee did not vote for those very six artists of the opposition? His friends were not elected, it is true, but how does he know—how dares he insinuate, for whom the Committee voted? He does not know it.

As far as regards myself, no man knew, or knows now, my vote at that election. It was a selection from both tickets.

Where is the evidence of bad faith?

"Is it not plain that they acted in bad faith?"

It may seem plain to those who read, or hear, only *ex parte* statements—or see only one side.

The insinuation is made with or without the knowledge of facts. If without, it is only in part excusable, for the writer should have obtained correct information. If it is with a knowledge of the facts, I now state, the imputation is, to say the least, entirely unbecoming.

We have acted with rectitude, and without any view to self, in all matters connected with the Fine Arts; and it would argue well for the advancement of the Arts, and for those who profess them, if every one could as conscientiously say the same.

No, it was not bad faith. It was the insulted body of stockholders, who were indignant that they should be dictated to in the style of the unfortunate and arrogant notice that appeared on the morning of the election, that defeated the union. That notice prevented the union—if, indeed, it was ever seriously desired by the opposition.

I am not accustomed to write or act *anonymously*—nor do I choose to be drawn into a newspaper controversy; but I will not thrust my name upon the public, in connection with an affair, in which only about one in a thousand of our community feels or evinces any interest.

Those who do, shall have any explanation or information in my power to offer, by calling personally, not in the newspapers, upon

THE CHAIRMAN OF THE COMMITTEE OF CONFERENCE
Of the American Academy of Fine Arts.

"BOYDELL" appeared once more, and denied that Morse was the author of the letters signed "BOYDELL." "JOE STRICKLAND," the "WORKING BEES" and other writers' productions are not given. The ground is sufficiently covered by the acknowledged correspondence of the President, &c. That closes what may fairly be denominated the FIRST WAR of the TWO ACADEMIES.

Trumbull and Morse were reviewed by Dunlap, under the title of "DOCTORS DIFFER."

The days of peace arrived, there may be a return to matter of a more congenial nature.

Almost coeval with the National Academy, was founded the "SKETCH CLUB"—"THE OLD" *Sketch Club.* The immediate causes that led to its formation had escaped the writer's memory. C. C. Ingham, Esq., its President, favors the work with the following:

"The second Exhibition of the N. Academy was held in the room over Tylee's Baths in Chamber St. After the Exhibition, the room was fitted up with plaster casts and drawing-boards, and there the students of the Antique School met, to receive instruction from the founders of the Academy. One night the teachers were as usual assembled. Previous to the opening of the School, seated in a corner, were Morse, Durand, Cummings, and Ingham. The subject of conversation was the recent breaking up of that most agreeable Club, the 'Lunch.' Mr. Ingham remarked, that now there was an opportunity for the Artists to establish a Club. All agreed that such a thing was feasible. Mr. Ingham proposed that those present should consider themselves the nucleus of one, which, when established, should be called the SKETCH CLUB—to consist of Artists, Authors, men of science, and lovers of Art; and that Morse should be the first President. Mr. Morse highly approved of the idea, but declined being the President, saying that it was enough for him to be the President of the Academy; that the person best entitled to the honor of being President of the proposed Association was Mr. Ingham, who had originated the scheme. Mr. Cummings coincided; and after some further conversation on the rules to be adopted, it was agreed to postpone the further consideration of the subject to Wednesday in the following week, and that a meeting should be called at Mr. Ingham's. A meeting of the principal Artists was held there, and the rules of the proposed Club discussed, and adopted. The plan of the Lunch had been, for the members to meet at a Hotel, to be entertained at the cost of the host of the evening. This arrangement was supposed to have caused a rivalry in expense, which led to the breaking up of the Club. To avoid a like result, the Artists determined to have their Club as inexpensive as possible; and to attain this end, it was agreed that the Sketch Club should meet at the houses of the members, in rotation, and that the entertainment should be confined to dried fruit, crackers, milk, and honey.   Mr. Ingham was elected President, and Mr. John Inman, Secretary.

"On the ELECTING OF MEMBERS, it was agreed that a single black should exclude; for the reason that each member, in turn, entertain the Club in *his house*. It would therefore be improper to force into the Club one against whose admission *any one* had an objection.

"The first regular meeting took place at the rooms of Thomas Cole. It was a decided success. All the members exerted themselves to please, and everything was agreeable—even the figs, milk, and honey. But on the day after the feast, came the pangs of repentance—and many a vow was made that the refreshments of the Club should be changed."

It may be regretted that its early *minutes*, witticisms, essays, drawings, verses, papers, &c., have been neglected or destroyed. Not a vestige to be found of that, one of the oldest and most interesting of clubs. It was formed for the promotion of mutual intercourse and improvement in impromptu sketching. Drawing for ONE hour from a subject proposed by the *host*, whose property the drawings remained, was part of the programme *positive;* the poets and others frequently amusing themselves during *that* hour by passing round a subject, on which each, in turn, furnished four lines—no more, no less : and some truly amusing mongrels were the result. Its members comprised, in a high degree, the talent of the country. In its organization, *over* great care had been taken to guard against its destruction by EXTRAVAGANCE in its entertainments, in eating; and "*milk and honey, raisins, apples and crackers*" were the limitation, the prescribed bill of fare. The medicinal qualities of the one were appreciated on the first dose, and the dryness of the other was not relished. "The rule" was more observed in the breach than in the observance. The first great outbreak, however, occurred at member J****s H********'s, at his *then* up-town residence, viz., East side Broadway, between Broome and Spring streets. On that evening, at the appointed hour for refreshments, the drawing-room doors were thrown open, and an elegant supper appeared before the astonished guests. A general revolt took place. *Protests* were entered, remonstrances made; a compromise *finally*, or, it rather should be said, *speedily* ensued. It was decided that the supper should be eaten, but that it should be done "*standing.*"   "*Sitting down*" to supper, it was said, was prohibited by "THE *rules.*" The distinction was a very *nice* one; so was the supper.

Members did not long "*stand out;*" chairs were in demand, and, in less than fifteen minutes, the whole were as comfortably seated as if no such *prohibition* had ever in the rules existed, and looked as innocently unconscious as if nothing had occurred contrary thereto. More ample justice could not have been done to a feast. Milk and honey never again appeared at the festive board. Many, very many happy meetings had that CLUB. The usual mode of *assembly* was to insert in the newspapers of the day the initials of the member, the street, and the number of the house where the meeting was to be held—nothing more. That was understood. The mysterious initials were the cause of inquiry from the inquisitive. The papers, editorially and by correspondents, *conjectured* all manner of things; and ever and anon a witty piece appeared, without drawing out the secret, until the following:

" ☞ S. C.—T. S. C."

The above appeared in some of the evening papers yesterday as an advertisement. Similar ones were quite common a year or two ago, and were said then to refer to the meetings of a gambling club; the same, it was thought, that was afterwards broken up in Lumber Street.

[To the Editor of the Standard.]

MY DEAR SIR:—I am exceedingly grieved to perceive by your paper of this morning, that you have fallen into an enormous error respecting the nature and objects of the Selebrated Cociety to which I have the honor to belong, and the existence of which is occasionally made known to the public through the press, by the apparition of its formidable initials, S. C. You appear to be somewhat alarmed at the portentous aspect of the prodigy; but, my dear friend, let me entreat you to calm your fears—there is no cause for your uneasiness. We, S. C's, are not gamblers; and we entertain as virtuous and laudable a horror of Lumber Street, and its iniquities, as any of our fellow-countrymen. How should it be otherwise? Are we not Sober Citizens, and Sincere Christians? Do we not Sleep Coundly, Sing Cheerfully, Separate Coberly, Speak Censibly, Suffer Courageously, and Sup Comfortably? You seem to think we Shuffle Cards, too; but, upon the Spotless Character of an S. C., it is not so; and the man who says it utters a Scandalous Calumny.

Since you manifest so much anxiety on the subject, however, I will tell you the honest truth: we are, in fact, a Secret Combination of Sworn Conspirators; and Social Conviviality is but a Simulated Cover for the Sacred Cecrecy of our Solemn Cabal. We are Severe Colts; and our purpose is to outroot Jacksonism and the Republic together. We are pledged for the establishment of absolute monarchy, the U. S. Bank, and Anti-Masonry; and we have sworn the downfall of the Regency, the Cherokees, and the odious practice of making visits on New Year's day. We have seriously concluded to have Mr. Van Beuren for King, and Mr. Clay Viceroy over him; but Mr. C. must change his name for Stephen, that he may be,

Like your Sensible Correspondent,
To all intents and purposes, an

S. C.

[*From an Evening Paper.*]

ANOTHER SOLUTION.

We can inform the editor of a Morning Paper, who seems to be perplexed with some harmless initials in this paper of yesterday, that S. C. stands for *Senatus Consultum*. He will find it on any old Roman half-penny.

We thank the editor of the evening paper for his interest in our perplexities, but has he seen "it" himself on an old Roman half-penny? and if he has, will he produce the coin? Not that we doubt his word; but then, "seeing is believing." And besides, if he displays the half-penny, we will repay his kindness. The piece must be valuable as a "curiosity," and we will teach him how to turn an old coin into an "old joke;" it will exchange for segars and wine. The editor of the evening paper, however, means only to show his smartness; he dislikes secret societies too much to know anything of this one.

We have still another explanation, and this—for we gave the best precedence—this is the true one. We certainly spoke only of the "similar notices" a year or two ago, and the reports then current respecting them, but we learned from many additional sources yesterday that the same opinion was prevalent now. The explanation, therefore, may be useful to the parties concerned.

This, then, is the truth:—S. C., being interpreted, mean "*Sketching Club*"! A queer title, certainly, but that concerns only the members. Of them, several have been named to us; they are poets, artists, &c.—men of taste, wit, and good talkers, who meet occasionally at the house of a member, to Speak Sensibly, Sup Comfortably, Sing Cheerfully, and Separate Soberly, after Sketching —no matter what. It seems probable, however, as sketching and drawing are nearly synonymous, that the subjects are generally *long corks*.

Our correspondent S. C., a first-rate in the sketching way, is a member, and his explanation might be sufficient, perhaps, but, to guard against possibilities, we may as well state that the capitals "T. S. C." are those of the gentleman, a distinguished Artist.

The Club exists, but *sketching* has for years been abandoned; simplicity of entertainment has, at times, been fearfully violated; and from that, more than all other causes, did liability to dismemberment occur.

It was afterwards called the "TWENTY-ONE;" probably, from its members remaining numerically so long at that point; access to its ranks quite as difficult, perhaps, as election to the Presidency of the *United States*.

The writer has since been much surprised, on learning that the minutes of the Club are not only not lost, but are all carefully preserved. "A young gentleman by the name of INMAN was in the Harlem Railroad Company, of which Mr. Jno. H. Gourlie, a *member*, was a Director. He, hearing Mr. Gourlie mention the Sketch Club, remarked that he was the son of Jno. Inman, the former Secretary, and that his mother *yet* had the records of the Club, and no doubt would be willing to part with them. That, on inquiry, did not prove to be the case. Mrs. Inman valued them as a relic of her departed husband. Mr. Gourlie then asked permission to have them copied, which was granted. The *copy* is in his possession.

April 12th, 1827. The late Colonel Stevens, of Hoboken, commissioned several Artists to paint pictures to adorn the cabin of the steamboat ALBANY, then building, and to run from New-York to Albany. That was a novelty—true art—as a steamboat embellishment, a specialty. The talent of the country was enlisted. Vanderlyn's " Ariadne," Sully's " Mother and Child," Morse's " Una and the Dwarf," Cole's " Catskill Clove," Doughty's " Juniata River"—all ?—where are they ?

Another incident between art and steam at the " early periods :" Mr. H******n M****n had promised to furnish the steamboat Rip Van Winkle (then building) with a representation of " Rip" for the exterior of the wheel-house. When its appalling proportions became apparent to him, he fled from the task, and applied to Inman for *help*. It happened to " *take*," and he offered to " officiate." A huge canvas was taken to Ackerman's, then a prominent sign-painter, in whose shop Inman worked up the great " Rip," rising from his sleep. Ackerman describes the fervor of Inman on the occasion " as immense." As soon as Inman left, Ackerman essayed to copy it, on a small scale. Inman, on returning, unwittingly highly complimented Ackerman, by remarking : " *Why, I do not remember that I painted a study for that picture*"; with which Ackerman was highly pleased. The work, when finished, was placed on the wheel-house, and long remained an attraction to the passengers and others of the Rip Van Winkle.

July 14, Died Gilbert Stuart, the American Portrait Painter, and Honorary Member. The Academicians were assembled. A eulogium, and resolutions of condolence with the family, were passed, and the usual mourning directed to be worn.

July 22, Died James Coyle, Academician. Born in England, 1798. Arrived in New-York August, 1824. He held the first rank in his branch of the profession, " scene painting." The scenery by him for the " Lady of the Lake" and the " Flying Dutchman," for the *Old* Chatham Street Theatre, will long be remembered.

September 26, Mr. Cummings presented a plan for the better accommodation of the School, which was adopted. Resolutions were passed calling on the members to act in turn as visitors ; and a printed programme of dates was served on each. There is nothing on the minutes as to the time of opening, or register of students in the Schools. Though clearly both were operative ; for arrangements were made for the usual lectures.

Mr. Morse, two each week, to end 1st January ; Dr. F.

G. King, Anatomy, during January; Mr. Bryant, Mythology, February; and John Neilson, Jr., Perspective.

December 6th, a communication was received from a foreign correspondent, announcing the DONATION to the Academy of *two large paintings.* A Donatory fever followed.

Thus was commenced the RECEIVING OF PRESENTS. A singular matter to complain of; yet it was one which came near destroying the Institution.

The writer must not be understood as making any comment on that separately, or other similarly generous acts, in themselves; but on the principle, and the RESULTS which followed. The presents were made abroad; and the expensive transportation brought the Academy deeply, almost IRRECOVERABLY, in DEBT. "In the above, and, indeed, in all cases, '*official thanks*' were returned to the Donors!"

March 12. The Clinton Hall Association tendered the Academy rooms in a building in course of erection **1829.** by them. Five hundred dollars a year was declared to be the full extent the Academy could *afford* to pay for "accommodations." Martin E. Thompson, Academician, and the Architect, was requested so to inform the gentlemen.

March 21. Died, Francis Johnston, Honorary Member, Architect, and President of the Royal Hibernian Academy of Dublin; a gentleman much distinguished in his profession, and beloved as a man.

March 31. The Schools, which had been well attended, closed. "The *Students* and *Council*" assembled, to determine to whom the premiums should be awarded—dissatisfaction having arisen on the previous methods. It was now to be done by a separate ballot by the Students, and the Council; if requisite thereafter, a *joint ballot.*

Each pupil was furnished with a slip of paper, on which were the numbers correspondent to the numbers on the drawings. The student's own work he was directed to enter as No. 1; afterwards, to place that one which, in his opinion, deserved that order of merit—number two, and so on.

The "lowest" "*footing*" *column* giving the "*highest*" merit.

The decision was, "No. 3 the best." Nos. 4 and 5 equal; but being the next two best drawings. It was referred back by Council for a further trial between 3 and 4; which decided it in favor of No. 4.

After which, the Council balloted in like manner. The

result was, a confirmation on No. 3, and a reversal of 4 and 5.

The premiums were given—1st. Geo. W. Twibill.
        2d. J. W. Paradise.
        3d. W. L. Ormsby.

It appears to have been satisfactory. An address was presented by the students, expressive of their obligations, and sense of gratitude; to which the President made suitable answer, and delivered the premiums.

Another effort was made at union of the two Academies, principally induced by Dr. J. E. Dekay, as one of a "Committee appointed by the American Academy, to confer with a Committee, if such should be appointed by the National Academy of Design."

In courtesy, such a Committee was appointed—Ingham and Dunlap—"To confer with the Committee of the American Academy of Fine Arts, on such subjects as may be proposed to them;" showing that the National had nothing to suggest. The time for a union had passed. Meetings were held, but nothing resulted from them.

There was comparative quiet in both Institutions. The animosities previously engendered had, to a great degree, died out.

The National Academy had gained gradual, but certain, strength—its opponents had proportionately dropped off, and many became friends—as is most usually the case, when LEAST WANTED.

May 6. The Annual Meeting. Samuel F. B. Morse was elected President; Henry Inman, Vice-President; John L. Morton, Secretary; Thomas S. Cummings, Treasurer; William Dunlap, Charles C. Ingham, Council; Horatio Greenhough, Professor of Sculpture; Robert W. Weir, Academician; F. W. Edmonds, Raphael Hoyle, James Whitehorne, A., L. De Rose, Associates.

May 9th. The fourth Exhibition was opened for the reception of invited guests, and to the public on the 11th, extending to the 13th July—fifty-five working days—and received $1,053.86—an average of $19.16 per day—187 works.

The Fall of the year opened unpropitiously. Mr. Morse, the President, was going to Europe, to be absent several years, and he felt it incumbent on him to resign the office, rather than encumber the Institution with an absent President. A unanimous request of the Council, that he would retain his office, and allow the duties to be performed by the Vice-President, happily induced him to change his mind.

Ball Hughes tendered his services to lecture on sculpture, which was accepted. There is no remembrance that he did so.

The schools opened with spirit, and arrangements were made by Dunlap and Cummings (a committee) for the usual course of lectures, which were only to a very limited extent delivered.

December 4, Dr. Jno. Neilson, Jr., was appointed Professor of Anatomy, in the place of Dr. F. G. King, deceased.

Drawing for the premiums commenced on the 4th January. The subject, "the Venus de Medicis."

There being no rooms in which the Council could assemble without inconvenience to the students, the meetings were directed to be held at the house of member Cummings "until otherwise ordered."

January 7th. Died, Sir Thomas Lawrence, Presi-
1830. dent of the Royal Academy, London, and an Honorary Member of the Academy.

March 22. The Council assembled to receive the ballots of the students on the premium drawings, which was made as stated for the last season. The Council differed with the students in opinion, and their decision was altered in one case—the third premium. They were then conjointly declared to be awarded as follows :

The best,	-	-	-	Mr. Torrey.
The second best,	-	-	-	Mr. Pratt.
The third " -	-	-	-	Mr. Packard.

The premiums were delivered by Mr. Inman, with the following address :

GENTLEMEN :—In congratulating the successful candidates upon the favorable result of their efforts, the Council have to express to them, and to all, their satisfaction at the decided improvement which characterizes their drawings, when compared with those of the last year. And while this circumstance should afford *them* an additional inducement to persevere in their studies, it demonstrates that the measures taken to extend the means of instruction, will not have been adopted without the happiest consequences. On this subject, I am enpowered to promise, that during the next season, in addition to the Antique School, *the living model,* and, that besides the usual course, practical lectures on portrait painting, architecture and engraving, will be delivered by able professors of these several departments. In the absence of our President, it becomes my duty, to offer a few remarks, naturally suggested by the occasion for which we have met ; and I can conceive of none more mutually interesting than that of dispensing and receiving rewards of successful competition.

I address myself particularly to those among you who are about to enter on the profession of either of the branches of art. I would urge upon your attention the great importance of the studies in which you have been engaged. Your proficiency in them will influence, in a most singular degree, your future success.   *   *   *   *   *   *

In conclusion, permit me to add a few suggestions respecting the government of your conduct towards each other as fellow artists. *Never* forget that you are professing a *Liberal Art.* In that sense of the term, avoid all disposition wantonly to quarrel with the works of your cotemporaries; but rather seek for their merits, and profit by them. Especially, be not too ready to depreciate the great master pieces of art, which have come down from olden times, and which have challenged the admiration of succeeding ages. On the contrary, prefer rather to doubt the justice of your own impressions, should they be unfavorable, than to impeach the decisions of the great tribunals of taste, which have pronounced on their merits, and be guided by that golden rule of criticism—"He only has the best right to censure, who himself excels." In the hope that these crude remarks may lend a new impulse to your professional ardor, I beg leave to tender you my warmest wishes for you welfare and improvement.

March 15. Was on exhibition, in the Old Academy Galleries, one of the finest collections of old paintings ever brought to the City, known as the Abrahams Collection.

It was a matter of record that the pictures were surreptitiously obtained. It was said that they were intrusted to him to be cleaned, and were removed here. It contained a beautiful "Hobbiman," a "Claude" of great excellence, a "Murillo" superb—indeed, the whole good.

By process of law the works were stopped, and Abrahams imprisoned. After a time the exhibition was continued, and, as then understood, for the benefit of the proprietors. Abrahams was subsequently released, and returned to Europe, where a compromise was effected.

He left in this country, from that collection, an original miniature portrait of Oliver Cromwell, by Cooper, which he presented to William Roome, the deputy-jailor of the City Prison, for kindnesses rendered during his confinement.

March 22. Wm. Dunlap, Thos. S. Cummings, C. C. Ingham, C. C. Wright, F. S. Agate, Jno. Inman and A. J. Davis were appointed "Lecturers."

April 30th was the Reception, and May 1st the Opening Day of the Fifth Annual Exhibition. It continued to the 5th July—fifty-six working-days; receiving $1031.79—an average of $18.42 per day: one hundred and eight-five productions.

May 5. The annual meeting opened by the reading of the Council's report.

"The Council report, That, since the last Exhibition, they have concluded with the Clinton Hall Association for the upper part of the building erecting by them, and in which building they will have ample accommodations, viz.: One large room for Exhibition, fifty feet square; one for the School, fifty by thirty-eight; one for the Library, thirty-six by twenty; and one of the same dimensions above it for the use of Mr. ——, who has been appointed 'Keeper.'

"That the Antique School has been well attended, and that premiums have been awarded to the successful candidates, and lectures delivered. * * * The Council have also made arrangements for a more extended Course of Lectures, by members of the Academy, in those particular branches of the arts considered by them as useful. * * * The connection made with the mercantile interests of the City, induces us to believe that the most favorable views may be entertained of our future prosperity.

H. INMAN,
C. C. INGHAM,
W. DUNLAP,
THOMAS S. CUMMINGS,
JNO. L. MORTON.

"The Treasurer reported on the condition of the Institution, and the increased interests taken in the Exhibition, as manifested by the augmentation of its receipts, which for the year had amounted to $1204.79 ; the disbursements, to $1101.16 : leaving a balance in the Treasury of $103.63."

Samuel F. B. Morse was elected President; Henry Inman, Vice-President; John L. Morton, Secretary; Thomas S. Cummings, Treasurer; William Dunlap, C. C. Ingham, Members of Council. No Academicians.

The placing of Mr. Bennett as "Keeper" was injudicious. "He soon" reported "his inability to control the students," "and requested the appointment of an assistant."

October 8. Removal of the Schools was made to Clinton Hall.

The Exhibition did not open there until the Spring of 1831. The building was opposite the *old* Brick Church. The Church has, however, winged its flight to 5th Avenue and 39th Street, and its former place occupied by splendid edifices devoted to Mammon.

Measures were immediately taken to fit up the apartments. Mr. Cummings was the Committee. The School was arranged on a (then) entirely new plan—to answer the double purpose of lectures and school. On one end of the room was a platform, on which three or four full-length statues were placed, and between them pedestals for heads. In the centre, and front of the platform, a neat reading-desk for the lecturers. The seats were arranged in amphitheatre form—each row in succession rising a few inches above the one preceding it. The backs of the one serving to hinge the drawing-boards on of the ones next following; to which back rail was also affixed for each draftsman a hooded lamp. Gas lighted the models, but not the drawing-boards.

On the commencement of a lecture, the drawing boards were allowed to drop from the lap, and then remained suspended by the hinges on the rail perpendicularly, and out of injury.

The season was prolific in students and lectures, the attendance remarkably good, and the interest taken in the Institution never better; though of too much excitement for long continuance.

May 5th to December 13th, no minutes.

December 13th.   Mr. Robert W. Weir was elected Professor of Perspective.

An order was made to change the *color* of the Galleries —apparently a very unimportant matter.   It will be found to be one of difficulty, and on which there has always been a great diversity of opinion.   Many changes have been made in the Academy Galleries.   The first choice was a "*negative* tea-green"—a light and admirable color.   After some years, and many discussions, it was changed to a "*deep red.*"   In 1859 it was ordered, and made of the deepest olive-green: little less than black.   That, however, was quickly abandoned.

April.   The Vice-President had removed to Phila-
1831. delphia, Morse was in Europe, and the Institution was left without either of its regularly elected presiding officers.

Dunlap was made chairman "*pro tem.*" and Weir was chosen to fill the vacancy occasioned in the Council.

April 26.   On the termination of the school-season, the students assembled, and, ALONE, decided on the relative merits of the drawings presented.   Dunlap delivered the premiums, and an address; the latter was published, and it is much regretted that it is too long for admission.

Morse's absence, Inman's removal, and a general lukewarmness pervading the art body, induced, perhaps, by the want of its officers, and more so by the enemies of the Institution, many of whom prophesied that the end had NOW COME, and that it was well known it could not survive Morse's leaving; and *that* sentiment having taken strong hold on the *body corporate*, it was greatly feared that a sufficient number of new works, originals by living artists, not before exhibited by the Academy, would not be obtained, wherewith to fill the greatly increased galleries.

Hence was introduced by the writer the device of a "REVIEW EXHIBITION."   Resolutions were passed authorizing such an arrangement, and circulars immediately issued.   The Sixth Annual Exhibition, it was declared, "*should*" consist "*only*" of works "*previously*" exhibited; and it was announced that such a *Review Exhibition* would be held every sixth year.

Thus was Clinton Hall pictorially inaugurated.   The result was highly successful; it was, at once, a "*Renovator,*" a "*Reviver,*" and a "*Restorer.*"

To the public, an admirable reminder of the good works exhibited in the past Exhibitions; advantageous to the

Artists, by presenting them in their cumulated strength; and to the Institution, a pecuniary benefit.

The drawbacks were, that it would present unfavorable comparison and preponderance over the ensuing Annual Exhibition, which would consist only of the works of the year, and that the younger artists, who had not been ex-hibiters for the five preceding years, were prejudiced by want of material from which to select.

Much force in the arguments, but completely outweighed by the good it did. It was, however, not repeated; it never proved necessary that it should be.

April 27. The Review Exhibition opened by private invitation, and to the public the next day. It closed July 9th. Its receipts were $1115.84; open sixty-three work-ing days, and averaged $17.87 per day; two hundred and one productions.

May 4. The annual meeting was held. Mr. Inman ab-sent, and likely to continue. He tendered his resignation of the Vice-Presidency, and resolutions expressive of regret at parting with him were passed. In the following, and indeed in all the future Reports inserted, all matter pre-viously given in the body of the work, and all mere rou-tine recitations of the academic year, will not be admitted. New or interesting extracts of matter, and suggestions for the future, only, will be retained.

From Report of the Council.

The School for the Study of the Antique has been attended by the usual number of students. Lectures on the several subjects provided for by the Constitution have been delivered by the Professors in each Department—Mr. Dunlap, Mr. Cummings, Mr. Mason, Mr. Jno. Inman, Mr. Wright.

   *   *   *   *   *   *   *   *   *   *

The premiums have been drawn for and awarded to the successful candi-dates, and the students generally have evinced great progress in their studies.

Several valuable additions have been made to the Casts since the removal to the new rooms. *   *   *   *   *   *   *   The expenses have been neces-sarily much increased by the extensive arrangements for the schools, light-ing with gas, carpenters' work and painting for the rooms; but these expenses are not to be considered as of the year in which they occur.

For these expenses, we have only the Exhibition to look to; but, from the favorable feeling shown by our mercantile community since our connection with the Clinton Hall, there is every reason to hope that they may be met.

The Council have made an arrangement with Mr. Governeur Kemble, on behalf of Mrs. Meade, to open an Exhibition of Pictures of the old masters, belonging to her, as soon as the Annual Exhibition closes, and this may be calculated on towards the extinguishment of our debt.

Mr. Cummings, the Treasurer, reported in detail the condition of the finances. The total receipts of the year had been $1,335.42; the total payments, $1,285.76; leav-ing a balance in the Treasury of $39.66.

S. F. B. Morse was chosen President; William Dunlap, Vice-President; Jonn L. Morton, Secretary; Thomas S. Cummings, Treasurer; Charles C. Ingham and Robert W. Weir, Members of Council.

The following were appointed PROFESSORS N. A.:

Samuel F. B. Morse,	Horatio Greenough,
Thomas·S. Cummings,	Jno. Neilson, Jr.,
Dr. Bush,	Robert W. Weir,
William C. Bryant,	William Dunlap,
	Gulian C. Verplanck.

Jno. L. Morton, James Frothingham and Raphael Hoyle were elected Academicians.

W. G. Wall, an Academician in 1826, was transferred to the list of Honorary Members, having taken up his residence abroad, at Dublin, his native place. In the first Exhibition he displayed a number of his beautiful landscapes in water-colors. He has since become a painter in oil, and returned to the United States, making Newburgh his residence, and still painting professionally (July, 1862); advanced in years, afflicted in his family by sickness, and discouraged for want of employment, he again returns to his native town.

Mr. Durand was called to the Council to fill the vacancy during Mr. Morse's absence.

May 4. Two resolutions, of more import than at first meets the eye, were proposed and passed, viz.:

" *Resolved,* That no picture shall be received for exhibition, at any Annual Exhibition, and marked for sale, unless the same shall be the property of the artist."

And the following:

" *Resolved,* That whereas the funds arising from the Exhibition are the support of the Schools of the Institution, and consequently the foundation of the usefulness not only to the Fine Arts, but to the manufactures of the country which must emanate from the Academy: And whereas the amount of those funds must depend upon the novelty as well as the excellence of the works exhibited:

" *Resolved,* That the works of those Artists and others, who devote their time and talents to supporting the credit, influence, and attraction of the Exhibitions of the National Academy of Design, and reserve their paintings, sculptures, designs, and engravings for those Exhibitions, are entitled to, and shall receive, a preference with the Council at the time of receiving and arranging the works of art sent in."

May 23. The Secretary informed the Board of his having received advices from the President, Mr. Morse, then abroad (at Rome), of the DONATION of casts from artists and amateurs, friends of the Academy, in that place.

May 23. Presents arriving from abroad. Little did the generous donors (the members, willing recipients) th'nk of the fatal consequences of the gifts to the Academy.

The statues were donated in Rome, and Rome is far from New-York. They had to be and were transported and directed to the Academy; the arriving statues frequently being their own heralds, and with bills of expenses on their backs surpassing all belief. It was soon found that the rapid arrival of *presents* was plunging the institution into DEBT far beyond the possibility of payment; and it was by that rendered BANKRUPT. The most urgent remonstrances were forwarded to send NO MORE PRESENTS.

The money which should have been used to pay the running expenses of the institution, had been consumed in paying freight and charges on the statues already received, and further large indebtedness on the same account was yet unpaid.

The Vice-President and Secretary were authorized and directed to negotiate a loan on the plaster casts ; but, unfortunately, "*imagery*" was a security unknown in the market. And it was an "*academic grief*," that, long as they had been in the "school," they did not "*draw well*"—at least, not "*capitally*."

June 7. Died, Peter Maverick, one of the "*originally*" elected Academicians. An engraver, of great excellence in his line—the bank-note—and was, to that day, what the AMERICAN and NATIONAL Companies are to the present. He did all the work of the kind required in his time. The excellence of his lettering, especially his "*round*" hand, was a conceded preventive to counterfeiting; and it has seldom been equaled, not surpassed, to the date of publication.

Perkins followed Maverick, and, in some lettering, perhaps more than equaled him ; though, as a whole, that can scarcely be admitted. They both stood pre-eminent in their art. Durand was a pupil of Maverick's, in line-engraving.

Mr. Maverick left a large family; two of the daughters, Octavia and Katherine, possessing talent in art. One of these ladies is Teacher of Drawing and Painting in the Packer Institute, in Brooklyn ; the other occupies a similar position in Mrs. Willard's Seminary, in Troy. Mr. Augustus Maverick, the only issue of Mr. Maverick's second marriage, is in the editorial corps of the *Evening Post.*

November 1. Mrs. Richard W. Meade's collection of old paintings was exhibited.

The collection was looked upon as one of an extraordinary character. It contained works from the Italian, French, Flemish and Dutch Schools, to the number of about one hundred, collected in Europe by Richard W. Meade, Esq., at very high prices. The works were given in the catalogue, viz. : $7000 for the " Calling of St. Matthew," by Lucca Jordana; $5000 for the " Martyrdom of St. Lawrence ;" and from $1200 to $1000 each for the greater number of the principal works—few below $500.

The most interesting feature was the original bust of Washington, by Ceracchi, " the only sculptor to whom he sat."

When finished, the artist offered it to Washington, then President of the United States. The President declined its purchase. The Spanish ambassador hearing that Washington declined it, after having ascertained that fact from personal application, eagerly paid the price, and carried the treasure to Spain.

From the widow of that gentleman, Mr. Meade purchased the bust for $2000, and restored it to the country. After the Exhibition, the works were sold or otherwise distributed, in the settlement of the estate of the owner.

Richard W. Meade, above mentioned, was the father of General Meade of the Army of the Potomac.

The schools had been opened for the season at the usual time, and it was

Resolved, That the School of the Antique be opened for a class of ladies, on Tuesdays, Thursdays and Saturdays, from 12 to 3 o'clock; that the instruction in the classes be performed by the *Council in turn;* that it be gratuitous.

November 10. " The turn " on " attendance " was arranged. Ingham the first day; Weir and Cummings the second; Durand and Morton the third; and so on—weekly repetition.

Admirable in theory, but poor in practice. The attendance of the scholars was " *irregular*," as almost all attempts at free instruction in Art, under such circumstances, will demonstrate to be the case. The pupils were not of a class requiring free instruction, and they were therefore, perhaps, not even too well pleased at receiving it. As a novelty, it took for a time—it was partially successful. The artists assigned to duty did their part well; but nevertheless, long before the season was over, it was found onerous.

Most of the Professors delivered their lectures, which were well attended; indeed, the little lecture-room was often overcrowded.

Dr. Bush's lectures on anatomy were of great value. The demonstrations of the most masterly execution, and the description clear beyond comparison. Those on mythology, by Bryant, were likewise very interesting. Early history simplified—viewed with originality, and pronounced on and filled with a fervid poetic fire, that interested all.

Dr. Hamilton Morton was elected Professor of Anatomy, in place of Dr. John Neilson, Jr., resigned, in consequence of ill health.

Charles E. Edwards's course of four lectures on the most famous of the Antique Statues were highly interesting and instructive. They were privately published for the use of friends, and their perusal afforded instruction and pleasure. A copy fell into the hands of Chantry, who spoke in very high terms of them.

February 13. The drawing for the premiums commenced. The subject, Thorwalsden's " *Mercury.*"

1832. The premium, the Works of "Burnett," elegantly bound, and the Works of Sir Joshua Reynolds for the second best.

Seven competitors entered, and in consequence of great dissatisfaction by the students in their own DECISIONS, as well as on that of JOINT DECISION, and its alteration being asked of the Council, it was " *Resolved,* That in future the Council ALONE shall determine on the merits of the drawings."

On the 23d April the premiums were accordingly so determined, and awarded—

1st. To J. W. Cassilear.

2d. To ——— Lawson.

It was resolved that the seventh Exhibition should open to the public on the 15th of May. It was not opened until the 21st, at least twenty-five days later than it should have been.

That was done to meet, and, if possible, reconcile the great diversity of opinion as to what was a proper time for opening a " *Spring* Exhibition." Circumstances determine it which cannot be foreseen—viz., the weather: if the Spring is a backward one, the later date is most acceptable; if warm and forward, the early one is preferable: though on no account so late as the 25th May. Experience points to the 10th to the 20th of April as a proper period.

In consequence of the late beginning, the Exhibition did not close until the 8th of July—*too late.* Open 43 working days, and received $862—averaging $20 per day. It contained 239 works.

"Public Opinion" assumed an exceedingly high moral tone. In the Exhibition was a beautifully chaste creation of Greenhough's—little statues in "cold white marble"— two figures base, and all about three feet high—"The Chanting Cherubs." It is true the little innocents were "*nude,*" and that was fiercely assailed by "*Modistus,*" who effervesced through the press on the subject for some time. Shortly after that, there was exhibited in the city two gorgeously colored French pictures by De Bœuf—"*Adam and Eve*"—life-sized "*nudes*"—"THE TEMPTATION," and "THE EXPULSION." THEY were pronounced "GREAT MORAL PICTURES," and their exposition made a fortune for their exhibiter. At the fire which occurred in the old American Academy building in Barclay Street, they were supposed destroyed. Such was not the case.

The records of the American were thought to have shared the same fate. That was likewise an error. They were saved, it seems, and placed by Colonel Trumbull in care of Alexander Jackson Davis, Esq., who has them, and who proposes to donate them to the Historical Society, as their proper depository.

The writer has heretofore made strong objections to "*Presents,*" and their reception. The following is admitted an exception: Miss G****r, one of the lady students, hearing of the Academy's wants, generously inclosed a fifty-dollar bill.

That was a substantial testimonial—an assistance. It was at hand free of charge; and even had it, "*statue-like,*" been presented at a distance, it would have cost little in transportation.

May 2. The Annual Meeting of the Academicians. The Council made no report. The Treasurer reported "in full." The receipts and disbursements were—the former $1,604.99; the latter $1,567.27—leaving a balance in the Treasury of $37.52.

S. F. B. Morse was elected President; Wm. Dunlap, Vice-President; Jno. L. Morton, Secretary; Thomas S. Cummings, Treasurer; Chs. C. Ingham, R. W. Weir, Council.

The same Board for so many years chosen, is certainly a contradiction of the "Doctors' asseveration" of the "uncertain and unreliable character of the artists." They— "the *Doctors*"—long since, in Rutgers College history, quarreled themselves out of corporate existence. It may in justice be added, that legislative interference, in refusing them the bestowal of diplomas, must have proved highly irritating, and destructive of their interests as a Medical School.

No Academicians were chosen; but at an *adjourned* meeting, Wm. S. Mount, Henry C. Shumway, were elected Associates, and nine Honorary Members.

That adjournment naturally led to the inquiry, Is such a proceeding legal, or the acts under it valid? It was clear that the intention was to confine the voting for members to but once a year. Such a proceeding would entirely set aside and negative that intention. If one adjournment was legal, it is certain that a dozen would be equally so; and if so, the annual meeting could, by adjournment, be held every day in the week.

It led to an alteration in the By-Laws. Though the writer never could see that it was required. The language was clear, and could in no reasonable manner be otherwise distorted in construction.

Orders were passed to the Treasurer that he should pay, as soon as "he may have sufficient funds," sundry indebtednesses. But, alas! he had no such "funds."

The Antique School was opened in the evening, in October, and to the ladies in the first week of November.

And another order passed that Dunlap, Ingham, Weir, Cummings and Durand should attend to it in turn, with the singular introduction, as regards Mr. Dunlap, " That he attend the first day; after which, he is not expected to attend *regularly.*" Subsequently, the Academicians were apportioned off " in pairs," and, by twos, directed to attend the evening school, according to programme. It was a small attendance. One or two did attend, for half an hour or so, the early meetings; but rarely, indeed, did the school see the countenances of the apportioned. Without compensation, from pure love for art, it was not to be expected. Few will be found, for a continuance, so far to sacrifice their comfort. It was a repetition of a previous delusion, or want of knowledge of human nature. Such an arrangement is understood to exist in the "Royal Academy." Very true; and each gentleman receives two guineas a night, &c., for his services. That is another affair, and, it is said, singular fact, that there is a prompt attendance; without it, probably, the salary is deducted; that may account for it.

October 31. At a meeting was passed what has ever been termed "the fig-leaf resolve." On a motion of Mr. Ingham, it was resolved, "that the statues in the Antique School suffer mutilation," and "that a plaster leaf be placed in lieu thereof." It excited no little mirthfulness; indeed, it extended further—derision; and, lastly, some acrimonious feeling; though the resolution was adopted. The writer participated in the general tone at the "*mover's*" expense.

His motives and his earnestness were always respected; and the writer can add, that he now admires his taste, and fully concurs with him in the desirableness of the change made, and regrets that he ever lent an aid in its derision.

It has before been remarked, that an endeavor to obtain a loan of $2000 on the statuary was not very successful. On long-continued efforts, of the Vice-President and Secretary, it was fully proved, nothing else was to be expected. Money, it is true, could be had on "*plaster,*" if not "antique," not in the "*round,*" not "imagery," but modern, and well spread out on the "*flat,*" on an indefinite number of bricks piled on a small portion of mother earth.

In the matter of plaster alone, without the two latter, a loan on it was decidedly at a discount; it had no votaries; it was nowhere to be obtained. That fully proven.

December 24. Mr. Cummings offered the following, which was carried unanimously :

Resolved, That it be proposed to the creditors of the Academy to receive on their several bills the interest, and fifteen per cent. of the principal the first year; the interest and 20 per cent. on the remaining indebtedness the second year; the interest, and 25 per cent. on the residue of indebtedness the third year; the interest, and 35 per cent. on the same on the fourth year; the interest, and 50 per cent. on the remainder the fifth year; and the remainder in full the sixth year. The first payment to be made on the 1st July, 1833; the subsequent payments to be made on the first day of July. Interest from 1st January, 1833.

After the manner of the familiar fable, the writer was left to tie the bell round pussy's neck—the *honor* to carry it out.

The creditors were seen, and it was explained to them that to *live,* the Academy *must pay* its *yearly* expenses; that it *had nothing* in store; that no one Exhibition would pay the creditors all, even though everything else was left unpaid; that it was no use to disembowel the institution, there were no golden eggs to be had; that if they wished to be paid, they must prolong, not destroy its existence; that the institution, by its Exhibitions, could, it was believed, pay its running expenses, and, by economy, leave sufficient yearly surplus to meet what was promised, judging by the past; and that to press any further, was to destroy the Academy, and thus lose the debt. Some acceded at once, some blustered and threatened, some asked the writer's personal security. The ultimate result was, that seeing they could do no better, they fell into the measure, as they said, from "personal respect, and belief in the responsibility of their humble servant." They *were* all paid—not only as asked and granted, but principal and interest, two years within the time named; and the institution once more, by *that* means, placed on its feet, and out of debt.

January. Another call was made by the American **1833.** Academy for a "*conference.*" A union! nothing could be more absurd than such a proposition.

The American Academy had been dying for years, and only required to be peaceably let alone to drop into its grave.

The National, on the contrary, had survived all its enmity and enemies, and overcome all its own pecuniary difficulties. Was it to be supposed that it would encumber itself with a dead load for nothing? Yet, out of respect to the parties, such a conference was acceded to; and, on their part, extreme sensitiveness was manifested as to who should appear to make the advance.

January 7. The ball was then put in motion. A communication was received from the Secretary of the American Academy, stating, "*that in consequence* of a communication made to that body by Dr. Hosack (*who had a conversation* with Mr. Morse on the subject of a union of the two Academies), that a Committee of three be appointed to meet a similar Committee from the National to consult on the subject of forming a union."

It was resolved that Messrs. Morse, Durand and Dunlap be "that Committee."

January 14. The Secretary of the American notified the National that such a Committee, viz.: David Hosack, Pierre Flanding and James Herring, had been appointed "*to pursue the negotiation commenced.*" (How ridiculously worded, "*negotiation commenced;*" to give the appearance of the National having sought the conference.)

And, for some cause or other, it was "requested" that Mr. Cummings should be added to the Committee, which was assented to.

It was stated that there was every disposition on the part of the American Academy to forward a union of the two Academies. The Committees met, and a joint report was agreed to, and which it was supposed would be ratified by the parties so opening negotiations by their emissaries. The joint report was submitted to the Council, and by them agreed to. A copy was duly authenticated, and delivered to the American Academy Committee, which was to be similarly signed by them, and, when so completed, to be by them laid before the *Directors* of the American, at a meeting to be held for that purpose. The Committee of the American repeatedly informed the Committee of the National "that ALL was a mere MATTER of FORM," as they had been authorized to act entirely at their pleasure; that the terms agreed upon were well known to the Directors, and would be "UNANIMOUSLY RATIFIED." On the day of meeting, the Committee of the National, by previous mutual understanding in the two Committees, assembled at the house of Dr. Hosack, at which place the Committee of the American were to meet them. After the mere form of presentation to the Directors, to declare the result and further talk over matters.

Dr. Hosack and Mr. Flanding did so meet them, directly from the meeting of the American, and reported, "not that the project was ratified—not that the joint report had been laid before the Directors of the American—not that they had discussed and adopted, or rejected it; but that, on the meeting being organized, Mr. Trumbull had taken from his pocket a paper, which he had brought with him, and read it to the Directors, and that THEY HAD ALL AGREED TO IT; that it was unanimously adopted, and ordered to be printed."

Dunlap says: "How these gentlemen answer this to themselves, cannot well be imagined."

The report of the Committees was not even presented. Mr. Trumbull had probably been informed of its contents, and was prepared. Trumbull rejected it, and it was rejected by all. It had been repeatedly asked during the conference, "in case there was a union, would Trumbull be elected President?" and was always answered, that it would depend solely on the electors. It was well known that he would not. He was thought "incompetent, or worse." The American Academy would have been long since out of existence, but for the continued friendship of Dr. Hosack, who, on its being ordered to vacate in the Park, rendered his assistance in its removal to Barclay street, where he erected a building for its use, and where the same unchangeable Exhibition was represented. It there sunk into still further neglect, or even contempt; and the rental of the building, if obtained at all, was only so obtained by letting to others than the Academy.

February 5. The Committee of the National requested to be discharged from the further consideration of the subject; and the President of the National was requested to answer the communication of the President of the American.

Thus did Trumbull once more defeat the desires for a union of the two institutions.

Frequent reference has been made to "Dunlap's History of the Arts of Design in the United States." Another and second effort (after his Dramatic Festival, in which the writer took an active part) was made to assist Mr. Dunlap, by the publication of a History of the Arts of Design in the United States. That emanated in the Academy, and principally from the writer, whose proposition it was. It had often been suggested to Dunlap, but by him declined, for want of means. In one of the conversations, the writer proposed a subscription for that purpose, drafted a heading, and at once set to work; and, alone, caused the subscription to nearly double what Dunlap had named as the amount requisite to enable him to complete the work. The material for the work was found to be more than anticipated. John L. Morton took the subscription list, and nearly equaled the writer's efforts. The contemplated work grew in size, and it was proposed to extend it to two volumes.

Dr. Jno. W. Francis and Geo. P. Morris then took the matter in hand, and the amount was again doubled. Thus encouraged, the work was soon published and the author handsomely remunerated.

A little singular, perhaps; Dunlap, in his preface, publicly acknowledges the assistance of Francis and Morris, but forgets to include his earlier friends Cummings and Morton. Why that gentleman should have shown such preference was never very clear to the writer's mind. The work is valuable, and the only one that can be turned to for early art record.

February 28. The schools were in successful operation, and the students commenced drawing for the premiums. Subject, "The Genie Suppliant." Drawings to be in black and white chalk.

The first premium, "Cunningham's Lives of Painters."

The second, "The Life of Benjamin West."

They were awarded—the first, to Allen Smith; the second, to James Clonney—by the decision of the Council alone.

Mr. Morse delivered the premiums, with "an *appropriate address,* before the members of the Academy and students assembled, when *the following resolutions,* by Mr. Dunlap, were unanimously approved and signed by those present."

But, alas! the resolutions do not follow; they are not there. The meeting was without date, and the resolves without record. Query. Was it on April the 1st? More so, as it might be asked on what date in "*April*" could it have occurred, as the next succeeding meeting, supposed to be a week afterwards, is recorded to have been held at that date.

April 8. Died, Raphael Morgan, a distinguished engraver, and Honorary Member.

May 1. The Annual Meeting of the Academicians. No report appears to have been made by the Council; one was made by the Treasurer, embracing the yearly receipts and expenditures, as also the indebtedness, and partial liquidation thereof by the Academy, which was approved.

The Secretaryship was divided. Samuel F. B. Morse was elected President; William Dunlap, Vice-President; Jno. L. Morton, Corresponding Secretary; A. B. Durand, Recording Secretary; Thomas S. Cummings, Treasurer; Charles C. Ingham and Robert W. Weir, Council; George W. Twibill, Anthony L. De Rose, James Freeman, Robert E. Launitz and Miss Ann E. Hall, Academicians.

It was resolved that it be left with the Council to communicate to Mr. Leslie the gratification experienced by the Academy, on learning that he had accepted the appointment of Professor of Drawing at West Point; and to make suitable arrangements for testifying their respect to him, by a dinner, on his return to this country. Leslie left England 21st September, 1833; arrived here October 12th. On his arrival, that was declined. A meeting was held; Mr. Leslie and his friend Washington Irving attended. There was no public demonstration.

May 8. Opened the Eighth Annual Exhibition; closing on the 6th July, and receiving $1387; fifty-two working-days, averaging $26.66 per day; works, 218.

Nothing transpired from May to October.

October 14. The School of the Antique was opened three afternoons in the week.

November 7. Was entertained a proposition to dispose of the lease of Clinton Hall, "and procure a more eligible location;" and a Committee was appointed to make inquiry and report.

January 15, died Eliab Metcalf, one of the oldest of the New-York artists—a portrait painter of standing, **1834.** and Honorary Member of the Academy—less known, perhaps, in consequence of his generally residing in a Southern climate, in consequence of ill health.

April 14. Leslie returned to Europe, with his "good friend, Captain Morgan"—circumstances connected with the prosperity of his labors, and the support of his family, compelling him reluctantly to leave this country. "Last evening, at the invitation of the Academy of Design, a large number of artists and literary gentlemen of this city met him at the rooms in Clinton Hall, and partook of a parting collation prepared for the occasion. The character and variety of the talent assembled on the occasion were as honorable to the city as to the highly distinguished gentleman. With the exception of the venerable Col. Trumbull and Mr. Dunlap, who were prevented by indisposition from attending, all the painters, sculptors, and engravers of note of the city were present. Among them, we recollect Messrs. Morse, Wier, Ingham, Bennett, Fisher, Cole, Cummings, Durand, Frazee, and a number of younger artists. Of the literary gentlemen, were Mr. Washington Irving, Mr. Verplanck, Mr. Halleck, Mr. Hillhouse, and several others of note. A very agreeable evening was passed."

One of his best pictures, "*Ann Page and Master Slender,*" was in the country; where it is at present, is unknown to the writer; it originally belonged to the late Philip Hone, and was only disposed of in the necessary settling of his estate.

April 25. The Ninth Annual Exhibition opened to the public, and remained open until the 5th July—62 working days—its receipts $1,215—an average of $19.60 per day—175 works.

May 4. The Annual Meeting of the Academicians. There was no report from the Council. The Treasurer's Report announced the total receipts of the year, $1725.07; the expenditures, $1,692.09; balance, $32.98; and that a payment had been made on the extended debt, which reduced it from $2,140 to $1,658. Samuel F. B. Morse was elected President; William Dunlap, Vice-President; John L. Morton, Corresponding Secretary; A. B. Durand, Recording Secretary; Thomas S. Cummings, Treasurer; C. C. Ingham, Thomas Cole, Members in Council.

There were no Academicians elected.

The Academicians were called on to mourn the loss of two of their oldest members and friends—Hugh Reinagle and John Paradise. Mr. Reinagle was principal scene painter in the Old Park Theatre, then in its palmiest days, under the management of Price and Simpson, and was a highly distinguished artist in his line. John Paradise died June 16. He was an Academician in 1826. He was not of a brilliant or extensive reputation. Though a portrait painter of merit, he possessed a very correct eye for drawing—hence he generally produced strong resemblances in his pictures. His color was rather dry and uninteresting.

June 26. The Academicians, Associates, and Honorary Members assembled to take part in the funeral solemnities in honor of General Lafayette, and a place was assigned them in the general programme.

There was a full attendance.

Columbia College had before that included the Academy in its annual Commencement procession, &c. Other than it, that was the first public recognition of the Institution, as a Society, to be cared for, in public demonstrations.

October 15. The School of the Antique was opened, and it was announced that a School of Ornament, for industrial art purposes, would be added, and it was so, but it met with no response—none attended.

The Life School was ordered to be opened, if a sufficient number of persons subscribed to pay the actual cost of models.

The early lectures by the writer, on "The Arts of Design as applicable to the Mechanic Arts," delivered before the Mechanics' and other Societies—and preceding the action since become so successful in England, which led to the establishment of Government Schools of Design—perhaps first awakened attention here to that branch. By request, the lectures were repeated on successive winters. The latter season, the writer, who had been furnished with the English Government reports, was enabled to enlarge on his remarks with valuable extracts from that source.

"The establishment of the Government Schools in England, it is said, has done much good to the manufacturing interests. The only really tangible complaint against them being their diversion from the regular course and intention—a school of ornament."

What truth there is in this, the writer is unable to say. If the objection is there well taken, Americans might naturally be expected, from similarity of temperament, to fall into the same mistake. In France, it has, however, not proved so. Many of the most able designers are found at the head of the manufacturing department. They are content so to be, and their power and influence have greatly contributed to advance the manufacturing interests of their country.

There is found no record of the doings of the Academy from November, 1834, to March, 1835; though there is scarcely a doubt but meetings were held. Probably nothing of importance transpired.

The Schools were opened free of charge on the 15th of October.

May 4, was held the Annual Meeting. A verbal report was made by the Council, (so say the Minutes,) "stating

1835. that the School had been open as usual. The students in the Antique numbering 22, and in the Life 14. The latter defrayed the expense of models by a contribution. No lectures or premiums were delivered."

The Treasurer reported the total receipts from all sources at $1,665.23, and the expenditures at $1,664.09; and that it left but $1.14 after payment of the installment on back indebtedness, which was reduced from $1,658 to $1,358.

Samuel F. B. Morse was elected President; Wm. Dunlap, Vice-President; A. B. Durand, Recording Secretary; John L. Morton, Corresponding Secretary; Thos. S. Cummings, Treasurer; Chas. Ingham and Thos. Cole, Council.

There were no members elected.

James J. Mapes was appointed Professor of Chemistry and Natural Philosophy of Colors, and delivered a course of lectures on that subject before the body. They were of the highest advantage to the students, members, and to the profession. Several colors not in use were reproduced, many tested as to permanency, and new ones added. Some of the specimens are with the writer, and are exceedingly brilliant and durable.

An invitation was received from the AMERICAN LYCEUM, inviting the members of the Academy to attend their meetings, which was accepted, and the *usual* vote of thanks rendered. Few availed themselves of the privilege.

The writer, by invitation from the LYCEUM, delivered his course of lectures on the Arts of Design as applicable to the Mechanic Arts, and the *officers, members*, and delegates of the Lyceum were, by resolution in Council, invited to visit the Exhibitions and Schools of the Academy.

May 5. The Annual Exhibition was opened to the public, continuing until the 4th of July—54 working days. It received $2,381.75—an average of $44.10 per day— nearly doubling any previous year's receipts. 233 works.

At that Exhibition occurred, for the first time, a necessity for the appearance of the Academy in a court of law. An exhibiter, from real or imaginary cause—dissatisfaction, probably, at the disposition of his work—thought proper to take the remedy into his own hands, and remove it from the walls. It was a production of no moment, or of any possible consequence whatever—a small architectural outline. The principle involved was ALL that was worth contending for. The determination of that point was deemed of vital importance to the future interests of the Institution. It was therefore contested. The trial lasted but a short time. The trespasser was defeated. As the object was the settling of a point of law, and not vindictive, or, indeed, any damages, it was so stated to the Court. The judge, at the Academy's request, awarded the mere nominal sum of six cents.

The Minutes show no work performed from May until October. The Summer vacation with artists, as with others, is found widely extending.

October 10 the Schools opened, and, as usual, three evenings to the Life and three to the Antique in each week; and, as the Institution was still in debt, at a small charge to the student, sufficient to pay the expenses of models and lights, rent and attendance, were yet provided by the Academy as heretofore. The classes were well attended.

During the year, the date unknown, died G. Stuart Newton—a highly distinguished artist, and an Honorary Member.

It has before been stated that the Institution was brought to the very verge of ruin, by being the "*recipient*" of presents from abroad, and the Academy's action thereon on 15th November; yet another resolution was passed, directing the discontinuance of "*receiving any presents whatever*" from abroad, unless the freight and charges were paid. Notwithstanding that and previous resolutions, two cases, containing casts unpaid as before, were forwarded, and had arrived. On resolution, the Secretary was directed "to refuse them."

In the latter part of the Winter there was opened for inspection and sale a remarkably fine collection of the old masters and other works, in the rooms of the (old) American Academy, "Barclay Street," and were thus heralded forth by the introducer:

"John W. Brett cannot omit this opportunity of calling the attention of *connoisseurs*, *patrons* of the arts, and *artists*, to the high character and *rare merits* of the collection. It will be found to contain specimens of nearly *all* the *cherished masters*, and to exhibit the *meridian* powers of their authors in their respective styles, many of which are in nearly as high a state of preservation as when taken from the easel."

The favorite project of GOVERNMENT purchase was tried. The collection had been offered at the last session of Congress, (so says the Catalogue); and lastly offered to the public as a special favor for sale by auction. The estimated value of the whole, $60,000. It certainly possessed many productions of merit, whether originals or not.

The writer and Dunlap, in favor of the Government purchasing modern American works rather than old masters, made a strenuous effort to the effect that it should not be so purchased. How far their exertions had influence, was not known. They were not purchased. That is certain.

December 15. Morse, Cummings, and Morton were empowered to make arrangements with the Society Library for accommodations for the Academy in their building erecting on the corner of Leonard Street and Broadway. And it was "*Resolved,* That the large Exhibition Room of the Academy, Clinton Hall, be tendered gratuitously to any of the public bodies, sufferers by the *fire,* who may desire it, until the same shall be wanted for the Annual Exhibition on the 15th March."

That was immediately following the fire of December 5, 1835, which desolated the lower part of the city, and long to be remembered as "THE GREAT FIRE."

December 23. Died, Dr. David Hosack, Honorary Member. That distinguished physician and gentleman was a true lover and encourager of art; and was one of the founders of the old American Academy, in 1804, and, in conjunction with Clinton, Jay, Francis, Murray, &c., bestowed his time and purse on its interests.

January 18. Premiums were offered in the schools, 1836. and they were extended so as to embrace " ORIGINAL COMPOSITION." A GOLD medal was offered "for the best original design of a single figure in "*chiaro scuro,*" painted in oil or "drawn in black and white chalks," and the large silver palette, for the best drawing of the " Genie Suppliant;" the small silver palette for the best drawing of the "Anatomical Figure." The productions to be exclusively the work of those offering them. No instruction to be received during their execution, either directly or indirectly.

February 15. The death of Mr. Twibill, an Academician, was announced. Suitable resolutions were passed and forwarded to the family of the deceased, and the usual badge of mourning worn for thirty days.

Of the young artists of the day, there were none more promising than Twibill. His portraits in oil in small were of excellence seldom equaled. His full lengths of " Gen. Cummings" and " Col. Trumbull," exhibited the same season, attest his excellence in that branch of art; and won him not only good opinion, but substantial recompense.

March 2. A union of the Academies proposed again. A communication was received from the (virtually deceased) American proposing to unite with the National. In respect, alone, to its members—for no prospect of union could be expected—a Committee was appointed, corresponding in number with that appointed by the American—viz.: Morse, Dunlap, Cummings, Morton and Durand—to confer, &c., &c.

The drawings for the premiums closed on the 18th of March, and on the 20th the premiums were decided on by the Council ALONE.

Five contended for the gold medal. It was awarded to Edward Mooney, since well known to fame. The second premium, to Charles H. Parker; the third, to Lewis P. Clover. Of that class, Clover has entered the ministry; Boyle is a distinguished artist in the West; Purcell of much merit; and Bannister is an engraver of the highest order, and still continues one of the most faithful attendants on the schools of the Academy.

April 2. Death again enters the ranks, and the members are called on to part with another of their number—A. L. De Rose—an early Academician; an artist of merit, but not distinguishedly so. The Academy attended the funeral, and the usual mourning was worn.

April 12. A communication was received from the Committees of Conference on the part of the two Academies, on the subject of "*union*," which "was read, and ordered to be put on file;" no other action being had on it. What it was, or where it is, is a matter of conjecture. Putting it on file, may as well have been putting it on the *fire;* there is nothing of the kind to be found, or the "file" either.

April 27. The Annual Exhibition opened, and continued to the 9th day of July—sixty-four working-days; receiving $3758.50—an average of $58.75 per day; contained 237 productions.

May 4. The Annual Meeting of the Academicians. Business opened by "the reading of the law passed in 1834 placing Academicians who should fail to exhibit for two successive years in the list of Associates." A list of delinquents was called for, and on examination it appeared that the following gentlemen were in that category: John Frazee, Robert Launitz, Wm. Main, Nath. Rogers, M. E. Thompson, Ithiel Town, Charles C. Wright. What action was had on it, is not found. Some of the names appear in future catalogues as removed, some not.

At that meeting the law was so amended as to read, "be placed on the list of Honorary Members." And again, at a later hour, the amendment was rescinded, and passed "that the law stand in its original form." And another was passed, "that any Associate who shall cease to exhibit any of his works for two years in succession, shall be considered as having resigned his membership (unless he gives a satisfactory reason to the Council for not exhibiting), sickness and absence only to be taken as satisfactory excuses."

The validity of the excuse was generally determined by the ability or popularity of the offender. Some were removed; others, doubly amenable, were never touched. All was, very properly, abolished—rescinded.

The next business in order was the reading of the Report of the President, from which extracts are made:

* * * * During the last Autumn and Winter, *the School of the Antique* was as usual opened, and thirty-eight students were enrolled. Their progress in the elementary department of drawing has been highly commendable.

* * * * * * * * * *

During the past year, also, the School for the "Living Model," which, in a former year, was altogether supported by private subscription, has been this year continued, and the expenses partially assumed by the Academy, preparatory to eventually adopting it altogether; and the time for thus taking this important school under our superintendence, and wholly at the expense of the Academy, it is believed, has now arrived. * * * * I cannot help congratulating you on the flourishing state of our Treasury. * * * * In the prospect of a surplus, it is deemed worthy of your consideration in what way it can be expended in the best manner to promote the objects for which we are associated; and I would recommend what, indeed, I believe will best meet your own views, that our objects be as general as possible; for the more general the objects can be for which we unitedly exert ourselves, the less liability will there be of a disturbance of that harmony which it is so gratifying to know has for so long a time existed, and still exists amongst us. * * * * Let us ever bear in mind, that union has been our strength.

The national motto is quite in point, and should be ours also: "United we stand; divided, we fall."

Let us glory in the success of the whole body; knowing, for a truth, that while the whole body is prosperous, each individual member partakes of the general prosperity; and that each member suffers, when the general body is not in health.

It is recommended that schools of the "antique" and the "living model" be made still more efficient; and that the "school of ornament" be continued.

* * * * * * * * * *

I would bring to your minds, gentlemen, that, with the increase of the City in numbers and wealth, the arts we profess will be more and more encouraged: and we shall therefore need a permanent establishment of our own, and on a scale suitable to our rank in the community, and worthy of this metropolis.

Academies of Arts in all countries have a suite of buildings, of necessity very extensive. We ought to cast our glance forward, and provide the ground upon which shall be marked out the foundation for the great institution of our country. It will be glory enough for us, who are the pioneers in this enterprise, if we can see this foundation well laid, even if we may not, in our time, see the institution raised; and yet, so rapid in growth is everything in the arts, as well as in commerce, in our country, that we are by no means to despair of seeing with our own eyes the institution an honor to the arts, and to the country, finished on the foundation which we may lay.

The Treasurer made a report embracing the details of

the finances, accompanied with a supplement of advisory recommendations.

The total receipts of the year were $2692.39
The total disbursements,   -   -   2497.23
                                   ————
                                   $195.16

May 4. Samuel F. B. Morse was elected President; Wm. Dunlap, Vice-President; John L. Morton, Corresponding Secretary; A. B. Durand, Recording Secretary; Thomas S. Cummings, Treasurer; Charles C. Ingham, Thomas Cole, Council.

William Page and John G. Chapman were elected Academicians.

June 9. Death again! And the shaft fell with more than ordinary fatality to Art. It removed one of the most beloved, most benevolent, and best friends to art and artists New-York City ever had—*Luman Reed,* who died on the 9th June, 1836.

The *usual*—and there, indeed, deeply felt—resolves were passed, and forwarded to his sorrowing family, and mourning worn by all, as a reminder that a friend had gone.

Dunlap says Allston writes: "My nephew, G. Flagg, has " met with a most munificent patron—munificent for any " country—not a *quid pro quo,* as I suppose you know." That patron was Luman Reed, who sent young Flagg to Europe to complete his studies, and supported all his expenses.

"Mr. Reed has built a large picture gallery at the top of his house in Greenwich Street. There already may be seen some of the unrivaled Landscapes of Cole. He has likewise commissioned Morse to paint an historical picture, (and he might have added Inman, Mount, and Durand.) To our princely merchants Luman Reed, Esq., has set an example of expending the gifts of fortune very different from the ostentatious displays of the dining or the drawing room."

He left a handsome collection of paintings, principally the result of his encouragement of resident talent. These have, by the heartfelt gratitude, liberal contribution of money, and untiring industry of his friend and partner in business, Jonathan Sturges, been kept together, and now stand as a memento of that valued friend. They formed the New-York Gallery of Fine Arts, since removed to the Historical Society, Second Avenue.

It may be mentioned in connection with Mr. Reed, and the "*first* painted" picture by William S. Mount, that there was an absurd story going the rounds of the newspapers, to the effect, " That Mr. William S. Mount having finished his '*first picture*,' came down to the city to exhibit it. That he was called on by Mr. Luman Reed, among others. That Mr. Reed, having long examined the picture, said, 'Mr. Mount, I am not rich enough properly to reward you for that picture, but if one thousand dollars will purchase it, I shall be happy to give you that sum for it.' Mount, having scarcely even heard of such a sum, was lost in amazement—but accepted it. *A check for that amount was given.* Days elapsed before he (Mount) could realize that he was not in a dream—or could muster courage enough to present it for payment; and that, when he did so, and received the money, he immediately *rushed* to Stony Brook, to live forever on that vast sum. It is a pity, perhaps, to spoil so pretty a bit of fiction, but it must be done—there is not a word of truth in it. The first picture Mr. William S. Mount exhibited was '*Husking Corn*,' and was purchased by Mr. Kemble. The first picture he painted for Mr. Reed was a commission. In justice to both the gentlemen, we deem it proper to contradict the statement. Mr. Reed was a gentleman of large wealth, and given to no such nonsense. Mr. Mount by no means so ridiculous a person as these statements would make him appear to be."

Mr. Jonathan Sturges, the late Mr. Reed's partner, is the judicious collector of a gallery of paintings for himself. Avoiding the "old master course," he at once struck into the encouragement of his townsmen and modern art. He commenced contrary to the general rule—and wisely so— and his collection embraces works of most of the known American Artists—and affords a fair index of the progress of American Art. He has three very fine works by Cole— " Catskill Mountains "—" Catskill Creek " and " View on the Thames "—"Faith " and a "Child's Devotion," by R. Weir. Ingham's " Flower Girl " and " Bertha "—remarkably fine works—the perfection, perhaps, of those qualities which gave that artist his high reputation. Edmonds' " Caught in the Act," and the " Bashful Cousin." Inman's " News Boy " — Durand's Landscapes of " Shakespeare's Church," " Alpine Scenery," " Valley of the Oberhalse." Copy of Titian—" In the Woods "—Huntington's " Italian Girl "—Gray's " Proserpine," and the " Young Poetess " — William S. Mount's " Farmers Nooning"—"one " of his " *good ones* "—" Ringing the Hog " — " An Axe to Grind " — Chapman's " Etruscan Girl "—Church's " Sunrise in the Cordilleras."

September 10. The Treasurer is ordered to purchase ten shares of bank-stock, as an investment for the National Academy of Design. The first amount funded by the Academy; probably so, by any art institution in the City. *Par excellence*—THE investment.

October 5. The schools opened for the season, under an admission fee of five dollars.

October 15. Mr. Cole made an exhibition of his " COURSE OF EMPIRE," the series executed for the late Luman Reed; originally a commission from that gentleman at twenty-five hundred dollars, but voluntarily augmented during the progress of the work to FIVE THOUSAND.

The exposition gave fame to the artist, but, strange to say, not pecuniary recompense; it did not pay its expenses. It was understood to have been Mr. Reed's intention to have had the works engraved in the first style of art, and, after the taking of a limited number of " proofs," the plates destroyed; thus enhancing the value of the impressions. Death put an end to the thought; and that which would have proved a monument to Cole's genius, and Mr. Reed's generous liberality, was left unaccomplished.

December 3. Died, Major-General Jacob Morton, Honorary Member of the Academy, in the 76th year of his age. That venerable gentleman was truly a man of the century. He was commissioned in the militia in 1786, and so continued, until the day of his death, fifty years. He was on duty and acted as one of the marshals of the day at the inauguration of General Washington, and served through the war of 1812 as a brigadier-general. In civil capacities, General Morton was a member of the Legislature from 1795 to 1797; afterwards, one of the associate judges of " the Court of Justices of the Peace" in the City of New-York, and Alderman of the City; subsequently, First Comptroller, City Inspector, and, finally, Clerk of the Common Council. It is in the latter capacity, and in the military of the City, that he is most generally known; and there are yet many who remember with pleasure his gray locks, venerable and urbane manners, and gentlemanly appearance. Perhaps to him, more than to any other, is due the enthusiastic reception of General Lafayette. On the announcement of his intended visit, the Common Council oft debated on the most suitable manner of receiving him, which debate was continued, and was undecided almost even until the day of his arrival—until the guest was at the door. In that state of the case, at one of the meetings, the veteran Morton arose and said, as he left the Council Chamber: " He," alluding to Lafayette, " is the NATION'S

GUEST; and if no one else will turn out to receive him, the First Division shall do it alone!" The words struck a chord. He was recalled, and action immediately had; all then joined in doing honor; and thus was obtained the enthusiastic *reception* in New-York—the key-note to the United States. The rest followed suit.

He was also the father of the Academy's Secretary, Jno. L. Morton, one of the institution's best friends; and shall it (in truth) be said, that while all other institutions in the City were rendering respect to the deceased, the Academy uttered not one word—passed not one resolution?

During the latter part of the year—the exact date not attainable—Died, Raphael Hoyle, Associate Member in 1829, and an Academician in 1831. Though young, he was an artist of merit in his department—landscape. He was of unassuming manners, and of a congenial disposition, and much beloved.

At the date of his death, he held an appointment as draughtsman to an exploring expedition; probably, that of Captain Wilkes.

January 30. The premiums for the schools were **1837.** determined upon and offered.

A gold palette for the best original design of a single figure (in *chiaro scuro*), "Epaminondas."

The large silver palette, for the best drawing in black and white chalks, from the "Venus Victrix."

The small silver palette for the best drawing of "Hudon's Anatomical Figure." In each case, the figure to be of not less than eighteen inches in height.

The galleries in Clinton Hall proving inadequate, even after the removal of the school-furniture, to the demand for exhibition-wall, it was resolved to prepare the "antique" room for exposition purposes, by a temporary or movable partition in front of the statues, shutter-like, with pivots to enter the floor, and a finished cornice binding the top; thus making an inner room, or small gallery, for water-colors and architectural drawings; leaving the statues encased within the temporary inclosure. It was successful, and saved the necessity of contemplating a removal for a time.

March 10. Of the students who entered for the Gold Palette, but two remained at the close of the contest; and the drawings were found not to come within the terms dictated. The premium was withheld.

The large Silver Palette was awarded to John J. Megarey, then a promising young artist; the small Silver Palette to E. Dunnell.

In the Spring of the year, the exact date unobtainable,

died John Blake White, of Charleston, S. C., an Honorary Member. He was originally intended for the law, and commenced that study. Afterwards he studied art under Benjamin West. That was changed again, and in 1804 he resumed his original profession, still continuing art practice as an amateur. He exhibited the "*Grave Robbers,*" and "*Marion Entertaining the British Officer.*" The latter was engraved.

March 17. Employment of President Morse by the artists to paint an Historical piece.

Congress passed a law (24th Congress, 1st Session, Resolution 8,) authorizing a Committee to contract with American artists for the execution of four paintings to fill the vacant panels in the Rotunda of the Capitol; and they were awarded to Vanderlyn, Chapman, Inman, and Weir—to cost twelve thousand dollars each, payable in two thousand dollar installments, if so desired by the artist.

Morse had long looked forward to such an awardment with solicitude, and was greatly disappointed at not receiving one of the commissions; the more so, as he had been the better part of his life preparing himself for the execution of such a work, and for which there were none, perhaps, better qualified.

The unfortunate result was, at the time, attributed to the enmity of John Quincy Adams—with what degree of truth, is unknown.

Be that as it may, the disappointment was great, and severely felt by Morse.

Artistic brotherhood sympathy was thought of.

The writer called a meeting of artists at his house, March 17th—suggested and arranged an Association for the purpose of raising funds, in $50 shares, for procuring Morse to paint an Historical Picture—the title, "A Joint Stock Association of Artists for procuring Morse to paint an Historical Picture." Certificates were immediately prepared, and subscribers solicited.

In a few days the writer had the satisfaction of the obtainment of such to the amount of five hundred dollars. John L. Morton, by his exertions, added another five hundred. The efforts of others in a short time increased that amount to two thousand dollars. At that point a great addition was at once made to the fund. A gentleman, *well known*, but who declined to have his name made public, subscribed *one thousand*—thus making a total of THREE THOUSAND DOLLARS; and Mr. ———, of Brooklyn, generously offered to contribute, free of charge, canvas, and all materials required in the execution of the work.

Thus armed, the writer and John L. Morton waited on Morse, and communicated the result—the first knowledge he had of the undertaking. The effect was electrical—it aroused him from his depression, and he exclaimed, "that never had he read or known of such an act of professional generosity;" and that he was fully determined to paint the picture—(his favorite subject, the signing of the first compact on board the Mayflower)—not of small size, as requested, but of the size of the panels in the Rotunda. That was immediately assented to by the Committee, thinking it possible that one or the other of the pictures so ordered might fail in execution—in which case it would afford favorable inducements to its substitution, and of course much to Mr. Morse's profit—as the artists from the first never contemplated taking possession of the picture so executed; it was to remain with Mr. Morse, and for his use and benefit.

Two or three installments were collected, and paid him, when his departure for Europe, in the furtherance of his TELEGRAPH, the success of which has "won him world-renowned reputation," caused a suspension of the painting, and delay was requested, and acceded to by the subscribers.

To THOMAS S. CUMMINGS, ESQ., *President and Treasurer of the Association for procuring* MR. MORSE *to paint an Historical Picture.*

DEAR SIR:—Circumstances relating to the Telegraph, invented by me in 1832, will require my attention for an indefinite time, and I am about to visit Europe, principally in reference to matters connected with this invention. At the same time, indeed, I have in view some studies connected with the Picture which the Association have commissioned me to paint for them. Yet, I ought not to conceal from the gentlemen who have so generously formed the Association, that circumstances may arise, in relation to the Telegraph, which may make it a paramount duty to myself and my country, to suspend, for a season, the commission with which they have honored me. In this state of suspense, I have to request that no further collections of the installments be made, until my return from Europe, in the Autumn, at which time, I shall doubtless have it in my power to acquaint you with the course which it may be thought advisable to pursue. If possible, I wish as soon as practicable to relieve myself of the cares of the Telegraph, that I may have my time to devote more strenuously than ever, to the execution of my Picture, and the benefit of the Academy, and of the Arts.

With sincere esteem, truly your friend and servant,
(Signed,)   SAMUEL F. B. MORSE.

NEW-YORK CITY UNIVERSITY, ⎱
    March 15th, 1838.   ⎰

A little later, and the complete absorbment of his mind and time in the Telegraph put an end to "THE PAINTING."

Mr. Morse finding he could not execute it, and wishing to relieve himself of the unpleasantness of the position in which he then stood, November 30, 1841, returned to the stockholders the amount in full subscribed, with interest; and canceled the obligation.

Thus, while the world won a belt of instantaneous communication, the subscribers lost the pleasure of his triumph as an artist. The Artist was absorbed by the Electrician; and there are none more rejoiced thereat than the writer.

April 21. The Twelfth Annual Exhibition was opened to the public, closing on the 4th July. The receipts were $4,587—sixty-four working days—averaging $71.50 per day. 304 productions.

May 3. The Annual Meeting of the Academicians.

The President reported:

GENTLEMEN—

I take great pleasure in congratulating you on the flourishing state of the Academy. Most of you are familiar with it from its birth; and you know the various trials and difficulties with which, in its infancy, it had to contend, until its youthful vigor now promises a healthy and useful maturity. * * * *

The gradual improvement of the Academy in its pecuniary affairs will appear from a comparison of the results of each successive Annual Exhibition, to be laid before you in a supplement to the report by the Treasurer. * * * *

The schools this year for drawing from the antique and living models have both been open. * * * * It has been thought advisable to continue the practice of requiring the sum of five dollars for the entrance-fee, for the reason that a privilege purchased is often considered by its purchaser more valuable, and therefore more likely to be used for his benefit than a privilege given. Some have supposed that the Treasury of the Academy derived a surplus from this fee. That this is erroneous, will appear from an estimate of the expenses of the schools submitted by the Treasurer. * * * *

I cannot too often repeat, that "union is strength." This has been our motto hitherto, and I hope will ever continue to be. Whatever difference of opinion may arise as to the best modes of administering the affairs of the Academy for the general good of the arts, I would fain hope that no Academician will ever carry his own predilection to such an extent as to endanger the Academy itself. The same spirit of submission to the will of the majority, which thus far has preserved our harmony, will carry the Academy safely through any evil which I am now able to anticipate.

In the prospect of an increasing surplus in the Treasury, it is very desirable that the views of all the Academicians should be concentrated upon one general plan. To effect this, it is only requisite to advert to the necessary wants of the Academy. We can never be truly an independent institution until we possess a building properly adapted to the purposes of an Academy, and wholly under our own control. * * * * This makes it imperative upon us to contemplate a building. In considering where we should build, we have to consult the effects of its location upon the Exhibitions of the Academy, which is the life-blood of our institution; and, in the construction of the building, not only the safety from fire, and other damage of the treasures of art, which will be necessarily under its roof, but also its prospective enlargement. The great aim, therefore, of the Academy should be, to prepare for a permanent location and construction of an Academic building.

The Treasurer reported the Academy as *entirely out of debt;* a surplus in the Treasury, the greater part of which has been invested to form a fund for the future use of the Academy, in the promotion of its welfare, as circumstances may dictate.

To the question frequently asked, " Do not the receipts from the Schools leave a large surplus in the Treasury, after defraying their expenses?" The answer is, No:
they ever were a cost to the Academy, which was as intended it should be.

The matter was given in detail in the report of the year,
and thus condenses—viz.: The total of attendance, gas, oil,
coal, &c., &c., $551.44; the receipts, $240; leaving a balance against the Academy of $311.44—without including
rent of rooms, or any permanent expenses.

The total receipts of the year were $4,198.66; total ex-
penditures, $3,004,99; investment, $1,000; balance, $193.67.

Samuel F. B. Morse was elected President; William
Dunlap, Vice-President; John L. Morton, Corresponding
Secretary; A. B. Durand, Recording Secretary; Thomas
S. Cummings, Treasurer; Thomas Cole and C. C. Ingham,
Members of Council.

There were no Academicians elected.

The month produced its events. Dunlap was directed
"to collate and publish the LAWS of the Academy," *for the
use and government of the members.*

A request was made to the *Common* Council to send Institution, members and all, to Bridewell, in plain ver-
nacular.

Application was made to the City Authorities for that
building, for the uses and purposes of the Academy. However deserving the members may have been of that distinction, they did not receive it. The request was not
granted.

June 6th. Morse and Dunlap were added to the Building Committee—then to consist of Morse, Dunlap, Cummings, and Morton—and were directed to apply to the Corporation of the City for a lease of that portion of the buildings fronting on Chambers Street, lately occupied by
"Scudder's Museum."

That was not granted.

November 1. The Life and Antique Schools opened for
the season.

In the latter part of 1837, or beginning of 1838, was established the "Apollo Gallery," afterwards known as "THE
AMERICAN ART UNION."

Its origin and originator are but imperfectly known, and
in course the credit not often correctly awarded. It is due
to Mr. James Herring, a highly respectable gentleman,
portrait painter, and publisher of the "National Portrait
Gallery of Distinguished Americans." He established the
"Apollo Gallery," and by his unaided efforts opened and

continued it for some time, the first exhibition consisting of works of modern artists. Mr. Herring kindly furnishes the following:

Notes on the Foundation of the Apollo Gallery, and the "Apollo Association," from my friend General Cummings.

The establishment of a permanent Gallery for the Exhibition and Sale of Paintings, Statuary and Engravings in the City of New-York, was contemplated by James Herring and John C. Chapman: the former a portrait painter of many years' standing, and Secretary of the old "American Academy;" the latter, a *universal* genius—a painter, engraver, modeler, &c.—at that time engaged on "The Baptism of Pocahontas," for the Government. Chapman's illness, his visit to Europe, and subsequent removal to Washington, broke up the arrangement. James Herring then ventured on the enterprise alone.

The Apollo Gallery, No. 410 Broadway, was filled with a very handsome collection of works of art, originals and copies, from every section of the country; mostly, for sale.

The financial embarrassments, which pervaded the whole country, prevented *sales;* and the projector was made the daily witness of the distress, and even, in some instances, destitution of artists of merit, whose works were upon the walls, followed by very natural importunities for temporary loans. His subscription library ("The ENTERPRISE LIBRARY"), of ten thousand volumes, his rare historical and scientific books, superb specimens of shells and minerals, on sale, were equally overlooked, but the expenses were unfailing and increasing.

At this time he received a report from "The Edinburgh Association for the Promotion of Fine Arts in Scotland," which had then successfully accomplished its second experimental year; and he adopted and drew up, on that model, a constitution for the institution, which was afterwards known throughout the Union as "The Apollo Association for the Promotion of the Fine Arts in the United States." After a consultation with those philanthropic friends of the arts, sciences and public education, Dr. John W. Francis, Joseph G. Cogswell, and a few others, a meeting was invited at the Apollo Gallery, on the 8th of January, 1839, by which the Association was put into working order. After that year, Mr. Herring could no longer sustain the expenses. The Association, however, energetically met the crisis, changed the name with the abandonment [of the location, and adopted the title of "The Art Union."

In 1839 the venerable Dr. Francis was installed President, and in 1840, its first anniversary, he delivered an address, which it is much regretted there is not space to admit.

The Apollo was not a success: it resuscitated, as "The American Art Union," after many severe trials; flourished, bore fruit, culminated, and in its turn died.

During a portion of its existence it had a widely extended sphere of action—was extensively known, controlled and distributed large sums of money, *as was said,* for the benefit of art and artists. It probably accomplished a portion of the objects aimed at, whatever may have been the final result.

There is no question but that it was established and maintained with the sincerest intent of doing good, and for which purpose many of the first citizens enrolled themselves and labored. That such was fully obtained, is questionable. The writer always held the opinion that art, to be successful, should be of natural, not artificial growth—should be let alone, like other trades, to be governed by the rules of supply and demand. If too highly stimulated, it necessarily finds a correspondent reaction. So it proved.

The Art Union congregated the art patronage into its own hands—it made the demand and furnished the supply; and, it was averred, had its favorites in the distribution of its favors.

It was said generally "to rule the artists"—they became jealous of its power, and thus neither the serving nor the intended to be served seemed satisfied.

It may, however, be remarked, that some were unreasonable, and especially so in the money matters, purchases, and payment. The purchases were frequently made with the full knowledge of both parties that they were "on time"—necessities of the seller frequently required money—money was to be found, but commanded a premium—necessity obtained it—the premium had to be paid—that was frequently complained of—and attributed to the management of the Society—where it really did not belong.

The Art Union had an influence not originally contemplated by the artists—not unlike capital in political economy—"inflation and contraction"—and correspondently controlled the regular flow of "trade"—art, it is supposed must be said. That was severely felt by those who relied wholly, or even partially, thereon for support. Its sudden stoppage was therefore highly disastrous, and seriously felt for several years—indeed, until the purchasing current returned to its proper and natural bed, from which it had been diverted. At the time, its downfall was attributed to distinguished Editorial hostility. Whether so or not, the writer had no means of knowing. Certain it was, that some offence had been given in that direction—not courted, perhaps—Editorial counsel not heeded. It was assailed as a LOTTERY, and a judgment obtained against it as "ILLEGAL." It was ridiculed by the reigning direction—but it proved but too correct a decision—higher courts confirmed it, and the American Art Union had to succumb. Its transactions would fill volumes, and it is not intended to give its history here, but merely to remind those not informed to whom they owe its origin.

It was honorably closed. The last remnant of its funds—proceeds of sale of its works of art—for which there were no claimants—were transposed to the uses and benefit of the New-York Gallery, then removed to the Historical Society, Second Avenue, where it is on exposition.

        January. The Schools had been open during the **1838.** Fall, and well attended. More applied than room could be found for.

The close of the season was the 19th March.

The premiums offered were—

The Gold Palette for the best original design of a single figure of "Epaminondas"—of not less than 18 inches in height.

The large Silver Palette for the best drawing in black and white chalks of the Apollo Belvideref—of similar size.

The small Silver Palette for the best drawing, as above, of Hudon's "Anatomical."

February 2. A special meeting was called for the purpose of taking into consideration the publication of a periodical to be devoted to the advancement of the Fine Arts. To contain fine "original" etchings from the best American pictures, effusions of American poets and prose writers, and particularly so of the members of the "Sketch Club."

A plan was given, and divided into 14 articles each, with numerous sections; and a Committee was appointed to offer the prospectus and obtain subscriptions—three dollars per annum. That ended the matter. It was never after heard of; and it is much to be regretted, as the talent promised in its support was very great, and little doubt could be entertained as to its success, either as an art journal, or pecuniary recompense.

March 20. The Council alone decided on the drawings offered for the premiums, and awarded as follows:

The Gold Palette to William H. Jewitt.

The large Silver Palette to Thomas H. Stevenson.

The small Silver Palette to Jeremiah Nims.

April 23. The Thirteenth Annual Exhibition opened to the public, closing 7th of July. The receipts were $4,699.23 —68 working days—averaging $69.10 per day—337 works displayed.

May 2. The Annual Meeting of the Academicians.

The President reported:

The tendency among our young artists is to premature and false facility; in reality, the apology both of indolence and ignorance: a fault which, more than all others, has well-nigh ruined the English School, and which it behooves us to eradicate from our own in the early stages of its existence. Something of the Continental schools of art, in the elementary branch, might with advantage be introduced into our own Antique School, while the bestowing too much time on one elementary branch, which experience has shown to be connected with the academic systems of Europe, are properly guarded against. It is therefore thought it will be, for us, the best policy to appropriate a proper sum for the payment of the nightly attendance and services of a competent person.

The Treasurer will present you with his Annual Report, by which you will perceive that our income is on the increase. Our funded capital drawing interest is already $3300. The Exhibition this year is more numerous in works of art, by more than thirty pictures, than that of any former year. When we look back, as most of us can, to the total receipts of our first Exhibition, and find that we now receive, in two days, as much as we then received in three months, the contrast is striking, and the result in the highest degree gratifying. We must not forget, that it is by the exercise of mutual forbearance and a conciliatory disposition that any association can concentrate its energies and maintain a healthy corporate existence. I do not mean, that differences of opinion may not exist and be controverted; but it is the manner in which this is done that mainly affects the harmony of a society. And may I not point to your own experience, for a proof that the disposition of the heart, more than any extraordinary exercise of talent, has been the salt that has preserved us ?

I am about to leave you, perhaps for a few months, but, considering the uncertainty of human affairs, it is by no means impossible that I now address you for the last time; and I therefore most earnestly enjoin upon you to let no differences ever alienate you from each other. If, in the warmth of discussion, or in the moment of forgetfulness, words should escape which our cooler moments condemn, learn the luxury of a frank confession. It is human to err; but, remember, it is Godlike to forgive.

* * * * * * * *

You will not, I hope, consider these remarks out of place. Hitherto, adversity and the necessity of common defence have united us. We have now PROSPERITY to try us, which, all experience shows, requires more moral courage to bear than adversity.

* * * * * * * *

The state of our funds is such as very rationally to make us fix our minds upon some plan of building, either permanently or temporarily, with others. The City Library is about to build, and, in conversation, we have been led to believe that such arrangements might be made with them.

* * * * * * * *

I have the pleasure of presenting to you this evening the books of the Academy, the accounts and minutes regularly made up to the present time under the care and diligence of the Treasurer and the Recording Secretary respectively.

The Report of the Treasurer showed that the total receipts for the year had been $5,195.07, and the payments $5,102.44—balance, $93.92; and that in the above, $2,300 was an investment, $519.90 the expenses of the Schools.

There had previously been an investment of $1,000.

Samuel F. B. Morse was elected President; Henry Inman, Vice-President, (Wm. Dunlap declined); John L. Morton, Corresponding Secretary; James Whitehorne, Recording Secretary; Thomas S. Cummings, Treasurer; James Frothingham and Henry C. Shumway, Members of Council.

Morse, on the eve of his departure for Europe, and Dunlap, retiring by ill health, were both requested to sit for their portraits. Dunlap did so, and the Academy possess one of the best likenesses of him ever painted—faithful beyond description—one of Ingham's finest specimens. Unfortunately, Morse did *not* comply, and the likeness, therefore, is less vivid.

An article was directed to be prepared for publication, setting forth the condition of the Institution, and views of the "FOUNDERS"—"To aid in the future government of the Institution." A rather singular article, certainly. It was not done—at least is not to be found.

May 8 marks an era in the Academy—viz., the formation of an Art Library, for the use of its members.

The President was commissioned to make purchases while abroad for the empty cases already decorating the Council-Room.

24th. The Building Committee reported an engagement with the Society Library for the upper floor of their proposed building on the corner of Broadway and Leonard Street. That was deemed extremely venturesome—extra hazardous—too high up town—too high up stairs—too everything wrong—"*risky,*" in fact. Yet it was taken. The accommodations were doubled in extent—the rent so in amount. The rooms were to be received in the rough, and would require from four to five thousand dollars properly to finish and furnish them—which would more than exhaust the Treasury—and nothing could exceed the fears with which the proceeding was received.

Cummings and Agate were the Committee to prepare them for use.

The largest Exhibition receipts ever taken were taken in that building. The rooms were handsomely proportioned, imposing in appearance, beautifully decorated, and not difficult of access. The stairs grand and easy, and the whole building one of excellent fitness.

June 16. Died, Hugh Swinton Ball, of South Carolina; a lover of the Arts, and an Honorary Member.

It is not often that the full-grown oak and the acorn from which it sprung are permitted to be seen by the same person. The following, the writer thinks, however, is an instance:

MORSE'S ELECTRIC TELEGRAPH.

Professor Morse requests the honor of Thomas S. Cummings, Esq., and family's company in the Geological Cabinet of the University, Washington Square, to witness the operation of the Electro-Magnetic Telegraph, at a private exhibition of it to a few friends, previous to its leaving the City for Washington.

The apparatus will be prepared precisely at 12 o'clock, on Wednesday, 24th inst.

The time being limited, punctuality is specially requested.

NEW-YORK UNIVERSITY, *June* 22, 1838.

An early message on the wire was given the writer, which is yet in his possession. It is in cipher. The words are (said to be—" Attention the universe—By kingdoms—Right wheel—Facetiously"—given by Morse on the writer's having just received military promotion to the command of a Division.

At a special meeting, sixty copies of Dunlap's History of New-York was subscribed for, and immediate payment of $300 ordered. A highly worthy and meritorious cause, no doubt, but certainly not within the objects of the Institution. It was objected to, but approved at a subsequent meeting—silencing all opposition.

November. "A number of the friends of the artist and of art—Hon. Gulian C. Verplanck, Hon. Aaron Clark, Philip Hone, Thomas Cole, Dr. Francis, General Lloyd, General Cummings, John J. Morgan, Daniel Kingsland, W. C. Bryant, C. C. Ingham, A. B. Durand, and some thirty others "—formed themselves into a Committee for the purpose of making an exhibition of Dunlap's and other works of art, the proceeds to aid him "in completing" his " History of the State of New-York."

Fostered and advanced by the members of the Committee and others, the Exhibition proved in a measure a success, and contributed somewhat towards the object, though not to so great an amount as was anticipated; for a meeting was called to receive a report, and to extend the time of its continuance :

☞ THE DUNLAP GALLERY—WEDNESDAY EVENING —STUYVESANT INSTITUTE. —At a meeting of the majority of the owners of Paintings now on Exhibition at the Stuyvesant Institute, for the benefit of Mr. Dunlap, and to enable him to complete his valuable " History of the State of New-York," a report was received from which it appeared, that owing to the expense of the Exhibition, and the low price of admission, only two hundred and nine dollars have as yet been realized towards the objects of the Exhibition. Whereupon, it was, on motion of Mr. Van Schaick,

Resolved, That after the close of the present season (which expires on Saturday evening, the 15th inst.), the Exhibition be continued for four weeks longer, with the addition of such cabinet pictures as have been already tendered to the Committee, and that our fellow-citizens be invited to contribute such choice modern paintings as may enrich the collection.

GULIAN C. VERPLANCK, *Chairman.*
D. KINGSLAND, Jr., *Secretary.*

It was so continued, and the pecuniary result was much improved.

The Exhibition was held in the then SUBURBS OF THE CITY, in a large room of the " *Medical College*," since more readily known as " Stuyvesant Institute."

November 12. The Schools were opened free of charge,

and VISITORS were declared *non-admissible*—a measure deemed absolutely requisite to the preservation of the means of study—the opposite having become ruinously impeding.

On the 20th of March the premiums were awarded.

The first premium, 2nd Class, to C. H. Thomas.

The second to Jeremiah Nims.

The second of the 3rd Class to W. Creighton.

January. A special request was made to appoint a Committee to take into consideration the alterations
1839. necessary to be made in the By-Laws of the Institution. It was appointed—Cummings (Chairman), Ingham, Durand, Whitehorne, Shumway, and Morton; and they were directed to examine and report such changes as, in their opinion, the exigencies of the times and the wants of the Institution required. A long report was made, a subsequent meeting held, and many changes suggested.

January 14. Died, John Wesley Jarvis. Mr. Jarvis was not a member of the Academy—he was, however, one of the best portrait painters of his day—eccentric, witty, convivial—and his society much sought by the social. He died in extreme poverty, under the roof of his sister, Mrs. Childs.

April. The Fourteenth Annual Exhibition opened to the members on the 23d inst., inaugurated by a supper, in the best style of Messrs. Hodges' art, to the public on the 24th. It closed July 6. Open 64 working days. Receipts $3,944.40—averaging $61.63 per day—296 productions.

The Exhibition was one of interest, and the public much pleased; but nothing—not even the supper—appeared to appease the wrath of *Middle-Tint*. Perhaps he had none of it.

NATIONAL ACADEMY—THE TEE-TOTAL DEPRAVITY SCHOOL OF PAINTING.—
It is most amusing to see the fever into which " Mr. Henry Inman, portrait painter, President of the National Academy, and brother of the sub-editor of the 'Commercial Advertiser' " (as he not unfrequently subscribes himself), lashes himself about the independent criticisms that have lately appeared in several of the city papers, relative to many of the miserable daubs now exhibiting at Clinton Hall. Mr. Inman has thrown down the pencil, which he uses with very moderate ability, and taken up the pen which he uses with no ability at all.

*   *   *   *   *   *   *   *   *

There is a clique in the Academy, at the head of whom is Henry Inman, Charles Ingham, Cummings and Durand; and this clique at present control the entire institution. The fact is, they are afraid of rivalry, knowing that if they allow honorable competition, they must go down. Durand is one of those men, of mediocre talent, that dabble in everything, and consequently excel in nothing; no greater proof of the truth of this can be given than by referring to the miserable head of Joe Hoxie, painted by him to produce a sensation, which is the best thing he ever painted, and which is no more like to Hoxie than it is to the artist. He has a sort of Caleb Quotem talent—

" Plumber, glazier, auctioneer—
In short, he is factotum."

Cummings never aspired to anything greater than portrait painting—the very lowest grade of the art—and in these he caricatures humanity most abominably. Ingham will go down to posterity as the painter of "The Great Adirondack Pass," and the laughing child with the cat-fish face, both now in the Exhibition. Mr. Henry Inman will not be remembered as a painter; for, in our opinion, his portraits are the most perishable things we ever saw; * * * * all his work will peel off the canvas in less than ten years, and leave no trace of a single feature. Nor are we singular in this opinion; for it is entertained by the best artists in the city. It is a style of painting to get a living by, and turn a quick penny, and was adopted by the pot-boilers in London, to enable them to buy a dinner; they painted against time, as Sheridan wrote against it, for his daily shoulder of mutton. And this is the clique—the leaders of the tee-total depravity school of painting—that at present control the National Academy of the city.

The history of their present elevation is a curious one: previous to the opening of the institution this season, the clique met in solemn conclave and resolved upon a juggle to elect Henry Inman President, and by trickery to put Mr. Morse out of the chair; they also bound themselves solemnly never to elect another Academician; no matter what his talents, or how eminent his productions, no more members were to be elected; the black balls of these four men could effect this, and faithfully have they stuck to their text. The dinner within the walls of the Academy was like the orgies of some miserable politicians we have heretofore chronicled, and many persons left the place disgusted. It was here that the consummation was given to their contemptible design of creating a monopoly; it was here that the leaders of the tee-total-depravity school elected themselves censors of painting, of the press, of wine, of anything and everything.

The Council were called on to give an opinion on the originality and merits of a work of an old master, then on exhibition, which was declined. "That, as a body, they had uniformly refused to give any such endorsements."

Mr. Morse declined, on the ground that "he had reason to believe his opinion, if favorably given, would be of no service, and probably positively injurious to him in Boston, where the picture was going." So the gentleman went without either.

May 8. The Annual Meeting was held. A report was made by the Council, which, as it embodied little else than details of the yearly proceedings, is not of sufficient general interest to require insertion.

The Treasurer reported the total yearly receipts, $5,170.86; total payments during same time, $5,170.86.

Samuel F. B. Morse was elected President; Henry Inman, Vice-President; John L. Morton, Corresponding Secretary; James Whitehorne, Recording Secretary; Thomas S. Cummings, Treasurer; William Page and Frederick S. Agate, Council.

There were no Academicians elected.

October 3. Death took one of the oldest and most faithful adherents—a beloved member; an original founder of the Institution, an artist of ability, a writer well known to fame—William Dunlap, Academician. He departed this life September 28th.

Was Vice-President in 1831. An historical painter of merit. His "Christ before Pilate," the "Bearing of the Cross," the "Crucifixion," and others of similar character, attest his merit in that department. They were exhibited throughout the country, and proved, in their day, a support to the artist.

Resolutions of condolence were sent to the family, and crape worn.

The Summer vacation probably prevented the official passage of the resolutions until the date given.

October 9. For the purpose of promoting "social intercourse among artists," QUARTERLY meetings were instituted, and held. Simple refreshments were directed to be served, and they were for some time agreeable, and well attended.

Like most of such schemes, it lasted but a short time; the novelty exhausted, the attendance fell off. It dragged, lingered, and died.

October 30. The Schools opened successfully. The attendance throughout the season was good. Four premiums were awarded: two in the "Life"—two in the "Antique."

In November an exhibition was opened by Alexander Vattemare, founder of the "International Literary Exchanges."

Mr. Vattemare was a remarkable man—of an active, untiring spirit in *Literary Exchanges*—the main pursuit of his life. Had his plans been carried out, they would probably have produced highly favorable results.

He supported himself while pursuing his favorite object by exhibiting his powers as a ventriloquist, and the receipts derived from that source were immediately invested in the former.

His National Album; his collection of sketches from artists of almost every nation in the civilized world; his autographs from thousands of celebrities, and from every crowned head who had ever written; medals of every nation and period, constituted his exhibition, for which the Academy gave the use of its rooms. It was at once historic and instructive, and one of the most remarkable ever presented in the city.

It appealed principally to the contemplative—to the scholar. It was therefore, as might have been expected, *unsuccessful* in a pecuniary point of view. The receipts were but $140; though Mr. Vattemare lost nothing—the Academy carried the difference.

Several medals and prints have since been received from

that gentleman, showing that he still carries on the "International Literary Exchanges."

Mr. Vattemare's visit is remembered with pleasure. On his leaving, the artists generally contributed to his "National Album"—the writer, a view of the Hamilton and Burr dueling-ground. In the last interview had with him, in company with Bryant, he was imbedded six feet deep in newspapers—packing and forwarding to France, copies of every publication in the United States. Quite an extensive undertaking. He is since deceased.

On the conclusion of his exhibition, the following correspondence took place:

To M. Alexander Vattemare:

Sir—I have been requested, by a unanimous vote of the Council, to express to you the thanks of the National Academy of Design for the generous offer and loan to them of your superb and unique collection of drawings and paintings by the collected talent of European artists, for the philanthropic purpose of creating a fund for procuring an annual medal, to be awarded by the Academy in promoting the arts.

In performing the gratifying duty in behalf of the Academy, I beg leave to say that the extent of our obligation to you is not measured by the degree of success with which the public have rewarded our efforts. Instead of producing a sum for the purpose proposed, the Exhibition has abstracted a sum from our Treasury; but although your noble intentions have been frustrated in the principal object, the instruction and the gratification which the artists and amateurs of this City have received from the study of your rich collection (emanations from some of Europe's most gifted minds) have amply repaid the Academy for any expense or labor to which they may have been subjected.

Wishing you every success in your philanthropic labors to promote literature, science and art, I remain, sir, with the highest consideration,

Your obedient servant,

S. F. B. MORSE, P. N. A.

Daguerre.—The extension of the daguerreotype—"singularly termed the marvelous process of drawing"—and the many varieties which have sprung from it, broadcast throughout the land, makes anything connected with its introduction a matter of interest. The following letter gives its presentment; and from its peculiar phraseology, is preferable to anything that might be given in its place.

Could Daguerre's pupil see the beautiful specimens which now adorn the galleries of such establishments as Brady, Gurney, Fredericks, and others, and compare them with the feeble specimens he brought with him, he might well be astonished.

Thomas S. Cummings:

> Dear Sir—As the friend and pupil of Mr. Daguerre, I came from Paris by the British Queen, with the charge of introducing to the New World the perfect knowledge of *the marvelous process of drawing*, which fame has already made known to you under the name of "The Daguerreotype." Having the good fortune to possess a collection of the finest proofs which have yet been made, either by the most talented pupils of Mr. Daguerre or by that great artist himself, I have thought it my duty, before showing them to the public, to give the most eminent men and distinguished artists of this City the satisfaction of having the first view of perhaps the most interesting object which has ever been exposed to the curiosity of a man of taste; and therefore, if agreeable to you, I shall have the honor of receiving you on Wednesday next, the 4th December, from the hour of 11 o'clock to 1 o'clock, inclusive, at the Hotel François, No. 57 Broadway, where this invitation will admit you.
>
>   I remain, sir, your most obedient servant,
>
>   François Pamsel.
>
> New-York, 29th of Nov., 1839.

The students of the Life and Antique Schools derived great benefit from the discourses of Dr. Watts on Anatomy. The Schools had been well attended, and premiums had been offered for the best drawing from the living figure, and from the "Antique."

The successful competitor for the first was Jeremiah Nims, and the second best, S. S. Fanshaw.

The first premium, Third Class, best drawing from the full-length figure, "Antique," was awarded to W. Jay Bolton. The second to F. E. Jones.

"They were delivered on the 16th of March, with appropriate remarks." The drawings, as a compliment to their authors, were ordered to be framed, and exhibited in the Council-Room, for ONE *year*.

W. J. Bennett, an English artist of merit, had a few years back been appointed "Keeper," and, as such, had charge of the Schools. Although an artist of considerable and varied ability, he was found entirely unsuited to the charge, and it became necessary to remove him. Frederick S. Agate was appointed in his place; an equally unfelicitous appointment, but from a very different cause—too much amiability.

The removal of Mr. Bennett brought forth a display of his natural disposition—selfishness—which self-interest had caused for time to be dormant. He had no sooner been removed than he put in a claim for a thousand dollars, stating "*that squeamishness and false shame*" had been the causes of his not having sooner called for his salary. It was well understood that he accepted the rooms he occupied as compensation as Keeper. Yet suprising as it may seem, the Academicians awarded him two hundred and fifty dollars in settlement of his claim, which he accepted.

January 14th. At the "Quarterly Assembly" was inaugurated the " *Costume Department.*" Mr. Ingham
1840. presented a suit of *olden times*, as a nucleus for the
undertaking. It was at *once* in ideal an extensive
"wardrobe." The costumes were to be loaned to members, to the great encouragement, as it was thought, of historic composition. It was, however, uncalled for; few additions were made. The work of the moths proved, *if
anything*, in advance of the supply of material, and the
wardrobe disappeared. It deserved, and, properly attended
to, would have had a better fate. The idea was a good
one. It required care in its use, and strict attention in its
care, neither of which it had.

April 27th. Was opened the Fifteenth Annual Exhibition, with a *reception* prior to its public exposition. It
closed on the 8th of July—the receipts $3,239. Sixty-three
working-days, and averaged $51.41 per day; 307 produc-
tions.

May 13th. The Annual Meeting was held.

The Council respectfully report:

They are happy in being still able to present you favorable accounts of its
condition. The state of the finances you will learn from the Report of the
Treasurer, by which you will perceive that, notwithstanding the difficulties
and embarrassments which have palsied the energies of the community at
large, it is a matter of thoughtfulness and congratulation that we are comparatively exempt from the troubles which have depressed our fellow-citizens;
still, it will be perceived that our expenses have increased, while our income
has temporarily diminished. The appropriations for the quarterly and annual suppers have added an item which will probably be an annual drain to
the treasury; an expenditure, however, for an object which, if kept within
its proper sphere, is worthy of the sacrifice. Every project that tends to the
harmony and social intercourse of the artists is worthy of the special adoption and fostering care of the Academy.

During the past winter the Building Committee, after encountering many
obstacles in the negotiation of conditions, have at length succeeded in settling the terms of the lease of the new rooms. The lease is duly executed by
both parties, and is herewith presented to you. It is proposed to take possession the present Summer, and have them arranged immediately for the offices
and schools of the Academy. The expenses of the removal of our property,
and arranging the apartments in a style suitable to the existing state of the
Academy, will be great—so great as to probably nearly exhaust our treasury; yet it is believed that our surplus funds cannot at present be better
applied than in preparing new attractions for our Exhibitions, and greater
facilities in our schools to our students, better accommodations for our social
meetings and general improvement.

The Treasurer reported. Receipts and expenditures of
the fiscal year, $5,798.28. There was no balance left in
the Treasury.

Samuel F. B. Morse was elected President; Henry Inman, Vice-President; John L. Morton, Corresponding Secretary; James Whitehorne, Recording Secretary; Thomas

S. Cummings, Treasurer; Andrew Richardson, Robert E. Launitz, Council.

Daniel Huntington, Edward Mooney, and T. W. Edmonds were elected Academicians.

July 1. A project was announced to unite the Apollo Association with the National Academy of Design—or the N. A. Design with it—"and Union"—and on July 6th the following was adopted:

"WHEREAS, The President has communicated to the Council that he has had an interview with several members of the Committee of Arrangements of the Apollo Association, in which interview it was mutually agreed that the general interest of the Fine Arts, which both institutions were formed to promote, would be more surely promoted by a harmonious action of the two, each in their separate sphere; and that, for the purpose of producing this harmonious action, it is desirable that a clear understanding of each other's views and plans should be ascertained: Therefore,

"*Resolved*, That a Committee be appointed to confer with a Committee of the Apollo Association, to ascertain the wishes of said Association, and to communicate those of the Academy, to devise a plan which shall not only prevent collision between the two institutions, but one which shall be promotive of mutual benefit, and report the same to the Council at as early a date as possible."

Messrs. Cummings and Page were appointed, who, with the President, composed the Committee.

July 13. Pleasing and gratifying courtesies pass between the AMERICAN INSTITUTE and the ACADEMY. The Institute offer the gold medal for the best design for a DIPLOMA, and requested the Academy to name two members, who, in connection with Martin E. Thompson, Academician and member of Institute, should be a Committee to decide on the designs. Messrs. Cummings and Ingham were appointed.

July 20. A statue of Minerva was presented by the. Academy to the "MERCANTILE LIBRARY," and Messrs. Morse and Cummings made Honorary Members of that Association.

REPORT.

Your Committee, to confer with a Committee on the part of the Apollo Association, report:

That the two Committees met, and on free discussion of the objects of the respective Societies, learned the views of the Apollo Association to be:

First. To hold frequent Exhibitions of the works of the artists of the country.

Second. To select from such Exhibitions, according to the amount of funds at their disposal, and to purchase for distribution by LOT occasionally, for the formation of a PERMANENT gallery.

Every subscriber to the Association to pay five dollars. For this he obtains free admission for himself and family to the Exhibitions, also a chance of acquiring one or more of the works selected for distribution.

The purchase of works to be confined to their own EXHIBITION.

"That the Association are desirous of obtaining the use of our rooms for *their Exhibitions.*"

It appeared to your Committee that the general objects of the Apollo Association are in the highest degree laudable. That in place of being antagonistic, its general objects come in aid of those of the Academy. That with a single exception, there is not the appearance of collision in the institutions, or their operation.

The exception demanded attention. It relates to the exclusiveness in the selection of works for distribution, &c.

We represented to the Committee the danger we apprehended from this source—inducing artists, in their necessity, to give their works to the Apollo Exhibition, instead of the Academy. Thus vitally destroying our Exhibitions, which are the life-blood—the source of the whole support of our Academic system.

With the frankness and liberality to be expected from such gentlemen, they acknowledged this tendency, and said that in the NEW Constitution which they were about to frame, that objectionable feature should be removed.

The adoption of such will put the Academy on equal footing, and take away all possible objection to the plan of the Apollo Association—indeed, it does more—puts the Association in a position to command our cordial co-operation; and your Committee, therefore, respectfully submit whether it is not now in the power of the Academy to give a proof of the estimation in which they hold the efforts of the Association to aid in the promotion of the Fine Arts in the United States.

They are now in search of accommodation for their FALL EXHIBITION. They are desirous of obtaining our NEW rooms in Broadway.

These, unfortunately, are not ready, but our rooms in Clinton Hall can doubtless be vacated in season to accommodate them. It is therefore submitted that the Academy offer the use of the rooms in Clinton Hall, rent free, for the remainder of their lease.

In further approval by the Academy of the plan of the Apollo Association, the Committee recommend that after our next Annual Exhibition, that such portions of the new rooms in Broadway as are not wanted for the schools and the offices of the Academy, shall be loaned annually, *rent free*, to the Association, to be occupied by them for the purposes set forth in their Charter—which loan shall be subject only to the renewal each year by the Academy, assembled at its Annual Meeting.

Free admission of the members of the "Apollo" to the Exhibitions of the Academy was under discussion. It was thought that the interests of our Exhibitions would not suffer if admission was extended to the members of the Association, on such easy terms as should furnish those solicited to subscribe additional inducement to do so. This part of the subject was, however, postponed for future consideration.

In conclusion, the Committee would express the high gratification they have had in the conference with the Committee of the Association, in perceiving the disposition to adjust their plan of operation, as not only not to interfere with those of the Academy, but, on the contrary, to unite with it in promoting the great interests of the Arts in the country—an object at which both profess to aim. Your Committee felt that they would have done injustice to the Academy, had they not met the liberal disposition of the Association by the same spirit.

SAM'L F. B. MORSE.
THOMAS S. CUMMINGS.
WILLIAM PAGE.

The writer seriously objected to the manner and matter of the Report, but was overruled.

August 13. R. E. Launitz offered a plan for the encouragement of Historical Composition by "premiums," which, after almost unceasing importunities, was adopted—viz. :

MR. LAUNITZ'S SCHEME.

In order to promote more effectually the advancement of the higher branches of the art of painting—to foster an honorable emulation among the younger artists, and also to secure the future prosperity of this Institution—

Resolved, That the Academy grant a premium of $100 for the first best, and another premium of $50 for the second best Historical Painting, on a subject to be determined by the Council.

Resolved, That the Council adopt the following Regulations for the carrying out of the foregoing:

Regulation 1.   All artists, except Academicians of this or any other Academy, to be allowed to concur.

Reg. 2.   All paintings for competition shall be sent to the Academy on or before the last day of ———, free of expense.

Reg. 3.   All paintings represented shall be arranged by themselves.

Reg. 4.   Premiums to be decided two weeks before the close of the Annual Exhibition of the Academy, by the Council, at a special meeting called for that purpose.

Reg. 5.   The sketch of the painting receiving the premium shall be presented, to become the property of the Academy.

Reg. 6.   No picture will be received unless a written declaration shall accompany it, stating that it is in for competition, and that the same is the *bona fide* composition and execution of the artist so presenting it.

Rule 7.   If none of the pictures should, in the opinion of the Council, possess sufficient merit to be entitled to the premium, the Council may, in their discretion, withhold it.

September 14.   Messrs. Launitz and Whitehorne were appointed a Committee to select A SUBJECT, to report at the next meeting of the Council—the pictures to be not more than 8, nor less than 7 square feet each—who reported:

Your Committee have given the business intrusted to them their careful consideration, and in coming to their conclusions, they have been guided by the following principles: As the subject was to be from American History, it should have reference to transactions between the "first lords of the soil" and its present rulers, possessing not only a higher interest, but giving also to artists a wider scope to exhibit their knowledge of the beauties of the human form, and an acquaintance with the manners, customs, character and history of the Aborigines of their native soil—the grandeur of whose original wild and lofty scenery should also not be excluded.   Your Committee is also of opinion that the subject should be one of matter-of-fact history, (not fiction,) representing both races in their predominant character.   The hate of the Indian for the white man, and the conscious strength and superiority, with the advantage of civilization, of the latter, relying on these for his protection; and the maintaining and enlarging of his foothold in the country. No subject has presented itself to your Committee in which these could be more interestingly exhibited than in the following—(from Thatcher's "Lives of the Indians," Vol. I., pp. 181, Harpers' Family Library Edition.)

Canonicus, Chief of the Narragansett tribe, sent a herald to Plymouth, who left a bundle of arrows inclosed in a rattlesnake's skin—the customary challenge to war.

The Governor dispatched a messenger in return, leaving the same skin, stuffed with gunpowder and bullets, in return—assuring the chieftain that if he had shipping, instead of troubling him to come to Plymouth to gratify his wish for fighting, he would have sought him in his own country; and furthermore, that whenever he did come, he should find that the English were ready for him.   This resolute message had the desired effect, and the Sachem's superstition confirmed it.   Fearful of some mysterious injury, he refused to touch the skin, and would not suffer it even to remain in his house.   It passed through several hands, and at length was returned to the Colony unopened.

Your Committee think that the above anecdote possesses an unlimited stock for the power of invention of an artist. It may be represented with only a few figures, while it allows of an introduction of hundreds.

The preparation of war of the Red Man—the barbing of arrows—the sharpening of tomahawks—which is stayed by the appearance of the English messenger.

Again, the anxious curiosity of the untutored son of the forest—the surprise and fear of the Sachem—the secret exultation of the messenger at seeing the effect he had produced—these, and the contrast of costume of the Indian and the English of the early part of the 17th century, afford material for a composition of interest. It may be objected, that this is a subject but little known. Your Committee would with deference reply,.that they deem it the business and duty of the Historical painter to snatch from oblivion, and transmit to posterity, facts in history that have not already been recorded by other hands, or made familiar to the mass of mankind.

All of which is respectfully submitted, by

ROBERT E. LAUNITZ,
JAMES WHITEHORNE.

Which report was accepted and adopted.

The paintings submitted were one by an amateur, W. J. Bolton, a pupil of Morse, and at Mr. Morse's express solicitation—a highly meritorious picture—another for which fifty dollars, the second premium, would have been an over-valuation, and which amount it did not bring on sale, with all the Academic endorsement. The third was so badly executed it could not possibly be permitted on the walls ; it was beneath contempt. The scheme proved a ridiculous failure—hastily adopted and permanently regretted—the originator as much, or even more disgusted than any one; and the Council, from that time forward, were free from solicitations to offer premiums for historic compositions. The award was made at a special meeting held on the 21st of June—the first to W. J. Bolton, the second to D. O. Browere, who, after the *rejected picture*, were the only competitors.

The system of premiums seems never to have found favor in the American community, whatever may have been the result elsewhere. Years ago the Fire Department offered one thousand dollars for designs for an "admission" and "discharge certificate." The result was unfavorable ; there was an abandonment brought about by " the want of merit." The work was given to Henry Inman, who designed those in use. Many years back the students of Columbia College made similar efforts for a commencement ticket, with like results ; and lastly, the Art Union tried the system, with the like or equal disappointment.

It is a matter of interest to trace the after course in life of some of those who made art their early profession. W. J. Bolton has become a clergyman in the Episcopal Church in England, and enjoys high distinction. Jared B.

Flagg, Academician, an Episcopal clergyman in Brooklyn.

September 14. Mr. Cummings pressed his resolutions to purchase for each of the Academicians a share in the New-York Society Library, in lieu of establishing a library in the institution, with its necessary expenses, believing it more advantageous to the members and less expensive to the Academy; it was lost. It is, perhaps, much to be regretted ; the advantages would have been with the members.

October 5. The rooms of the Academy in Clinton Hall, previously vacated by them, were loaned to the Apollo during the residue of the Academy's lease, free of expense. Singular generosity for one institution to pay another institution's, and that their opponent's, expenses ! A mistake occurred in naming 1841, in place of 1840, as the expiration of said lease, and the Academy graciously offered to pay the year's rent, from '40 to '41, to make good their error. That, however, was refused. Very agreeable and courteous resolutions were passed and repassed on the occasion ; the Academy, however, paid some three hundred dollars for that part of the term during which the Apollo occupied.

Extravagance again in the Academy. The floors in Clinton Hall had been painted and stenciled, and were handsome; yet the *noise* of walking on the bare floors in the exhibition rooms had become offensive to increasingly sensitive wealthy citizens' ears ; carpets were in demand, and ordered for the whole of the galleries, and they have of course, like every other luxury, ever since maintained their post, no longer luxuries—actual necessities, indispensables.

Mr. Cole occupied one of the rooms of the Academy, for the purpose of examining and completing, under that more favorable light, his series of the " Voyage of Life."

" A special quarterly meeting was ordered to be held for the purpose of promoting social intercourse, punctuality in attendance, and cordiality when assembled"—matters especially desirable, doubtless, yet doubtful if to be cultivated by legislation. Oysters and champagne were ordered to be procured for the occasion—much more likely to produce the desired result. It was a success for the time, though the writer has ever doubted the advantages of any such stimuli.

November 16. The Antique and Life Schools were opened—the first entries, Edwin White, Thomas A. Cummings, Charles Weir—names familiar.

A speck of war on the horizon. Matters in the Apollo

did not appear to be working quite so well as was anticipated; a conference again called for, and Morse and Cummings, the greater portion of the previous Committee, were sent on that errand, and instructions given to confine themselves to the consideration of such plans alone as shall be based on the principle of the discontinuance, on the part of the Apollo Association, of exhibiting any works of modern artists, not previously exhibited by the National Academy of Design—any other arrangement being deemed a vital interference with the interests of the Academy, and cannot, on that account, be entertained by this Board."

A memoranda left by the Committee of the Apollo Association with the Committee of the Academy had been read, to which Mr. Morse prepared a reply, which was not read in committee until about a quarter of an hour before the conference. On its reading, the writer objected to all commencing and after ("if then an association is subsequently formed"), as irrelevant, advisory and uncalled for. There was no time to alter it; the members of the Apollo had come in, even during the conversation. When read, one of that committee immediately rose and objected to all commencing from the same point and following.

The meeting abruptly terminated.

The report of the Academy Committee was as follows:

The Academy of Design has been in operation for fifteen years. One of the distinguishing features the following rule, which has ever been considered as fundamental, to wit—"WORKS OF LIVING ARTISTS only, and such as have never BEFORE BEEN EXHIBITED BY THE ACADEMY, will be received at the Annual Exhibition." To this was added the exclusion of *copies*—all must be original. This adopted on the well-understood principle that novelty is attractive; and it has been adhered to amidst much discouragement. The principal difficulty encountered at first was that arising from the habits induced in the community by the opposite system long in use in the American Academy. It was not until after many years that the public were impressed with the fact that each Annual Exhibition was composed of an entirely new set of works. When this was understood, the soundness of the principle upon which it was based was shown by the anticipation and inquiries expressed before each Annual Exhibition, and the eagerness with which the public thronged the rooms on its opening. We consider the experiment successful. The plan has operated well, and we have therefore no desire of change. On the Exhibition the Academy is vitally connected—its very existence. We have no stockholders—no subscribers to create a fund for our use; our sole revenue is the Exhibition. By that we defray all our expenses.

All the funds are expended for the advancement of Art. The officers, with the single exception of Keeper, perform their duties without salary. The schools have been a cost to the Academy of upwards of $5,000. Each student of the Antique School a yearly cost of $12.50, and each student of the Life School at an annual expense of $40. The encouragement given to our Exhibition has thus far enabled us not merely to defray the annually increasing expenses of our extending plan, but has given us the means, for several years past, of investing each year a liberal sum in the public funds for the purpose of gradually extending our means of usefulness, and of making the

National Academy what it has from the first professed to be—a truly public and National Institution.

*   *   *   *   *   *   *

Having shown the nature of the connection between the Annual Exhibition of the Academy and all its other plans of operation, it will not appear strange that the guardians of its interests should scrutinize with some concern anything that is likely to affect the Exhibition favorably or unfavorably.

It will be observed that from the beginning the Academy has confined itself to a very limited class of works of Art—to wit: to original works of living artists never before exhibited by the Academy. It will be seen that the large class of *copies* from fine works of art, the large class of works from *deceased artists*, the annually increasing class of works once exhibited are by our laws excluded from our Exhibition.

These are left for others to use as they may deem expedient. We have no interference with them on that account.

If, then, an Association is subsequently formed, professing to promote the Arts, and with an Exhibition system, might we not expect that justice to us would lead them so to adjust their Exhibition system as to avoid interference with our previously established system? Interference would occur if the Association thus formed should adopt our plan of Exhibition, in whole or in part. If it selected for exhibition such works as come not in our plan, there is no interference; even more—there would be a positive gain to the Arts by such a system; for it would cultivate a field upon which we do not profess to enter.

The only circumstances in which such Association could, with any public advantage, select the same class of works for exhibition, is either when these works shall have so multiplied that a single Exhibition will not fairly contain them all, or when mismanagement on the part of the Academy shall be so manifest that the proper encouragement of the Arts requires the opposite. We presume that the latter exigency will not at present be pretended. Have, then, the annual productions of our artists so multiplied that our Annual Exhibition will not contain them? Our experience on this point is conclusive to us. From 250 to 300 new works are the natural production of the year; our walls have been filled, and we have not included more than two or three works for many years. We have now in our new rooms an increased surface of wall to cover our Annual Exhibition, with the accommodations now at our command, will, we think, contain all the new works that are produced for exhibition within the year. Another Exhibition that should take the same class of works for exhibition must diminish the interest of the Exhibition, and consequently injure the Academy in all its interests.

The more these Exhibitions are multiplied during the year, the feebler will be each Exhibition, and in the end must break down the system. This reasoning applies to the present state of the Arts in this city: when artists and their works are so multiplied that an exhibition will not contain their annual product, then other Exhibitions will naturally be called for. This, then, is the state of the case. The principal and previous point to settle is that when the Apollo Association has adopted a plan which interferes with that of the Academy.

The opportunity for stating the subject of interference to the Association, sought our aid in procuring the use of our rooms. The points of interference were alluded to, and briefly but informally commented on, in conversation, between members of the Academy and the Association.

To manifest the disposition of the Academy towards the Apollo Association, whose exigencies require immediate action. The Academy waived for the time being the formal discussion of the subject of interference, and in the mean time gave the use of their late rooms in the Clinton Hall to the Association gratuitously. The opportunity of conferring on the subject having at length arrived, by the appointment on each side of a Committee for that purpose, and having given our views of the matter, may we not expect from the Association a removal entirely of the ground of interference, caused by their adoption of a plan of Exhibition which the Academy conceives to affect vitally its interests? Will, then, the Apollo Association so modify its Exhibition system as to remove entirely all interference with our previously established exhibition system? Will they confine their Exhibitions to those works, vastly more numerous, excluded by our laws from our Exhibition, and leave us the exclusive exhibition of the works of living artists never before exhibited in the City of New-York? Is not this a reasonable request? We think it should be granted, as a matter of common justice; it would scarcely be complimentary to the sense of right in the Association to offer privileges for a simple act of justice. This act, then, would put us on eligible ground for the reciprocation of favors.

S. F. B. MORSE,
Chairman of the Committee of Conference.

In the course of a few days the following resolution of the Committee. of Management of the Apollo Association was received and ordered to be inserted in the minutes of the proceedings of the Council:

Resolved, That the Chairman of this Committee be requested to communicate to the President of the National Academy of Design, that it is inexpedient to continue further negotiations in regard to arrangement between the two institutions, on the basis submitted in the communication by the President of said Academy.

That ended the matter.

January 4. The drawing for the premiums commenced.

The gold palette was not offered. The large silver **1841.** palette—the "FIRST" premium in the third class—for the best drawing from Thorwalsden's Venus; the small silver palette the second premium, third class, for the best drawing from the "Anatomical Full-Length" by Houdon.

An effort was made to secure to mechanics "a COPYRIGHT for their *ornamental designs*," in furniture and manufactures. Morse and Cummings were appointed to confer with the Mechanics' Society, and to endeavor to awaken an interest on the subject. It was without success. A petition from the artists and mechanics was submitted to Congress, but it met with no response.

January 18. Died, Henry S. Mount, Associate.

Resolutions of condolence with the friends of the deceased were passed, and the usual badge of mourning ordered to be worn. He, in his department, sign painting, stood deservedly *high*, and many of his works might have justly received a far better place than they met with "on the outer walls."

January 25th. A resolution was passed for the purpose of disseminating a knowledge of the arts of design to the mechanic and artisan, and the privilege was granted to the

Mechanics' Institute to send any three of their pupils to the Academy schools, of which they never availed themselves.

The premiums of the season were awarded:

The first—the large silver palette—to A. Seeley; the second—the small silver palette—to I. S. Pierson.

March 29. Died, Frederick W. Philip, Associate, an artist of promise. Resolutions of condolence were offered, and the usual mourning was worn in his memory.

April 7. The Academy was called on to participate in the funeral solemnities of President Harrison. They assembled under their leaders, and entered the procession on that occasion. The day was one of extreme severity.

April 9. Another effort, and a final one, on a "UNION" of the "TWO ACADEMIES."

APRIL 9th, 1841.

To T. S. CUMMINGS:

Dear Sir—At a meeting of the members of the Academy of Fine Arts, at the New-York Society Library Rooms, on the 7th inst., Mr. David Colden, Mr. T. Cummings, and myself, were appointed a Committee to collect information of the debts of the Academy, of the compromises the creditors may be willing to make, and if any agreement can be made with the National Academy of Design to take the property and assume the debts.

Although long a member of the Academy of Fine Arts, I know but little of its affairs. It is not so, I have reason to think, with yourself and Mr. Colden. When you and he have done all that can be done in reference to the matters referred to the Committee, I think a meeting of the members should be called to consider the report which we may be then prepared to make.

Yours,

JOHN L. MORGAN.

May 3. The Sixteenth Annual Exhibition opened in the new galleries on the corner of Leonard Street and Broadway.

The exposition surface was increased to over four hundred feet, that was fully covered by three hundred and sixty-six works of art; the rooms, which were far superior to anything ever before presented, gave an effect that was truly gratifying to the artist and visitor. Closing July 5th; receipts $4902; fifty-five working days, averaging $89 per day.

May 10th. The Annual Meeting. The report of the Council contained nothing beyond the details of removal and fitting the new galleries. The Treasurer reported the yearly receipts $8762.69, the expenditures $8748.69, leaving a balance of $14 in the treasury.

Samuel F. B. Morse was elected President; Henry Inman, Vice-President; John L. Morton, Corresponding Secretary;

J. Whitehorne, Recording Secretary; Thomas S. Cummings, Treasurer; Cornelius C. Verbryck, Academician.

At the meeting a slight testimonial was awarded to the ever-present *Mrs. Croker*, for "faithful services," who, though but officiating as door-keeper to the Exhibitions, has been so long at her post that she has become an Academic "fixture"—"an Institution." Still on duty—not quite so young as once, or so active, yet still as inflexible in the discharge of her vocation.

July 14. Dubœuf's large painting of Haidee and Don Juan, the Princess of Capua, and several other fine works, were exhibited in the Academy rooms. In a pecuniary point of view it was unsuccessful, though a highly attractive and beautiful display of art.

October 4. Financial troubles. The Commercial Bank had been made the depository for the National Academy of Design funds, probably from its central position and convenience, the Academy possessing few to execute its errands. Afterwards it proved to have been not the best selection; the Bank stopped payment.

REPORT.

The Treasurer regrets that he is called upon to report that the funds of the Academy which had been retained for the purpose of defraying the expenses of the Institution, deposited in the Commercial Bank, had become unavailable—an injunction having been placed on that institution by the Chancellor.

That he had taken immediate steps to make himself acquainted with all the particulars in relation to the matter within his power. That he had called on the Commissioners, and from them had received the assurance that NO ULTIMATE LOSS would be sustained; that the assets of the Bank were amply sufficient to more than meet its debts; and further, that in the event of its not proving so, that the State Safety Fund was liable, and would make good the deficiency.

He therefore refers with pleasure to these assurances, and requests the order of the Board.

T. S. CUMMINGS, *Treasurer.*

It was referred back to the Treasurer, " to do his best." The promises held out, of future reimbursement, were REALIZED. No ultimate loss was sustained, though the locking up of the Academy funds for some two years, and receiving it only by installments, was a serious inconvenience.

It is a fact worthy of notice, that in the many money pressures, or commercial revolutions, through which the institution has passed, and particularly that memorable panic of "thirty-six," that it has not in any instance lost one cent.

October 15. The Life and Antique schools were opened, the attendance " good," and the improvement of the pupils highly spoken of. Premiums appear to have been offered as usual; *singularly*, no notice of such is recorded. They were silver palettes only, and were awarded—one to Benjamin F. Childs, the other to Thomas Augustus Cummings, son of the writer.

October —. Died, Jeremiah Nims, Associate. The precise date is unobtainable.

Resolutions of condolence were passed and forwarded to the relatives of the deceased, and the usual badge of mourning worn.

October 5. A bust of Morse was ordered; it was placed in the Council chamber, and yet remains a reminder of the artist. An admirable likeness.

November 1. Thomas Cole exhibited many of his works—the Voyage of Life; a figure piece; " His Angels," a large landscape, and some smaller works. The Exhibition did not prove attractive or remunerative, and was not of long continuance. It is worthy of inquiry, whether an artist can be his own best exhibiter. The writer would say NO. In such cases the artist appears under great disadvantage. " Third parties" can do for him what he cannot, with " modesty," do himself, or even if done, with the same effect.

November 21, was enacted the last act in the drama of the American Academy of Fine Arts *vs.* the National Academy of Design. The property belonging to the first was brought to the hammer by sheriff's sale, to satisfy a judgment obtained by the heirs of Dr. Hosack, for rent due. The Treasurer was a committee to purchase, and did so for the sum of four hundred dollars; there were few persons present—no bidders save the National. The auctioneer's " Going—going—for four hundred dollars—going! going!! GONE!!!"—the only sounds that disturbed silence. Their reverberation the only response.

Alas poor *American!*

The galleries of the Academy were given to the American, in which to make sale of their remaining stock, much of which had been damaged by fire. It was singular how much valuable property, belonging to that institution, escaped its custody—Leslie's copy of the Gate of Calais. " The Roast Beef of Old England," after Hogarth, was purchased by a boy, at an auction, for a few shillings, who afterwards disposed of it for a few dollars to Rich'd B. Fosdick; both purchaser and seller highly delighted with the transaction, though not then knowing its value or author. A superb fruit piece was likewise sold for a trifle at the same auction, but it cannot be similarly traced.

January 17. A union with the Apollo Association again brought forward by Mr. F. W. Edmonds, Academi-

1842. cian, and member in both institutions, who had at all times been desirous that a harmonious course of action should be maintained, and who now intimated "that alterations and modifications in the constitution of the Apollo should be made, of such a nature as to prevent all interference with the Academy, and as the rooms occupied by the Apollo were about to be given up, and that they might not be without *a place to meet ;* "whereupon the use of the Council Room was immediately tendered to them for that purpose."

March —. Died, William Gracie, Honorary Member, a merchant of the city, and an amateur noticeable in early art history in the city, and the possessor of several fine works.

April 27. The seventeenth Annual Exhibition was opened to the public, remaining so until the ninth of July, sixty-four working days. The receipts were $3949, averaging $61 70 per day ; works exhibited, three hundred and fifty-seven.

May 11. The *Annual Meeting* of the Academy was opened by Mr. Morse remarking :

" According to custom, I have the gratification of laying before you the Annual Report, and proofs of your continued prosperity.

" In the course of the last winter two events of deep interest to the Academy have occurred. The American Academy of Fine Arts, for so many years the obstacle to our progress, has ceased to exist ; and we have purchased, and have in our possession, the casts from the Antique, which were owned by it. The other event which interests us, is the modification of the plans of the Apollo Association, by the present board of management, so as not to interfere with our exhibition system.

" It will be perceived that in our present rooms we are necessarily at more expense than we were at Clinton Hall, while the receipts of exhibitions have not increased in the same proportion. Many expenses to which we have been subjected, are of a nature not to be repeated, and we hope that in future (at least for some years), we may, with proper economy, be enabled again to find a surplus for future operations. The present year we thought it expedient to omit our "ANNUAL SUPPER," in consequence of the demands upon the treasury. * * * * * * * *

" Thus, gentlemen, we are now free, for the first time, from any associated opposition. It remains for us to show the public that we can maintain our union after the external pressure (which, it may be, has, to some extent, kept us together) is removed."

TREASURER'S REPORT.

To the Academicians of the N. A. D.:

In presenting this, the seventeenth Annual Report, I cannot but call the attention of the body to the greatly increasing expenditure of the Institution, amounting the past year to within a very little of the total receipts of the last and most successful Exhibition, and which in all probability may be looked upon as the maximum receipts for some years to come, and greatly exceeding, so far as can be judged, the probable receipts of the present Exhibition.

This is worthy to be reflected on. I would impress on the Academicians the necessity of endeavoring to lay up some portion of the receipts, to provide against periods of great embarrassment, which may naturally be expected, more or less, to exert an influence on the Institution.

So sensible am I of this, that, under advice, I have reduced as far as practicable all expenditures, and omitted everything capable of being dispensed with without injury to the interests of the Institution.

*   *   *   *   *   *   *

Another and more effectual relief may be had by letting of the galleries during the periods they are not wanted by the Academy.

*   *   *   *   *   *

The stoppage of the Commercial Bank should be a useful lesson, and cause the Academy to look, in their investments, for SECURITY, rather than profit. The Treasurer is therefore induced to recommend the sale of the Bank Stock owned by them on the first suitable opportunity, and that future investments be made only on bond and mortgage, or such other security as may be deemed equally permanent and trustworthy.

THOMAS S. CUMMINGS.

Samuel F. B. Morse was elected President; Henry Inman, Vice-President; John L. Morton, Corresponding Secretary; James Whitehorne, Recording Secretary; Thomas S. Cummings, Treasurer; Asher B. Durand and Edward Mooney, Members of Council; Henry Peters Gray and Shepard A. Mount, Academicians.

The Treasurer's Report verified. The receipts dwindled down to twenty-five hundred dollars, showing the necessity for a fund, to prevent the barque occasionally running aground. It would scarcely be necessary to dwell on such, to business minds; yet some there are, of the Academic body, who think a SURPLUS a POSITIVE INJURY—an INCUBUS on art and the institution. As for the writer, HE is not of that opinion; he thinks it a very comforting auxiliary, and would much rather they should have than be without it.

From summer until October no minutes—no doings of the Academy recorded.

November 1. The schools opened for the season, and about the same time several amendments were offered, and added, to the *Constitution and By-Laws.*

November 17th. Died, George Washington Lee, an Honorary Member of the Academy—one of its earliest friends.

April 10. An official application was made by the Apollo Association, "to append to the Academy's Catalogue **1843.** a statement of the design and prospects of the Apollo Association, and to make some convenient arrangements by which SUBSCRIPTIONS might be received in the rooms of the Academy." Another committee was appointed to confer with the Apollo Association, with what result the author is unable to say; nothing appears on the records.

April 27. Opened the eighteenth Annual Exhibition, closing July 4th, sixty working days, and received $4631, making a daily average of $77 20; three hundred and eighty-seven works.

May 10. The Annual Meeting of the Academicians was held. President Morse reporting: "It may not be uninteresting to remark, before closing, that the Apollo Association, whose form, early in its organization, threatened a serious interference with our exhibitions, has been so modified that the Academy and the Association now mutually aid each other."

Nothing of further interest in the report; the Treasurer's yearly receipts, $4532 60; the disbursements, $4041 78; balance in the treasury, $490 82.

Samuel F. B. Morse was elected President; Henry Inman, Vice-President; John L. Morton, Corresponding Secretary; James Whitehorne, Recording Secretary; Thomas S. Cummings, Treasurer; and James H. Shegogue, an Academician.

July 12. Death again entered the ranks. A special meeting called. Washington Allston died on the ninth instant.

The President, in a very feeling manner, communicated the event to the Council, which was received with a deep and solemn feeling seldom witnessed. The following were unanimously passed:

Resolved, That in the death of Washington Allston we acknowledge the hand of a mysterious but just Providence, who, in his wisdom, has by this event deprived the Arts of Design of one of their most brilliant ornaments, and the profession of one of the richest sources of instruction.

Resolved, That we hold in the highest veneration the noble traits which distinguished the deceased, and which were manifested uniformly in his professional, social, and Christian character, and commend him as one of the loftiest examples for the imitation of all artists.

Resolved, That as an expression of our deep sympathy with the relatives and more immediate friends of the deceased, we will wear the usual mark of mourning, crape on the left arm, for thirty days.

Resolved, That a Committee be appointed to wait on the Honorable Gulian C. Verplanck, and invite him, at as early a period as his convenience will permit, to prepare and deliver before the Academy a eulogy on the distinguished deceased.

Resolved, That a Committee be appointed to inquire if there be any good likeness of Allston; and if so, to report at the next meeting of what kind, and the cost of procuring a bust in marble of the same for the Academy. Messrs. Edmonds, Gray, and Chapman were appointed the said Committee.

Resolved, That the President be requested to transmit a copy of these resolutions to the widow of the deceased, and that they be published.

A bust by Cleavenger was procured for the Academy.

During the fall was exhibited Weir's picture, painted for the Government and Capitol; the scene a group of part of the congregation of John Robinson on the deck of the Speedwell, at the moment of embarkation—the GERM of the republic.

On the completion of Mr. Weir's picture a story obtained circulation, extensively copied throughout the country, that Mr. Weir had devoted the WHOLE of the proceeds arising from the execution of his work to the erection of a chapel at West Point.

That Mr. Weir contradicted, stating that while he took a most lively and Christian interest in the erection, he did no more than a number of other gentlemen—contribute towards it. The story circulators did not so readily submit to contradiction, nor would they spoil a good article, and it long continued to be repeated.

October 16. John R. Smith applied to be appointed a *Professor* in the Academy—that, too, in an institution which he had so much abused. The institution had become a success, and "success makes the man." So John R. Smith seemed to think; but the Council had no such power. Messrs. Cummings and Agate, both his former pupils, with Mr. John G. Chapman, were appointed a committee to report on the merits of his "Perspective-exemplifying apparatus," which he desired to be submitted to the Academy. Three months' use of the room was given to him for its trial. There was no "exemplification." That was probably not the object in view. There was of course no report of the Committee.

October 30. The Life and Antique Schools opened, and an effort was made by the Mechanics' Institute to establish a Polytechnic Exhibition, and the co-operation of the Academy was solicited. Cummings and Chapman were appointed delegates to a convention; nothing, however, grew out of the effort.

November 13. Departed this life, the venerable Colonel Trumbull, aged eighty-seven years—an artist and a gentleman. Whatever differences of opinion may have existed as to his policy as President of the old American Academy—however he may have proved deficient in his estimate of the rising generation of artists in his day—there is no doubt he acted in the full belief in the wisdom of his views. If fault there were, the fault was doubtless in his education. He was of the old school; his courtesy and urbanity of manner were worthy of imitation; his want of heartfeltness for the professional was severely felt by the youngest artist. On the 14th Mr. Morse communicated the fact to the Council, as follows:

DEATH OF TRUMBULL.

Scarcely four months have elapsed since you were convened to receive the sad intelligence of the decease of the most distinguished of American painters, the noble and well-beloved Allston; and now it is my melancholy duty once more to convene you, to announce to you the death of Colonel John Trumbull, another artist, whose name and works are amongst the earliest associations of our childhood, and whose fame is interwoven, not merely with the history of the arts of design, but also with the political history of the country. Although not enrolled as a member of this Academy, yet I believe I express your sentiments, gentlemen, when I assert that we render a sincere, willing homage to the character of Trumbull, as one of the brightest ornaments of his country in the arts of design. On numerous paintings connected with our Revolutionary history, Colonel Trumbull's fame as an artist may securely rest. But my duty before you has not been completed in announcing the loss of the venerable Trumbull. Death has been busy in our ranks; and, even before the call for this meeting, it is announced in the public journals that the young and gifted Clevenger has also departed. Trumbull descends to the grave in the fullness of age and of fame; but Clevenger is cut down in the morning of life, and the flower of his fame is blighted in the bud.

"THE ARTISTS' SKETCHING CLUB."

January 2. At a social meeting of artists, consisting of Messrs. Chapman, Ingham, Cummings, Durand, 1844. Gray, Morton, Edmonds, Agate, &c., it was proposed to organize a "Sketching Club," and Mr. Cummings was called to the chair; whereupon the meeting organized, proceeded to declare that there should be an association, and that the same should be known as the *"Artists' Sketching Club."*

Thus was formed one of the most agreeable and instructive little clubs that ever took share in art matters in the city. its members were: Chapman, Ingham, Cummings, Durand, Gray, Morton, Edmonds, Agate, Cole, Mount, Cassilear, Shegogue, Baker, Prud'homme, Jones, Gignoux. The meetings were held once a week in the Council Room of the Academy, the use of which was given for that purpose.

At the designated hour the company sat down to work—everything ready but the "subject," which was to that moment unknown. "It was then given." The sketchers were allowed *precisely* ONE HOUR to make their drawing, and at the termination of that the bell rung. The works were all gathered up by the gentleman who gave the subject, whose property they were to be. At the end of the season the sketches were all exhibited, and then distributed to their proper owners. Pleasant and agreeable as it was, the Club lasted but two or three years.

The first subjects drawn from by the record are stated to be "Too Late," "Charity," "Too Soon," "Just in Time," "Surprise," "Hard Case, "Catastrophe," "Trying Hour," &c. It may not be confounded with the New-York Sketch Club, of more recent date, nor with the OLD Sketch Club, which preceded it many years. It was of the middle age, and stands alone in its short-lived glory.

December, 1843, to March, 1844. Was exhibiting, in the galleries, Cole's duplicates of his Voyage of Life, his rapidly painted "Mount Ætna," "Past and Present"—two of his most beautiful productions—and a number of his other works.

It would appear a little singular, in regard to the two series, "The Course of Empire" and "The Voyage of Life," that Mr. Reed, who gave the commission for the first, died shortly after its completion—Mr. Ward, who ordered the second, shortly after its commencement.

The Exhibition was not pecuniarily successful; it did not pay its expenses, and the "*rent*" was remitted, or canceled by the Academy, on account of "an unpropitious Exhibition."

As before stated, the original Voyage of Life was painted to the order of the late Samuel Ward, Esq. On the settlement of his estate it became the property of the American Art Union, and was one of the offered prizes of the year. The subscription list was said to have been increased by it, from less than eight hundred to more than *sixteen thousand!* and it was estimated that something like half a million of visitors attend the free exhibition of the gallery, of which it formed so important a part; and yet withal the writer cannot but think that the purchase of that and other very valuable prizes had much to do with the downfall of that Institution. It was too much to be continued, and led seriously reflecting minds to question their own motives in subscribing, and probably drove some away, which certainly contributed to the *inquiry* of its being a LOTTERY, which afterwards proved so disastrous.

In December of 1847 or 1848 the series was distributed, and fell by lot to a Mr. J. F. Bredt, of Binghamton, from whom they were purchased by the Rev. Goram D. Abbott, and placed in the gallery of the Spingler Institute, his splendid school, then in the building on the corner of Thirty-fourth Street and Fifth Avenue. The gallery of that, one of the first educational institutes in the country for young ladies, was free, and formed a distinctive feature of attraction in the establishment. The little gallery was rich in other works of art.

The series by J. B. Stearns—" Four Great Periods in the Life of Washington, as Soldier, Statesman, Farmer, and the Christian in Death"—paintings of great merit. The last—the death-bed scene—extraordinary in feeling and treatment; should the writer's judgment be of value, he would place it amongst the very foremost in the American school of art.

In the face of the physician, in that work, the writer fancies he can discover the lineaments of the beloved Francis, and has no doubt it was the type—a delicate compliment, and deserved. In the Braddock's Defeat, the face of the colonial officer supporting the dying and baffled Braddock, can be readily recognized as a "STERN" *portrait* of the painter. That is not without authority. The wounded young dying officer occupying the foreground in Trumbull's Sortie of Gibraltar, is a portrait of Sir Thomas Lawrence, who was said to have been one of the handsomest young men of his day, and the portrait warrants the reputation.

The copies of the old works which graced the walls are :

The Transfiguration of Raphael; The Madonna di Foligno; Domenichino's Sibyl, from the original in the Borghese Palace; Guido's famous Aurora, from the fresco in the Rospizlioso Palace; The Annunciation, by Guido, the original of which is in the Quirinal Palace; A copy of the Madonna by Murillo, from the one in the Corsini Palace; An original painting of Judith with the head of Holofernes, by Houthrost.

Variable New-York ! The beautiful building on the corner of Thirty-fourth Street and Fifth Avenue has been removed—TORN DOWN—probably to make room for a still more magnificent one—and Dr. Abbott's Young Ladies' Collegiate Institute has been removed to the corner of Park Avenue and Thirty-ninth Street.

January 21. The following extraordinary resolution was passed:

> *Resolved,* That in consideration of THE KNOWN benefits to the Arts of Design from the present course pursued by the Apollo Association, the National Academy of Design present to them for distribution among their subscribers three hundred season tickets for the Exhibition of 1844.

Admission to the Academy Exhibition was asked for, to add an additional inducement to persons to subscribe to the Apollo Association, and it was so given by a season ticket of admission; thus adding fifty cents on each subscriber of five dollars, and probably so much loss to the Academy. Did the Academy receive any thanks even for it? On the contrary, in the following yearly report their constituents were informed "that they had made arrangements by which the subscribers to the Apollo Association would be admitted to the Exhibition of the National Academy of Design." Not a word in reference to the donation.

March 13. A special meeting was called, and the following resolution in reference to a Permanent Gallery was passed:

> *Resolved,* That the Council of the National Academy of Design, believing that the proposed establishment of a Permanent Gallery of paintings and other works of art in New-York is an object greatly to be desired, as leading to promote the Arts of Design, and willing to aid the effort to establish such an institution, as far as the means within their power may allow, and understanding one of the difficulties presented, to be the want of a suitable place for their safe keeping and exhibition—do hereby tender temporarily the use of their large Exhibition Room for that purpose, until other arrangements can be made for their disposition.
>
> *Provided,* The net proceeds or profits that may arise from such exhibition be converted to no other purpose than the establishment of a Permanent Gallery in the city; and further, by such occupation of said room for the purposes of the National Academy of Design, be in no manner interfered with.

From whence that application came, or to whom to be given, does not appear in the Minutes. By a resolution of a similar import passed in May next following, it is seen to be for the "Society" forming for the purposes of establishing a Permanent Gallery of Fine Arts in the City of New-York, and which afterwards became the "New-York Gallery of Fine Arts." It was for the Luman Reed Collection, and it was on exhibition six months. It was ultimately purchased on a truly democratic principle, of a ONE DOLLAR SUBSCRIPTION.

> The following are the conditions on which the Association is to be formed:
> 1. The Gallery shall be commenced by the purchase of the Reed Collection of Paintings.

2. The property of the Association shall be vested in a Board of Trustees, who shall have power to adopt a Constitution, to appoint officers, Executive and other Committees, and prescribe their powers and duties; to fill vacancies in their own body; to preserve, enlarge, and exhibit the Gallery; to procure suitable premises for the exhibition; to obtain a Charter, and in general to manage and transact all the affairs of the Association.

3. The Trustees shall have no power either to create any debt or liability on behalf of the Association, or to sell, exchange, or lend any of its property, or to do or suffer anything by which any of the same can in any way be encumbered.

4. The property of the Association shall be fully insured.

5. The exhibition of the Gallery shall be opened, as soon as possible, in a central situation.

6. The Trustees shall give special attention to the works of American Artists, and to the formation of a collection of casts from celebrated statues.

7. Every person paying one dollar shall become a member of the Association, and shall receive a Certificate of membership, which will entitle him to free admission to the Gallery for life, subject to such regulations as shall be adopted by the Board of Trustees.

8. Certificates of membership shall not be transferable, but the rights conveyed by them shall attach solely to the person named therein.

9. The following gentlemen shall be the first Board of Trustees:

William H. Appleton, Horatio Allen, John H. Austin, James Brown, Wm. C. Bryant, Wm. B. Crosby, Thomas S. Cummings, William S. Conely, Stephen M. Chester, Peter Cooper, J. A. Clark, Orville Dewey, Charles Denison, Frederick De Peyster, Nicholas Dean, Francis W. Edmonds, Robert Elder, Thomas H. Faile, Walter C. Green, George Grundy, Richard Irvin, William H. Johnson, Wm. Kent, James G. King, Shepherd Knapp, Charles M. Leupp, R. E. Lockwood, Jos. N. Lord, Charles E. Minor, William B. Minturn, Henry S. Mulligan, Stewart C. Marsh, Hamilton Murray, James McCullough, Lora Nash, Alfred Pell, Eleazer Parmly, J. Smyth Rogers, Peter A. Schermerhorn, Jonathan Sturges, William L. Stone, Benjamin D. Silliman, Francis Skiddy, Charles A. Stetson, Moses Taylor, Thomas Tileston, James Warren, Jr., Fredcrick A. Wolcott, John Wiley, Jacob A. Westervelt.

It was not incorporated until 1845.

March 24. Died, Chevalier Albert Thorwalsden, Honorary Member, a truly distinguished sculptor, the only one enjoying the reputation of "approaching" the "Antique"—the "august" standard. Why not at once say equaling it? He deserved it.

April 15. Died in Boston, G. Bullfinch, aged eighty-one years, a distinguished architect, of Washington City, and an Honorary Member.

April 25. The nineteenth Annual Exhibition was opened to the public, preceded by a reception, on *invitation* by the Council ONLY. It continued open until the sixth of July. The receipts were $4964 86; open sixty-four working days, averaging $77 58 per day; contained three hundred and eighty-seven works.

April 28. Died, James Devaux, Honorary Member, a young artist of great promise, then in Rome, a Southerner by birth—a student of the late Henry Inman.

May 6. At the Annual Meeting of the Academicians Mr. Cummings announced the

DEATH OF F. S. AGATE, ESQ., N. A.

GENTLEMEN OF THE ACADEMY—It is my sad province to announce to you that, in addition to the usual business of the Annual Meeting, we have a melancholy duty to perform. I allude to the recent death of our lamented friend and fellow-Academician, Frederick S. Agate. To his excellent qualities as a member of the Institution, we can as a body bear ample witness. To his virtues as a man, and the uniform kindly deportment which characterized his intercourse with us, we can all individually bear truthful testimony. I would suggest that a suitable record be made of our regret at his loss, together with an expression of condolence and sympathy with his relatives and friends.

Resolutions were passed and forwarded to the family of the deceased, and the usual mourning was worn for thirty days.

A very beautiful tribute was offered up and published by his friend and brother artist, F. W. Edmonds—a chaste biography, and a polished production, which it is much regretted there is not room to insert. It may be found in the " *New-York Knickerbocker,*" of August 1st, 1844. The following is from a brief notice published by the writer in the papers of the day:

OBITUARY.

It is with most sincere regret that we are called to the painful task of noticing the demise of our much esteemed and talented fellow-citizen, Frederick S. Agate, who departed this life on Wednesday last, May 1st, at the residence of his brother-in-law, Mr. Carmichael.

Mr. Agate was born in the year 1807, in the village of Sparta, and at an early age evinced a genius and propensity for the Fine Arts; and at the solicitation of Mr. Rollinson, the engraver, he located in the City of New-York when about thirty years of age, and commenced the study of portrait painting, and in a few years, by hard study and industry, placed himself in the first rank of his profession. In historical painting and composition, Mr. Agate also possessed talent of the highest order, as may be seen by his "Dead Child and Mother," "Columbus and the Egg," "The Samaritan," "The "Ascension," and "Count Ugoleno"—most of which have been engraved for the Annuals.   *   *   *   *   *

He went to Italy in 1835, where his intense application to his studies seriously impaired his health, from which, however, he had apparently recovered, when, about three months since, he was attacked by his fatal complaint. Mr. Agate was equally esteemed for his amiability and Christian virtues, and to this circumstance we may mainly attribute the fact that he was never known to have an enemy. He is cut off in the prime of life, with glowing prospects before him had he lived. But he was prepared for the change of worlds, and left this with happy assurances of a glorious immortality in the next.

The Academicians proceeded to the transaction of their yearly business, previous to which Mr. Inman addressed the meeting, declining a re-election to his present office, or any other in the Academy, and assured the members that "he should always be proud of the title of National Academician, in whatever country he should spend the remainder of his days."

A vote of thanks was tendered Mr. Inman for his past services, and in like manner to John L. Morton, who declined re-election, and who had faithfully served the institution some eighteen years.

The Treasurer reported the total receipts at $5544 63, the payments $5208 72, the balance $334 91.

Samuel F. B. Morse was elected President; A. B. Durand, Vice-President; James Frothingham, Corresponding Secretary, "who consented to serve, provided the office was abolished as soon as a meeting could be convened for that purpose;" James G. Chapman, Recording Secretary; Thos. S. Cummings, Treasurer; Charles C. Ingham and William S. Mount, Members of the Council. There were *no* Academicians elected.

May 15. A special meeting was called, to receive the announcement of the death of Academician W. J. Bennett. Suitable resolutions were passed, and forwarded to the friends of the deceased; and the members wore the usual badge of mourning.

Mr. Bennett was born in London in 1787; was a pupil of Westall; entered the British army, and served in Egypt. Resident here from 1816, he was elected Associate in 1827, and Academician in 1828. He was an artist of very diversified talent, distinguished in water-colors, and an engraver of ability in aquatint.

That meeting was scarcely over when the Academy was called on again to perform the same melancholy duty, caused by the death of Cornelius Ver Bryck, Academician, which occurred *abroad*, April 30th. The following tribute to his memory was offered by Mr. Gray:

Resolved, That in consequence of the death of Cornelius Ver Bryck, we meet here to testify our deep sorrow for the loss of one of the most accomplished members of the Academy, and one who, by his gentle virtues as an individual, was personally endeared to us.

Resolved, That in expression of our sympathy with the relatives of our deceased Brother, we will attend the funeral in a body, and wear the usual badge of mourning (crape on the left arm) for 30 days.

Resolved, That Mr. Cole be requested to prepare for publication a biographical sketch of our deceased friend.

Resolved, That a copy of these proceedings be transmitted to the bereaved relatives, and published.

THE LATE MR. VER BRYCK.

In compliance with a request of the National Academy of Design, the writer has attempted a short memoir of Cornelius Ver Bryck, the third member of that Institution, whose remains they have been called upon to follow to the grave within a few months; and if the departure of one gifted with the highest moral and intellectual qualities should ever call forth the expression of sorrow, we are now emphatically called upon for our tribute of grief.

The life of an artist is proverbially barren of those stirring incidents and strange vicissitudes that interest the reading multitude, and his biography consists, in a great measure, of an account of his birth and death, and a description of his works; and to this the life of Mr. Ver Bryck will furnish no exception.

Yet, if the expression of what those who knew him feel for his loss, were such matter as would interest in the columns of a public journal, their hearts could easily dictate a tribute to the memory of one so much loved.

Mr. Ver Bryck was born at Yaugh Paugh, New Jersey, on the 1st of January, 1813. In childhood he discovered a predilection for the fine arts, which strengthened with his years, and at length caused him to become an artist by profession. The present writer is not informed of the time when he undertook the art of painting professionally; but in 1835 he studied for some time under Mr. Morse, President of the National Academy. His health failing him, he went to Mobile in the Fall of 1837, and a much esteemed friend of his, to whom I am indebted for much of the information in this memoir, says that he carried with him several pictures, among which were one of Bachante, and another of a Cavalier, which were much admired, and purchased from him at Tuscaloosa, Alabama. He remained in that place two months, and would have made a longer stay had his health permitted, as his encouragement was equal to his wishes.

He returned to Mobile, and early in the Spring sailed for New-York. In 1839, stimulated with the desire to behold with his own eyes the wonders of ancient art, and scenes that, through history and poetry, had long been familiar to his mind, he sailed for London, in company with his friends Huntington and Gray, and for a time enjoyed, as such a mind as his can only enjoy, the works of the great masters, and the works of art to be found in London and Paris. But unfortunately, his stay in the Old World was too short; for he was called home by the illness of a sister—his brother was at the point of death when he left New-York, and died before he arrived in London.

After his return home, he was occupied in landscape and historical pictures. Among the latter was one whose subject was, "And one was taken and the other left." This picture was finely conceived: it represented a blessed spirit ascending towards Heaven, with enraptured expression, in the midst of light; while below, in murky gloom, was seen one of the accursed ones, with demoniac face, descending.

The writer believes that in the year 1840 he was elected as a member of the Academy, having previously been made an Associate—a tribute due to his talent and character.

For a few years he pursued his art, struggling against ill health and unfavorable circumstances, until 1843, when his friend Huntington, with his lady, who was the sister of one to whom Mr. Ver Bryck was deeply attached, proposed to visit Europe again. Suffering from disease, and in hope that a voyage might restore him, Mr. Ver Bryck determined to accompany his friend. To accomplish this was difficult, but generosity and devoted love accomplished it. Miss Richards, the sister of Mrs. Huntington, became the wife of Mr. Ver Bryck on the eve of his sailing for Europe. The party sailed for England in May. The voyage was favorable, and as far as health would permit, Mr. Ver Bryck enjoyed the scenery of the Isle-of-Wight and England exceedingly. The cathedrals, castles, abbeys, and exhibitions seemed to fill his mind with delight; but, alas! the beauties of nature nor the charms of art could check the inroads of disease, and even the ever-hopeful eye of affection could perceive in him no change for the better, and with his lady he left England, and arrived in New-York in the Autumn. Return brought no relief; the air of his native country had no healing balm; he lingered through the Winter, suffering much, but at times cheated into hope by the deceitful slumberings of his disease, until, on the 31st May, he expired. His mind was clear and calm to the last, and his soul, which through religion had been blessed and purified, was freed from its mortal tenement.

The principal circumstances of Mr. Ver Bryck's life have been thus hastily related, in order to dwell more particularly on his character, which is endearing to all who had the good fortune to be acquainted with him. It would seem that the higher the intellectual qualities possessed by man, the less fitted he is for encountering with success the stormy passage of life; that he whose mind is cast in Nature's most finished mould, the mould of genius and taste, is least capable of withstanding the asperity of actual life; and we frequently find that the possessors of these fatal gifts become early tenants of the tomb. Of this class was Mr. Ver Bryck: the flame burnt too bright to burn long. Endowed with keen sensibilities, his heart responded to every call. The love of the beautiful was the law of his being; the beautiful in nature and in art his chief joy. A sight of the mountains moved him with unutterable thoughts; he could truly say,

> " To me, the meanest flower that blows, can give
> Thoughts that do often lie too deep for tears."

Himself of poetical temperament, his taste for poetry was exquisite; but he loved most those antique songs in which simplicity of sentiment and style were combined with mystic grandeur of olden time. He had deep reverence for antiquity; and what poetical mind has not? for it clothes the dim and shadowy forms of the past with drapery of its own.

Music was a passion with him; his voice was low, but sweet, and he accompanied his songs on the guitar with great taste; and in his hours of quietness and solitude, many a plaintive song of Ver Bryck's steals like an Æolian strain on the mind's ear of the writer of this memoir. Speaking, in a letter written during his last visit to England, of the pleasure he enjoyed in visiting Winchester Cathedral, he says: "We remained and heard the service chanted. To me it seemed very impressive—the sweet, plaintive tones of the boys—that long-drawn 'Amen,' so often repeated in rich harmony—the touching words of the Psalm, 'Have mercy upon me, O Lord, for I am in trouble; mine eye is consumed for very heaviness—you, my soul and my body.' I thought I had never heard true chant-music before." Alas! he could too well feel the words of the Psalmist, for disease was then fast consuming him.

With all his artistic feeling and enthusiasm for art, the productions of Mr. Ver Bryck's pencil were not numerous; and perhaps, when we consider the obstacles that rose in his path, there will be little reason for suprise at this. Portrait painting, frequently the last anchor of the artist, which he casts out when all others have failed, was not to him lucrative; and although it occupied many of his most valuable hours, and stole him from precious moments which ought to have been employed in embodying the creations of his poetical mind, it scarcely furnished him with the means of support. He was of all men the least fitted for the potrait painter. The disappointment—the delays —the pert criticisms—the tantalizing caprice of sitters and their friends, were hard for him to bear, and they wore upon him.

His landscapes, which were simple productions—views or compositions sketching Nature in her tranquil moments—as well as his historical pictures, too frequently remained without a purchaser. The high qualities of his works, which ought to have brought him encouragement and profit, were passsed unnoticed by the multitude; and the coarse scenes of the tavern could frequently find purchasers, while the chaste works of Ver Bryck had no attractions. The hand of the artist is palsied if he once feels that his works produce no glow or sympathy in the minds of the beholders. Mr. Ver Bryck needed a more ample practice than he ever had, in order that his executions should be equal to his conceptions; but difficult it is to toil on works which, when completed, will in all probability meet with the same cold reception from the world that their predecessors have done. "Hope deferred maketh the heart sick," and this Ver Bryck had often felt. Hope itself died within him, for he had other and more unconquerable obstacles in his path than those of which I have spoken. There was a great shadow over him; for Melancholy "marked him for her own," and "solitude to him was next to death." Consumption, which had swept away brothers and sisters, until, of a numerous family, but two or three remained, hung like a spectre over him—pointing to the grave.

In the language of a friend who has been speaking of the absence of selfishness in Mr. Ver Bryck, is not comprehending that his society fully compensated others for their kindness to him. His guitar was his never-failing companion, and made him companionable to all. Melancholy and plaintive were the songs he loved best—characteristic of thoughts and feelings too often controlling him; the absence of these were always forced. Yet when among friends, no one could enjoy more, or add more to the pleasures of others. No one needed more the excitement of society to make him forget the spectre which so closely followed him. Illustrative of the tone of his mind is a passage in one of his letters: "They may say what they will of Hope and her pleasures. O, oft has she cheated me! But Memory—I love her: she is kind: doth she not make the pleasant seem more pleasant—the good better—the beautiful still more lovely? And even our past sorrows—she hath a way of softening them till they are almost sources of joy. A river—a pile of stones and mortar, are unsightly: but time covers it with moss and ivy, and it is beautiful."

In another letter he says: "I believe I am getting old, f r my pleasures are more of Memory than Hope."

But as the sands of life wasted away, the flame of hope burned more brightly in his bosom, and lifted by religious faith above the shadowy vale of tears, his eye caught glimpses of a glorious future, which made the past seem dim, and he longed to depart.

His mortal remains rest in Greenwood Cemetery, in a spot chosen by himself—in a quiet dell, beneath the shade of trees; and where he was interred, flowers, which he loved so much, were growing near the child of genius. Cut off, also, in the early promise of his years, "it might make one in love with Death, to think one should be buried in so sweet a place."

It is ours to regret that disease and death should have checked the development of powers which seem to have been of the highest order; but the works of his pencil were few, his virtues were many, and his friends will ever cherish the memory of them. And there is one, whose widowed sorrow will be softened by the consciousness that her pure, self-sacrificing love did much to soothe the passage of his spirit to the tomb.

> Peace !—Peace !—he is not dead—he doth not sleep—
> He hath awakened from the dream of life.
> 'Tis we—who, lost in stormy visions, keep
> With phantoms an unprofitable strife.

T. COLE.

August 3, 1844.—[*Post.*]

Was inaugurated a very highly proper, advantageous, educational measure—invitation to all "Schools to visit the Exhibition. It was done by *card*, procurable on application, and the Library was OPENED TO THE MEMBERS.

June 13. Died, Ithiel Town, a distinguished architect and bridge-builder, Academician in 1826, and transferred by non-residence to the Honorary Members' list.

Mr. Gray was called to supply the place of William S. Mount, on the Council, and Mr. Shegogue that of James Frothingham—" non-residents."

Nov. 13.   Very stringent though proper regulations, (which had become an absolute necessity,) were passed for the government of the schools.   The "Life" was opened Monday, Wednesday and Friday, at 2 P. M., in place of 7, as before, and the STUDENTS in *succession* were charged with SETTING the MODEL, which did not answer the expectations formed of its advantages.   During the months of December, February and March, the large gallery was occupied by the New-York Gallery, and one of the smaller by the exhibition of the portrait of Abdel Kader—the latter somewhat of a curiosity.

December 6.   Died, Nathaniel Rogers, an Academician in 1826, and by non-residence retired to Honorary Membership—an artist of merit in his line (miniature), and painted most of the "fashionables" of his day.

January.   Dr. Watts, Professor of Anatomy, offered the students an opportunity to pursue their studies under **1845.** his instruction at the Medical College.

At that time what may be considered a rather curious piece of legislation was enacted, viz. :

Resolved, That a "Special Agency" be established for the sale of works of art in the forthcoming Exhibition, and that NO commission be charged the " ARTIST."

There always was such a ONE, viz., the person in charge at the door, and who had, and ever had been especially directed *not* to receive any commission or payment for any pictures sold.

February 3.   The Quarterly Meetings, which had been somewhat thinly attended, were resuscitated, and notices were sent "that a supper would await the members' attendance."   The attendance at the meetings was greatly improved.

February 11.   A Special Meeting.   Mr. Cummings communicated the death of Geo. W. Newcombe, a highly meritorious artist, a benevolent, good man, and an Associate member.   He was born September 22nd, 1799, and died February 10th, 1845.   Resolutions of condolence with the family of the deceased were passed, and the members wore the usual badge of mourning for thirty days.

The attendance on the schools pronounced in the minutes to have been good.   No premiums were offered.   They closed on the eighteenth of March.

February 21. Died, Henry Sargent, Honorary Member, aged seventy-four years.

April 2. The "black-ball ballot" was introduced into the Hanging Committee, viz.:

Resolved, That any member of the Hanging Committee having objection to the hanging of any picture for the Exhibition, may place the number of the same (as designated in the reception-book) in a box to be provided for that purpose, to be opened at the beginning of every day or evening of hanging; and such picture or pictures, the number thereof that may be thereon found, shall be balloted for. A majority of votes deciding on its or their admission.

It was protested against by the writer, and as the result of its operation showed, was a most ill-advised movement. A number of pictures—some deserving, some not, of such treatment—were alike dropped in the box, and black-balled.

In retaliation, others—the supposed markers—were similarly specked. The members of the Committee black-balled each other; some of the best works were passed through the ordeal, probably in derision. Ultimately, scarcely anything—from one motive or another—escaped the black-ball; it became a farce in everything except its consequences; it was near breaking up all good feeling, and was then abandoned, and never should have been admitted.

April 8. It was decreed that the Art Union notice be published in the Catalogue free of charge; and the different Committees of Management of the Art Union, New-York Gallery, Faculty of Columbia College, and Board of the Mercantile Library, were presented with season tickets of admission to the ensuing exhibit.

April 17. The Twentieth Annual Exhibition opened to the public. Closing July 5. The receipts, $5,163.24; 69 working days, and realized an average of $74.83 per day. 369 works exhibited.

May 11. Died, Carl Weinedel, Associate Member of 1839; and on the 14th, Henry J. Megarey, Associate Member of 1844.

Resolutions of condolence with the families of the deceased were passed, and the usual badge of mourning worn as a token of respect.

May 14. Was held the Annual Meeting. A report of the year was prepared by Secretary Chapman, from which extracts are made.

REPORT.

Our Library is beginning to be appreciated, and appropriations of a liberal portion of our surplus funds to its increase, may justly rank among the primary objects of the Academy. It is an investment productive of immediate and perpetual interest, of which every member may enjoy his portion, without diminution of the amount to be transmitted to his successors.

* * * * * *

In connection with this is another object hitherto overlooked, but well deserving your attention, in support of whose direct practical utility, no argument is needed—a Wardrobe: that is, a collection of such articles, whether of costume, or other matter as would serve to facilitate the labors of the artist.

* * * * * *

The school for the study of the living model, which was unavoidably closed during the preceding year, has been successfully reopened, and that of the Antique well attended; and both these departments continue to demonstrate their great usefulness, in diffusing the all-important knowledge of the language of art, which it is their province to teach.

* * * * * * *

Among other acts, a Diploma or Certificate of Membership has been prepared, in a style in accordance with the present dignity of the Academy, and measures are in course to put every member in possession of this testimony of his connection. * * * *

The Council have to regret that another year has passed without carrying out the intention of the Academy with regard to the delivery of lectures on some of the various subjects connected with art.

* * * * * * *

The history of our Institution from its origin is but the progress of an experiment; ALL its laws have accordingly, from time to time, undergone various changes and modifications. In the year 1839 a general revision was established. In the course of the two following years other amendments were deemed necessary, and the usual course pursued for their accomplishment. So that in 1841 and subsequently, until within a few months past, we had supposed the Institution firmly placed on the basis of a tolerably good Code of By-Laws. But, singular as it may appear, on investigation they are found to be a most questionable authority, if not, in fact, a mere nullity—never having received the indispensable sanction of approval by two-thirds of the whole number of Academicians.

* * * * * *

If, then, we love the Institution that has nourished and sustained our dearest interests; if we would not ignobly yield the vantage-ground gained for our beloved arts, by a siege of toil and conflict, supported through many years, let us strengthen and renew the bond of Union which has hitherto been our tower of strength; let us sacrifice all individual interests, and every selfish impulse, not consonant with the good of all, and come with generous zeal to the defence of our common cause.

By the Treasurer's Report, it appears that the total receipts were $5,724.24, and the outlay $5,107.81; leaving a balance in the Treasury of $616.43.

Previous to balloting for officers, Mr. Morse declined a re-election as President of the Academy, in consequence of necessary absence from the city, on duties connected with the Government of the United States; and the following resolution was passed:

"*Resolved*, That the thanks of the Academy are due, and are hereby tendered, to Samuel F. B. Morse, Esq., for the faithful and earnest performance of his duties as President of this Institution from its earliest foundation, and that we deeply regret his unavoidable absence from the city and the profession, and by which we are deprived of his valuable services."

A. B. Durand was elected President; Charles C. Ingham, Vice-President; John G. Chapman, Corresponding Secretary; Francis W. Edmonds, Recording Secretary; Thomas S. Cummings, Treasurer; Robert E. Launitz, Henry Peters Gray, Council.

No Academicians were elected.

The Annual Meeting was adjourned to the 15th, for "special business."

May 14. The following resolutions (in the absence of the writer, which was adroitly procured for a sufficient length of time,) were offered, and passed unanimously:

TESTIMONIAL.

Resolved, That the thanks of the Academy are due, and are hereby presented, to Thomas S. Cummings, Esq., for the faithful and correct manner in which he has executed the duties of the office of Treasurer of this Institution for twenty years.

Resolved, That in token of esteem and regard, the Academy present to him a service of plate;   *   *   and that the Council procure said plate;   *   *   and that the Secretary transmit to Mr. Cummings a copy of the foregoing resolution.

The above very unexpected compliment was received with much pleasure. A service was selected, and decorates the writer's table—he trusts a memento to himself, and an incentive to his children.

The following notice appeared, with many others, at the time, which from, he trusts, excusable vanity, he may be allowed to insert:

DESERVED COMPLIMENT.

The National Academy of Design has presented to its Treasurer, General Thomas S. Cummings, a service of plate, in token of the approbation merited by his long and valuable services. The General has been elected to that office unanimously, some twenty years in succession, and as the *Commercial* says— "During which period the financial affairs of the Academy have been managed with a business ability that is not often exhibited by artists, who are generally more noted for disregard of pecuniary interests than for undue attention to the prosperity of their worldly affairs. Mr. Cummings is an exception. Although an Artist eminent in his line, he is as prompt, as correct and clear-headed in business matters as any merchant or financier in the country."

We may add to the above, that he has also served some twenty or more years in Commission in the Militia of our State; and here the *Commercial's* encomium is equally applicable:—"He now holds one of the highest military offices, and with ability and reputation as deserved as enviable."

June 20. Died, Charles E. Weir, for many years a student of the Academy, who had endeared himself to the members generally by his estimable character, and high promise in his profession. Resolutions of condolence were passed and forwarded to the family of the deceased, and published in the daily papers.

June 23. Was announced the death, on the 22d, of Mr. Carey, Honorary Member, of Philadelphia, a distinguished amateur in art, and publisher of one of the most beautiful of American Annuals; a friend to artists, and a sympathizer in their necessities. His purse was ever ready to respond to their wants. His gallery contained some of the most beautiful specimens of American art. Resolutions expressive of the high estimation in which he was held, and in condolence with the relatives of the deceased, were passed and published.

There were no meetings from June 23 to September 15.

In October was exhibited, at the Academy, a statue in marble—"Nymph entering the Bath," by De Keypers—one of the most exquisitely beautiful creations of the chisel that ever appeared in the city. It was pecuniarily unsuccessful; it did not receive a sufficient attendance to pay one quarter of the door-keeper's expense. Probably the exhibiter lacked a knowledge of the external management necessary to success.

The New-York Gallery removed to the *Rotunda* in the Park, granted to its use by the Corporation, for the purpose of introducing a permanent Gallery of Art in the city. Even there it was not successful as a paying exhibition; it did not derive sufficient revenue to insure its continuance.

November 3. The Life and Antique schools were opened for the season, three evenings in the week to gentlemen, and in December following, to ladies in the daytime.

December 9. A special meeting was held for the purpose of passing amendments to the CONSTITUTION, authorizing the payment of annuities to widows and children of deceased Academicians. Several efforts had been previously made to procure the attendance of the constitutional number of the Academicians without effect, and it had then become an indispensable requisite, to give Mr. Inman's family the benefits of its results (it being well known that Inman's days were numbered.) That it should be done, extraordinary efforts were resorted to. The late Miss A—— H——, an Academician, the only lady Artist in the executive, (in course had never attended the meetings of the body,) was solicited by the writer, in view of the extraordinary nature of the case, to attend the meeting, and after great persuasion consented, and did so; and further, as a *last resort*, arrangements had been further made with Mrs. Inman, by which the Academy might adjourn to the *sick-room*, thereby making Inman one towards procuring the desired quorum, if by so doing *only* a quorum could be obtained. Such a contingency did occur; at 9 o'clock in the evening, after exhausting all other sources, a quorum within one had been obtained, and the meeting adjourned in mass to *Inman's chamber.* Never will the writer forget that evening. Sitting up in bed, supported by Mrs. Inman and the writer, poor Inman surrounded by his brother Academicians, and within a few days of his death, listened to the hasty reading, by his old friend Ingham, of the amendments, that were to give his wife and family the prospect of something, after his decease. The resolutions were quickly read and unanimously passed in mass, and the meeting silently withdrew to the Academy rooms in Broadway—after seeing Miss Hall, Miss Leslie, daughter of Major Leslie, U. S. Army, and Miss Rebecca Cummings, the daughter of the writer, who accompanied Miss Hall on her mission, to their respective homes. He returned long after midnight to the *waiting* Academicians.

On calling on Miss Hall the next morning, to congratulate her on her effort, the writer received the very flattering assurance that although she had very reluctantly consented to attend, that, knowing what she then knew, she would rather have attended a dozen such meetings, even to the whole night to each, than the object should not have been accomplished.

January 5. Died, Alfred T. Agate, Associate Member, brother of Frederick S., the Academician. He was an **1846.** artist of promise, and died young. He accompanied Capt. Wilkes as one of his draughtsmen on his expedition, and on his return was continued in the service as assistant in completing, arranging and making the more finished drawings of the survey for publication.

January 17. Died, Henry Inman, and on the nineteenth a special meeting was convened. The President announced, in a feeling manner, his death, whereupon Mr. Cummings offered resolutions expressive of the high estimation in which the deceased was held, and condolence with the family, as also one to appropriate one hundred and fifty dollars to defray the funeral expenses, which were passed unanimously. Alas, that such talent should have required such assistance !

The following notice of the funeral, and the proceedings which followed it, are cut from one of the daily papers of the time, and afford a concise but accurate account:

INMAN'S FUNERAL.

The procession moved in the following order, and extended from Murray to Reade Street. The reverend clergy, Rev. Drs. Alexander and Potts, in a carriage; next, the members of the Independent Order of Odd Fellows; then THE BODY, with the following gentlemen as pall-bearers:

A. B. DURAND—President N. A.

C. C. INGHAM,
JOHN L. MORTON, } Members of Council.
THOMAS S. CUMMINGS, }

JAMES J. MAPES.
F. W. EDMONDS.
RICHARD B. FOSDICK.
GEORGE BUCKHAM.
JAMES McMURTRIE, of Philadelphia.

Then followed the brother, son and son-in-law of the deceased; next, the physician; following them, the Academicians; and lastly, the numerous friends of the distinguished artist. The interment took place at St. Mark's, where, at the close of the ceremony, the benediction was pronounced by the Rev. Dr. Potts. The body was placed temporarily in one of the vaults, but will be removed in the Spring to the Greenwood Cemetery.

" Yet his funeral ! Never, never has been witnessed a more striking scene than that of the long and compact procession, comprising some of the most prominent persons both from this and other cities, following the bier of the artist on foot, for two long miles, on a cold winter evening. No splendid pageant to the memory of the eminent painter could have been so balmful to his hurt mind as that unerring tribute to his acknowledged worth as a man; and if his spirit still hovered near till the earth closed over his mortal remains, it must have soared away at last, content that his name and his fame would be alike shielded and cherished by his mourning countrymen."

" The artist' dead; the gifted's task is ended ;
The brush and canvas lie all useless now:
Life's picture finished—light and shade are blended
By the great Master to whom all must bow."

OPENING OF THE INMAN GALLERY.

At a meeting of the friends of the late lamented Henry Inman, convened on the evening after his interment, at the residence of General Cummings, it was thought proper, while offering earnest and heartfelt condolence to the afflicted family of the departed, that the occasion should be improved to invite the friends of Art generally to unite in some more substantial token of interest in their welfare.

From that meeting a notice was issued, inviting the friends of the artist to meet at the Globe Hotel.

The same authority continued : " There has seldom been a nobler display of kind and generous feeling among our citizens, than was manifested at the Globe Hotel. A few evenings after Inman's death a notice was published in the city journals, inviting the friends of the late artist to assemble at that place. The high character and the number of the assembly bespoke the feeling death had awakened.

General Cummings, his former pupil, was unanimously called on to preside over the meeting, and opened it with a fervid address and eulogy on the deceased. The proceedings were brief, to the point, and characterized by the utmost dignity. It was resolved that all the works of the artist, which could conveniently be brought together, should be obtained, and an exhibition made thereof, for the benefit of his family.

The committee alone appointed on the occasion consisted of over a hundred of the oldest and most respectable members of the community, and all so named were present. The Art Union rooms were generously tendered free of charge, and the Art Union Secretary offered his services as door-keeper in like manner, which were accepted."

The Exhibition was ordered to open in the Art Union rooms, 322 Broadway, on the tenth day of February, and all persons willing to loan works were requested to report to the Chairman, T. S. Cummings. The exhibition was held, and was a success. On its termination the following resolutions were passed :

INMAN EXHIBITION.

At a meeting of the Committee on the Inman Gallery, held at the Art Union Rooms on the 8th day of April, instant, the following resolutions were passed unanimously—viz. :

Resolved, That the thanks of this Committee are pre-eminently due to those who have loaned the valuable productions of Mr. Inman's pencil to the Exhibition which has lately closed, and that they would in the strongest way show their sense of obligation to the gentlemen from other places, and particularly the City of Philadelphia, who have sent some of the most *valuable* paintings that enrich the collection.

Resolved, That the thanks of this Committee be given to the Art Union, for the all-important privilege of using the rooms of that Association for the Inman Exhibition, and for their zealous co-operation in promoting its success.

Resolved That to Mr. Fraser, the Secretary of the American Art Union, our best acknowledgments are especially due for the liberal service he so cordially rendered during the whole time the Inman collection of paintings was upon the walls of the Gallery.

Resolved, That this Committee, while making full acknowledgments of their estimation of the handsome manner in which the public have responded to their call, feel that the success which has attended their efforts is chiefly due to the generous warmth with which the public *Press* of New-York has gratuitously seconded their exertions.

And after reading the Treasurer's and other Reports, it was

Resolved, That the net proceeds of the Exhibition be paid over to the widow of the late Henry Inman, and that the Executive Committee be requested to recommend to *"invest"* the same in such manner as they may think will be most conducive to the interests of herself and family.

Adjourned.

THOMAS S. CUMMINGS,
Chairman of the Committee.

In accordance with the instructions contained in the above resolutions, the Committee paid the amount over to the widow of Mr. Inman, as the following correspondence shows :

ART UNION ROOMS, *April* 13, 1846.

Dear Madam:

The tribute to the memory of Mr. Inman, which has been so feelingly and zealously accorded in the city, where he and his works were best known, cannot but be most grateful to yourself and his bereaved family.

The Committee of his friends who ventured to interpret the general sentiment at Mr. Inman's loss as calling for an Exhibition of his paintings, have no reason to regret their choice. They have in every instance found but one feeling of sympathy and interest pervading the community to whom it was thrown open.

Notwithstanding the difficulty of collecting more than a portion of Mr. Inman's works in the brief period allowed for arranging the Gallery, the ultimate result in no way disappointed the expectation of the Committee ; and in their behalf I have the honor herewith to inclose you the Treasurer's statement of the collections and disbursements of the undertaking—viz. :

Receipts, $2,340.17. Expenditure, $426.85. Net balance, $1,913.32—for which amount, in accordance with the resolution passed by the Committee, you will please receive the Treasurer's check—trusting, dear madam, that the same may be in some measure the means of aiding you in advancing the interests of those now dependent on you for protection and support.

I have the honor to remain, with the highest sentiments of regard and respect, your obedient servant,

THOMAS S. CUMMINGS,
Chairman of the Inman Committee.

To Mrs. HENRY INMAN.

P. S.—The Treasurer reports that there are still some tickets out, of which you receive a memorandum—the returns from which will be made to you, personally, by the parties, and cannot be expected to yield less than $100 in addition to the above $1,913.32.

REPORT OF THE EXECUTIVE COMMITTEE.

To Mrs. HENRY INMAN—

Madam—In pursuance of a vote of the General Committee, we, as the Executive Committee of the late Exhibition of the pictures of your lamented husband, beg leave respectfully to suggest that it is the opinion of your friends, the General Committee, that the amount accruing from the Exhibition should be invested on *Bond and Mortgage*—which could probably be done on property of double the value, at 7 per cent. per annum—thus securing both the principal and interest, without the ordinary risk of loss contingent on personal securities.

We remain your obedient servants,

THOMAS S. CUMMINGS,
JAMES J. MAPES,
RICHARD B. FOSDICK,
Executive Committee

To T. S. CUMMINGS,
  Chairman of the Committee of the Inman Gallery, and others.
GENTLEMEN—
  I acknowledge the receipt of $1,913.32 from the Treasurer of the Committee, which I have invested according to your kind advice, and for which I return you my most grateful thanks, and with feelings of deep and lasting obligation,
  I remain, Gentlemen, your most obedient servant,
                                             JANE INMAN.
  RAHWAY, *April* 27, 1846.

After the death of Inman, who, it is well known, had received two or three payments on account of the picture he had engaged to paint for the Government (and on which no progress had been made), Mr. Daniel Huntington then offered to complete, or it should rather be said, to paint the picture for the balance then due and unpaid on the original commission, and thus save his brother artist Inman's reputation, and Congress' loss. It was a truly generous offer, but for some reason or other, it was not accepted. The commission was given to Mr. Powell, who furnished the vacant panel with his De Soto—now in the Capitol.

January 1st was established "CUMMINGS' SCHOOL OF DESIGN"—a Private Institution covering the course pursued in public academies, adapted to the wants of amateurs of either sex.

The course of study announced to be " the General Education of the Eye, in its appreciation of form, light, shade and color; *Elementary Drawing* in lead pencil and crayon, from 'examples,' from the '*round*,' from '*nature*,' and the '*living models;*' Painting in oil and water-colors, and the general principles of Composition, with lectures on Anatomy, Perspective, and other subjects connected with art, by competent professors, if sufficient demand appeared for their appointment." The school met with marked approval. The New-York University appointed the writer their Professor of the Arts of Design, and many other institutions followed their example.

Drawing schools there were in the city long previously; but they aimed at little or no more than copying, from *examples*, and artists of standing especially eschewed teaching, or even being looked upon as teachers.

The establishment was successful, and the press teemed with articles in its praise. It received the commendation of the first artists in the country, and the writer thinks he is fairly entitled to be considered the introducer and founder of THE better and more enlarged PRIVATE SCHOOL OF ART.

The example has been followed by many; suffusion, and

not dearth of instruction, appears to be the dilemma; and so far from FEW being willing to receive amateur pupils, the exceptions are rare, though some have tried, and relinquished the experiment.

March 14. The schools of the Academy were closed; no premiums were offered.

April 16. The twenty-first Annual Exhibition opened to the public, preceded by an "invitation" reception. The receipts were $5665 18; the Exhibiton open sixty-nine working days, averaging $82 10 per day; it closed July 14; 346 works exhibited.

April 27. Messrs. Durand, Edmonds and Cummings were appointed a "Standing Building Committee."

The body generally had become discontented with the rooms they occupied, and desired a change, and the public clamored for less stair ascent.

May 13. The Annual Meeting of the Academicians was held, and opened their proceedings by the reading of the Report of President A. B. Durand.

GENTLEMEN OF THE ACADEMY—

While, in reviewing the occurrences of the past year, we find much that calls for the most sincere congratulation, as evincing our continued prosperity and advancement, we are suddenly checked in our joy by the reflection that, in the midst of our gain, we have to acknowledge and lament a loss of proportionate magnitude—the decease of one of our most conspicuous members.

When a name like that of Henry Inman is stricken from our living record, we must deeply feel that there is left a vacancy that cannot easily be supplied. Nor is that vacancy apparent only in our ranks; it is perceived and felt throughout the community. But it is not my purpose here to attempt an estimate of the extent and character of the loss thus sustained; nor is it my intention to pronounce his eulogy; that has already been done in eloquent and most appropriate language by the expression of public and private sympathy, commencing with the funeral solemnities, and continued by the unprecedented interest attendant on the subsequent exhibition of his works. These circumstances constitute a high tribute of respect to the memory of Inman, and we regard it as a tribute paid to the art in which he excelled—a public acknowledgment of the value and evidence of more enlightened appreciation of the character and influence of the Fine Arts in our country.

Honors thus paid to the dead are virtually shared by the living.

The most prominent act of the Academy since our last Annual Meeting is the adopting of a new Constitution, by which many difficulties which have for years past obstructed our operations, are, we trust, effectually removed. This instrument may not be as perfect as we could wish in all its points, yet its deficiencies are but of subordinate import. It contains at least one provision that should serve as a ready passport to all the rest. I allude to the clause which established an Annuity Fund. It is a stimulus to the continuance and increase of our productive labor, inasmuch as it clearly illustrates the broad principle, that the interest of self is inseparable from the good of all.

* * * In the schools it is proposed to receive and enforce a former regulation of the Academy, unwisely fallen into disuse, and which, prop-

erly observed, could not fail to insure the best results to the labors of the students, in the preservation of good order and well-directed industry—that is, the appointment of Visitors from the body of Academicians, one or more of whom should be always in attendance during the session of the school.

   *   *   *   The subject of Lectures naturally follows, and renews the call for some efficient action. The presence of our Professor of Anatomy, even, has again been wanting in our rooms.

   *   *   *   *   *   *   *

We are aware that any measures involving additional demands on our Treasury would at present be inadmissible, since, as will appear from the Treasurer's Report, retrenchment in our expenditures, as he states, is actually indispensable; still, the subject is submitted for your consideration, whether some steps may not be taken towards the desired end without liability to this objection.

   *   *   *   Reference to the eighth Article of our new Constitution (providing for the growth of the Annuity Fund) naturally suggests the exercise of all due precaution relative to the future outlays of the Academy. But if there be any one object more imperative in its demands than all others, on our resources, at least of a prospective character, it is the securing of a permanent local habitation. Under these considerations, a Committee of three of your officers has been appointed to inquire into the feasibility of procuring the erection of a suitable building, on conditions that shall meet the requirements as well as the means of the Institution.

The revenue from our Annual Exhibitions is gradually increasing, and, what is not less gratifying, is the general concession that the present Exhibition is characterized by a higher order of merit. The older contributors sustain their reputations, and the younger evince fair progress. New claimants to notice are springing up, and the general prosperity will ere long, if not at once, dictate the propriety of limiting the number of works presented by each contributor for exhibition—say to eight or thereabouts—not only that each may be more fairly exposed, but also with reference to a due regard to variety and interest in the aggregate. This suggestion may well deserve the attention of the present meeting.

   *   *   *   *   *   *   *

We are happy to say that our relations with the other institutions of our city, devoted to the common cause, continue on the grounds of cordial co-operation, and our satisfaction is increased in the assurance that no year of our public existence has opened upon us under more favorable auspices of encouraging prosperity than the present. And who does not perceive that unanimity of feeling and action within and without our body has been largely tributary to this condition? So also must its continuance depend on the maintenance of that harmony.

From the Treasurer's Report it appears that the total receipts of the year were $6,508.51, and the disbursements $5,708.52; leaving a balance in the Treasury of $799.99.

A resolution was passed in accordance with the Presidential recommendation, " appointing *tutors* from the body of Academicians, whose duty it should be to *attend the schools in rotation;*" though there was no pay attached.

There is no change in human nature; there was little or no compliance. The " novelty" induced one or two to drop in for a time, but virtually there was no attendance.

A. B. Durand was elected President; Charles C. Ingham, Vice-President; J. G. Chapman, Corresponding Secretary; F. W. Edmonds, Recording Secretary; Thomas S. Cummings, Treasurer; J. Frothingham and H. C. Shumway, Council; F. R. Spencer, J. F. E. Prud'homme, Charles L. Elliott, V. G. Audubon, and N. Jocelyn, Academicians.

May. The following resolution, in view of extending the knowledge of American art abroad, was passed:

> *Resolved,* That a complete set of the American engravings, *now in the possession of the Academy for distribution to foreign Institutions,* &c., be sent to the Archæological Society of Belgium, and that the Secretary be directed to carry this resolution into effect.

That was very well, but to what engravings it applied is certainly a matter of conjecture. There were none such in the Academy, nor does the writer remember their ever possessing a collection of such engravings, or any that might be used for that purpose. Of course it was never carried out.

September 24. Died, W. G. Williams, U. S. A., an amateur artist, Honorary Member, a gentleman of considerable ability in art. He was killed at the "Taking of Monterey."

October 11. Mr. Vanderlyn called for the use of the Gallery for the exhibition of his painting of the Landing of Columbus. It was offered to him on precisely the same terms authorizing its rental to any one else. Singularly enough, twenty years had in no way altered that gentleman's notions in relation to "artistic hostility towards HIM." In his interview, although he exempted the writer from his sweeping denunciations, he declared that the whole Academic body were his most deadly enemies (they elected him a member in 1826, and he threw it back in their teeth), and for years the writer scarcely ever heard his name called up, or in any way whatever referred to, or even, as he believes, thought of. Yet during the whole period of his painting being on exhibition, that monomaniac never failed to introduce to every one attending it, his belief in the deadly "Academic animostic poison," and the baneful effect of it on his exhibition, in which respect he fared better than twenty similar instances which preceded him.

November 2. The Life and Antique Schools opened, and a catalogue of the statues was prepared by Secretary Chapman, beautifully gotten up. Forty-two students entered.

It is to be regretted there is no authentic record of the first enrollments of students; it would be interesting. The portraits of the Associate Members, required at their admission, have resulted in forming one of the most interesting collections, and years hence will, perhaps, be deemed *invaluable!*

November. An Exhibition of the works of H. K. Brown, the sculptor, was held in the Galleries. It was a beautiful and chaste exposition of talent, and gratified his friends, although with little pecuniary success to the artist.

December, 1846, or the beginning of January, 1847, produced one of the many flowerets of the National Academy of Design—the " Century." To John G. Chapman, Secretary of the Academy, belongs its credit and paternity.

At a meeting of the "SKETCH CLUB," it was proposed by Chapman to found a club of artists and men of letters, for gentlemanly and social intercourse, the difficulty of admission into the "Sketch Club" being such as almost to amount to "prohibition"—the new association to have a permanent local habitation. The plan was acceptable, and in January, 1847, a code of by-laws was adopted. Gulian C. Verplanck, John L. Stephens, A. B. Durand, John G. Chapman, David C. Colden, and Charles M. Leupp, were elected a Committee; Thomas S. Cummings, Treasurer; Daniel Seymour, Secretary. The whole formed the Committee of Management, and at once was organized the " Century."

The upper part of a house in Broadway was rented, and furnished in the most modest and inexpensive manner; no games of any kind were permitted. From its commencement it was a success, and continued prosperity has attended it. It has embraced the highest talent in every branch of art, literature, and science, and the gatherings were looked upon as the most desirable of all the New-York winter entertainments. To its full-blown lustre perhaps the artists may have but little claim; in its founding merely it is "Academic." It has achieved a reputation, and its history has been given by J. H. G., the talented author of the facetious papers of " No. 197 Wall Street"—a myth—at least one number more than is to be found in the street.

February 25. Died, John Stephano Cogdell, Honorary Member, of Charleston, S. C., a gentleman of refined
1847. and extensive acquirements, who devoted much of his leisure to practice in art. In the early records of the Academy he was enrolled as a student in its schools, and is well remembered as modeling in clay from the Antique.

March 1. It was reported by Council, that the number of pupils of the schools of the city, who visited the last Annual Exhibition free, was nearly six thousand.

March 12. A special meeting was called by the President,

who announced the object to be to decide on a question that had arisen with regard to the election of S. B. Waugh as an Associate, and Nathaniel H. Jocelyn as an Academician; both gentlemen appearing to have been ineligible, as they were not at the time of their election strictly, and legally speaking, permanent residents of the City of New-York, which, by the Constitution of the Academy, is an essential qualification in all who may be elected into the body of Associates or Academicians.

As the executive officer of the Academy, I have considered the grounds of their disqualification sufficient to authorize the omission of the name of Mr. Waugh as an Associate, and that of Mr. Jocelyn as an Academician, in the next Catalogues. At the same time, anxious to have the approbation of the Academy before the Catalogues were printed, it has been accordingly convened. Their elections were declared " null and void."

That accounts for what had escaped the writer's memory, viz.: the reasons why Mr. Jocelyn's name, who was elected in 1827, did not continue to appear in the list of Academicians.

April 2. The twenty-second Annual Exhibition was opened to the public, after a reception given the previous day to invited guests, to which the "Members of the Sketch Club, Century, Society Library, Mercantile Library, American Art Union, City Gallery, Columbia College and New-York University," were invited.

The receipts of the Exhibition amounted to $6278.22; it was open eighty working days, at an average of $78.47 per day; 375 productions. The largest receipt from an Exhibition ever obtained by the Institution. It will, however, be also observed that it was of the longest duration—nearly three months—from April 2d to July 3d.

May 3. The Annual Meeting was held, and a report was made by the Council, recapitulating the general events of the year, which, as they have been chronicled, are omitted.

From the Treasurer's Report it is gathered that the total receipts were $7,005.11; the investments, $1,886.83; the expenses, $4,385.93; total, $6,272.76: balance in the Treasury, $732.35.

A. B. Durand was made President; C. C. Ingham, Vice-President; J. G. Chapman, Corresponding Secretary; F. W. Edmonds, Recording Secretary; Thomas S. Cummings, Treasurer; Charles L. Elliott, Daniel Huntington, Council. There were no Academicians elected.

A resolution was passed, "that hereafter the proceedings

of the Annual Meeting be published in pamphlet form, for the use of the members." A matter which seems to have been neglected. But one such was published.

May 17. A Special Meeting was summoned, at which the following preamble and resolution were offered, which have been embodied in the By-Laws:

WHEREAS, It is important to preserve the novelty of each Annual Exhibition of the Academy, by a strict exclusion of all works of art that have been previously exhibited publicly in the City of New-York: It is therefore

Resolved, That in future, no work of art, that has been publicly exhibited in the City of New-York, be admitted in the Annual Exhibitions of the Academy, and that due notice be given to exhibiters to that effect.

It was not done at a meeting legally constituted to do it. No notice, as required, was given. There was not the requisite vote given to constitute it a law. It has, therefore, no legal existence. It previously stood: "No work previously *exhibited by the Academy* should be re-eligible to an Annual Exhibition." That was well, and it never should be otherwise.

The resolution appears to have excited considerable discussion; the ayes and nays were called for, when it appeared that 12 voted in the affirmative, and 4 in the negative; on which latter the writer was one.

The resolution fell into disuse, though it does not appear to have been rescinded, as was naturally to be expected it would. It was too stringent. If no other impediment offered, the difficulty of proof or knowledge on the part of the Committee as to what had been "publicly exhibited" in the city, or what should constitute public exhibition, was sufficient to annul its operation.

And the first Exhibition after its passage made that apparent to all. The doors of the Gallery were no sooner opened, than two or three most flagrant instances were pointed out, which had escaped the Committee's vigilance. The next question that presented itself was, "What shall be considered public exhibition?" And after much discussion, it was decided that the exhibition "for MONEY" should be the determining point. It was very clear that that decision only rendered the matter worse. For while a picture exhibited for money had perhaps been but little seen, and possessed freshness, by that ruling was excluded; while a picture that had been publicly exhibited in a store window in Broadway for months, and having lost all its exhibition interest, was admissible. That actually occurred. A painting by a German artist was presented, which had been so publicly exhibited in a store window for months, and could not, under the rule, be excluded; while

Mr. Cole's beautiful series, which was offered and which had been exhibited but a short time at a large admission fee, and consequently seen but by few persons, was ruled inadmissible! After that there could be no question as to the fate of the resolution; yet it still remained in the *printed laws.*

May 17. Non-previous exhibition by the Academy is undoubtedly the only point at which such a rule should stand. The Hanging Committee possessing the power to reject any work which, in their estimation, may be deemed from any cause unfit or undesirable in the Annual Exhibition. The rule as last given, if rigidly carried out, from "Artist receptions," "Club receptions," "Store receptions," where pictures are sent, two-thirds of all the city pictures that are painted would be excludable. Yet it has been equally clear that unless some method could be devised—the *esprit du corps* of the Art body touched, or in some manner reached—the Annual Exhibitions would fall into disrepute for want of NOVELTY; and such has grown to be the case.

June 21. A letter was received from the Washington Monument Association, returning thanks for the *loan of the Fourth of July*—a singular article to loan, certainly; but, seriously, the writer has no remembrance of any loan to the Washington Monument Association at all. One day's receipts from the Exhibition was appropriated to that object, but that could scarcely be called a loan.

Again the number of children attending the Exhibition by invitation was announced, and declared to be largely over six thousand! Gratifying.

September 6, was received by the Academy, an invitation to attend the laying of the corner-stone of the Washington Monument.

As the writer believes, that is the extent of its progress. That must not be confounded with the Washington Statue at present gracing Union Square. For that the city is indebted to private munificence and the untiring exertions of Col. Lee, who justly deserves the credit of the enterprise and its successful carrying out. As he truly remarks, "it is no myth now."

August 23 to January, 1848, was exhibited in the Academy Gallery, Power's "Greek Slave." A work of art too well known to need comment. In a pecuniary point of view it met with great success, receiving from its first exposition in the city, it was said, ten thousand dollars—for a single statue or work of art, probably the greatest success on record.

In September Quidor's historical pictures were exhibited by the owner, with the avowed intention of making his fortune by their exposition, which, it is believed, was not accomplished. A lawsuit between the parties was instituted on the subject, but on what ground, or for what purpose, is disremembered.

September 24, was established the "NEW-YORK SKETCH CLUB." That is in no way to be confounded with " THE *Sketch Club*"—the institution of 1826—or the subsequent or second *Sketch Club*—an *older* institution. The named are the *younger* artists. It proved a highly interesting society, and contributed much to the enjoyment of those professionals.

Its first officers were : T. Addison Richards, President ; J. H. Cafferty, Vice-President ; Thomas A. Cummings (generally called Junior), the writer's son, Secretary. Unlike its older prototype, it elected a list of Honoraries, of which the writer was one, who frequently had the pleasure of inspecting the works of the "Evening," and can speak in praise of their general artistic excellence.

Whether they commenced on "milk and honey," and gradually slid into the oysters and champagne, in imitation of their older model, the writer cannot say ; he never witnessed anything of the kind, but had, however, frequent misgivings.

October 4. A resolution that the Antique School should be open daily, from nine A. M. until dusk, was passed. That proved a failure ; that which can be procured at ALL times is scarcely ever valued or sought. The attendance was nominal—seldom more than one or two at any one time throughout the day. Under the gallantry of the polite Curator, the Ladies' School was rather more of a success : at a great personal loss, he devoted to it much of his valuable time. In return for his kindness, the ladies very prettily "presented a silver pitcher to Mr. Prud'homme, as a souvenir of their appreciation of his attentions. It was remarkably well deserved."

The truth is, there is little CALL for an Art Day School in the Academy. During the day artist students are generally engaged in their painting, and amateurs in their other business. The evening classes meet with success, and suit the wants of the people. The day school was soon abandoned ; it was closed by a resolution passed on the 29th of November, as follows :

Resolved, That the Antique and Life Schools be closed in the daytime, there not being a sufficient attendance, and that they be opened in the evenings as heretofore.

November 24. A meeting of the Academicians was called, on the subject of a location for a building.

The Treasurer reported several propositions, with rough estimates of the cost of ground and buildings.

Whereupon it was

Resolved, That the question of THE LOCATION of the National Academy of Design from and after the expiration of the lease of the rooms now occupied by them, be referred again to the Committee heretofore appointed, with thanks for the exertions they have taken in regard to this important subject, and that the said Committee be requested to make a report to the Academy on or before the 10th of February next.

December 3. It was decided that the drawings for admission to the schools should be made "*in the schools of the Academy*," probably to prevent assistance being rendered in the execution of the work, and to test the actual merit of the applicant.

Such an arrangement never works well, the removal of a party on trial always producing much ill feeling. It is better not to admit until the merit or demerit is decided.

January 1. At that time an application was made by the students for an additional Life School, to be under **1848.** their own charge. That was granted by resolution apportioning the alternate evenings of the Life School of the Academy to their use, making six evenings per week.

That was granted while the Academy was furnishing, under its own management, as good a school as could be offered, and while in the resolution it declared that they thought the accommodation ample, with one of the best models of the French Academy. Its granting was a little singular, and even equally so that it should have been asked. It was not of long duration; no real benefits, not previously given, were derived, love of change or independence probably the leading features of the desire for it; these satisfied, it declined. The Academy was left to be at the cost, while its direction was removed from their hands.

January 3. A communication was received from the newly-organized Art Union of Philadelphia, stating that it was laid down as a principle, "that subscribers who draw prizes may select their pictures from any accredited public gallery in the United States." And whereas this Academy believes such a course to be highly beneficial to the artists of the country, it is therefore

Resolved, That we fully approve of the objects and plan of the Philadelphia Art Union, as admirably adapted to the general promotion of the Fine Arts, and that we cheerfully give it our co-operation.

Resolved, That the subscribers to the Philadelphia Art Union have free admission to the Exhibition of the Academy of the current year, of their membership.

The resolutions were forwarded to the Philadelphia Art Union.

The plan appeared feasible, and calculated to satisfy the artists. How it succeeded is not within the writer's knowledge. No advantages were derived by New-York artists—THAT is known—nor any advantage taken of the free admission to the Exhibition granted here.

In January was opened, in the galleries of the Academy, a collection of paintings by the old masters, owned by Mr. Nye, a gentleman of taste and fortune. His object is set forth in the introduction to his Catalogue, as follows:

"This Exhibition is intended to be for the period of six weeks only, and is, as the proprietor of the collection hopes, merely preliminary to the formation of an association of gentlemen to relieve him of individual responsibility, and insure the retention of it in this city as a nucleus of a Gallery worthy of the position held by New-York. He esteems himself fortunate to be the possessor of what is, at once, a source of pleasure to himself and a mean of the advancement of art amongst his countrymen; and trusts to a due appreciation of the value of the collection, as a mean of higher advancement in art and an embellishment of the city, to enable him to retain it here permanently."

Mr. Nye was doomed to disappointment. The collection contained about sixty works, large and small, and was said to have cost over one hundred thousand dollars. There were many paintings claimed to be the undoubted works of the masters by whom they purported to be from; and, indeed, as a whole, the collection contained great excellence. A Titian—the Martyrdom of St. Lawrence—was critically examined by the best judge of that artist among us, G——y, and believed by him to be an original picture. Mr. Nye continued the exhibition of his collection before the public for several years, at an expense to him of from $3,000 to $5,000 per annum, without recompense, the receipts from the exhibition amounting to comparatively *nothing*. But what distressed him most appeared to be the non-attendance; the pecuniary loss did not appear to incommode him in the least. His leaving the country to attend to his vast business in the East Indies was the signal for its closing—his subsequent death for its dismemberment. In the closing up of his estate, it was distributed under the hammer of the auctioneer, and the last portion was sold in the galleries in Tenth Street and Fourth Avenue.

DEATH OF COLE.

To the Council:

It is my painful duty to announce to you the receipt of the intelligence of the death of Thomas Cole, one of my dearest friends—one of our fellow-Associates in founding this Institution. A friend deeply endeared to us all by the high and Christian qualities of mind and heart which ever distinguished him through life, as a dutiful son, an honorable man, and an affectionate husband and father. As an artist, pre-eminently an ornament to his profession and his country.

In offering to you these few and feeble remarks on the merits of our deceased friend and fellow, permit me to express the hope that all that can be done to render a proper tribute of respect to his memory will be done, and that the Academicians be immediately convened for that purpose.

Respectfully,

THOMAS S. CUMMINGS.

February 18. A Special Meeting was called, and the President addressed the meeting as follows:

Gentlemen:

It is indeed a mournful occasion upon which we are at present assembled.

The death of Thomas Cole, rendered the more impressive by its suddenness, is a dispensation which cannot but spread far and wide a deeply saddening influence; and it falls upon the Academy with more than ordinary severity.

One of its early members, from first to last a constant and most efficient contributor to its maintenance, it would be difficult to overestimate our loss. But it were well if this were all; for when we reflect that he is cut off in the height of his maturity, in the full enjoyment of his high fame, and under the influence of its responsibilities; exerting unimpaired all the faculties of his gifted mind, where shall we limit the loss sustained in common by the Arts and by the country? It was ever his great aim to elevate the standard of Landscape Art, and he has been eminently successful; he has advanced far beyond the point at which he found it among us; and more than this, he has demonstrated its high moral capabilities, which had hitherto been at best but incidentally and capriciously exerted. Hence he is richly entitled to the name of Benefactor.

While we unite, then, to lament his untimely end, and to attempt some expression of our heartfelt sympathy in behalf of his bereaved family and friends, it becomes us to testify our regard for his services and character, by such tribute to his memory as shall in some measure accord with his signal merits, and serve in some degree as a stimulus to emulation of his brilliant example.

On motion, it was

Resolved, That we have heard with the profoundest feeling of regret of the untimely death of one of our earliest and most distinguished members, Thomas Cole. That the Secretary be desired to convey to the bereaved widow and family of the deceased the expression of our deep sympathy.

Resolved, That William C. Bryant, Honorary Member, be invited to deliver before the Academy an oration on the life and character of the deceased.

Resolved, That the usual observance of mourning be adopted by the Academy, and that these proceedings be published.

Mr. Bryant's oration was delivered on the 4th of March following. Some year or more after his decease an interesting memorial volume was published by the Rev. Mr. Noble, of Catskill—his intimate friend.

Many were desirous of a public exposition of his works. Messrs. Cummings, Durand, Huntington, Sturgess, Leupp and Edmonds, from the Academy, and Messrs. Wetmore, Cozzens, Hopping and Austin, from the Art Union, were appointed a Committee to forward that object.

The Art Union tendered their rooms, and an exhibition of his works was held. The merit and interest manifested are better understood than can be expressed.

March 13. Mr. Chapman going abroad to reside, he resigned the office of Corresponding Secretary. A resolution expressive of regret at parting with him, as also a vote of thanks for his valuable services, were passed. Mr. Chapman must have also acted as Recording Secretary for several years, as the minutes are in his handwriting; the beauty of which, and the clear exposition of the proceedings, are prominent proofs of his ability in that department. A testimonial to Mr. Chapman was ordered. Was it ever carried into effect?

April 3. The twenty-third Annual Exhibition opened to the public, closing July 8th, eighty-four working days, receiving $4446.91—average $53.06 per day—three hundred and seventy-three works.

May 10. The Annual Meeting of the Academicians was held. The Council reported:

"That in pursuance of the recommendation in last year's report, the Library has been opened daily during the season, with a Librarian in attendance. This arrangement will be continued in future, and we trust that its benefits will be duly appreciated.

"For the past season the schools of the Academy have *not* evinced an activity corresponding with the efforts of the Council in that direction. The number of students is somewhat diminished, and other signs of apathy, at variance with a just appreciation of their importance, have appeared. The inefficient operation of the Antique School may be safely ascribed to the change of its sessions from evening to daytime. Although the superior facilities thus offered cannot be questioned, and notwithstanding the Council has been petitioned to continue it, it is evident that the change is not wanted, and that from the nature of their daily avocations the great majority of students have been compelled to forego this advantage. We therefore returned to our former regulation, and for the future will open the school for the evening only.

   *   *   *   *   *   *   *   *   *

" The Life School commenced operations early in the season, and that nothing might be omitted to satisfy the wants of students in that department, it was furnished with the best model that could be procured—one experienced in the schools of Europe, and engaged at double the usual rate of compensation. This school also was at first opened during the day, but lacking attendance, its sessions were soon transferred to evening. Still failing to receive due encouragement, the Council became convinced that further exertion on their part would prove unavailing, and submitted to the discouragement, satisfied with having discharged their obligations.

"Late in the season a number of students of the Academy and others, chiefly young artists, formed an association with the avowed object of awakening a livelier interest in the study of the living model. They believed that this interest would be more effectually awakened and sustained by the institution of a new and independent Life School, subject to such regulations only as they chose to adopt, and supported by individual subscription among its members. Instead of availing themselves of the facilities already offered by the school of the Academy, and conforming to its regulations, this association solicited from the Council merely the use of an apartment. This, together with all the necessary accompaniments, was readily conceded, and their school has been carried on to the end of the season with commendable zeal and activity.

" The Council advert to this circumstance, not only to show the disposition of the Academy, consistently with its constitution, to favor every laudable effort to promote the study of art, but also to suggest whether there be any feature in the structure or administration of the Academy, that warrants the existence of such an association, or calls for measures of reform, or indeed dictates any movement that may tend to awaken the desired interest in, and more effective operation of, our schools.

"This inquiry has already occupied the attention of the Council, and the result of their mature deliberation is the conviction that the Academy is amply endowed with the power, and in possession of means fully adequate to the present wants of students and professional artists, in all that relates to practical education in drawing, both from the living model, as well as from the Antique.

" If these powers have not been fully exerted, it is more chargeable to the students' delinquency than deficiency on the part of the Academy; and further, we are satisfied that this delinquency originates mainly in the too prevalent repugnance to any species of restraint, even to an extent amounting to entire exemption from wholesome and necessary restrictions, required to secure the efficiency and stability of academic order. Of course to tolerate such a laxity of government would be fatal to the existence of an institution; at the same time we are willing and anxious to fix the limits of restrictive rule at the very verge of safety, if in so doing we can extend the Academy's advantages.

"We may with propriety here refer to the popular prejudice and antipathy, even to appearances of exclusiveness in the operations of public bodies; and if we would not have our course embarrassed by such imputations, we should be admonished to exercise the utmost liberality in the admission of new members. Indeed, we cannot lay too much stress on this point. Granting the necessity of an Academy for the cultivation and protection of art, such an institution, administered solely by artists, should necessarily embrace the interests and claim the support of the entire profession.

"Its course, therefore, should be to encourage and not to repulse the deserving aspirant for its honors, and even to invite every accession of the talents requisite for the active exercise of its usefulness.

"The paternal attachment of its founders, that has hitherto insured a lively interest in its welfare, will with them have soon passed away, and its safety may hereafter depend on less disinterested feeling. Among the dangers to which it is exposed, not the least, perhaps, are those of negligence and inaction. To guard against these liabilities, suitable talent and activity are required in our business department (in the common understanding of that term); the proverbial scarcity of this talent among our fraternity is an additional motive for the exercise of a discriminating liberality in the elective franchise.

*　　*　　*　　*　　*　　*　　*　　*　　*　　*

"The Building Committee, though not prepared to report definitively on the business before them, entertain confident hopes that the erection of a suitable edifice will be effected in time to meet the desires of the Academy; the Council has accordingly postponed, for a few weeks longer, the decision on the renewal of the present lease.

"A Committee has been appointed on the part of the New-York Gallery of Fine Arts to confer with your Committee on the subject of uniting the two institutions under one roof, and we are encouraged to hope that this plan will be finally carried out—a speedy determination is expected, when the matter will be laid before the Academy.

The Treasurer reported the total receipts for the year, $8058.57; disbursements, investments, &c., $7638.77; balance in hand, $419.80; and submitted an appendix, from which is extracted the following:

GENTLEMEN:

Herewith I deliver to you the drawings and estimates for a building for the Academy and other purposes, to be erected on a surface of 50 by 200 feet, drawn agreeably to plans I submitted, together with suggestions for carrying the same into effect.   *   *   *   *   *   *
Having passed these matters to your consideration, I beg leave, in consequence of circumstances not properly within my province to mention, to be permitted to retire from the said Building Committee, feeling fully satisfied that my remaining can in no way be serviceable or advantageous to the Academy.

Respectfully,

T S. CUMMINGS, *Treasurer.*

A. B. Durand was elected President; Charles C. Ingham, Vice-President; J. H. Shegogue, Corresponding Secretary; F. R. Spencer, Recording Secretary; Thomas S. Cummings, Treasurer; H. P. Gray and V. C. Audubon, Council. There were no Academicians elected.

May 26.   The drawings for a building to be erected on Broadway, above and north of the Bond Street House, presented by Mr. Cummings, were acted upon, and it was

Resolved, That the plans for a building for the National Academy of Design submitted by the Treasurer be, and they are hereby approved, and that immediate measures be taken to carry the same into effect.

The Academy subsequently built on the stables of the old Broadway line of omnibuses, between Bleecker and Amity Streets, and next southerly to the marble buildings known as the Bond Street House. The first-named property was *northerly* adjoining—fifty feet front by two hundred feet deep, running through to Mercer Street, and was purchased of the late Mr. Lafarge for fifty thousand dollars. After the agreement had been signed, a difference arose on the subject of a party-wall on the north side of the Bond Street House, which had never been released, or its existence even known to the seller, but which the Academy deemed included in the purchase. The seller thought otherwise, and the parties were at issue; and although the Academy had incurred the expense of searching the title, and of having full architectural plans drawn for the building, costing several hundred dollars—a sum probably equal to more than double the purchase money of the wall—yet, as the seller refused to include it, the Trustees refused to accept without it, both parties were a little excited, and had passed the point of judicious reasoning.

The owner was willing to leave it to referees, and named parties who, for some cause, (the *referees*, but not a reference) were rejected. The Academy accepted reference, and in turn named referees, who were in like manner refused, probably because the first-named referees by him had been rejected. Mutual choice was offered by the seller; that was singularly rejected. Mr. Lafarge then drew off altogether, and the whole matter fell through, which no sooner occurred than the first party purchased the wall at a mere nominal sum, and Mr. Cummings retired from the Building Committee.

October 3. The Life and Antique Schools were opened, free of charge, and in the minutes the attendance pronounced good. There were no premiums offered.

During the Fall of 1848 some beautiful paintings of the German School were introduced, which led to the establishment of the *Dusseldorf Gallery;* at least that importation formed the basis of it. The works were exhibited with success; it received frequent additions, and for years continued to attract attention, and obtained the support of the community—far beyond any other similar collection.

A proposition " to *lease* the Racket Court Building, Nos. 594 and 596 Broadway, for the purposes of the Academy," received considerable support, and much opposition; the ayes and nays being called on every question proposed. It was not taken.

November 20. A resolution was passed:

" That the plan of an International Art Union, submitted by Messrs. Goupil, Vibert & Co. to the National Academy of Design, and soliciting their co-operation, meets with the approbation of the Council, and will receive their cordial support."

The plan, as it appears, must have been materially altered from the original draft, for after the passage of that resolution it was (in December)

Resolved, That the resolution in relation thereto, passed on the 20th November, be, and it is hereby rescinded.

The plans, unfortunately, cannot be given; they are not to be found on file.

December 31. Died, Robert Gilmore, aged seventy-five years, a distinguished merchant of Baltimore—a lover of the fine arts, and an Honorary Member of the Academy.

The Adam and Eve paintings returned, after a general exposition throughout the country. They were exhibited in the galleries of the National Academy of Design, and were successful, though not to the extent of their previous *earnings*.

January 23. Died, Frederick Fink. The subject of our remarks was born at Little Falls, in the Mohawk **1849.** Valley, December 28, 1817, and lies interred in a beautiful knoll not far from the cottage of his birth.

He was a descendant (grandson) of Major Andrew Fink, of Revolutionary fame, whose services were highly eulogized by Washington; and he likewise received a vote of thanks from the Provincial Congress. He was in the battles of Monmouth and Saratoga. After the war he was one of the earliest settlers of Tryon County, where, while in the peaceful cultivation of his farm, he lost his life. Near his plough, left standing, he lay dead, with the murderous knife still in his heart. But the brave man had not died unrevenged; by his side lay two Indian warriors, one of whom he had felled with a blow that laid bare his brain, while his hand still clinched the hair of the other, who had driven the knife into his bosom.

Andrew A. Fink, father of Frederick Fink, was reared a farmer, inheriting a large tract of land through his grandfather, Major Fink, on the banks of the Mohawk River—which he continued to cultivate, and where the subject of this sketch was born and reared. He was an honorable and very active man, and in early life was foremost in all the enterprises of his native town. He is still living, at the age of eighty, in comfortable health, with an unclouded intellect, on the farm where Frederick was born.

Frederick, the artist, was destined for the medical profession, and after leaving the district school of his neighborhood, at the age of thirteen, he was placed with Dr. Beck, of Albany. There he remained three years, as he said, his love of art becoming stronger and stronger every day, until eventually that connection was severed; subsequently he was placed with his brother—a prosperous merchant—but it suited Frederick no better. Frederick desired to be an artist, which was not deemed advisable by either his father or his friends; which opinion was, however, only admonitory—not mandatory. He had determined to be an artist, and despite that advice, "steamed" for New-York.

Once in the city, he devoted himself to the study of art, somewhat financially assisted by a friend of his father's family. He made the acquaintance of Trumbull, Morse, Cummings, Crawford, and others, and received friendly advice from them. His father, finding Frederick determined, allowed him the bent of his inclinations—to draw pictures, and to " draw" on him for funds wherewith to enable him to do so in comfort and to advantage. Frederick was placed in the studio of Morse, to study his chosen profession therein three years. At the age of eighteen he started for himself, finding good employment at from fifty to one hundred dollars for a portrait, according as it was a half-length or only a bust.

His portrait of W. S. Parker was much admired, and induced in him a desire to go abroad for further and higher study. That picture introduced him to Mr. Schoolcraft, who, hearing of his desires, at once gave him a commission to paint for him, during his absence, a subject—whatever he pleased, how he pleased, and at what price he pleased. That determined him to visit Italy, and while painting Mr. Schoolcraft's portrait, he was offered by that gentleman five hundred dollars in advance on his commission, to enable him to proceed at once, and Mr. Parker subsequently gave a thousand dollars for the same purpose.

Fink had married in Albany in March, 1838; in May, 1840, he sailed for Havre, taking with him his wife and infant.

He copied for his friend Parker, Titian's Christ at Emmaus, and Murillo's Magdalen. His " Old Man's Head" and " Peasant Girl," exhibited at the National Academy Gallery, were much admired. He copied works of art, but not long or many, soon executing originals—"An Old Soldier of Napoleon," and " The Death of Raphael," for Mr. Schoolcraft. His " Greek" was much eulogized abroad and at home. " The Holy Family"—a copy of Paul Veronese— made at Venice for Mr. Henry Bleecker, of Albany, brought him many encomiums. After several months on the Continent, the young artist started for England, and from thence, after a three years' absence, once more returned for home. His pictures painted after his return gave him increased reputation ; and he was made an Honorary Member of the National Academy of Design, May 10th, 1839.

Among the " *original*" works he left are: " The Artist's Studio," " Shipwrecked Mariner," " Young Thieves," "Negro Wood Sawyer," "A Female," "A Greek," "Death of Raphael," " Before the Virgin," " Cigaretta," and " Napoleon's Old Guard."

The " *copies*": " Magdalen" by Murillo, " Madonna" by

Raphael, "Madonna" by Paul Veronese, "Presentation at the Temple" by Titian, "Aurora" by Guido, "The Miracle" by Tintoretto, "Christ at Emmaus" by Titian, "Deposition from the Cross" by Titian, "Madonna and Child" by Raphael, and many less important works.

April 3. The twenty-fourth Annual Exhibition was opened to the public; closed July 7th (eighty-three working days), and received $2753.47, averaging $33.17 per day; it contained three hundred and seventy-three works of art.

April 30. The President was authorized to sign an agreement for the purchase of the property on Broadway, south of the Bond Street House, and the rear property in the centre of the block—"Brower's Stables." On it was erected the well-known splendid Galleries. Many, indeed, were the difficulties encountered in that undertaking, although ultimately a source of great advantage to the Academy.

May 9. Messrs. Sturges, Leupp, and Edmonds resigned their positions on the Building Committee, and Messrs. Ingham, Shegogue, and Gray were appointed to supply their places—the Committee was then Messrs. Cummings, Durand, Ingham, Shegogue and Gray. A commencement was scarcely made before a difficulty occurred between one of the Committee and the Medical College of the Stuyvesant Institute, on the subject of their wall, below which the Academy had proceeded to excavate, and in which premises he had made certain promises or concessions, which greatly exceeded his powers and embarrassed the proceedings, and caused delay and expense. More money than was at the disposal of the Committee was wanted, and scrip or bonds had to be issued. There appeared to be but little confidence in the business ability of the Committee; they were all artists, and at that time, whether justly or not, artists had not a high reputation for business capacity. The completion of the front building exhausted the funds, the bonds did not produce more, and no advance whatever had been made towards preparing the Art Galleries in the main building, which alone was looked to for the support of the Institution. The Academy was a second time bankrupt.

At that stage of the proceedings Messrs. Sturges, Leupp and Edmonds were again consulted, and their aid solicited. They returned, the prior Board resigning for that purpose. Under their assistance money was raised on the bonds of the Academy, but more so from the liberal private purses of Messrs. Sturges and Leupp. The buildings once more progressed, and under their influence were carried to completion.

Died, Carey R. Long, Architect and Honorary Member. He built the Union Bank and the St. Paul's Church, in Baltimore—works of rare merit and originality. He met with a sudden and melancholy death, unsurrounded by friends, unaided by their comfortings in his last extremity. At the time of his death he was engaged in Morristown, New Jersey, superintending the completing of the interior of a church which he had designed and erected. There, while at his work, he was taken sick with the cholera. His affrighted fellow-workmen and comrades running away—deserting him—for want of assistance, it was said he actually died in the church.

The writer cannot help placing the following in juxtaposition. Louis Lang was taken sick in New-York; his friend Darley heard of it, and immediately went to him—only to find his room-door shut, and entrance refused, apparently with some one within. Darley called, and was answered from thence by his friend, to "Go away; that he (Lang) was very sick with the small-pox, and not to come near him." At once Darley's foot was at the door, and it yielded to his impetuous charge; he stood in the presence of his friend, and remained to nurse and cherish him in his misfortune. In turn he took the disease even worse than Lang. They, however, both recovered, but Darley carries with him, and *will* carry with him to his grave, the HONORABLE marks of his devotion.

May 9, was held the Annual Meeting of the Academicians, the Council reporting:

REPORT.

GENTLEMEN:

The condition of the Academy at the close of another year may justly excite your anxious solicitude for its future welfare.

The sudden decline in our revenue which appeared in the course of the last Exhibition was the commencement of a series of adverse circumstances, which has continued, with but brief intervals, up to the present time.

A deficiency of near two thousand dollars, compared with the income of the preceding year, could not fail to cripple the operations of the Academy, although its immediate effect was chiefly confined to the Annuity Fund; but an accompanying calamity, the loss of one of our most valued members, not only renders any curtailment of that fund the more to be lamented, but also extends the evil into every department of the Institution. Notwithstanding this deficiency, the most essential purposes of the Academy have not been impeded; on the contrary, the schools have flourished beyond preceding sessions—the annuities, though doubled, have been paid—the Reserve and Library Funds have received their usual appropriations. These, and other details relating to our finances, will, as usual, be submitted in the Report of the Treasurer.

*   *   *   *   *   *   *

A prominent object kept steadily in view for the last few years—that of providing a suitable location on the expiration of our present lease—has more especially occupied the attention of the Academy during the past year.

* * * * * * *

At a meeting convened on the 22d day of November last, a proposition to purchase lots, together with plans for the erection of suitable buildings thereon, as reported by the Building Committee, were approved, and said Committee instructed to proceed in carrying the same into effect. At this meeting two other members were added to this Committee, for reasons deemed indispensable.

* * * * * * *

An important feature in the resolutions passed was the creation of a Trusteeship, by constituting the Building Committee a body of Trustees on the part of the Academy, with full power to carry out the intended object.

* * * * * * *

Another object deemed of paramount importance engaged the attention of the Academy—that is, a general revision of the Constitution. For this end, due measures were taken early in the season, and earnestly pursued, resulting, at present, in the attainment of but two essential points—one affecting the Annuity Fund ; the other relating to the conduct of our elections.

These amendments cannot fail to exercise a beneficial influence, in harmony with every other measure conducive to our future prosperity.

As already stated, other important revisions are in progress, under charge of your Committee.

* * * * * * *

The Academy has, in all its relations, a healthy and vigorous action, and from its continuance through a period of more than twenty years, in connection with the collateral aid of progression in popular Taste, not less natural, they had a right to entertain confident expectations of the final and firm establishment of a great National School of Art. This confidence is at length shaken, if not completely prostrated ; for it is no longer a question that the seductive influence of Free Exhibitions, encouraged and sustained by far other motives than the love of Art, is the primary cause of our embarrassment. To this we owe the decline in our revenue, commencing with the last, and continued into the present season. We may be permitted to hope that the evil is but temporary, and destined ultimately to develop its own remedy.

* * * * * * *

If there be any available means to counteract this evil, in addition to the attractions of our Exhibition, they may perhaps be found in the adoption of measures corresponding with those that have produced it—that is, the incorporation of the Art Union principle into the structure of the Academy. We are constrained to recommend this suggestion to your earnest consideration. It is recommended on the ground that it is politic, and indeed imperative, to adapt our movements, as far as consistent, to the habits and susceptibilities of the community.

* * * * * * *

We must render our Exhibition Room more easy of access, and put on all suitable extrinsic decorations to attract the *multitude*, instead of relying on the inherent beauties of Art, perceptible only to the enlightened few.

* * * * * * *

For this reason, we deprecate every effort to create a demand for works of Art beyond the power of Art, as circumstanced, to supply, by the full exercise of healthy and intelligent action. Anything beyond this must degrade its standard, and retard its advancement. The more we reflect on this subject, the more we become convinced that it is the duty of this Academy, if possible, to wrest from incompetent hands an agency so powerful as the Art Union principle is proved to be, and, by a judicious direction, preserve it at least from the destructive sway of ignorance and pretension.

By the Treasurer's Report it appeared that the total receipts were $5780.48; disbursements, $5306.92; leaving a balance of $73.56 in the treasury.

A. B. Durand was elected President; Charles C. Ingham, Vice-President; James H. Shegogue, Corresponding Secretary; Frederick R. Spencer, Recording Secretary; Thomas S. Cummings, Treasurer; William S. Mount and William Page, Members of Council. Thomas P. Rossitter, J. B. Flagg, J. B. Stearns, F. E. Church, Edwin White, Christian Mayer, and J. F. Kensett were elected Academicians.

At that meeting it was

Resolved, That the Council be requested to draw up a plan by which the Art Union principle may be applied to the advancement of the interests of the Academy.

August 18. A Review Exhibition was resolved on by the Council, to take place in the fall. It did not meet with a response, and was abandoned; it was to have consisted of pictures previously exhibited.

August 21. Died, John R. Smith.

"His death was sublimely, beautifully quiet. At the age of about eighty, he had become quite infirm, but was able to sit up several hours each day.

"He rose one morning, ate his breakfast, read his morning paper, and, according to his custom, fell asleep in his chair. His wife sat by his side, but thinking he slept longer than usual, looked at him more attentively, and found that he had quietly passed away."

He had labored for nearly forty years as a Teacher, devoted his whole time, and was devotedly attached to his art. He was a sarcastic writer, and author of a series of articles in the *National Advocate*, on the Academy, under the title of NEUTRAL TINT. He published a "Juvenile Drawing Book," "A Compendium of Anatomy," and "Chromotology," his favorite work. In his early days his classes were large—included many since distinguished artists—Sully, Cummings, Agate, Leutze, and many others. His love of truth was his failing; he gave offence, and his influence was widely felt; he was a severe and uncompromising critic.

"His personal appearance," says a cotemporary, "was very curious. His short figure, large head, peculiar one-sided gait and indescribable expression of countenance, with its queer significance, while uttering his rare and spicy witticisms, will long be remembered."

August 31. Died, George W. Bruen, a distinguished merchant, and an Honorary Member.

From August to October there were no meetings.

October 25. There was a rearrangement of the Trust,

with full powers, and a Trust Deed was executed, to enable them better to proceed with the work. The fiscal management was placed in the hands of the writer.

November 5. There appeared to have existed considerable difficulty on the "ALTERATION AND AMENDMENT OF THE CONSTITUTION," that well-worn subject; many meetings and hot contests on the proposed *amendments*, perhaps safer to say alterations.

Cummings, Gray, and Ingham resigned from the Committee; but whatever may have been the *difficulties*, the Academicians seemed determined to proceed in the undertaking, and conquer them. Cummings, Durand, Huntington, Proud'homme, and Launitz were immediately reappointed, and directed " to proceed with the work, and likewise to lay before the body a *complete exposition* of the *laws already passed and operative.*" (No very slight work, certainly.)

Alteration of the Constitution appeared to have become a periodical mania.

As a general principle, the difficulty will be found in the following: *that* no sooner did a law become operative, than there was a desire to change or abrogate it; it pinched somewhere.

November 25. Messrs. Goupil, Vibert & Co's proposition, made through Mr. Shaus, to establish a fund by their house, to send an American art student abroad for study for two years, was again brought before the Academy, and it was

Resolved, That the Council accede to the proposition to act as judges on the designs or pictures to be executed in competition for the prize offered to send an American artist abroad to study for two years.

On the 27th of March then next following a decision was given on the paintings in competition submitted. In that decision there was an utter disregard of the strict construction necessarily required to be put on the offered terms, which did a manifest injustice to one of the contributors, Thomas Augustus Cummings, and to whom, under strictly legal ruling, the premium would have fallen.

In the stipulations offered, and published, to govern the judges and contributors, a date was fixed and given for the reception of works, and beyond which, it was stated, no contributions were to be received.

The painting which obtained the award was not received within that so specified date, nor was it present or in for *many* days thereafter. Though it WAS in before the much-delayed meeting of the Council, to decide on the merits. Had the decision been made on the day of closing, or had that point, which was argued and which was entirely disregarded, been correctly ruled, it is clear that the picture which received the premium would have been excluded ; and as it was unanimously conceded that the contest rested between Thomas Augustus Cummings (all names then unknown) and the one which received the award, it is equally clear that a correct construction would have given the premium to Cummings. An appeal to a legal tribunal, to decide the question, was advised and seriously thought of; but as the writer was the father of the contestant, and a member of the Council which decided, and withal not particularly anxious for the award for his son, he allowed it to pass. It therefore went to Mr. Rutherford, who received the $1200 money or $600 per annum, and started on his course of study under its advantages. Unfortunately, that young gentleman was not destined long to profit by its advantages; consumption, deeply seated before his departure, cut him off in his youth. He died abroad, much regretted by his friends.

The plan submitted by Mr. Ingham, for the establishment of an Art Union by the Academy, was approved, but unfortunately it does not appear in the record, or file; its excellence or its advantages are, therefore, left to conjecture. No further action appears to have been had in the premises. It was to have received the title of the "Painters' and Sculptors' Art Union." A reference to Mr. Ingham was of no better avail; he answered that he did not remember the slightest fact connected with it.

December 26. The Huntington Exhibition. A number of the most distinguished citizens solicited an exhibition of his works, as gratifying to themselves and many friends. The proposition, so kindly made, was acceded to, and arrangements were immediately made and carried out, for their exposition in the Art Union Building.

The collection embraced one hundred and thirty productions, extending from his first composition—" Ichabod Crane"—to his most finished and latest productions, not excepting, perhaps, his finest work—" Mercy's Dream." The Exhibition was most gratifying to artist and public.

January 20.   Died, Bartolini ———, a distinguished sculptor of Florence, and an Honorary Member.

1850.   February 2.   The rooms were offered to the City Gallery for their Exhibition during the intervals of the "Academic Annual," with the restrictions, that the Exhibition should contain only the works owned by the Gallery, or such others only as should receive the assent of three members of the Council; nor was the City Gallery to open the Exhibition free of charge.

In the early part of April died, David C. Colden, Honorary Member. He was the son of Cadwallader D. Colden, one of the early Mayors of the City of New-York. Mr. Colden was a gentleman of taste and refinement, and delighted in the society of artists and literary men. He was a member of the old Sketch Club, and likewise one of the founders of the " Century."

Success had attended the efforts of the Trustees, and the Brower's Stables had been converted into a beautiful suite of Galleries.

April 13. A Reception was had to inaugurate the new rooms.

On the day following the twenty-fifth Annual Exhibition opened to the public.

The long-wished-for reduction of the stair ascent was obtained; the rooms were only thirteen feet from the street line, and through one of the most eligible and easy-of-ascent staircases that could be devised. That staircase was A FEATURE; in fact, it had been Mr. Ingham's hobby, and was ever known as the "Ingham Stairs." It was a very beautifully-designed piece of work. The rooms were the handsomest the Academy had ever had, or probably ever will have, and covered an area of one' hundred and sixty-four by fifty feet in one line—over six hundred feet of wall. They were well lighted by day, and in the evening by three hundred gas-burners—one hundred and fifty-seven feet of running wall—more than the Leonard Street suite, and the number of gas-lights more than doubled—then decidedly the finest Art Galleries in the country. Yet, with all such advantages, the twenty-fifth Annual Exhibition received only $3066.61—open seventy-two working days, and averaging $42.60 per day ; three hundred and seventy-three works of art—far less in amount than had been obtained under much less favorable circumstances. The falling off was undoubtedly attributable to the Art Union Free Exhibition (open at the same time). It was scarcely to be expected that one Exhibition should be attended at *twenty-five cents* admission, if an equally good one was obtainable, at the same time and equally convenient, for nothing.

During that exhibition occurred one of those unpleasantnesses which, more or less, are ever found to disturb the academic course—the right of an artist to exhibit his work with, or without the consent of the party ordering it. The artist exhibiter who sent the work claimed that he had the consent of the reputed owner, and moreover, that ownership was not complete—that he had not been placed in possession, that no delivery had been made, and finally, that *he* (the *artist*) had not been paid for his work. The other party denied all the points as set forth, and claimed for himself directly the reverse.

As is usual in such cases; and he *peremptorily* demanded of the Academy the *immediate removal, from the walls* of the Gallery, of the painting to him belonging, and the delivery of it to him. As before stated, the Academy had received the work from the artist, and had no knowledge whatever of any other possessor. To deliver to the complainant would make them liable to the artist—to deliver to the artist, probably equally so to the opposing party. The demand was refused, and the complainant at once replevined, and Charles S. Roe, Esq., was retained to conduct the case for the Academy.

The Sheriff immediately demanded the work delivered to him, and it was sent, under a strong escort, to his office. The Sheriff, after a hearing of the case and receiving a bond for the safe-keeping of the picture, remanded it back to the Academy's care, and it was replaced on the walls of the Exhibition, under extra watch, which was onerous and expensive, and it was taken down and placed in the Council room, and a ticket stating the cause of removal thereof put up in its place.

A litigation was then commenced, which lasted many months—nay, some two years or more—and during which time the painting remained in the custody of the Academy. The complainant was successfully resisted. It was subsequently settled by the sudden and unannounced removal, for permanent residence abroad, of the artist painter—the Academy's only witness; and as he appeared to be, and *was* willing to relinquish all claim and interest in the work, the Academy had little more to object to—the matter ended. The painting was then delivered to the claimant, who, it is said, had originally ordered it.

April 25. A Special Meeting was held, pursuant to notice, to amend the Constitution, and a full and successful attendance was had.

The Constitution *was* amended, and the body was then and there notified again to assemble on the first Monday in November, for the reception of still farther emendations. The *amendment fever was at a high point.*

May 8. There appears to have been no schools, consequent, probably, on "removal," and there being no apartments ready for use.

The Annual Meeting was held.

Business commenced with reading the President's Report.

REPORT.

Immediately after the purchase of the property on Broadway, Trustees were chosen from our own body, empowered to raise funds for the erection of the buildings, on bonds issued by the Academy, based upon such security as the Academy had it in their power to offer. After encountering many and unforeseen difficulties, the Trustees succeeded in collecting some four thousand dollars, which, with about three thousand remaining in the treasury, enabled them to erect a two-story building on Broadway, including an entrance, vestibule, and staircase to the Exhibition Rooms, according to plans approved of and adopted at the time. The object of this front building was to secure at the earliest date its quota of revenue to meet the demand of interest on the investment; its style and dimensions were unavoidably restricted by the limited means in the hands of the Trustees, but notwithstanding the strictest economy, before the building was completed their funds and resources were exhausted. In this dilemma, assurances were given by the former Trustees that they would relieve the Academy from their embarrassment on certain conditions, which were finally made satisfactory to the respective parties. Accordingly, your Trustees resigned, and the former Trustees were reinstated in the Trusteeship.

By the more ample resources at the command of these gentlemen, the buildings have been so far completed as to furnish accommodations for the present twenty-fifth Annual Exhibition, as well as to place the remaining portions in such a state of forwardness as to insure their completion by the first of June next. The premises have all been favorably rented; and from the income, it is expected that the Academy will be able to meet all claims for interest on the investment, as well as to carry a surplus annually towards the liquidation of the principal.

An accompanying statement of the Trustees will show the amount of receipts and disbursements on the property up to this date.

The Annual Report of the Treasurer will present you with the financial condition of the Academy, from which it will appear that the depreciation in the receipts of the last Annual Exhibition has required the suspension of our schools, and rendered the Academy unable to meet the demand for rent.

      *   *   *   *   *   *   *

In compliance with the request of the International Art Union, the Council have decided on the claims of the competitors for the prize offered by that Institution—viz., the sum of $1,200, for the support of an American student for the term of two years in Europe. The Council have awarded the same to Mr. Rutherford, of this city.

From the Treasurer's Report it appeared that the total receipts were $12,159.84, and the total expenditures $12,025.54; leaving a balance in the Treasury of $134.30. And the Treasurer received a vote of thanks from the body for his long and faithful services in the discharge of his duty.

At that stage of the meeting, an injunction was served on the body assembled—issued by the Court of Common Pleas, on the complaint of the Vice-President, to restrain the members present from proceeding in the election of Academicians, or of increasing the number thereof beyond thirty-five.

That such a proceeding should have been sought by Mr. Ingham, with his views on the matter, would probably not have excited surprise, or even been without advantage, as a slight reminder to the Academicians that they, too, were subject to higher tribunals than their own, and even prove a salutary lesson—but the abruptly unannounced demonstration, not received until the evening of meeting, thereby depriving the body of *counsel*, or thought, was the subject of much complaint.

The suit was defended by the Academy. Ultimately it was abandoned by the complainant, who found the contest unprofitable; and there ended the matter, except as to feeling, which fortunately has been all healed.

The election of officers was proceeded with.

A. B. Durand was elected President; Thomas S. Cummings, Vice-President—(Mr. Edmonds consenting to allow his name to be used as Treasurer if Mr. Cummings would continue to discharge the duties of the office, to the end that he, Mr. Cummings, should take the place of Mr. Ingham); J. H. Shegogue, Corresponding Secretary; J. B. Stearns, Recording Secretary; F. W. Edmonds, Treasurer (nominally). J. F. Kensett and Thomas P. Rossitter were elected to the Council.

The meeting adjourned for half an hour, and after some consultation, proceeded with the election of Associates.

No Academicians were elected.

The party then at issue was one of the oldest artists—one of the longest-tried and firmest supporters of the Academy—one who was never found wanting—one who was fearless in its defence—one to whom the scathing beam of justice offered no fear of short weight against him. Something, it seems, of more than ordinary import must have occurred to arouse such a man, and in such a manner; the more particularly so, as he, with many others of the Academy, were together the previous evening, and no notice whatever was given of the intention. As he has furnished the writer with a written explanation, he shall be heard for himself.

MR. INGHAM'S EXPLANATION.

" Mr. Ingham's difficulty with the Academy arose from the following cause: A majority of the Academicians thought that as this is a democratic country, the Academy should be based on principles of equality; that all artists should be admitted; that a *bare majority* should elect members, and should have the power of altering the Constitution. In opposition to this doctrine, Mr. Ingham maintained that, as many artists had no means of adding to the income of the Academy, those who earned, should alone have the power of disposing of the money. The leaders of the majority determined to make a radical change in the Constitution of the Academy, and for this purpose called a meeting. According to the provisions of the then existing Constitution, it required a concurring vote of *two-thirds of all the Academicians* to make an alteration in the instrument. From the number of *absent* members, Mr. Ingham calculated that not more than two-thirds of the body could attend the meeting, so that one or two opposing votes could stop any alteration; and there being three members who held Mr. Ingham's conservative views, he was sure of retaining the existing laws. The meeting took place in the Exhibition Room over the Library in Broadway. The proposed alterations were put to the vote. One of Mr. Ingham's friends remained silent, which was equivalent to *no;* another, Christian Von Mayer, voted no. The President declared the measure carried. Mr. Ingham said it was not—that the requisite number of members were not present, and demanded the call of the yeas and nays. *This was refused,* and then the President *broke up the meeting.* Mr. Ingham being confident that the alterations in the Constitution had not been legally carried, had an injunction served on the Academy at the Annual Meeting to stop all proceedings under the altered Constitution. After the controversy had been carried on for some time, he reflected that his opponents required only two or three votes to carry their measures at any time, and he could hope for no new converts to his conservative opinions; therefore he withdrew his suit, *each party paying their own expenses.*"

May 28. Died, at Rome, Richard Wyatt, Honorary Member, and sculptor of great excellence.

June —. A resolution was passed "that the two statues of Canova—" THE BOXERS"—be placed, one on each side of the library door, on the entrance to the building, provided it was not objected to by other tenants." Alas! it was objected to. Their love of art was by no means equal to their love of space; they voted them a nuisance, and they were removed. The Bacchanalian figure, "colossal," was placed on the stairs, in a niche previously built for that purpose and encroaching into the Council room, although facing and open to the stairway; but the ruthless tenants *"below"* papered the hall across, and thus excluded the art display from view. His Bacchanalianship remained thus incased until the removal from the building, when he was released from his thraldom. He has never since been put together, and is a part occupier of a temporary storage-house.

From that forward there appear to have been six successive meetings without a *"quorum."*

June 8. Died, Daniel Seymour, an accomplished scholar and lover of art—Honorary Member of the Academy, and one of the founders of the "Century."

August 30. Died, John Inman, brother to the lamented Henry Inman, Artist: Honorary Member of the Academy. Mr. John Inman was a distinguished writer, Secretary of the *Old Sketch Club,* and was for many years, and up to the time of his death, the assistant editor of the *Commercial Advertiser.* His pen was wielded with effect, and to the advantage of the Academy, in its early struggles.

September — was exhibited in the Gallery a life-size group in marble—"The Bard's Curse." The work possessed a high degree of merit, yet did not please. It was pecuniarily unsuccessful; it did not, perhaps, possess the requisites essential to move the people; nor did it appear to excite the lovers of art. Its want of success proved a subject of depression to a young and meritorious artist. It was exhibited in the Crystal Palace, after thence sold at auction, and lastly returned to Europe, where it was more fully appreciated, and holds, it is said, a high rank.

September 4. Died, Gerlando Marseglia, Academician of 1826, an Italian artist of much merit. His works are scarcely known, or himself remembered. The first Exhibitions contained many of his productions—remarkably peculiar in style; and unlike anything other than themselves, they were glittering, even to a metallic lustre, in surface. He was a kind, good-natured man, had few enemies and many friends.

October 18. Died, Theodore Allen, Honorary Member—a gentleman of refined taste, a lover of the arts, and devoted much of his leisure to the society and encouragement of artists. He was the son-in-law of the late Leuman Reed, and was a member of the Sketch Club.

October 28. Owing to the depressed condition of the funds of the Academy, it was resolved "that the Life and Antique Schools should not be opened;" and at the same time, one loaning the rooms and statuary to such artists and others as should associate together for the purpose of study, they (the scholars) bearing all expenses. The schools were then left under the exclusive control of the students. One member of the Council attended for a time, and took care of the establishment and the preservation of order; and while so conducted it answered a good purpose. On the remission of his superintendence the matter assumed a far different aspect, and from that period "*lost favor.*" Was it to be wondered at ?

October 30. An Exhibition was held at the Gallery of the Academy, by Baron Arnstein, purporting to be "original works," and of GREAT VALUE. The most exorbitant views were entertained by him, of its success. The Treasurer, however, insisted on the rent being paid in advance. The exhibiter "had astonished foreign courts, had created a *furor* wherever he displayed in European art-knowing cities," and, as he supposed, would, in New-York, receive adulation and "golden" recompense.

As a part of the programme, the proprietor wished at once to engage six gentlemen ushers, who were to be "dressed in black"—"white cravats and white kid gloves" —"their object to herald the public, to announce greatness, and direct the parties to the more prominent works." That the writer prevented by stating that he could allow no such nonsense to take place in the rooms—that it would be a source of ridicule to all parties. That was fortunately listened to. The Exhibition was opened without success; it received no support whatever—it was unworthy of it—

and the receipts, as the BARON himself stated, did not pay his *advertising bills*. It was not long before he humbly thanked the writer for saving him the mortification which would necessarily have followed his projected outset. He did not, he said, *know* the American public. That was true.

Some were cruel enough to say the pictures were copies; and if the prices they brought at public auction should be taken as a criterion, they were so ! They scarcely brought dollars—where thousands were "the Baron's" estimated valuation. He was disgusted with the Americans' want of taste and love of high art. The writer consoled him by the assurance that they certainly knew either too little, or *too much*, to *appreciate his* works.

October 30. A meeting of the Academy was called for the purpose of "devising some means whereby to discharge a small floating debt of the Institution, which was embarrassing, and required settlement."

The meeting was addressed by Edmonds and Cummings, both of whom gave full statements of the causes that had provoked the circumstances related, and urged a united effort to discharge the obligation. Several suggestions were made—the more prominent, that each member should contribute a work of art, to be disposed of by raffle or sale—the proceeds to be used to discharge the debt incurred.

Mr. Abraham S. Cozzens, President of the Art Union, then present, stated that if the pictures were furnished by the members, the Art Union would purchase them in mass. That method was adopted; the pictures were produced by the following gentlemen, pursuant to the call:

A. B. Durand, Thomas S. Cummings, T. P. Rossitter, Regis Gignoux, V. F. Audubon, D. Huntington, J. B. Stearns, John Evers, F. E. Church, James Boyle, P. P. Duggan, William S. Mount, E. H. May, Joseph Kyle, T. A. Richards, S. S. Osgood, J. H. Cafferty, J. W. Audubon, George A. Baker, S. R. Gifford, Thomas Hicks, Thomas Thompson, C. Cranch, H. C. Shumway, J. H. Shegogue, J. F. Boyle, S. A. Mount, Jared B. Flagg, H. P. Gray, William M. Pratt, G. W. Flagg, C. L. Elliott, Mrs. Spencer, J. F. Kensett, and H. Dassell.

A Committee—A. B. Durand, A. M. Cozzens and F. W. Edmonds—appraised the pictures, when finished, at two thousand dollars, and that amount was at once paid for them by the Art Union. A united effort, and good friendship, saved the Institution from embarrassment. The transaction reflected the highest credit on all parties. Suitable resolutions of thanks were offered to the contributors and to the purchasers.

Dr. Watts delivered his lectures on Anatomy to the students of the Medical College, to which the art students were invited.

November 4. Was exhibited Mr. Healy's picture of the Senate Chamber—Webster addressing the Senate in his "great speech"—the likeness remarkably good, impressively so, of the grandeur of the great man—statesman—one whom, more than any other, the nation delighted to honor, and to whom even a presidential election could have given no additional renown. The Exhibition was attractive, but not remunerative.

January 13. Died, Thomas Birch, Honorary Member— a marine painter of merit. His residence was in
1851. Philadelphia, where his works were best known.

The freshness of his atmospheres, and the clearly-painted waves, were generally the marked features in his pictures—almost always a ship in the distance, heading in. These will long be remembered by his admirers. He was a large contributor to the EARLY Exhibitions of the Academy.

January 27. Died, J. J. Audubon, the great ornithologist, and Honorary Member, at his residence, Audubon Park, One Hundred and Fifty-fifth Street (Carmansville), in the City of New-York.

April 6. Mr. Cummings presented to the Academy fifty-eight etchings by Piranisi.

April 8. The twenty-sixth Annual Exhibition was opened to the public, closing on the fifth of July. It was open seventy-seven working days, and received $2,918.30—averaging $37.90 per day. It contained four hundred and sixteen productions; the Exhibition yielding less than that of 1850, although the display was universally pronounced one of much more than ordinary excellence.

June 9. Occurred a pleasing little ovation. The writer had, some time previously, painted a copy of Stuart's head (from the original study) of Mrs. Washington. While painting the portrait of the Governor-General of Canada, he mentioned to him his intention, at some time or other, of presenting it to his sovereign, the Queen, which appeared to gratify him, and he strongly advised its being done at once. Mr. Barclay was that day sending dispatches, and advised the writer then to address a note to Her Majesty, asking that permission, which form was an imperative necessity. It was done, and by return steamer the permission was given. The picture was framed, and sent.

The following letter will give the result:

CUMMINGS'S PORTRAIT OF MRS. WASHINGTON.

FOREIGN OFFICE.

Sir—I have received and laid before the Queen your letter of the 9th of June, inclosing a portrait of Mrs. Washington, the wife of General Washington, which you have painted from the original portrait by Gilbert Stuart, and which you have offered for the acceptance of her Majesty. The Queen commands me to acquaint you that she has very much admired the portrait, which, as a work of art, is of a very high order, and will form a valuable addition to her Majesty's collection of historical portraits. The Queen desires me to convey to you her thanks for the portrait, together with the assurance of her Majesty's gratification at this proof of that kindly feeling towards her Majesty which has been so often expressed by citizens of the United States.

I am also to transmit to you the accompanying gold medal, bearing the portrait of the Queen, which her Majesty requests you to accept as a mark of her regard.

I am, Sir, your most obedient, humble servant,

PALMERSTON.

THOMAS S. CUMMINGS, Esq., New-York.

May 4. Died, Philip Hone, Honorary Member, one of the old school of merchants, Mayor of the city at a time when the office was an honor, and in which he discharged the duties with gentlemanly and marked ability. He was one of the early encouragers of art, and possessed the beautiful paintings of "Ann Page" by Leslie, and "The Sleeping Student" by Newton. He died deeply regretted.

May 14. The Annual Meeting of the Academicians was held.

PRESIDENT'S REPORT.

GENTLEMEN:

The removal of the Academy to its new building last year, caused high expectations among its members and friends, that the combined advantages of a superior location and more convenience would have produced a corresponding increase in the revenue from the Annual Exhibition. These expectations were NOT realized, while the increased expense attending that removal, and the fitting up of the Galleries, added largely to the debt of the Academy. Still requiring the suspension of our schools as on the preceding year, and confining all its operations, in short, to the most rigid economy.

Seeing no means of relief at hand in the ordinary course of events, a general meeting of the Academy was called, and a sufficient number of the body agreed to contribute a picture each, to be disposed of for the purpose of raising a fund for the payment of the debt referred to above, and we are happy to state that the aim has been entirely successful; and we are hereby enabled to commence the present year released from all pecuniary embarrassments.

But as our new location involves the necessity of greater expenses than heretofore, and as, from present prospects, the proceeds of our Exhibition will still be inadequate to sustain the Institution, it remains for us to resort to some other means to meet the emergencies till better times. Among these, and perhaps the only resource available, will be that proposed by Mr. Cummings—to let out, as occasion may offer, such of our Exhibition Rooms as may at any time be unoccupied by the Academy. This course becomes the more necessary, as other important portions of our buildings have failed to realize the anticipated revenue required to meet the interest and other expenses on the investment made by our Trustees. Although our schools have been suspended on the part of the Academy, in consequence of its inability to maintain them, they have still been conducted by the voluntary subscriptions of students. But it is proposed by the Council that they hereafter be continued by the Academy, subject to such admission fee as shall be found necessary to defray expenses, until such time as the Academy shall be enabled to re-establish them on a free basis.

     *   *   *   *   *   *   *

The election of new members, which is about to engage your attention, is the first to take place under certain revisions of our Constitution, having an important bearing on the proceedings of our Annual Meeting. By these revisions the number of the Academic body is extended to fifty instead of thirty-five, its former limit, and candidates for this and other classes of membership are admitted by the affirmative vote of two-thirds of the member-present, in place of the larger majority heretofore required. The list of cansdidates before you for the first class is more numerous than usual, and of unexceptionable qualifications.

     *   *   *   *   *   *   *

We trust that no feeling of individual interest or prejudice will be permitted to prevail against the welfare of the Academy, and that the charge of our exclusiveness be henceforth heard no more.

A. B. DURAND, *President.*

By the Treasurer's Report it appeared that the receipts for the year were $6449.67, and the disbursements $6341.96; balance in Treasurer's hands, $107.71.

A. B. Durand was elected President; Thomas S. Cummings, Vice-President; J. H. Shegogue, Corresponding Secretary; J. B. Stearns, Recording Secretary; F. W. Edmonds, Treasurer (consenting to serve as named last year); Daniel Huntington and F. E. Church, in the Council. Thomas Hicks, G. A. Baker, H. K. Brown, J. F. Cropsey, Regis Gignoux, P. P. Duggan, Alfred Jones, T. A. Richards, R. M. Pratt, J. W. Cassilear, J. Smillie, and G. W. Flagg, were elected Academicians.

From June to October there appears to have been no business transacted, the writer being the only attendant.

June 8. Died, deeply regretted by a large circle of friends, John R. Murray, a distinguished merchant of New-York— one of the founders of the old American Academy of Arts, a true lover of art, an accomplished critic in his day, and an Honorary Member of the National Academy of Design.

July 2. Died in Paris, L. J. M. Daguerre, Honorary Member—the well-known-to-fame artist and discoverer of the type which bears his name.

July 24. Died, John Town, of Philadelphia, Honorary Member of the Academy.

September 14. Died, James Fennimore Cooper, the distinguished author, an Honorary Member. As a novelist, Mr. Cooper is too well known to fame to need comment. As a friend to artists, and one who has furnished an abundant harvest for art illustration, he deserves, and will receive, the lasting remembrance of the American artists.

September 22. Died, John Neilson, Jr., one of the early friends of the Institution—a gentleman distinguished for his urbanity of manner, literary taste and love of art. He drew with skill, and his sketches from nature bore marks of ability far beyond the generality of such efforts. He took particular pleasure in the society of artists, and was one of the original members of the old "Sketch Club."

October 19. Died, Christian Mayer, Academician—a foreign artist. His works are but little known. He was a man of merit, but not of marked ability. As an American artist by education, he probably would not have commanded election into the body of Academicians.

October 27. Arrangements were made for the opening of the schools, although it did not appear, even at that late date, that a quorum of the Council was in town. The greatly-extended Summer vacation, and the almost entire absence of artists during the Summer and early Fall, calls seriously for consideration, and the adoption of such means as will give the business of the Institution attention during that interval. That has heretofore fallen on the writer, who never has been absent; but he may not be expected to last forever. The matter is of much institutional importance.

The students of the season, in consequence of want of funds, were charged five dollars each for the same, and the schools were well attended. The writer's experience in old times had always been in favor of a small charge to students, as favoring the interest of the student even more than that of the Institution.

November 20. Died, Dr. James E. De Kay, Honorary Member, a gentleman of high standing and extensive acquirements—one who took a lively interest in art and the early progress of the Academy—indeed, wrote several articles in its behalf when it had but few friends or adherents. He was a geologist of standing, and was one of the corps which surveyed New-York State, where his name appears to advantage.

January 8. Died, Charles Henry Hall, Honorary Member,
a gentleman of wealth, refined taste, and one of the
1852. earliest and truest friends of the Institution—much
regretted by a large circle of artists and other
mourners.

February 21. Died, William Cumming, an artist of high
repute—Member of the Royal Hibernian Academy, and an
Honorary Member of the National Academy of Design.
Little is known of his works. He becomes more a matter
of interest, from the fact of his having been the instructor
of C. C. Ingham—one of the oldest members of the
Academy.

February 26. Died, John Frazee. Mr. Frazee was one
of the first enrolled Academicians, and under the unwise
and unconstitutional law of 1834, was removed to the list
of Associates, and subsequently to the Honorary Members.
The action, or rather the execution of that law, was " a
convenient decapitation" or retention, according to the
pleasure of the administration, or merit and popularity of
the party infringing it.

Mr. Frazee executed many creditable works in marble,
although not of sufficient merit, perhaps, to place him
amongst the highest in order of excellence. He was the
architect, and superintended the erection, of the New-York
Custom-House, and was generally considered a man of
originality; he was entirely self-educated, and therefore,
perhaps, wanting in that exterior refinement which would
have rendered him popular.

Those who desire a more full account of Mr. John Frazee
are referred to No. 31, volume 6, of the *North American
Quarterly Magazine* of 1835, in which a very full autobiog-
raphy is published—too long for admission.

March 28. Died, John Haviland, architect, Honorary
Member—a resident of Philadelphia. Mr. Haviland was
born at Gundenham Manor, England, in 1792, and died in
Philadelphia. He lies in a crypt of St. Andrew's Church,
of which he was the architect.

After a very long neglect of business, there appeared at
last some interest excited in a very "*high cause.*" A resolution
was passed, providing for "*a grand reception*" *evening* DRESS
party, prior to the opening to the public of the Spring
Exhibition, and choice refreshments were ordered to be
furnished in the galleries, during the evening. Cummings,
Church, and Stearns were appointed Grand Usher Mana-
gers. It proved a success, and there was a brilliant assemblage.
It became the father-founder of that species of entertainment—"artists' receptions," &c., since so popular, although

the plan was not then, for the first time, introduced. The first, second, third and fourth Exhibitions were similarly inaugurated.

Splendid suppers subsequently took the place of that more refined entertainment, in course decidedly more popular in "THE BODY." The seasons, however, even then, varied: sometimes they had, and sometimes they had not, entertainment—sometimes with ladies, sometimes without, &c., &c. It was not even the first "*full-dress*" artist "*reception*" at the Academic Halls; yet it deserves, in its extent and elegance, to bear the palmy designation of "THE Academy Reception."

April 13. The twenty-seventh Annual Exhibition was opened to the public, closing on the fifth of July, seventy-four working days, and received $2849.45, averaging $38.50 per day; four hundred and seventy-one productions. Notwithstanding the brilliant inauguration, it fell short of the receipts of the preceding year, and showed conclusively, that "cause" existed for that falling off, beyond the artists, galleries, or location, as the Exhibition was far superior to that of 1847, and at which double the amount was realized, even under all the unfavorableness of stairs and the height of entrance to the rooms, which had been so strenuously urged—a most discouraging circumstance.

May 3 appears, by the record, to be the date of the return of the contested picture, two years before referred to.

May 12, was held the usual Annual Meeting of the Academicians.

PRESIDENT'S REPORT.

For the last five years the Annual Reports of the Academy have been merely a review of its struggles to maintain an existence. It has done this, however; and in doing it, has proved the soundness of its vitality, as well as its capabilities to realize the anticipations of its founders.

The sudden decline of its revenues after 1859, and the embarrassments brought on by providing for the erection and possession of our new buildings, sufficiently account for its present apparently passive condition. Our operations since the last Annual Meeting have been few, and are briefly stated; yet they may be introduced, because interesting.

* * * * * * *

The management of the schools, which for two years has been left in the hands of the students, has been resumed by the Academy.

* * * * * *

In entering on the duties of the ensuing year, the most important subject for consideration is a revision of our schools, to render them worthy of the Academy, and adequate to the wants of the students. Important changes are imperative. * * * The standard of merit regulating the admission of students should be of a more elevated character, and one or more from the body of Academicians should be appointed to give instruction and maintain order.

From the Treasurer's Report it is found that the receipts from all sources for the year were $4300.88; and the disbursements during same time, $4247.26; leaving a balance in the Treasury of $53.62.

TREASURER'S REPORT, MAY 12, 1852.

GENTLEMEN:

I congratulate you on the successful termination of the fiscal year. The affairs of the Institution are growing into a more prosperous and healthful condition. Your yearly expenses (this is to be understood as apart from Trustees) have all been promptly met, and a small balance remains.

On the purchase of your property and bonds no payments have been made. The indebtedness remains the same as at the last report.

The rise in the value of property since its purchase cannot but equal your most sanguine expectations.

*   *   *   *   *   *   *

The general expenses are $4,247, and may, I think, be taken as a fair average of the yearly expenses of the Institution. Slight reductions may be made, but to no great extent, as due economy has undoubtedly been practiced. The "Annual Supper," or "*an opening*," would perhaps form the most important item that could be dispensed with, and the omission of that meets not with the approval of the members, or even those friends most deeply interested, and for whose interest it is our DUTY to exercise the most watchful economy. The arrangements only have been changed, and, as it is believed, with great success. The fullest approbation has been generally expressed.

I would call your attention to the necessity of some extra efforts on the part of the body to aid the Trustees in their generous endeavors in our behalf. Certainly something should be done to show that we feel our obligations, and spare no exertion likely to aid in the good work.

As one of the means to accomplish this, I would recommend a Review Exhibition in the coming Fall, to commence as early as the 15th of September.

Such an Exhibition will in no way impair the Annual Exhibition, and yet, from the excellence of the works that may be brought together, will prove highly remunerative, and materially aid us in the liquidation of the debt incurred in the erection of our buildings, to which purpose I propose the receipts be devoted.

Let the effort be made, and well made; and should it prove a failure in every other particular, it cannot fail in showing that we are willing, at least, to do all in our power to aid.

*   *   *   *   *   *   *

T. S. CUMMINGS, *Treasurer*

TRUSTEES' REPORT.

The amount of money received by the Trustees between the 1st of January, 1851, and the 1st of May, 1852, is $4,973.68. The amount paid out during the same period is $4,289.15.

[Here follow the details of account.]

By which it may be seen that the revenue from the real estate pays all its expenses—interest money, taxes, and charges against it, except the debt due to two of the Trustees. This debt, with interest, amounts to $13,000.

If the Institution has the ordinary support during the present year, there will be means sufficient to pay the *interest* due on that.

It may therefore be safely said, that at no period since the Academy purchased its property has so favorable a state of things existed.

A. B. Durand was elected President; Thomas S. Cummings, Vice-President. James H. Shegogue, declining a re-election, T. Addison Richards was chosen Corresponding Secretary; Junius B. Stearns, Recording Secretary; F. W. Edmonds, Treasurer; Charles L. Elliott and George A. Baker, on the Council.

F. O. C. Darley and Louis Lang were elected Academicians.

D. W. C. Boutelle, W. J. Hays, Thomas Augustus Cummings, son of the Vice-President, and F. B. Carpenter, were elected Associates.

Some of the members having left the room, the meeting was without a quorum, and all further business was stopped.

May 24. Another effort was made in Council to carry out the Vice-President's recommendation of a Review Exhibition. The artists were notified to send in their lists of pictures on or before the thirty-first instant. There was no response. A second meeting was called for the 17th of June, at which five only were present. It had evidently gone too far in the Summer vacation to hope for its accomplishment in time to meet the object in view. Thus discouraged, the effort was abandoned.

The pupils of the private and public schools, Deaf and Dumb Asylum, and other charitables, were invited, and attended the Exhibition—a judicious " *investment.*"

During the Summer, as usual, there had been "no quorum." In October a resolution was passed, that the schools open for the season on the first of November. That is too late; the first of October experience points out as a better time. The first of the Fall, immediately after the Summer vacation, there is a freshness and an attendance not found later in the Winter and early Spring.

July 14. Died, W. J. Wilgus, Honorary Member; born January 29th, 1818. He was a pupil of Samuel F. B. Morse, and a man of much promise. He is said to have gone South, after which no information is had of his future career.

July 28. Died, A. J. Downing, Honorary Member—a distinguished rural architect and agriculturist—one of the unfortunate victims who perished on the " HENRY CLAY."

August 25. Died, Daniel E. Tylee, Honorary Member. He was a lover of art, and gave encouragement to the Academy in its days of infancy—befriended it in its early progress. On the Arcade Baths, in Chambers Street, he built an extra story for the use of the Academy, and it was there the second Exhibition was held.

September —.   After the purchase of Brower's old building, and after it had been fitted up and occupied, the writer,
in view of the rapidly-rising condition of property on Broadway, had advised his friends, Mr. Sturges and Mr.
Leupp, of the possibility of the Academy realizing a handsome
sum by a real estate transaction which he named, and
which was, the purchase of the whole line on Mercer Street,
in rear of the Academy building—five or six old houses
and lots, &c.—and thus unlock the property, and control
the rear lots for attachment to the Broadway line, which,
it had now become evident, they would be required for,
and thus make, as he estimated, many thousand dollars.

The idea was kindly, but rather credulously, listened to ;
yet they promised to inquire into it.   They did so, and the
result was, further interviews and *"more"* belief, until, ultimately, they authorized the writer to make the purchase,
and their purses were from thence opened to its fulfillment.
To make the purchase, as it proved, was more easily said
than done, even—and it required much labor and patience
to obtain it.   The Manhattan buildings, &c., were bought
October, 1852.   To obtain a clear title to other parts of the
property after a sale had been offered, a suit had necessarily
to be commenced, which did not terminate until nearly two
years thereafter.   With its terminus the purchase was accomplished.   In the Summer, when the effort was made in
the Academy's favor, the Academicians were away, and as
innocent of even any such good intention, as if it had never
existed.

September 15, was founded the School of Design for
women.

It was the writer's intention to have introduced a record
of the early history of that most meritorious, beneficent
and successful institution.   It was repeatedly and in several
instances applied for, and was even promised, although it
has never come to hand.

October 4. Died, John Vanderlyn, the well-known artist.
The following notice of the event is from the pen of Mr.
Lewis McEntee :

"One pleasant morning in October, 1852, while on his way from Rondout
to Kingston, he was met by a friend, (and the only one with whom he was on
terms of perfect intimacy,) from whom he craved a shilling, with which to
pay for the carriage of his baggage from the steamboat to Kingston.   He was
ill then, and shortly after his arrival at the hotel was taken to his bed.   The
friend referred to went about quietly and collected the means to pay his board
for a time, but it was never needed.

"Requesting that he might be left alone, he abandoned himself to the lone-
liness of his situation, and on the next morning they found him dead in his
bed, in his low room that looked out into a stable-yard without even a cur-
tain to shield the sunlight from his dying eyes."

So departed that truly excellent artist.

October 25. Again was a resolution passed, that the Academicians superintend the schools in rotation—another programme, "another service." The attendance was as sparse as ever. A paid officer—and that one, too, of proper nerve for the office—is what is required in the schools, with the occasional attendance of a "Visiting Board"—perhaps once or twice a month—is the only plan, within the writer's experience, likely to prove of practical utility.

Such is human nature everywhere; men will not—cannot—give a great portion of their valuable time and attention through all weather, and privation from society, for nothing, or at most for "*honor*," which is much the same thing. It ought not to be expected; if it is expected, it will not be found, or the work well done, if done.

A charge of five dollars each was made on the students, and from the same cause as last year—the Academy's want of funds.

The schools closed for the season February 28th. No premiums were awarded.

November 15. The death of Thomas Thompson, an Associate of the Institution, was announced. Suitable resolutions were passed, commemorative of the loss the Institution had sustained, and the sympathy felt by the members with the relatives of the deceased. The Academy attended the funeral in a body, and the usual badge of mourning was worn.

Mr. Thompson was an aged, nay, a venerable gentleman of the old school, distinguished in his department—liberal in his views—and came promptly forward to aid the Institution by taking its bonds. In the settlement of that gentleman's estate, and consequent sale by auction of his assets, his two hundred dollars worth of the bonds of the Academy, put up at auction, were knocked down at about twenty-five to thirty cents on the dollar, to a well-known friend of the Institution, *with a whistle* among the knowing ones, as they supposed themselves, accompanying the transaction, even at that low figure. They were not *exactly* knowing ones. The Academy, at that time, was reducing its indebtedness, "*paying off* its smaller scrip," and Mr. H—— M——, the purchaser, in a few days after received the face of his bonds and seven per cent. interest.

Who paid for that whistle? The property of the Academy had, and ever had been, under the charge of the writer; its condition was sound; interest had been paid on every indebtedness *promptly*, and even, too, at a time when dividends on almost every security in the market *deemed valu-*

able had been passed; and yet, in the face of all that, the bonds, secured by property to ten times their value, had depreciated in public estimation. No faith. There was no better security in the market; they have all been paid—principal and interest.

The rapid rise of property, which had been anticipated by the writer, had occurred, and he looked forward to the period of sale and realization; and by resolution, the Vice-President, Thomas S. Cummings, was appointed and directed to act in behalf of the Academy, in endeavoring to effect that object. *That*, although highly regular, was scarcely requisite, as the Vice-President had never ceased his endeavors to effect that object. It was, however, a record of authority, and definitely settled the Academy's views.

The property was supposed sold, but it did not turn out a successful fulfillment.

Died, in Boston, Horatio Greenough, the distinguished sculptor, and Honorary Member of the Academy.

January 17. A Special Meeting was called for the purpose of completing and giving all necessary powers **1853.** to the Trustees (if such were required); and further, by the creation of a *new trust*, viz., Sturges, Leupp, Cummings, Edmonds and Durand, to receive the funds arising from sale under the prior trust, and by said trust and concentration thereof, more fully, readily, and certainly insure the purchase of a site and the erection of buildings for the Academy of Design.

April 18, was the inauguration of the twenty-ninth Annual Exhibition, by a " Supper" to the *members*, exhibiters, and the press. Ladies and poetry dormant. The selfishness of the flesh in the ascendency. It, too, was an ovation, and certainly a very splendid one. Dr. Bellows, Dr. Chapin, and others entertained the company. The writer was called on, and, as it was said, was felicitous in his remarks—of course. If he made any remarks at all, they were felicitous. Durand actually made a speech, and *a good one*.

The Exhibition opened to the public on the day following, the nineteenth, closing July 9th—seventy-one working days—receiving $2306.58, an average of $32.48 per day—yet a further reduction, and over five hundred dollars below the receipts of last year. The number of works exhibited, three hundred and ninety-eight.

May 11. The Annual Meeting of the Academicians. The President reported :

That the Council, in connection with the Trustees, have been engaged since our last Annual Meeting in effecting preliminary arrangements for the final disposal of the ground and buildings now in possession of the Academy. It was expected that a satisfactory sale would have been effected during the Winter, but more advantageous prospects have induced farther delay, leaving little room to doubt, however, that this object will be accomplished in the course of the ensuing year. The general prosperity of our city has at length thus far reached the Academy, affording assurance, ere long, of a condition of comparative independence, by which its field of action will be greatly enlarged, together with the demand and the encouragement for the more efficient exercise of all its functions.

For the last few years the scanty income of the Academy has confined its operations within a very limited circle, the revenues of the year just terminated being scarcely sufficient to meet the current expenses, although directed in their application, as far as practicable, by the rule of strict economy.   *   *   *   The schools exhibit the average number of students, and have been conducted under a proper attention to their order, according to the recommendations in our last Annual Report.

*   *   *   *   *   *   *

We have seldom been called upon to deplore the loss of one so sincerely and unreservedly lamented as Horatio Greenough. He may be justly regarded as the Father of American Sculpture.   *   *   *   Greenough has done much towards the establishment of an American School of Art, and there are others who still live, alike entitled to our gratitude for their services in the noble cause, who, while they acknowledge the advantages of study in foreign schools to complete their art education, choose not to surrender their identity, and pass away in the current of servile imitation. This is as it should be. Our national importance and power, our history and our scenery, exert an influence which, unimpeded by conventional schools, cannot fail to produce an original school of art worthy to share the tribute of the universal respect already paid to our condition of political advancement.

From the Treasurer's Report it is found that the year's receipts were $3904.74; expenditures, $3732.30; leaving in the treasury $172.44.

A. B. Durand was elected President; Thos. S. Cummings, Vice-President; T. Addison Richards, Corresponding Secretary; J. B. Stearns, Recording Secretary; F. W. Edmonds, Treasurer; C. L. Elliott and George A. Baker, Members of Council. J. H. Cafferty was elected an Academician.

After the election of Associates and three Honorary Members, (several members having left,) the Academy was without a quorum, and no further business could be transacted.

From that date to the seventeenth of October, nominal or no meetings—"no quorum"—"Cummings, Richards," "Cummings, Stearns," "Richards, Cummings"—and there was no legalized business transacted. It was well there were some to be found to do that which was absolutely requisite to be done; though there was doubtless but little except routine business to be attended to.

The schools opened on the first Monday in November, on an admission fee of five dollars.

Opened the Crystal Palace Exhibition in a building

erected for the purpose on Reservoir Square, between Fortieth and Forty-second Streets, Sixth Avenue, and west of
the Croton Reservoir. The building was totally destroyed
by fire October 15th, 1858. Its record is too well known to
need comment here; it will form part of the history of its
day; it is only in its art matters the writer adopts it. Art
Exhibition, in connection with other and "grosser material"
—"*manufactures*"—has always been repugnant to the
American artist, and even "The Crystal," with all the
European example, did not form an exception to that feeling. Many names of city artists graced the Catalogue; the
art works numbered over seven hundred, by some six
hundred contributors. It contained many productions of
great excellence. The "oil portrait of Shakespeare," "The
First of May," by Winterhalter—a much-admired picture,
the property of Queen Victoria, and loaned by her—
" Death of the Betrothed," by Horace Vernet, several
by "Hasenclever," "C. Sohn," "Scheuren," "Murillo,"
"Gessellchap," "Kraus," "Böcking," "Achenbach," "Stop-
ford," "Varley," "*Joseph Shaw*," "*George W. Flagg*," "W.
S. Mount," "*Havelle*," "*Fagnani*," "Rochart," "Fries,"
Rembrandt Peale, Carlo Dolci, Ruysdael, Teniers, Tempesta,
Van Laar, Joseph Vernet, Van Ostade, Poussin, Rubens
Coecoek, Bonheur, Schendel, Scheffer, Hubner, Spitzweg,
Leutze, Hurlstone, Rechlin—and yet but little appeared to
be thought of the Art Exposition; there were, perhaps, too
many productions.

The sculpture was equally excellent—" Combat with a
Serpent," Otten; "The Shipwrecked Mother," Lechesne;
" Bear and Hunter," Fremit; "The Amazon, in metal,"
Kiss; Canova's "Hebe," "Adoration," "Eve," "Hope,"
" Carrier." In marble, Queen Victoria, Napoleon, Wash-
ington, Sabrina (a beautiful work), Tambourina, "The
First Whisper of Love," "Ruth and Naomi," "Eve, Fisher
Boy, and Greek Slave," by Hiram Powers; "Minstrel's
Curse," by Muller; Hager, Erminia, Fisher Boy, Diana,
Flora; and in plaster, the Twelve Apostles, from the works
of Thorwalsden.

There certainly were some that were commonplace; yet,
much that was superlatively excellent. Had the works of
art alone been given as an Exhibition, it would have been
thought extensive—GRAND. As in connection with other
material, it was but a part—it lost its importance.

November 21. The "LIFE" School was ordered closed,
there not being a "sufficient attendance to warrant its
continuance."

There was on exhibition in the Galleries of the Academy,

Powell's " De Soto"—the Government picture, painted to supply the deficiency caused by the death of Inman.

" De Soto, who had served under Pizarro during the conquest of Peru, returned to Spain with immense wealth, and a reputation that had preceded him for glorious deeds in arms. He married the beautiful Isabella de Boab-dilla, the daughter of one of the most distinguished families of Spain. He was offered a high and honorable position in the Government by Charles V., and was surrounded by circumstances which would have in any other man produced contentment, ease, happiness. Not so with De Soto. His imagination, excited by the romantic stories of the conquest of Mexico, produced dreams of gold and glory concerning the unexplored regions of the Floridas. He asked and obtained permission of his Government to equip an expedition that was to exceed in the magnificence of its result everything that had yet been undertaken.

" When it became known that a new enterprise, commanded by one of the conquerors of Peru, was entertained, crowds of the most distinguished and wealthy hidalgos flocked to his standard. Soldiers of Portugal who had served in the wars on the frontiers came as volunteers, and we are told by the historian of the time—Garcillasso de la Vega—that ' when a muster of the forces was called, the Portuguese appeared in glittering, burnished armor, while the Spaniards looked very gallant, and were clothed with silk upon silk.' All that wealth could produce was lavished in the equipment of the expedition—arms, armor, blooded horses of Arabia, and slaves, were so numerous as to become cumbersome. The army, composed of a thousand men, sailed under the most favorable auspices ; they touched at Cuba, where the forces were mustered, and in 1539 they landed on the shores of Florida. * * * In the Spring of 1541 they arrived on the banks of the Mississippi River, where a Cross was raised, and formal possession taken of the country in the name of Charles V. of Spain. There they were met by a deputation of various Indian tribes, who brought presents to conciliate the conqueror of their country.

" It is this point of time Mr. Powell has selected for the subject of his painting."

December 5. John F. E. Preud'homme resigned his post as Curator, and a " vote of thanks was presented to him for his long and faithful services." He had devoted much of his valuable time to the Institution, as the writer well remembers, to the detriment of his own interests.

January 9. Died, Thomas H. Perkins, Honorary Member, one of the wealthiest and most distinguished of 1854. Boston merchants—one of her favorite sons, a lover of the arts, and philanthropist—at the advanced age of eighty-nine years.

February 15. A special effort was made to sell the Academy property. It was offered at auction unsuccessfully ; it did not receive a bid ! It was, however, sold on the eighteenth day of the month, at private sale, deliverable on the first of May, and a payment of ten thousand dollars received. Immediate measures had to be taken to obtain a place to hold the next Annual Exhibition. The *Apollo* Rooms were offered at one hundred and twenty-five dollars per *week*, the Dusseldorf Gallery at $4,000 per *annum*, the

Racket Court at $3,600 per *annum*; these were all deemed ineligible, and in lieu thereof the writer proposed an Exhibition for *one month only*, to be held in the old rooms, prior to the delivery of the property, on the first of May. That was wisely adopted.

March 1. A room was hired in Cummings's "Studio Building" in which to store the statuary, and to which it was immediately removed, to make way for the TWENTY-NINTH ANNUAL EXHIBITION, which opened to the public on the twenty-second of March, closing the twenty-fifth of April— thirty working days—and received $2584.87, averaging $86.18 per day. That, it was supposed, would be the last Exhibition held in the old building, which did not, however, prove to be the case.

The property, as before stated, had been sold on the 18th of February, deliverable on the first of May, which delivery, for the accommodation of the purchasers, was extended to the first of July. Difficulties were unexpectedly met with in its fulfillment.

Had the property referred to been under other direction than it was, it probably had long since been academically a matter of the past—so *variable*, so "conflicting" was the advice. During the necessary holding of the estate, the writer was frequently informed " that the Academy wanted no real estate—no property—a building only in which to exhibit art"—"that the real estate should be sold for anything it would bring"—"GET RID OF IT ANY HOW"—"that art needed not money wherewith to forward it," "and that the Institution should not possess it"—" that money STULTIFIED AND DEBASED ART," " and that it was a clog on progress, and for that alone, should be '*immediately*' sold." "Again, by others, that it should be HELD and leased, and the revenue ONLY taken for art purposes"—"that it should not be sold at all"—"that it would ultimately form a permanent support to art and artists."

Thanks to the manner in which the property was placed, the writer was able to disregard such advisory counsel—to mature and carry one plan to completion; and a success it proved—sufficiently so to pay for a building suitable for the uses of the Academy. But to the first of July delivery— on the day preceding the one named for the completion of the sale, and the receipt of seventy thousand dollars in cash, there came to light the great abstractions or strategical performances of one Schuyler, and a panic, such as is seldom seen, ensued in the money market. No belief in anything—no confidence in any man, or his means. Mammon's idol, gold, scarcely held its own; it too, perhaps, had almost to be tested before it was touched, so far was confidence lost. The purchasing parties could not pay the amount stipulated for, and greatly feared the loss of that already paid. After many methods had been discussed, it was agreed that on the deposit of additional securities, the purchasers should have the property on the amount of cash paid in, to enable them to make trial of its re-sale to the association for which they had originally intended it, and for which it had been purchased by them.

The proposition was to proceed at once in the erection of a grand Musical Hall, which should cover the whole ground previously occupied by the Academy, as well as that which adjoined on Mercer Street, and for which a joint-stock association was in process of organization. Circumstances ordered it otherwise. The company was, for some cause, never formed, and the property remained on the hands of those who had purchased it in view of that formation. Yet, so far had such an organization proceeded, that a proposition was received, inviting the Academy to become perpetual lessees of galleries which should be constructed in the proposed building, conditional with their becoming subscribers to the capital stock of the "Metropolitan Hall Association," to the amount of twenty-five thousand dollars. It is scarcely necessary to say that the proposal was not entertained.

The second promises were not fulfilled, and after giving some indulgence, a foreclosure was had, and a decree and order for sale obtained. At that sale an annoying and utterly inutile scene was enacted. The party purchasing failed to comply with the terms of sale, and there was left no other alternative but to go over the proceedings again— re-advertise and re-sell. At said sale the property, under authority granted by the court, was bought in by the writer in behalf of the Trustees.

It was subsequently sold at private sale to one of the original purchasers, who solicited that opportunity to reinstate himself; which to him, a deserving man, the Trustees were not unwilling to grant. Under their orders the sale was so made, though with little hope of its success. The result proved the justness of the fears. The building was scarcely altered to suit the purchaser's views, when a full stop was put to the whole by builder's liens and other claims.

The party tendered a return of the property. That could not be accepted, and a further foreclosure suit was "compelled." It was again sold under the Sheriff's order, and re-purchased in by the Trust—leaving an indebtedness of some ten thousand dollars, for which a judgment against the purchaser was recorded, and a further sum of ten thousand dollars was required, to settle claims that had become liens on the property. Again the premises reverted to the writer's management.

The money wherewith to discharge the liens that preceded the Trust was loaned by Messrs. Sturges and Leupp, and arrangements had still further to be made for the purchase of what had cost some six thousand dollars, in movable furniture for the various dressing, ball and concert rooms made in the building, and without which the business could not possibly, thereafter, be conducted, or revenue gained. Those were all obtained on "time" (calculated to be covered by the earnings of the Hall), and at little more than half their cost.

On taking possession in June, (a most unpropitious time in the year for letting purposes), the property was found in a neglected and most dilapidated condition—the few tenants in the buildings highly dissatisfied, and in possession without agreements or leases, and disposed to take advantage—some even holding over without paying rent or leaving the premises. By great efforts order was restored and control obtained; legal force, however, had to be used. Few surrendered until they found themselves unable longer to resist. Injudicious subordinates, and improper persons on the property, were removed, and the whole repaired and put in order for the "fall business." By attention and strict economy, it was made to pay its interest, expenses, and the greater part of the repairs and payments on the purchases made; and when sold, in April, 1860, it was yielding a gross yearly income of over ten thousand dollars. That, however, was accomplished under a laborious management, scarcely credible, though of little general interest; few of the *members* even appreciated it.

MODERN ART EXPOSITION.

March 1. Was inaugurated by the *old* and respectable house of Williams & Stevens, free exhibitions of European and American works of art in their Galleries. The exposition was for the double purpose of familiarizing the public with the original works, and the obtainment of subscribers to engravings. The latter doubtless the source of profit.

Some idea may be formed of the extent of that mode of exhibition by the following list of pictures in a short time exhibited by them, and politely furnished by that house:

Glimpse of an English Homestead..........................J. F. Herring.
Christ Teaching Humility..R. Scott Lander.
Landing of the Pilgrim Fathers..............................Charles Lucy.
Walter Scott and Friends at Abbotsford.....................Thomas Faed.
Shakespeare and his Contemporaries at the Mermaid ...John Faed.
The Twins ....Sir Edward Landseer.
Charles Edward Entering Edinburgh ....Thomas Duncan.
     Do.   in the Cave, Protected by Flora Mc-⎱ Do.
        Donald...............................⎰
Sporting Dogs and their Game—(7 Pictures)..............Richard Ansdell.
Milton in his Study ....John Faed.
Shakespeare in his Study ....   Do.
Last Judgment..John Martin.
Great Day of His Wrath..   Do.
Plains of Heaven...   Do.
Church's Niagara...F. E. Church.
Weir's Embarkation of the Pilgrims ....R. W. Weir.
Horse Fair..Rosa Bonheur.
"Il Corso"—(the Race-Course at Rome) ....T. Jones Barker.
Murillo's Immaculate Conception.
Winter View of Niagara...Regis Gignoux.

March 2. A number of artists assembled for the purpose of making an expression of their appreciation of the talents and many virtues of their President, A. B. Durand, Esq. After many plans had been discussed for accomplishing their wishes, a presentation of a service of plate was decided on. The amount requisite was immediately subscribed, and the service purchased; and after it had been seen for a short time in the Galleries, was presented to that gentleman. It was desired to make the presentation in a public manner, but that was declined by Mr. Durand. It may be doubtful if he would not rather have declined the present, than have complied.

LETTER OF PRESENTATION.

To Asher B. Durand, Esq.,
    President of National Academy of Design.

Dear Sir:—

In behalf of a number of your friends, whose names are herewith inclosed, I have the honor of presenting to you the accompanying Service of Plate.

We ask your acceptance of it as a testimonial of the high sense in which we hold your Artistic excellence, and as expressive of our grateful remembrance of your long and faithful services as presiding officer of the National Academy of Design.

Years of Academic and social intercourse have endeared you to us all; the high moral character you have sustained in all the relations of life, as husband, father, and friend, has excited our warmest approbation, and called for this remembrancer of the past; for the future allow us to express the hope that your career of usefulness will in no way be curtailed, that you may long continue to enjoy that happiness which is so justly your due, and that your health may permit you, for years to come, to discharge the duties of presiding officer of the Academy, a post you have filled with honor to the profession and Art.

In conclusion, my dear Sir, I must beg to say, that it would have afforded us sincere gratification to have made this testimonial of our regard to you in person, and in what we conceive to be a more suitable and public manner; but in yielding that point to your earnestly expressed desire, we only do, as we hope always to do, consult your wishes and happiness.

With sentiments of the highest regard, in behalf of your friends,

I have the honor to remain,

Your obedient servant,

THOS. S. CUMMINGS,

Vice-President N. A. of Design.

MR. DURAND'S REPLY.

To THOS. S. CUMMINGS, Esq.,

Vice-President of the N. A. of Design.

DEAR SIR:—

The beautiful Service of Plate, accompanied by your letter of presentation in behalf of a number of my friends, was placed in my hands on the evening of the 25th April, inst.

This signal evidence of their regard, coming as it does from so many of my brother Artists, as well as friends with whom we are all in habits of social intercourse, gives rise to emotions and feelings of such a character that I am at a loss in what terms to express my grateful acknowledgments.

In endeavoring to fulfill the various obligations, social and professional, which have devolved on me, whether in relation to the National Academy of Design or otherwise, I have never expected nor desired other recompense than that which results from conscientious discharge of duties and the sympathy of those who, with myself, are deeply interested in a common cause. If I cannot fully acquiesce in the generous estimate of such services, which my friends, through you, have expressed, I may, at least, claim all that is due to earnestness of purpose and the conviction that no unworthy motive has ever controlled the dictates of my heart.

Throughout my professional career, a period of thirty years and upwards, I have enjoyed the confidence and esteem of many true and generous friends— more true, more generous, few could boast. The memory of their kindness is deeply imprinted on my heart, and I should distrust my nature if any souvenir were needed to preserve or freshen the associations connected with their names.

In conclusion, let me assure you that this testimonial is most gratefully appreciated : both as a remembrance of the past and an earnest for the future, I shall always cherish it with sentiments in keeping with its pure material, and in harmony with the spirit of the valued friends who have delegated you to perform this pleasant duty.

With earnest wishes for the health and prosperity of yourself and those for whom you act,

I remain, with great respect,

Your obedient servant,

A. B. DURAND.

May 10. The Annual Meeting of the Academicians was held, and for the first time in the temporary rooms 58 East Thirteenth Street.

PRESIDENT'S REPORT.

The operations of the Academy since our last meeting until the beginning of last March require but a brief notice in this Report.

The receipts of the Exhibition of 1853 showed a continued decline, and the number of students in our schools has fallen much below that of any previous season. The School of the Living Model has been suspended on account of the limited number of applicants, while the resources of our Treasury have scarcely been adequate to meet the necessary demands, although expended under the most economical regulations. From this embarrassing condition we are happily relieved by the sale of our property. The result of this sale, by the judicious management of your Trustees, promises to place the Academy in the possession of means which will enable it to enjoy a more complete and unobstructed exercise of all its functions, and which, under proper directions, will eventually secure for it an independent position.

The profits of this sale are not yet realized, but $10,000 has been paid in cash, and we have every reason to expect a satisfactory fulfillment of all its conditions of the 3d of July. Measures will then be taken to procure a new location, with due regard to the lessons of experience so emphatically taught us during the last four years. In addition to this unlooked-for instance of good fortune, another circumstance for congratulation is found in the successful character of the 29th Annual Exhibition, just closed. Although limited, by the terms of sale just mentioned, to the short period of one month, the proceeds have exceeded by $300 the amounts of last year's receipts—a fact which recommends to your consideration the propriety of restricting the term of our future Exhibitions to a much shorter period than custom has heretofore established.

Apartments have been secured for the storage of our movable property. These will be retained until a new and permanent building shall be erected.

The following report and proposition were submitted by T. S. Cummings:

* * * The proceeds of the sale consist of $56,000 over and above all indebtedness; but it is at present in a measure unavailable, consisting of two mortgages on the property, dating from and after the original mortgage thereon, of $35,000.

A desirable site on Broadway and Twenty-fifth Street, Madison Square and Fifth Avenue, can now be procured; the amount of purchase ($52,000) to remain on bond and mortgage for years. The present assets of the Institution are sufficiently available to erect a building, which is estimated at $42,000—the revenues from the first story of which, it is believed, will fully support the Academy.

The following is a diagram of the property:

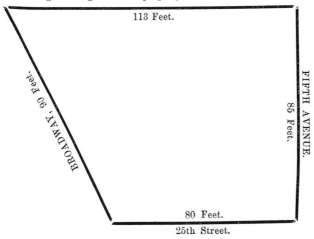

113 Feet.

BROADWAY, 90 Feet.

FIFTH AVENUE. 85 Feet.

80 Feet.

25th Street.

To accomplish the object, it is proposed to call on the friends of the Institution, and by the issue of bonds, in sums of $100 each, to raise a sum sufficient for the purpose. Said bonds to be a lien on the buildings, additionally secured by the mortgages, to bear interest at the rate of seven per cent. per annum, and to give to the bondholders the privileges of Honorary Members, and free admission for themselves and families to the Exhibitions, &c.

It is proposed to place the affairs under the care of the Trust—Sturges, Leupp, Cummings, Edmonds, and Durand—until all indebtedness is liquidated.

The following gentlemen have tendered a subscription of one thousand dollars each: Gilbert & Thomas, Mr. G. A. Conover, Mr. S. B. Cornell, Mr. T. A. Warner, Mr. D. C. Weeks, Mr. Lemuel Bangs, Mr. John Thompson, Messrs. Harper Brothers, Mr. Jonathan O. Fowler, Mr. S. M. Meade, Mr. E. H. Ludlow. And Mr. Meade is willing to guarantee to bring $10,000 more.

The Treasurer reported the entire yearly receipts to be $4,016.27; expenditures, $3,995.97: leaving a balance in the Treasury of $20.30.

A. B. Durand was elected President; Thomas S. Cummings, Vice-President; T. Addison Richards, Corresponding Secretary; J. B. Stearns, Recording Secretary; F. W. Edmonds, Treasurer (held as before); Henry Peters Gray, J. F. Cropsey, Members of Council; S. R. Gifford, Academician.

There had been no schools, and but little business transacted.

June 11. Died, Charles Cushing Wright. In his decease the Academy lost one of its earliest friends. He was one of its founders, and at his instigation was the meeting of artists called, as referred to in the early record. In its formation he was an Academician; afterwards, under a law of exclusion, decidedly unconstitutional, disfranchised, and removed to the list of Associates. He was the first die-sinker in the country. The seal of the Institution now in use is by his hands. His head of *Page* is a masterly work, and worthy of any period.

October —. Was exhibited, 663 Broadway, Leutze's large picture of Washington at the battle of Monmouth—a spirited picture, though perhaps a scene and moment of time the least expressive of the quiet dignity of the General's character that could have been selected. The foreground groupe, aside from the principal figures, a superb piece of composition. The painting belonged to Mr. Leavitt, and was intended to grace that gentleman's gallery at his residence, Great Barrington.

The exhibition was not made for pecuniary recompense; it was not even sought, and it was probably not obtained.

October 4. Died, Frederick Catherwood, Honorary Member. He was one of those who met death in the ill-fated "Arctic." He was a man of high attainments as an architect, and of great general information. He was on his way to construct a railroad abroad when he met his untimely death.

January 22. 1855. A Special Meeting of Academicians was called, on "requisition," on the subject of a building.

EXTRACTS FROM THE MINUTES.

Mr. Cummings made a verbal statement of the affairs of the Academy, and in reference to building a new edifice, suggested, first, "Shall it go on?" And if so, "Where and how shall the money be raised?"

Mr. Edmonds answered, and "was of the opinion that the times were adverse, and that we had no surety that the property 663 Broadway would not eventually come back into our hands, therefore a risk to attempt to build; and that the war in Europe was another reason why we should not attempt to do anything in the way of erecting buildings at present."

Mr. Cummings stated, in answer to a question, that "the lots on Madison Square (Fifth Avenue), Twenty-fifth Street and Broadway, could be bought without cash; purchase money could remain on bond and mortgage; and that the neighbors were willing to raise the most of the money necessary to erect the building."

Mr. Duggan "thought that, in connection with the Academy, an extensive paying school of art practice, in all its branches, is desirable; and, in anticipation of the probable increase in the value of property, he is of opinion that we should endeavor to erect a suitable edifice for such purposes immediately."

And it was asked to what extent negotiations had been entered into with the owners of the property.

Cummings replied, that "no obligations existed on either. That the property could be had, if desired; if not, there was an end of the matter. The parties were much interested, and would serve the arts."

On motion, adjourned to Monday, February 5th, at 7½ P. M.

At which time it was resolved that it is "inexpedient to enter into any arrangements for the purchase of lots, and erecting a building for the uses of the Academy;" and a vote of thanks was tendered to the gentlemen before named, for their kindness in offering to aid us to build. IT WAS DEEMED TOO FAR UP TOWN.

Thus was lost the best site on New-York Island for an Academy—the convergence of Fifth Avenue, Broadway, and Madison Square, (three fronts)—which property in a few years might be expected to advance a hundred thousand dollars.

The disappointments were borne with considerable fortitude.

It was promised that the Academicians should within another year have a building of "THEIR OWN" in which to exhibit. They were, however, not so soon to be gratified; though the most strenuous efforts were made to purchase, lease, or indeed in almost any way to procure more suitable accommodations for the Institution. Advertisements

HISTORIC ANNALS OF THE

on advertisements were put forth in the daily papers for months, and almost innumerable pieces of property, for sale or to lease, examined and reported on, but without obtaining the desired result. No "*Home*" was to be had, within the "*means.*"

May 8. Was held the Annual Meeting. "No quorum" present. Only such business, therefore, as could be transacted without that requisite, was entered into.

EXTRACTS FROM THE PRESIDENT'S REPORT.

Gentlemen:—The important business of the year has been the completion of negotiations for the sale of our property on Broadway and Mercer Street. By this arrangement of its affairs, the Academy is placed in a position the most favorable it has occupied during its existence; being freed from pecuniary embarrassments, and provided with means for future operations, which, with due caution in its application, may prevent the recurrence of all past troubles.

The Treasurer will furnish all the particulars of our financial condition.

It is important now that we should examine well our position, and if any changes shall be found wanting either in organization or modes of operation, let them be immediately undertaken and earnestly pushed.

It is the opinion that one important change, at least, in the "*Constitution*" is wanting, that might render the Academy more effective, or at least silence objections raised against us, and evidently too well founded to be disregarded—that in the removal of the restrictions which limit the number of Academicians. It is recommended, therefore, to abolish the restrictions, and leave their number unlimited. This appears to be a measure in accordance with our institutions. The conferring of exclusive honors and privileges is at least inconsistent with the democracy under whose influence Art seems to have thriven with its fullest vigor; and so far as they have any influence with the public, they are as likely to blind taste as direct it.   *   *   *

It is therefore desirable to remove all trace of exclusiveness or partiality in their arrangements, in order that the public may have some respect for them.   *   *   *

It may also be well to consider, with reference to our future plans, what provision may be made for increasing the efficiency of our schools, so that students in Art may receive the same advantages as those who go to Europe to study. Where objects fall naturally to the care of our Institution, established and conducted by artists, and we may be assured that its reputation as an Academy rests solely on this ground, we do not mean the introduction of any course of rudimental instruction, but something beyond the mere practice of drawing from the Antique and living models; some course, in short, that embraces the main features of the elementary principles of art-education.

As we now stand, the Annual Exhibition is the only feature which interests the public, and even with the artists the only visible evidence of its existence; and, unfortunately, the one least essential in the structure of the Academy, although a valuable auxiliary in its operations and influence.

No satisfactory location for the future home of the Academy has as yet been found, but diligent search for that object is being made.

A. B. DURAND.

The Acting Treasurer, T. S. Cummings, likewise one of the Trustees, made a full report of the affairs and condition of the Trust, which, being a matter of figures only, is omitted.

From the same officer's report, (the Vice-President,) who was officiating as Acting Treasurer for Mr. Edmonds, it appeared that the total receipts of the year amounted to $3429.17; total payments, $3168.56; balance, $260.61.

May 11. A Committee of seven was appointed to take into consideration so much of the President's Report as referred to the alteration of the Constitution, and to report thereon. Cummings, Stearns, Richards, Gray, Huntington, Cafferty, and Baker were appointed said Committee, who subsequently reported: "That they had given the subject earnest, patient, and careful examination, and that it is their mature and decided opinion that the proposed change cannot be advantageously or safely made."

June 28. A Special Meeting was called for the purpose of the consideration of the subject of a site and a building. The resolution which had suspended that operation had been rescinded, and Cummings and Richards appointed a Committee further to inquire, examine and report.

February 5. At an Adjourned Meeting of Academicians, that was again reversed, and it was "thought that we had better defer building for at least one or two years;" and therefore,

"*Resolved*, That at present it is considered inexpedient to enter into any arrangements for the purchase of lots and erecting a building for the use of the Academy."

Yet notwithstanding all that, Mr. Cummings was ordered to advertise and otherwise pursue, and did pursue, his inquiries for a site, and many pieces of property were examined and reported on.

On the 21st of May the Council ordered that the consideration of a building should be the special business of the meetings; and on the 11th of June "it was resolved that the Council meet every evening until the question of a location shall be decided on, unless it shall be deemed expedient to defer it;" and Cummings and Richards were again ordered to proceed in their inquiries.

June 28. Another *Special Meeting* of the Academicians was called to receive reports on sites examined by the Committee, and at which it appeared, by the record, six were submitted, and the one on the corner of Irving Place and Fifteenth Street received a large vote in its favor. On inquiry, it proved that the only terms on which it could be obtained were beyond the Academy's means, and all thoughts of it given up.

From June to October no meetings, or if any, no record, and no quorum was obtained until November.

August —. A writer on the History of the New-York
Gallery, in reference to its lease (nominally rent free) from
the Academy, during the interval between the Exhibitions
—some nine months in the year—remarks, that "the Exhibitions were held in the Academy buildings at a heavy
loss, and it was deemed advisable to discontinue them until
a more favorable state of affairs. The Exhibition then
closed, and for two years it did a more profitable business
as landlord therein, making sufficient money to pay all
claims against it."

Correct enough; yet, why did he not say who did it?
The writer suggested the arrangement, and did the letting
and collecting without charge or consideration, which was
well known.

October 22. Died, Nicholas Carroll, Honorary Member
—cut off in his early days. He was a young man of considerable attainments—a lover of art, a friend of the Academy,
a member of the Mercantile Library, and an active partici-
pator in many literary societies, in his day. He took an
active interest in the politics of his time, and was highly
esteemed; indeed, his zeal in that direction was much less
than beneficial to his pecuniary interests, and was so looked
upon by his best friends.

Although the attendance on the schools, for the preceding
two or three seasons, had been so greatly reduced in
numbers, and so little interest taken therein, as to produce
despondency on the part of the Council—almost even to
their doubting the utility of their continuance—yet, no
sooner were they closed, than a clamor was immediately
raised for their reopening; so much does it appear to be
the pleasure of some, to demand all to be open—all to be
free, if only for the opportunity or pleasure of neglecting
the advantages.

November 5. A resolution was submitted, that the Life
and Antique Schools be reopened, which was passed. The
room occupied in the Studio Building, and intended for storage only, was cleared of all incumbrances that could be conveniently removed—the full-length figures were retained—
and they were arranged as well as the accommodations
would permit, and the schools were opened, and the students
left, in purely democratic style, to govern themselves.
There appeared to have been ten students only, which cor-
responds with the school register. The attendance grew
less and less; joking, smoking, taking each other's seats,
&c., led to such confusion, that almost all of the more respectable were driven off, and three is noted as the average attendance; company then began to be invited for

amusement. Towards the last of the season "skylarking" was said to be very common, and on one evening one of the casts was thrown down and broken to pieces; and the school, that is, the one or two attendants thereon, returned no more to face their misdeeds. Indeed, before that, it had become a disgrace rather than a benefit, and the sooner it closed the better; and the writer freely expressed the hope that it would never again be opened under such disadvantages.

November —. The almost never-ending subject—a selection of a building site—was again brought up, and Mr. Cummings was directed to examine ALL POSSIBLE places, even unto the Crystal Palace, for the obtainment of a place for the Academy Building and its Exhibition purposes, and to report thereon. That was truly an extensive order—a most formidable work.

At the next meeting, (at which there was not a quorum,) Mr. Cummings made no report on a building site, but simply stated that for exhibition the gallery over Dr. Chapin's Church could be procured at two hundred dollars per month, and the rooms 663 Broadway at three hundred dollars per month.

The first named was again selected, and that miserable *room* was once more destined to be the recipient of Academic display.

December 22. Died, J. W. Glass, Honorary Member. It was not until some six years after that distinguished artist's death, that an exposition and sale of his works took place. They were sold by Mr. Dexter, but how favorably is unknown to the writer.

Exhibitions of Art—how precarious! Powers' Greek Slave, on exhibition in the city of *Paris, pecuniarily* a dead failure! In this city—in the Academy Gallery—it obtained, in a few weeks, some ten thousand dollars. The Paris correspondents say its expenses in five weeks had been fifteen hundred dollars, while its receipts barely reached one hundred and thirty dollars! The failure was attributed to the French journals.

January 1. Political honors bestowed on a member of the Academy—Thomas H. Mattison—elected to a

1856. seat in the New-York Assembly, as a Representative for Sherburne, his native place.

January 30. The Vice-President, Mr. Cummings, was urged—nay, directed—to procure plans and estimates for a building calculated for a lot in Lafayette Place, *to combine the greatest possible economy and income*—not a light undertaking.

Mr. Cummings facetiously retaliated by nominating the mover to that duty, or that he have an interview with the Trustees, and inquire into their views on the subject; which was passed.

They were seen, and it was subsequently reported "*that they* were not disposed to encourage the Academy in building there at present." And very judiciously advised—most particularly so, so far as THAT plot of ground was concerned. Acting under that advice, on the twenty-fifth of February, at a special meeting called for that purpose, *a resolution* was offered and passed, "that we deem it inexpedient to build on ———— or any other property, until such time as the Academy shall find itself clear of its present engagements. By that was meant its property on Broadway. It was not an ill-advised resolution. either.

The Rev. Doctor Dewey, Honorary Member, delivered a course of lectures on " Artists *as Educators*," before the Mercantile Library Association of New-York City. They were well attended, and the doctor discoursed in his usual eloquent and forcible style. Doctor Dewey expressed the great gratification he usually derived from music, and his ear-gratefulness therefor; but on the whole, on mature deliberation, he thought he even preferred the delight his "eye" experienced in seeing good works of art.

March 12th. The thirty-first Annual Exhibition was opened in the room in the Church, 548 Broadway, the same as occupied in 1855. The writer would have preferred the Exhibition omitted rather than held there; such was not the view of others. It was there held; it closed on the tenth of May—its receipts $2550.75, and was open fifty-two working days, averaging $48.05 per day—two hundred and eighty-eight productions exhibited.

March 10. The contingency contemplated in the resolution passed some time back, had become a reality.

April —. The purchasers of the property 663 Broadway had failed to comply with the conditions of payment, and the writer was of necessity compelled to another foreclosure suit.

May 1. Mr. Cropsey, Academician, previous to his departure for Europe, made sale of his sketches and some more important works. The sale realized over eight thousand dollars, and bears satisfactory testimony to the value of art material. The studies from nature brought favorable prices, and aided to dispel the idea that artists are not well paid for their labor.

Art as a material, if well selected, is as likely to prove an advancing property to its possessor, as other securities.

It must, however, be selected with the same wholesome judgment which is called for and given to other matters, or the reverse. will undoubtedly prove the case. Selectors without judgment had better not venture on art investment, any more than in Wall Street, in the expectation of a "rising market."

May 14. The Annual Meeting. The President read a report, that

"The operations of the Academy during the past year are chiefly of a financial character, and will accordingly be laid before you by the Treasurer.

"At a Special Meeting held on the 26th of February last, it was deemed inexpedient, in the present condition of affairs, to take any immediate steps towards the purchase of grounds and erection of buildings, postponing that measure until the final settlement of the matters connected with the sale of the property 663 Broadway.

"The Antique School, which, with that of the Living Model, was suspended the previous year, has been reopened, with an indifferent attendance on the part of the students, while the number of applicants for admission to the Life School has been too limited to authorize a renewal of its sessions. This palpable apathy in the direction of our Schools, taken in connection with the apparent indifference of our members, as shown by a lack of men and a quorum at our last meetings, has a significance that should not be disregarded; at least, it is the interest due the duty of the Academy to examine into the causes which have led to the condition thus presented, and, if possible, to apply a remedy."

 * * * * * * *

A. B. DURAND, *President.*

From T. S. Cummings, Vice-President, and the Acting Treasurer's Report, it appears that the receipts were $2906.86; disbursements, $2767.36; leaving a balance of $139.50 in the treasury.

A. B. Durand was elected President; Thos. S. Cummings, Vice-President; Francis W. Edmonds, Treasurer (nominal); T. Addison Richards, Corresponding Secretary; James B. Stearns, Recording Secretary; Edwin White and J. W. Cassilear, Members of Council. There were no Academicians elected.

From that until the twenty-seventh day of October there were no meetings. The writer, it is true, was on the premises, and attending to all that required attention. To such an extent has the artistic summer stampede extended, that if the existence of art itself depended on remaining, it would be doubtful if it obtained it—much less to attend to Academic routine.

Notwithstanding the previously-named resolution, Cummings and Stearns had again been appointed to the double task of looking after " *a suitable site,*" and " *to secure more eligible rooms* for the holding of the approaching Exhibition ! As it was well known there were none such to be had, it was imposing ·an onerous task on the Committee ; but in art matters, magical and not common movements are sometimes expected. The appointment was, however, not without its advantage.

The Vice-President was ordered to prepare a memorial on the imposition of duties on imported art works, and submitted the following :

To the Congress of the United States,

  in Senate and House of Representatives assembled :

The undersigned, Artists and lovers of Art, your petitioners, beg leave respectfully to represent :

That the present unrestrained introduction of foreign works of art, particularly paintings, is a subject worthy of your consideration and legislation.

As against the importation of works of art of excellence, your petitioners offer no objection, and wish no serious impediment imposed to their introduction ; such are of benefit to the artist, to art, and to its general diffusion.

Nor do your petitioners seek the imposition of any protective tariff to the benefit of general or individual interests. They simply beg to offer their protest against the unrestrained introduction of worthless trash, benefiting none but the importer, and to the great injury of the standard of taste for art, which it is hoped it is the pleasure and pride of American painters to promote, maintain, and cultivate. The remedy sought is the imposition of such a duty as shall virtually stop the one class, while it shall present no serious obstruction to the admission of the other.

And your petitioners, after mature deliberation, respectfully suggest that a duty of —— cents per foot square on the superficial measure, or per foot circumference, as a means of accomplishing that end ; or that your Honorable Body will pass such or any other measure as may seem fit to accomplish the object your petitioners have in view.

And for which your petitioners will ever pray.

It was numerously signed by the artists and others, and forwarded to the "Art Commission," then in Washington, who doubtless presented it. It, however, received no attention, and no benefit is known to have accrued from the effort.

The writer reported having obtained a lease for two months of the old rooms of the Academy, 663 Broadway, at a very reasonable rent—a most gratifying result—and that he had offered personally to lease the rooms at the same rate, for three years, which was declined. Indeed, it was only on very prompt acceptance of the proposition, and immediate execution of writings, that they were secured at all—the party almost immediately pressing to be released from his bargain. It was proposed by the writer, that a "*Review*" be added, to occupy one or two of the rooms, as an increased attraction and means of raising the financial condition of the Institution ; but it was unheeded. The sites on Broadway and Great Jones Street, Twenty-third

Street and Broadway, Twenty-second Street and Broadway, Thirteenth Street and Fourth Avenue, Art Union, Broadway, the old property, 663 Broadway, Tenth Street and Broadway, were all offered for consideration. The Vice was requested to examine and report the probable revenue that could be obtained on 663 Broadway.

July 4. Brown's Statue of Washington, erected in the space between Union Park, Broadway and Fourth Avenue, was, for the first time, exposed to public inspection, and duly inaugurated. The work was welcomed with that enthusiasm which pertains to everything referring to that great man. The Rev. Dr. Bethune, in an eloquent address, presented THE STATUE to the country, and to the citizens of New-York as its guardians, in the name of the patriotic gentlemen to whose liberality the city is indebted for it. The enterprise was started and matured by Col. James Lee, and to whose indefatigable industry and perseverance the citizens are indebted for its successful accomplishment; and it is but proper he should be awarded the laurels to which he is so justly entitled.

The subscription to the work doubtless embraces the names of some of the most wealthy and patriotic citizens. The work stands as a successful monument of private enterprise, and sheds a lustre on the city. It might almost be said, perhaps, but little deserved. The Empire City should *long since* have had such.

Had it been put directly on the cross-walk, it would have proved an advantage to its position, and a refuge for pedestrians from the complete sweeping of the crossing by vehicle drivers. As it is, it may yet be of great service in that particular, by extending a second railing from the present, on the north, west and south sides, accessible by openings to passengers only.

July 24. Died, Thomas Doughty, Honorary Member— a landscape painter of much merit, particularly to be remembered by the soft and sunny tones of his pictures, in which he seemed to delight. Sylvan scenes were his choice, and he painted them with great delicacy of touch. His pecuniary encouragement did not appear to meet his expectations, or, indeed, to have been important in amount, and was, doubtless, not without its effect in souring an over-sensitive nature.

September 10. Died, Seth Cheeney, Associate Member— an artist of superior excellence in his line of art.

October 17. Died, Luigi Canini, Honorary Member— officiated as Professor of Architecture at Turin, and conducted the excavations at Tusculum.

October 27.   The writer, fully aware of the shockingly-reduced standard of the schools, as also the importance of having instruction in such an institution, if at all, under subordination—to insure it to its proper uses—and believing that a great deal of the past difficulty arose as much from the want of proper care on the part of the Institution, as from any intentional neglect or disobedience on the part of the students, determined to sacrifice his personal comfort to the endeavor to remedy the evil and restore the schools to their proper usefulness.   He offered, and was placed in "SUPREME CHARGE," and immediately assumed the direction, submitting and having adopted the following few rules for the government of the schools:

The Schools for the season will open on Monday, November 3, free of charge to the students, and have been placed under the immediate direction of the Vice-President, T. S. Cummings, who will be constantly in attendance, and to whom the students are referred.

Admission can be obtained on application to the Council, by presenting a drawing from the "round" for their approval on every Monday evening; or may be left with Mr. Cummings during the week.

No strangers, or visitors, excepting the members of the Academy, will be permitted access to the rooms during study hours, except on express permission of the officer in charge.

Every student admitted will be furnished with a pass, and which must be shown to the door-keeper on entrance, or at least so until the party is known, when it may be dispensed with.

Every student will provide himself with a drawing-board and materials.

No conversation, noise, or smoking will be permitted in the rooms during study hours.

The Roll will be called each evening at $\frac{1}{4}$ past 7 o'clock, and the absentees noted.   Absence at Roll-call will be regarded as absence for the evening.

Absence from 3 successive evenings forfeits the seat, and the same may be taken by another.

Absence for 6 successive evenings forfeits the studentship, unless especially excused by the Council, on application.

The casts, models, and seats will be arranged by the officer in charge on the first evening of every month; and the seats will be chosen by the students, by lot, on that evening, or the first drawing evening thereafter.

Painting in oil in the Antique School will not be permitted.

The above arrangements and rules have been made solely for the comfort of the students, and to promote the efficiency of the School, and afford quiet means of study to those desiring it.   They will therefore be rigidly enforced.

Every student, on admission, is presumed to accede to these rules; and any one disregarding them, or in any other manner conducting himself other than as an artist and a gentleman, will, on examination of the facts, if proven, be by them dismissed the School.

The arrangements worked to admiration. The students were informed that the rules were few, and made exclusively for their benefit, and that they *would be enforced*. Seventy-five entered—fifty-two in the "Antique," and twenty-three in the "Life;" the average attendance forty in the "Antique," and twenty in the "Life." *No* confusion, NO disorder, NO disobedience, of any kind whatever, occurred to mar the school, or impede the progress of the pupil; and so complete the attention to the rule of silence, that a pin might have been heard in its fall during school hours; and yet the presiding officer never had occasion to call attention or admonish any one, during the whole term.

It was said that some of the playful and refractory of the preceding year came to the doors, and into the rooms even; but finding how matters stood within, either appeared no more, or fell into the rules, and became orderly, art-loving scholars.

At the end of the season a very pleasing testimonial was tendered the presiding officer by the students, and it was personally delivered by one of the oldest of their number— Mr. Bannister—in a most felicitous and happy manner. The following is a copy of the proceedings as published:

Life and Antique Schools of the National Academy of Design.
1856—1857.

PRINTED BY ORDER OF THE COMMITTEE.

Perhaps the least-thought-of person among the public, and too little regarded by the patrons and lovers of Art, is the Art Student. In this City of turmoil and bustle, where men rather "poke about for pence," than treasure up the beautiful and true, either in Nature or in Art, some account of the studies and doings of that quiet body—the Students of the NATIONAL ACADEMY OF DESIGN—may not be uninteresting.

The past, present and future of the NATIONAL ACADEMY—a theme now engaging the mind and pen of one of the ablest and most experienced artists, cannot be entered upon in a short space. But the Schools of this Institution, as they have been conducted during the past Winter, under the management and experience of the Vice-President, call for some notice, that the friends of Art, and the Art Student himself, may know where to seek that knowledge and guidance for which too many have long sought in vain.

The Life and Antique Schools, opened on the 1st of November, 1856, and to the 1st of April, 1857, went prosperously forward, with an attendance of over fifty pupils.

Mr. CUMMINGS, early in the season, seeing both the want of management and a ruling head, came forward, voluntarily, and took the charge, much to the honor of the Academy and the benefit of the Students. We might go on to enumerate the constant source of gratification and improvement in study on the part of the pupils, derived through this supervision, or tell of the kind rule and good order under Mr. CUMMINGS—

" The kindest man,
The best condition'd and unwearied spirit
In doing courtesies."

But the closing proceedings will speak more to the point.

Mr. BANNISTER, addressing Mr. CUMMINGS, observed :

SIR :—Towards the Academy, we might perhaps express our thanks by words ; but words seemed unfit and too cheap in return for the benefits we have derived from the kindly advice and encouragement received at your hands. In behalf of the Students, I beg the favor of your acceptance of this testimonial of our regard, in the shape of an autograph proof of the picture of Shakespeare and his friends, at the Mermaid Club. Whatever proficiency in Art I have made, I may properly attribute much of it to the advantages of the Academy Schools ; and while I allude to the past, and the rise of Art among us—to the long line of men who have gone from these Schools, whose names are now household words—remembering MORSE, and COLE, and DURAND, I can still think of none more worthy of being called the Student's friend than Mr. T. S. CUMMINGS. To him he would express his own grateful respect, and assure him of the hearty sympathy of all the Students who had the pleasure of receiving instruction and advice from one so high and honorable in the profession.

To these remarks Mr. CUMMINGS replied as follows :

Students of the National Academy :

GENTLEMEN :—It is with mingled feelings of pleasure, and I trust justifiable pride, that I receive the testimonial presented to me this evening. The very beautiful, and, indeed, eloquent terms in which you have been pleased to refer to many of my associates in the establishment of this Institution, some of whom death has removed from us, touches a chord of early recollection and friendship of the past which I had scarcely supposed could have been so deeply awakened at this far-removed date. The very flattering terms you have been pleased to bestow on my services in the Academy, and cause of Art, render it somewhat embarrassing to me, properly to reply to your kindness.

I will not affect the modesty that I deserve none of this. It is true I was present at the incipient formation of the Schools and the birth of the Institution, and I have been, I believe, at least a faithful laborer, to the best of my ability, in the cause, ever since ; now a period of some thirty-five years. Quite a sufficient time, you will say, to try the steadfastness of one's purposes, and the zeal you are pleased to attribute to me in your cause. I trust it may have served the cause of Art, and the good purpose of an example to you all hereafter.

You are now Students, but you know not how soon you, or at least some of you, may be called on to preside over these very Schools yourselves. Then, remember to do unto others as you have been pleased others should do unto you, and if you find your zeal abating, remember the term of service in your behalf of some of those who have long gone before you.

In conclusion, gentlemen, allow me to present to you my earnest thanks for the very beautiful present : as a work of Art it is of the highest excellence, and the taste of its accompaniments and manner of presentation worthy of the School. With the sincerest wishes for your welfare and happiness, I bid you all adieu—though, I trust, but for a season—for on the opening of the ensuing Fall classes, I hope to have the pleasure of meeting you all again, with renewed energies, and with increased facilities in the Schools for your improvement in the study of Art.

The season allowed for study being about to terminate, meetings of the Students were held on the seventh and fourteenth of March, when the following preamble and resolutions were adopted :

To the President and Council of the National Academy of Design :

About now to separate for the season, after enjoying, by your kindness and liberality, the privileges of the Life and Antique Schools, and an uninterrupted course of study therein, we feel it not only a sense of duty, but that we should do violence to our feelings, if we let pass the opportunity to express our gratitude for these strong inducements to study. And that in consideration of the selfishness of the age, and especially of individuals and associations having the ownership and control of collections of Art, we deem it due to the welfare of present, as well as prospective Art and Artists, to hold in venerable esteem all who offer encouragement, give opportunities, or hold out inducements to the rising Art and Artists of our country.

Resolved, That we, as Students of the NATIONAL ACADEMY OF DESIGN, of the City of New-York, feel that we have been highly privileged and much benefited by having free access to and instruction from the study of the beautiful antique casts, as also from the living models furnished by the Institution, for which we return our sincere thanks ; and that the many improvements and opportunities afforded, over those of former years, we hail as arguing for the future a bright career of usefulness and honor to the Academy.

Resolved, That we acknowledge our indebtedness to the Vice-President, Mr. T. S. CUMMINGS, for his constant attendance and attention to our many wants, his mild and courteous demeanor towards the Students, and the uniform good order which he has preserved, all of which have combined to render our course of study pleasant and profitable.

Resolved, That we shall await with rejoicing the opening of the Schools in the ensuing season, and hope they may be under the same good administration.

Very respectfully,

JAS. BANNISTER,
J. B. WHITTAKER,
J. L. DICK,
A. McLEES,
J. W. McEBEE,
W. P. MORGAN,
Committee in behalf of the Schools.

To which the Council replied as follows :

To the Students of the Life and Antique Schools :

GENTLEMEN :—The Council of the Academy desires to say to you, that they are exceedingly gratified by the terms and spirit of your communication on the occasion of the closing of the current session of the Life and Antique Schools, to which, as members, you have done so much honor.

It is through the Schools, more than by any other means, that the Academy hopes to accomplish its object of contributing to the advancement of the Arts of our country ; being persuaded that good and true works will be ever the best educators of the public taste, and that, among a people intelligent as ours, the understanding and estimation of Art will be always in full correspondence with its worth.

It is thus, with great pleasure, that the Council looks back to the long list of Students who have gone from the Schools in past years to add to the excellence and honor of their profession ; and yet with deeper interest to the future, with its promise of higher achievements, with enlarged facilities of study ; especially when the means are used with so much earnestness as in your labors of the past Winter.

With the highest anticipations from your assiduity and progress in the past, the Council bid you adieu, with the hope of meeting you all in the coming Autumn, and with every wish for your professional and personal success and happiness always.

In behalf of the Council,

I am, gentlemen, very truly your friend,

T. ADDISON RICHARDS,
Corres. Sec'y N. A.

The Committee would remark, that these facts speak for the honor of the Academy, and will strengthen its already well-established reputation for good, and usefulness for the Art Student. If used properly, as we have endeavored to do this Winter, it affords opportunity for study and profitable advancement, which we fear too few are aware are now within the reach of all, who will apply themselves diligently to the course of study and rules laid down for their good.

We may state that the next session will probably open with increased facilities for study, by the restoration of the professorships of Anatomy and Perspective.

With respect, your ob't serv'ts,

(Signed,)

JAS. BANNISTER,
J. B. WHITTAKER,
W. J. HENNESSEY,
W. P. MORGAN,
Committee on Publications.

November 3.   The meeting of the Council was mainly devoted to receiving reports on sites for a building.

Mr. Cummings reported favorably on the gore lot bounded by Broadway, Fifth Avenue, and Twenty-third Street, suggested last Monday evening—dimensions 131 feet on Broadway and Fifth Avenue lines, by 59 on the base—which, on examination, he found might perhaps answer all the purposes for exposition and schools, as per diagrams, plans, and drawings submitted.

The lot is, to all appearances, an awkward one, yet, on examination, sufficient room is found for all purposes, and a revenue may be derived from the lower part, as stores, sufficient to nearly or quite meet all expenses—with a prospect of that amount being greatly increased from year to year, as the neighborhood becomes more valuable for business purposes. It is recommended that the building be four stories high, which, under the plan of ascent, will be sufficiently easy to visitors, while it will greatly reduce the yearly cost to the Institution.   Estimate on revenue has been intentionally placed very low, and may soon so far rise as to place the Institution *free of any yearly charge*, and even be expected to yield a surplus.

The main points for consideration are its peculiar dimensions, the proper lighting of the Galleries, and satisfactory arrangements of wall to meet the wants of the Artist exhibiters. $38,000 is now asked for the plot, in place of $35,000, previously named.

It is hoped, however, that may be reduced. The owner will advance a builders' loan of $35,000 with which to proceed with the erection of the building, in consideration of its being for public purposes. The *terms* ALL *on mortgage.* $50,000, it is presumed, will cover it with suitable buildings. The device for increasing the revenue is the more necessary, as it is very evident that the *Exhibition of Paintings* for money may soon be profitless—or for the present, at least, not to be looked on as a source from which an income may be derived.

Respectfully,

T. S. CUMMINGS.

The site was not accepted. In the Fall of 1856, died, William Strickland, architect, and Honorary Member. He was born in England, and died in Nashville, Tennessee. He was buried in a crypt of the State Capitol, of which he was the architect.

November 4. Died, in Paris, Paul Delaroche, Honorary Member of the Academy.

During two or three months, sites almost innumerable were offered for a building, and repeated examinations made, of which only the most important have been enumerated—enough, however, to satisfy and answer the oft-repeated question by members of the society to the writer: "Why is the Academy doing nothing—making no effort towards obtaining a building?" The simple fact was, it was *their ignorance* of what was doing, or what had been done, and not what was left undone, that was the cause of the inquiry —a mistake that is of frequent occurrence, not only in art, but in other matters. It is not at all an uncommon thing to put the shoe on the wrong foot.

December 8. Premiums were ordered for the schools, and President Durand was requested to prepare an *address*, to be delivered on the occasion of their awardment. They were *not* publicly delivered, and consequently there was no address.

January. Mr. Cummings, Vice-President, was directed to make application to the Legislature for a renewal **1857.** of the CHARTER, which was done, signed by the Council, and forwarded; and after much delay, and the final assistance of Secretary Stearns, it was obtained, and THE CHARTER renewed.

February 23. The writer reported to the Council, "that if the Academy were sincerely desirous of repossessing their former property, 663 Broadway (as had been intimated by some), they had the opportunity to do so. The owner offers a resale of it to the Institution at the price he gave for it—receiving his mortgages in payment, to the amount of their face; the balance to remain on mortgage on the premises." And on the 3d of March it was

" *Resolved*, Whereas, after a careful consideration had on the proposed purchase of the property 663 Broadway, (and as the Trustees are opposed to the same): Therefore,
" *Resolved*, That any further consideration of the subject is at present deemed inexpedient."

It was declined! In fact, the proposition was offered merely to set at rest the importunate inquiries and statements by many to the writer, namely: "Why do not the Academy go back to their old rooms? The Academicians —the Trustees—the Council—ALL desire it." Which did not appear to be the case.

In the Spring of 1857 was erected the building known as "The Artists' Studio," in Tenth Street, containing a number of rooms, arranged in a manner most suitable for artists' purposes, with an exhibition gallery, in which to place their works when finished, or to hold public exhibitions in, if desired.

The building proved a great success, and supplied a desideratum long wanted. It has been fully occupied from its finish, and the proprietors enjoy the satisfaction of seeing, in one building, a considerable portion of the art talent of the city. It is also a well-known feature to strangers, and access to the separate studios of its occupants much sought.

Purloining from Art Exhibitions on the increase. The Academy of Design, it appears, not the only parties exhibiting paintings deemed worthy of being stolen. No less than thirteen productions are recorded "removed" from the Exhibition of the "Boston Art Club." The expertness in the removal perhaps only equaled by the *selection*, which was doubtless good!

May 13. The Annual Meeting of the Academicians was held in the rooms 58 East Thirteenth Street; and in consequence of ill health, the President made no written report, briefly referring to the good condition of the schools under the charge of the Vice-President, the renewal of the Charter, and to the Treasurer's report of the financial condition of the Institution. The latter was read and accepted, and the meeting adjourned for want of a quorum. No members felected. The officers held over.

May 18, was opened the thirty-second Annual Exhibition, in the old rooms, 663 Broadway. No alterations had been made in the galleries, and they were hired for that purpose. It received $3,861.75, closing on the 20th of June; thirty woking days, averaging $128.70 per day—the highest daily average on record. Works exhibited, 548.

June 1. An offer of twelve thousand dollars per annum was made for the "Racket Court" property on Broadway— ALL alterations at the Academy's expense. Although deemed a very full offer, it was not accepted.

June 11. Died, at New Dresden, Frederick August Moritz Retzsch, Honorary Member. He was born at Dresden, December 9th, 1799. As a painter, but little known; his reputation rests on his outline etchings from the German Ballads of Goethe, Schiller, &c. His prints of these, and the Game of Chess, stand pre-eminently among the foremost works in their department.

July 25. A meeting was called for the consideration of the leasing of the upper floors of a building in course of erection on the corner of FOURTH AVENUE and Tenth

Street—then up to *"roofing"*—which, although well known to present NO advantages that would be deemed acceptable as a permanent arrangement, was yet so far in advance of anything that had offered, within the Academy's means to accomplish, as to be desirable as a temporary arrangement. A portion was leased, and Cummings and Stearns were appointed to superintend the adaptation of it to the wants of the Academy. That was rather a difficult task; there was left for the Committee but to make the best they could of that which was but very partially adapted to the purposes, or likely to meet the wishes of the artists: the two upper floors were thrown into one, and the roof perforated for sky-lights. The space was divided into rooms wheresoever the chimneys of the houses over which the galleries extended would permit, and over several the galleries passed. Two more *salons* than originally contemplated were *called for*, and ultimately added; and a bridge was thrown across an interior court-yard, some thirty feet from the ground, to produce the continuousness of communication so much prized by the artists generally. The whole was painted, carpeted and prepared, and under all the unfavorable circumstances, certainly presented a very inviting temporary arrangement—far more so than could have been anticipated by Committee or Body when it was undertaken.

As before stated, the whole suite, as finished, was not originally undertaken; a little more than half was reported on, and at less than half the cost, and that accommodation was deemed sufficient, and, so far as the means of the Academy were concerned, all that should have been taken, and it is probable all that would have been taken, had it not been for the coming on of the *" English Exhibition,"* which perhaps unwisely determined the Academy on undertaking the WHOLE. The rent was then increased to *three thousand dollars*, while fifteen hundred dollars should have been its limit. During the four years the Academy occupied the building, it created a debt of about six thousand dollars, fifteen hundred dollars a year, and about the amount of the additions called for; though *sub*-letting the Galleries materially reduced the burden during some of the years of their occupation. That the rent was too great for the Academy's means, was beyond question.

September 17. Died, J. Dallas, Associate Member. The following obituary notice is from a daily paper:

DEATH OF JACOB A. DALLAS.—We regret to record the death of Jacob A. Dallas, the well-known popular artist. Mr. Dallas was born in Philadelphia, in the year 1825. He was the son of an eminent merchant, and the cousin of Hon. George M. Dallas, our present Minister to England. At the age of eight years he removed with his parents to Missouri, where he studied at Amos College, and after a due course of instruction, graduated at the age of eighteen. He then returned to Philadelphia, and attended the Life and Antique School, under Professor Otis, the celebrated portrait painter. About nine years ago he came to New-York, where he has since resided. His talents, which were of the highest order, were employed upon all the principal illustrated works that have been produced here for many years. He was one of the chief illustrators of *Harper's*, *Putnam's*, *Mrs. Stephens'*, *Frank Leslie's*, and other popular periodicals, while many of the larger volumes, issued by our best publishers, were wholly indebted to his pencil for the valuable engravings which they contained. Mr. Dallas married, rather more than a year since, Miss Mary Kyle, the daughter of Mr. Joseph Kyle, the celebrated artist. The union was a happy one. Miss Kyle was also well known as an artist, and was possessed of considerable literary ability. Everything promised well for the success of the young couple in life, when a few weeks ago Mr. Dallas was seized with dysentery, which, passing into consumption of the bowels, terminated his death on Wednesday afternoon last. His funeral took place from the residence of his father-in-law, Mr. Kyle, in Fifty-first Street, near Tenth Avenue. He was interred in the New-York Bay Cemetery, his body being followed to the grave by most of the artists and *literati* in the city.

As a man, Mr. Dallas was beloved by all who had the advantage of his friendship. A truer friend, a more genial companion, never existed. His early death is deplored by all who knew him, and is a loss to the profession which he adorned, that will not in a long time be repaired.

October 1. The Schools opened for the season, as before, under the charge of the Vice-President; (sixty-three students admitted to the Antique, and twenty-six to the Life School.) They were closed the thirteenth of March, after a most successful season. No premiums were offered.

October 10. Died, in London, Thomas G. Crawford. Mr. Crawford was a sculptor of high standing, and an Honorary Member of the Academy.

The remains of Mr. Crawford were deposited in Greenwood Cemetery, January 8th, 1858—the funeral services had been previously performed in St. John's Church; the Rev. Drs. Berrian, Dix, and Weston officiating. Resolutions of condolence were passed by the National Academy of Design, the "Century," and by almost every Art Institution in the country, and by the American artists at Rome. Thomas Hicks, Academician of the National Academy of Design, was selected by the "Century" to deliver a eulogy upon the deceased, before the Club. The writer did not hear it. It was highly spoken of by the press and society generally as a fervid and finished production.

The Central Park Commissioners attempt the old, well-worn practice of *premiums* for the obtainment of artistic excellence in design for their work; and it was

"*Resolved*, That this Board do advertise for plans for laying out the Central Park, and that they offer for the best plan chosen, $2,000; for the second, $1,000; for the third, $750; and for the fourth, $500. Said plans to become the property of the Board."

November 2. Died, William E. West, Nashville, Tenn., Honorary Member. Mr. West enjoyed a wide reputation. Most of his life was spent in Europe, where he stood at the head of his profession. He painted Byron, which was generally conceded to be the best likeness extant, and which the artist sold for two thousand dollars. He was engaged, up to within three days of his death, in painting portraits of many of the citizens of Nashville, and had two or three "historical pieces" on his easel at the time of his decease.

November 9, was announced the death of William H. Ranney, Associate Member of the National Academy of Design. Resolutions of condolence with the family were passed, and crape worn by the members, in token of their respect for his memory.

A number of the friends of the late William Ranney, desirous of expressing their sense of his abilities as an artist, and his character as a man, decided upon offering a testimonial to his memory, which, at the same time, might be of some permanent value to his bereaved family. The artists generally contributed works of their pencils, which, being added to the sketches left by Mr. Ranney, formed a collection sufficiently various for a public exposition, with the ultimate view of sale at auction, at the close of the Exhibition—the proceeds to be disposed of for the benefit of the widow and children of the deceased artist.

The thought, and the credit of carrying the enterprise to successful completion, belong to Nason B. Collins, A. F. Tait and William Hart—the two latter artists—the former a young merchant of the city, who voluntarily gave much of his money and time to the object. By their exertions the works of the deceased were collected, finished, and otherwise made acceptable for exposition and sale; works generously supplied by the artist contributors were, with those before mentioned, framed, and an Exhibition was held, consisting of over two hundred productions, in the Galleries of the Academy, given rent free for that purpose; Mr. Leeds, the art auctioneer, selling them without charge.

The result was highly successful. The works by Mr. Ranney sold for sufficient to discharge a mortgage due on a little homestead which he had erected, though not entirely paid for, in West Hoboken. The amount obtained from the sale of the sketches contributed by others was some five thousand dollars, which, by the unanimous determination of the contributors, was placed in the hands of Messrs. Cummings, Durand, and Edmonds, as Trustees for investment for the benefit of the widow and children, who derive the interest therefrom.

Attendant on that effort, and at the earnest request of many artists, the writer drafted a plan, which embodied "THE ACTION" in the Ranney case into a society or association form, for a permanency; and likewise a code of by-laws calculated therefor, which was deemed acceptable, and a society was immediately organized, under the title of "The Artists' Fund Society of New-York."

T. S. Cummings was elected President; C. L. Elliott, Vice-President; Nason B. Collins, Treasurer.

It was brought into action under the most favorable prospects of success. Unfortunately, differences of opinion, both as to the method of aid and the government of the Institution, occurred at the first Annual Meeting, and adverse to the existing administration. A printed ticket was suddenly sprung on the Board; and as the officers who were discharging that trust (not so much to benefit themselves as others) did not anticipate such a measure, and, if they had, would have taken no precaution to have prevented it, they were, of course, taken at vantage-ground, and defeated. The writer, the President—after several ballotings, and the opponent selected refusing to run against him—was elected. Others were removed; several changes were made, and there appearing no prospect of a united success, and the Board which had enjoyed the President's confidence removed, he declined to continue, and resigned.

The whole face of the matter was then changed. It was, however, continued, and under many modifications, became a highly prosperous society. The objects aimed at were worthy of obtainment, and highly charitable, and it is sincerely hoped may prove beneficial.

The first Exhibition and sale made a handsome fund to begin with. It was continued with marked success, has had several Exhibitions and sales, and has obtained a capital of some twenty thousand dollars for the performance of its work. It now embodies the form of a life insurance. Whether it be more profitable to pay a premium in pictures than money, to it or other institutions, must depend on the salability of the works of the artist. The clause making returnable to the artist whatever his picture may sell for over a certain amount, may contribute much to its prospect of successful continuance.

In November an Exhibition of paintings was made in the new Galleries, of works by "English artists;" and at the same period, a similar one at the Art Union Gallery, by "French artists." They attracted much attention, and afforded the American artists an opportunity of comparing their strength with many names of repute, without the necessity of crossing the water to do it—that is, provided the samples gave a proper representation of the foreign authors. The French collection was generally approved, but the English did not receive such unqualified approbation. It undoubtedly contained many specimens of excellence, held at a very high valuation; and a most extraordinary effort was made by the agent having them in charge—a gentleman well skilled in his profession, of plausible manner and excellent address—to engage the Academy in an enterprise, conjointly with the Philadelphia and Boston Academies, for their exhibition in the three cities, and also for the further importation of similar works, to be of still greater value, in like manner to rotate on exhibition in the three cities; the institutions so consenting, to give the use of their galleries free of charge, and pledge themselves for the expenses of importation and exposition of ALL kinds.

The National Academy was interested—nay, perfectly charmed. Resolutions were passed agreeing to engage in the enterprise. Conditions, however, were introduced by the Treasurer, Cummings, who opposed the whole scheme, which materially modified their power and extent.

December 5. The paintings, first exhibited here, were removed to Philadelphia, and, so far as sale thereof was concerned, was much more favored there than in New-York. Many of the principal works were sold, and the remainder were returned to England. For some cause or other, nothing more was ever heard of paintings or triple union exhibitions; and well may the Academy rejoice thereat.

January. Were organized several limited combinations for drawing from the human figure, aside from
1858. the schools of the National Academy of Design; though principally from draped figures—"*sketching*," rather than *critical* or laborious "*drawing*," the object. Facility—dangerous facility—the aim.

The plans, generally, were for a dozen or more artists to form a society to meet two or three evenings in the week in one or the other of the members' studios; each member in turn selecting the model to pose—mostly from street characters. The picturesque rather than *classic* purity of "outline," or elevation of "form," the leading points in the selections. Doubtless much *amusement*, and perhaps "some" "DRAWING," which might not otherwise have been had. Yet, though practice is at all times necessary, it may be questionable if such, with its attendant dangers, is desirable or improving.

January 10. Died, Hezekiah Auger, sculptor, of New-Haven, Connecticut—Honorary Member. A man of talent in his branch of art. He made an exhibition of one of his works in the Gallery of the Academy; but, like other such, it did not attract attention, or give pecuniary profit.

August Belmont, then Minister at the Hague, and long resident in the city, a gentleman of wealth, taste, and refinement, imported one of the best selected and most beautiful collections of works of art ever introduced in the country; and in the beginning of 1858 the Galleries in Tenth Street were open for the exhibition of the art purchases of Mr. Belmont. Public exhibition of the collection had been solicited by several gentlemen, and it had been assented to, to give the citizens an opportunity to see the collection prior to its final adjustment. The proceeds of the exhibition, which were large, were divided between several of the charitable institutions of the city. The works adorn his private gallery at his residence, where, under proper regulations, they are accessible to the public.

"ARTISTS' RECEPTIONS."

A meeting of the professional artists had been held, and resulted in the founding of "The Artists' Receptions." The first of the series was held on the 8th of January, 1858, at Dodworth's, Broadway. It proved a very agreeable and successful appointment—"took amazingly" with the artists, and their friends. Dodworth's Hall was never better filled, decorated, or supplied with a more brilliant and beautiful assemblage. Art gratified the eye, and Dodworth's music the ear. It was at once determined to hold three more such during the season; and the last of the set was held on the 12th of February, 1859, with increased interest on the part of the artists and the public.

The artists of the "Tenth Street Studio" followed the example, and held their "Receptions." Most of the Studios were thrown open, and the circulation through the building was another "agreeable," often *réunion*, recreation to visitor and artist, and increased the pleasures of the gathering. Lessening the number of receptions in a season would perhaps afford a probability of longer continuance of the pleasant arrangement—overdoing, or rather too much excitement, for continuance being a leading feaure in art, as in everything else, in the novelty-loving public.

Boston followed suit. The success quite equaled that of New-York.

Brooklyn was not to be outdone, and established her "Art Receptions," and with a decided success. The Academy of Music was brought into requisition, and, by the aid of a Committee of Amateurs, a subscription, or contribution in some form, was added. It was "eminently successful," and made an "Art fund for the advancement of the object," and its future support.

The writer would quote, "Abstain to enjoy." Too many may tire both artist and public, and leave both to mourn over their discontinuance.

March 22. Delegates appointed to the Artists' Convention.

"WHEREAS, The Council have heard with sincere pleasure of its being the intention of Messrs. Morse, Bellows, and Brown, members of the Academy, to remain in Washington during the present season, and in furtherance of the desire expressed by the Washington Art Association to the Academy: It was therefore

"Resolved, That the Academy hereby appoints and recognizes as its delegates to the Washington Convention, Messrs. S. F. B. Morse, H. K. Brown, and F. W. Bellows, and solicits the favor of these to confer with the Convention as to the best means of calling the attention of the Government to the most judicious patronage of American Artists, in reference to the decoration and adorning of the public buildings at Washington with works of Art; and that copies of the resolution be sent to the Convention."

The action of the Convention resulted in the appointment of "J. R. Lambdin, of Philadelphia, H. K. Brown and J. F. Kensett, of New-York, as Art Commissioners to superintend the decoration and enrichment of the Capitol with works of Art by American Artists." And it is hoped their efforts will be efficient in directing the enterprise over which they preside in a proper and legitimate direction. They since, by Doc. No. 43, 36th Congress, 1st Session, made an admirable report on its progress, and their recommendations; which is commended, but cannot, by reason of its length, be inserted.

It was determined to dispense with the "Annual Exhibition Supper," and to reinstate a "Reception," to precede the annual exposé in its place. Cummings, Stearns, Richards, Gray, and Cafferty were placed in charge of the programme; and they then and there, for the first time, introduced "Music"—full dress, as before; and on the 12th of April was inaugurated the Thirty-third Annual Exhibition, in the new Galleries in Tenth Street, near Broadway. To the public on the 13th, closing on the 30th of June. Its receipts were $4,297.25. Open 68 working days, and averaged $63.10 per day—of which twenty-six were wet days!

The number of works, 560. The new Galleries contained about 800 *"running"* feet of wall, and were lighted by over 300 gas-jets.

The Exhibition was deemed one of more than ordinary merit and interest, and was appreciated by the public, as its greatly advanced earnings—over $4,000—showed; the greatest amount received in any one year, for ten years, or since 1848.

May —. The Annual Meeting of the Academicians was held (the Minutes have no date beyond what is given—*May*) in Cummings's Studio Building in Thirteenth Street. In the unexpected absence of the President, Mr. Cummings, the Vice-President, presided, who informed the body that he had no knowledge of the intended absence of the President, whose duty it was to prepare the Annual Report— that under such circumstances of course he was unprepared. "A verbal report was made by the Chairman of the general features of the year's business—condition of the Schools, prospects as to property, Trusteeship, &c., &c.; after which he read his report, as Acting Treasurer, on the financial condition of the Institution; all of which was accepted." By the latter it appeared that the total receipts of the year were $5,315.44, and the total expenditures $5,324.91; balance in Treasury, $0.53.

A. B. Durand was elected President; Thomas S. Cummings, Vice-President; James B. Stearns, Recording Secretary; T. Addison Richards, Corresponding Secretary; F. W. Edmonds, Treasurer; William Hart, E. D. Greene, A. F. Tait, R. W. Hubbard, *Academicians*.

The Pennsylvania Academy reduced the price of admission to its Exhibition to 10, and the Catalogues to 5 cents. That assumed more than ordinary importance, from the fact that such action had been freely advocated in the "Academy Council," to wit—that they should on some proper occasion try the experiment of abolishing "season tickets"—always a vexatious annoyance—and lessen the price of single admission. During the Summer, and until October 5, there appears to have been nothing done—at least no record; and again from that to January 31, 1859, with the exception of one meeting—no quorum—there was probably nothing to do.

October 15. The Life and Antique Schools were opened, under the charge of the Vice-President, Mr. Cummings. Sixty-one students were enrolled in the "Antique," and 30 in the "Life." The order of the School was perfect, the general attendance good, the improvement correspondent with the industry and advantages—the whole fully fulfilled the expectations of the writer; and he deemed the Schools at that moment a credit to themselves, instructors, and Institution.

December 7. Died, Mrs. H. Dassell, Honorary Member—a distinguished lady artist. Her loss was much regretted by the profession, and deeply mourned over by the numerous friends who were endeared to her by her many Christian virtues—a fond mother, and an affectionate wife.

January 18th. Mr. Aspinwall had a private reception of his friends and lovers of art, on the completion and **1859.** arrangement of his paintings, and to inaugurate his new Gallery. The works presented were of universal excellence, principally by the old masters—many of the most valuable and authenticated of any, perhaps, to be found in the country; some for which princely prices had been paid, and come from the possession of kings. The collection, by the liberality of its possessor, is open to public inspection, under the simple regulation of procurement of tickets of invitation.

January —. Mr. Reichardt, an artist of some talent, opened to the public his works on exhibition and sale in the Galleries of the Academy. They were of more merit than seemed to be considered by the public. They were not numerously visited or enthusiastically received, and the writer understood the exposition did not pay its expenses, and that the *sale* did not meet the artist's expectation. It probably needed the trumpet. At all events, there was great disappointment expressed.

Discourses on Art subjects appeared to be more frequent than usual. Thomas Hicks, N. A., delivered one in Brooklyn—"The Mission of Art;" and the Hon. James T. Brady one for the benefit of the Ranney Fund — "American Art;" Mr. Remington, two lectures on the "Science of Beauty."

February 1. Was held in the Academy Galleries one of Leeds' interesting "Annual Sales of Works of Art"— "American and Foreign"—a specialty as to merit, variety, and value.

February 14. Died, Thomas Augustus Cummings, Associate Member—a young artist of merit, a student of the Institution for years, and son of the Vice-President. Dying young, his works are not numerous, or generally known.

Another meeting was called for the purpose of altering and amending the Constitution—and that oft-altered instrument was again destined to submit to emendation.

It were well-nigh time it should be perfect, or let alone.

A resolution was passed, "That there should be an exhibition in the Fall, to remain open during the Winter;" and another, "That after the transaction of the usual business at the Annual Meeting"—"That a *dinner be given to the members.*" The latter was carried out—"or down;" but not so the former.

The Vice-President proposed several sites for a building —viz.: The property and house on Fourteenth Street, between University Place and Broadway, and running through to Thirteenth Street—since the *Maison Dorée;* one on the south side of Twenty-first Street, and corner of Broadway, running through from thence to Fifth Avenue about 140 by 75 feet—facing the St. Germain Hotel; one on the corner of Thirty-fourth Street and Broadway, of about 100 by 125 feet. None of them were deemed acceptable.

March 7. That already well-manipulated document, the Constitution, received several "AMENDMENTS."

March 18. In Charleston, the collection of paintings belonging to the late Mr. Ball were sold at auction. Allston's picture of "Spalatra, or the Bloody Hand," bought originally for $500, sold for over $3,000.

In April was established the "International Art Institution," on Broadway, corner of Fourth Street, and the following circular issued:

INTERNATIONAL ART INSTITUTE.

The Professors of the Academies of Design at Berlin, Dusseldorf, Munich, and Dresden, in Germany, have long been desirous of making the American public acquainted with the works of their living artists of eminence, and they have finally concluded to establish a permanent Exhibition of Paintings in the City of New-York. For that purpose, they have made an arrangement with Mr. Aufermann to act as Director of this new Institution.

The collection of paintings now presented to the public is one of the finest and most valuable ever exhibited in this country. It will be kept up by new accessions, from time to time, from the hands of living masters.

Every painting exhibited will be offered for sale; and in order to secure the public against imposition, a Special Committee has been appointed for each of the cities from which the paintings are sent. Nothing will be shipped to New-York for exhibition which has not first undergone the inspection of one of these Committees, and they will scrupulously reject every painting not particularly deserving of merit. At the head of these Committees are the following well-known names:

Professor SCHRADER,
    " KRETSCHMAR,
    " MAX SCHMIDT,   } in Berlin.
    " MEYER VON BREMEN,
    " H. ESCHKE,

Professor Em. Leutze,
" Andr. Achenbach, ⎫
" C. Hübner, ⎬ in Dusseldorf.
" J. W. Lindlar, ⎭
" Robert Kummer, in Dresden.
" Dietz, in Munich.

By the adoption of the course thus marked out, and which is specially provided for in the contract between Mr. Aufermann and the various Academies, *The International Art Institution* will be placed on the same footing, and conducted on the same plan, as the Academies of Germany, France, Belgium, Holland, and Italy.

Amateurs in the Fine Arts who may be desirous to purchase, may rest assured that *originals only* will be found in this Gallery, and they will be warranted as such.

Eminent Artists in America, England, France, Belgium, Holland, and Italy, have kindly offered their encouragement to this Institution, by contributing their works to this Gallery, in order to make it what it was intended to be—*International* in the true sense of the word.

Information in regard to prices may be had at the office.

The second Catalogue issued contained a list of 200 works, mostly by men of great eminence in their respective schools.

April 13. The Thirty-fourth Annual Exhibition opened to the public, closing on the 25th of June—embracing 65 working days—and realized $5,888.92; averaging $90.60 per day—815 productions. The receipts, as may be observed, largely in advance of the preceding year, which were greater than any in the ten previous years : highly gratifying, and encouraging to the Academicians. The largest amount ever obtained from any Exhibition was $6,278.22; the lowest of any one year was the first—$300. The highest amount ever received in *one day's* Exhibition was in the year 1859—$324.25. The lowest ever taken was on the 11th of July, 1857—25 cents. Could not well have been less, raining all day; it was only surprising that it should have been anything. The highest daily average was in 1857—$128.70.

May 5. Died, in London, Charles R. Leslie, Honorary Member. Mr. Leslie was an artist of the highest excellence, a man of many virtues, and of a most congenial, affectionate, and retiring disposition.

May 13. The Annual Meeting of the Academicians was held for the transaction of the yearly business, and the election of officers. Thirty-two members present; the President making the usual Annual Report.

ANNUAL REPORT.

Among the circumstances affecting the condition of the Academy since our last Annual Meeting, the first in order is the repurchase of the old property.

Our interest in that property was secured by bond and mortgage on the property, subject to the usual condition of foreclosure.   Default having occurred, there was no alternative, to secure the Academy against loss, but to force a sale.

The sale took place accordingly, at public auction, in July last.   No purchasers appearing on terms acceptable to the Trustees, it was bought in by their order, and is now in possession of the Academy, subject only to the original mortgage of $35,000.   *   *   *

Another change, more directly affecting the legitimate operations of the Academy, appears in the amendments to the Constitution, unanimously agreed to at the Special Meeting held on the eighteenth of last month.

The principal amendment is that of the unlimited extension of the list of Academicians.   It is presumed that this liberal measure will greatly promote the welfare of the Institution.

It will at least silence the complaints growing out of the constitutional restrictions, and remove the charge, real or imaginary, of injustice towards the profession.   *   *   *

The enlargement of the Council, including two additional members on the Hanging Committee—another clause in the amendments—is of less certain benefit.   Its practical action will determine its merits.   Experience, however, indicates a reduction, rather than an increase, of that Committee.

A nearer approach to that end might be gained by the adoption of a rule that should limit the number to two or three, at most, of the works of any one exhibiter, occupying the line or the best places of the Exhibition, and require that every contributor of positive merit should have one or more of his works so placed, if practicable.

*   *   *   *   *   *   *

There is an increasing anxiety for the erection of a suitable building for permanent and better accommodation.   To this end, the Council have for many months been diligent in examining lots on private sale, and in the market, discussing their eligibility, and endeavoring to devise ways and means for purchase, and putting up the desired buildings.   Thus far their labors have proved unavailing; not that they have not been able to find an eligible site—for several have been offered—but for the want of funds to purchase and to build, without greatly exceeding the resources of the Academy.   In this state of things, it is proposed, by the issue of bonds, as on a former occasion, to raise the sum of $50,000.

It would perhaps be irrelevant in this Report to discuss the merits of this proposition, but the Council would not consider its failure a serious discouragement.   To borrow to this extent at the present moment involves the question how to meet the interest payments on the bonds without an increase of revenue.   Our property yields no available income, and the revenue from all other sources is barely sufficient to meet current expenses.   On the other hand, the commercial tide now running up Broadway must ere long absorb the Stuyvesant Institute, with our adjacent possessions.   The connection of that property with Broadway is inseparable, and must soon be occupied with stores, or some public edifice; and, besides, its actual value is on the increase, as well as the probabilities of an early sale.   Therefore, it is a matter of time only, and of brief time, whether, by such a sale, we shall escape the necessity of borrowing, and be exempt from its embarrassments and obligations.

In this state of things, is it not better to incur the charge of undue cautiousness, than, by incurring additional debt, diminish the hard-earned gains of many years of laborious and painful struggles, for no other object than a more speedy attainment of an end sure to be reached by a prudent, safe, and healthy, though slow action?

The establishment of a continuous Exhibition, for the purpose of exposure and sale of works produced in the interim of the Annual Exhibition, is proposed for the consideration of this or a future meeting. In theory the project is flattering, and a practical experiment may be recommended, under restrictions, securing the Academy against any considerable loss, in case of failure.

Our Schools continue in a flourishing condition.

*   *   *   *   *   *   *

We contend that, by a discreet use of the means already in our hands, we can advance the love of Art as rapidly as is consistent with its healthy growth, and, with the present artistic ability, to supply its sustenance. We contend that no sudden accession of Academic facilities would qualify us to present a stronger attraction to public sympathy than now exists; for the reason that these facilities cannot confer the genius or the earnest labor which are most essential elements to progress in Art.

We have to record the death of another of our Associate Members since our last Annual Meeting—Mr. Thomas Augustus Cummings.

In conclusion, we advert to a change in the offices of Vice-President and Treasurer, which circumstances seemed to render unavoidable.

The invaluable services of the present incumbents—Mr. Cummings, who declines being a candidate for re-election, and Mr. Edmonds, who also declines —are too obvious to need comment; and we cordially tender to these gentlemen our grateful acknowledgments. We should lament the necessity of this change, but for the assurance that their services will be retained, with but a slight modification in their direction; and we hope that our just appreciation of their value will be attested by the unanimous vote of this meeting.

From the Treasurer's Report it appeared that the total receipts of the year were $5,386.71, and the disbursements $5,542.50; leaving an amount due the Acting Treasurer of $155.19.

Mr. Cummings officially announced to the meeting that, as he was holding and performing the duties of two offices—viz., Vice-President, and acting as Treasurer—he might be presumed to have more than his share in the honors of office; and as Mr. Edmonds preferred to leave the nominal office of Treasurer—which he had only consented to hold for the good of the Institution and the advancement of the writer—made manifest to him at the meeting at which he had so consented—and the difficulties that then occurred having been amicably adjusted—he desired now to retire; therefore BOTH declined a re-election to their offices. That had been by them some time previously communicated to the members, to the end that they should be fully prepared to fill their places.

A. B. Durand was elected President; Charles C. Ingham, Vice-President; Thomas S. Cummings, Treasurer; T. Addison Richards, Corresponding Secretary; J. B. Stearns, Recording Secretary.

G. A. Baker, F. W. Edmonds, T. P. Rossitter, J. W.

Cassilear, P. Gray, A. F. Tait, the six Members of Council, as contemplated under the "*revised*" Constitution.

As will be seen, Cummings and Edmonds were both returned to their original positions—jocosely pronounced "*indispensables.*"

William Oliver Stone, L. R. Mignot, C. F. Blauvelt, James M. Hart, were elected Academicians.

Seven Associate Members were chosen; *no* Honorary Members.

Information was called for as to what amount of money had been obtained on subscription to the bonds of the Academy Building.

Mr. Kensett reported $5,000; Mr. Greene, $5,000; Mr. Cummings, $5,000.

No others offered anything.

Whereupon it was "*Resolved*, That it is not advisable at present to endeavor further to raise money for the purpose of building."

Complimentary proceedings were had in favor of Cummings and Edmonds, for past services.

An adjournment was "called" and obtained, and the members proceeded to "The Annual Dinner," which was "BY LAW" prepared for them. The meeting was graced by the presence of several of the elder members.

The "*di'ner*" was "*Parisienne*," and highly enjoyed. The members separated only at an "*early*" hour.

From thence commenced the usual Summer vacation, and there were no meetings, or *no quorum* with which to do business, until December.

August to the early Fall. Mr. Crafts presented his English Exhibition in the Galleries, and Rossitter and Mignot their "Home of Washington."

The Schools of the season were opened, as usual, under the charge of the late Vice-President. They were well attended—the order perfect, the improvement good. No premiums offered.

October 6. Death again entered the lines, cutting off one of the nearest and dearest of Art friends—Mr. Charles M. Leupp: one who had ever been endeared to all by a thousand acts of kindness received at his hands, and by the most intimate social relations, existing during a period of over twenty years; one who had nobly and generously opened his purse in the Academy's darkest hour of need, and relieved it in its troubles; one who SHOULD NEVER BE FORGOTTEN.

A memoir, by his friend, John H. Gourlie, was published, for private distribution. Unfortunately, a copy was not furnished the writer.

Consequent on the settlement of his estate, his fine collection of paintings, principally executed to his order by city artists, had to be disposed of. They were sold, on the 13th November, 1860, by Mr. Ludlow, in the Galleries of the Academy, which had been very properly tendered for that purpose.

November 28. Washington Irving, the distinguished writer, America's favorite author, and Honorary Member of the Academy, died at his residence, "Sunny Side."

His remains were taken to Christ Church, Tarrytown, where he was buried, in accordance with his oft-repeated wish. The services were "the beautiful form of the Church of England—no unusual address or ceremony."

Miss Sarah Cole presented the Academy with a copy of "Merimee's Art of Oil Painting," which had been the property of her brother Thomas, and bore his autograph. It was accepted, and a vote of thanks tendered Miss Cole for the memento. It had likewise been the property of F. S. Agate. "It is," says Mr. Falconer in his note, "the wish of Miss Cole that the book be given, at the discretion of the Academy, as a reward of merit in the Schools."

December 8. Died, Theodore Sedgwick, Honorary Member. Theodore Sedgwick was a distinguished member of the New-York Bar, and United States District Attorney for New-York District. He was widely and favorably known as a lawyer of ability, and also as the author of a "Treatise on the Measure of Damages," and another upon "Statistics." The first-named work has obtained a wide celebrity, not only in America, but in Europe. He was a lover of art, and his leisure was frequently given to its cultivation.

December 20. The sale of Mr. Rossitter's pictures, as previously advertised. The total amount realized was between five and six thousand dollars. Most of the pictures sold at low rates.

The following are some of the advertised amounts:

"NEW-YORK.—The sale of Mr. Rossitter's pictures took place at the rooms of the National Academy of Design, on the 20th ult. The principal pictures realized as follows: The First Lesson brought $225; Primitive Life in America, $260; Giorgioni going to the Lido, $180; Wise and Foolish Virgins, the largest in the collection, $525; Washington Reading to his Family, $175; Country Post-Office, $150, and City Post-Office, $141; At the Opera, $90; Isola Bella, $172; Coast of Italy, $125; The Patrician, $155; Moonlight in the Wilderness, $120; Joan of Arc in Prison, $105. The smaller pictures were sold chiefly at very low prices. The total amount realized from the sale was $5,222.50."

The following are the prices obtained for Mr. Leupp's collection, which may prove of future value as an art record:

SALE OF WORKS OF ART.

The admirable gallery of pictures left by the late Charles M. Leupp, Esq., was sold at auction at the National Academy of Design, last evening. The patronage bestowed by Mr. Leupp on American art was as judicious as it was generous. He strove to realize the capacity of native painters to illustrate the brilliant scenery and rich physical life of the land, and succeeded in grouping within a limited circle as many charming characteristic pictures as are to be found, perhaps, in any gallery extant. The attendance of ladies and gentlemen crowded the salesroom, the bidding was free and spirited, and the result of the sale could have been only satisfactory to all concerned.

There were 82 pictures sold. They realized the sum of $9,817.50. The highest price paid for any picture was paid for a bold and thorough landscape by Cole, the "Mountain Ford." Mr. Bowman Johnson got it for $875. The "Kenilworth Castle," by the same artist, found a purchaser in the same gentleman at $500. A noble memorial of the genius of Washington Allston, "Katherine and Petruchio," was run up to $640, and secured for that sum by Mr. Edwin Forrest, the actor. Great interest was shown in Mount's graphic paintings. "The Dance of the Haymakers," a perfect rustic American interior, familiar in the engraving, was sold to Mr. Wolfe for $430, and his "Banjo" to Mr. Sydney Mason for $260   Leutze's picture of "Mrs. Schuyler Firing her Wheat-Fields," a memorable incident of the Revolution, full of the bright life tints and masterly handling of the famous artist, was sold to Mr. Lieber for $385. A "View in the Alps," by Durand, started at $100, was taken by Mr. Johnson for $310, and a very natural and pleasant landscape of New-Jersey, by the same artist, was sold to Mr. McGuire for $220. "Henry VIII. and Holbein," another well-treated historical subject by Leutze, went to Mr. Johnson for $120. An "Autumnal Sunset View" by Church, delicious in color, was sold to Mr. P. Parsons for $115.

The other works were disposed of as follows: White Mountains, by Kensett, to Isham, at $35. Scene on the Mississippi, by Kensett, to Jessup, $215; Ruins, by Panini, to R. J. Brown, $35; Magdalen, by Giordano, to George Baker, $60; Sheep and Landscape, by Ommeganck, to J. R. Livingston, $40; Market Scene, by Wyck, to S. E. Eastman, $25; Goat and Kid, by Robbe, to Bell, $125; Sheep and Lamb, by Robbe, to Bell, $110; Landscape, by Robbe, to Pritchard, $90; Animal Life, by Robbe, to Royal Phelps, $320; Oak Trees, by Robbe, to Burrell, $50; Flemish Beauty's Toilet, by Eckhout, to J. McGuire, $100; Catskill Scenery, by Huntington, to J. McGuire, $220; Italian Mendicants, by Edmonds, to Morris, $45; Gil Blas and Archbishop, by Edmonds, to Johnson, $150; Facing the Enemy, by Edmonds, to Conover, $205; Sam Weller, by Edmonds, to Mason, $92.50; Sea-Shore, by Inness, to O. G. Hillard, $100; Landscape, by Inness, to Burrell, $45; Mother and Child, by Grey, to Grey, $250; Innocence, by Greuze, to Hewitt, $75; Landscape, by Chapman, to Cobb, $40; Landscape, by Chapman, to Johnson, $15; Italian Maid, by Chapman, to A. D. Palmer, $140; Italian Mother, by Chapman, to A. D. Palmer, $140; Landscape, by Chapman, to R. J. Brown, $50; Ferdinand and Isabella, by Chapman, to E. Forrest, $110; Dock Scene, by Clover, to A K. Brown, $15; Portrait of a Lady, by Page, to Eastman, $27.50; Portrait (Roman), by Page, to E. Forrest, $75; Duke d'Urbino (after Titian), by Page, to Eastman, $55; W. C. Bryant, by Page, to Fred. Cozzens, $40; Portrait, by G. Stuart, to Johnson, $150; Rocky Pass, by Cranch, to J. H. Cheever, $40; View in Venice, by Pritchard, to Blatchford, $90; View in Venice, by Pritchard, to Blatchford, $90; Harvesting, by Davidson, to F. Walker, $35; The Milkmaid, by Hepburn, to Goodrich, $25; Rydal Water, by Inman, to Johnson, $45; Rip Van Winkle, by Inman, to Cozzens, $210; Winter in Holland, by Vanderveer, to Johnson, $65; Fisherman's Luck, by S. Mount, to Sherwood, $45; Constantinople (watercolor), by Preziozi, to E. Forrest, $45; Henry Clay, by Linnen, to E. Forrest, $75; The Greenwood, by Wilhelm, to L. Lang, $20; Fête Champêtre, by Watteau, to Cozzens, $50; Fête Champêtre, by Watteau, to Cozzens, $50; Mailed Knight, by Vandyck, to Satterlee, $42.50; Napoleon at Isola Bella, by Christie, to Burrell, $20; The June Shower, by Durand, to Cozzens, $125; Landscape, by Boynham, to Goodrich, $15; Landscape, by Boynham, to Goodrich, $15; Landscape, by Boynham, to Schenck, $15; Landscape, by Boynham, to Schenck, $15; Philosophers, by Jordœns, to Johnson, $42.50; Interrupted Repast, by Venneman, to Mason, $15.50; John C. Calhoun, by De Block, to E. Forrest, $100; Chocolate Girl, by Liotard, $72.50; Ben More, by V. G. Audobon, to Eastman, $105; Landscape, by Baker, to W. Lee, $25; Marine View, by Gherardini, to Wagner, $135; Puss Sporting, by J. W. Audobon, to Conover, $120; Landscape, by Oddie, $105; Brambletye House—Unknown, to Johnson, $40; Winter Night—Unknown, to Burrell, $27.50; Marat—Unknown, to Mrs. Ward, $18; Portrait—Unknown, to Burrell, $12.50; Landscape—Unknown, to Melville, $7.50; Landscape—Unknown, $10.

A good bas-relief, "Contemplation," by Richards, was sold for $65. A lot of fine engravings, embracing 31 of the most popular copies, was also disposed of for fair prices. Messrs. E. H. Ludlow & Co. were the auctioneers.

January. From January the 9th to March the 12th, were called seven successive Council Meetings, and **1860.** no quorum obtained. The cause unknown.

February —. George H. Hall, the celebrated art fruitest, made a display of his works in the Galleries of the Academy, prior to his departure for Europe—winding up with a sale. The works were all of his peculiar department, of a high order of merit, and the prices obtained said to have been highly satisfactory.

March 12. The Schools of the "Life and Antique" closed for the season, after a most successful Winter's work; the average attendance on the Antique 40, and on the Life School 30.

The same order and regularity as before—great enthusiasm exhibited. One of the finest models (from the French Academy) ever presented to the School was placed on the stand, and the drawings corresponded in merit.

No premiums were offered.

March 16. Died, John Fisher, an Honorary Member. Mr. Fisher was born March 6, 1806. He died suddenly at his residence in New Rochelle, of disease of the heart.

April 14. The Thirty-fifth Annual Exhibition opened to the public, preceded by a "Reception," which was a brilliant and successful affair. The receipts of the Exhibition were $4,144.07. It was open 55 working days, averaging $75.34 per day, and contained 668 works of art.

During the month of May, and for two or three years previous, the number of wet days in the Exposition term had materially interfered with the receipts of the Exhibition: twenty such in the month of May last passed, and certainly called for the serious consideration of the propriety of changing the Exposition period—perhaps to the Fall. The Exhibition was unfortunate in more particulars than one. In its arrangements, it had the misfortune to displease one of the contributors—so far so, as to cause him forcibly to remove his production from the walls—a truly unfortunate occurrence, and carried with it the necessity of an appeal to the Law for the enforcement of the rights of the Body Corporate over the pictures placed in their charge. That, as on the first and similar occasion recorded, was carried to a successful issue. It was further unfortunate in the abstraction from the walls—LOSS of two works of art of considerable size and importance in merit.

May 9. Was held the Annual Meeting of the Academicians for the transaction of the yearly business—33 members appearing in their seats.

Mr. Durand (who was in the chair) stated, that in consequence of bad health, he had prepared no Annual Report, and was unprepared to say anything, and referred to the Treasurer for information, who had, on receiving that information on the morning of the day of meeting, prepared a report of the yearly doings, to submit to the meeting.

ANNUAL REPORT.

*   *   *   *   I have the pleasure, gentlemen, to report to you the sale of your property 663 Broadway, Mercer Street, &c., for the sum, leasehold and fee, of one hundred and ten thousand dollars, to responsible parties.

Realization of profit is therefore no longer a myth—it has become a reality.

The proceeds arising therefrom, after paying all indebtedness of every kind, cannot fall much, if any, short of $64,000.

You may very well conceive, gentlemen, how much this gratifies me. The original purchase was of the interior building. The subsequent additional Mercer Street line of property was made solely on my personal recommendation, and even without the knowledge of the body of Academicians, though with the perfect co-operation of the other Trustees; well assured of its great ultimate value, though at that time little expecting it so to the extent that has been realized.

Mr. Leupp and Mr. Sturges, advanced the means for the purchase, and for which they stood its paternity, and during the years it has been in litigation for the title, and had to be held. They, through all its troubles and perplexities, of which you yourselves have little idea, have been ever ready to sustain and hold it; and oft as the writer had been compelled to call on them for money, frequently tens of thousands at a time, he never met with a cold look, or a murmuring word. True friends they have been to you—such, indeed, as are seldom found, and you owe to them all you possess pecuniarily.

If not before, at least in the building it is the purpose to erect, I trust measures will be taken to preserve their semblance, and thereby to present a slight memento to their worth. Let their outward form be placed before all, as a reminder of their excellent qualities and worth.   *   *   *

On the completion of the sale, and settlement of the outstanding indebtedness of the Trust, it *ceases.* Your affairs will then again pass into the hands of Messrs. Jonathan Sturges, Thomas S. Cummings, Asher B. Durand, and Francis W. Edmonds, surviving Trustees—all, but one, your Academicians—who will no doubt, to your very great benefit, conduct their part of your business relations.

As you will be deeply interested, and consulted, so should you be prepared to advise, on the matter in question.   *   *   *

The building—when shall it be commenced? Where shall it be? *Shall it be proceeded with at once?* Or shall more time be taken for consideration?

It is scarcely probable—indeed, scarcely practicable—(though money may accomplish it)—that it can be done, suitably to your purposes, in time for the ensuing Exhibition.

If that is your desire, *there is not a moment to be lost.*

If that is not deemed *essential*—and it certainly does not appear to be—then there is no immediate hurry. There is another year at your discretionary disposal.   *   *   *

So far as your present leases may have any bearing on the subject, it is well you should be informed of their conditions.

In November, 1857, you ordered a lease of a part of the rooms now occupied in Tenth Street for "TEN YEARS"—bearing your interest in view, and the probable occurrence of the contingency which has arisen, viz.:—That you would not want it for so long a period—I deemed it advisable to vary, though not alter, the terms.

I leased for *three years and six months.* And in like manner, on your directing a lease of the additional and adjoining two rooms, that lease was made to conform to the first lease—viz., three years and six months; though both containing the covenants of continuance from *year to year, to a period not exceeding ten years in all, at the same rent.*

That more than fulfilled your directions, and on more favorable terms to you than you yourselves dictated. Everything you asked was obtained. The leases are therefore expirable, or continuous, at your option, from and after the 1st of May next.

The holding of the next Exhibition in the rooms will carry with it the continuance of the rent for the year.

As to the character and location of your building. In that I have seen no cause to change my previously-formed opinion or advice, as given to you years ago. The location conditionally purchased for you—Broadway, Fifth Avenue, and Twenty-fifth Street, facing the "Worth Monument," nearly one hundred feet square, for $52,000—and which you looked upon as in the wilderness—and *unanimously* rejected—and which could not now, without a brick on it, be considered worth less than $100,000—prospectively double—was the best ground on the Island for such a building; and would have yielded a revenue of not less than $20,000 per annum.

That is gone, and with it the best location on New-York Island for you! I yet adhere to the bounds I then gave you.

The *location* of your building presents two very important phases for consideration—viz.:

1st. *Off Broadway,* and sufficiently so to enable you to obtain ground at a greatly reduced rate; relying solely on Art accommodation, and revenue *for its support.*

2dly. *On Broadway,* or in its *immediate* vicinity; and sustaining the additional cost (remember the building costs no more) by commercial accessions, *or rental.*

The first named, in my opinion, is not to be *thought of.* It is undesirable for attendance generally, particularly so to strangers, and would in the end, though promising a lesser expenditure at first, ultimately prove comparatively a greater, and absorb the Institution by debt; slowly, perhaps, but insidiously, and certainly.

The second case calls for careful and deliberate consideration. You cannot expect to meet the wants of the present Art demand, let alone the future, with much, if any, less than an area of 100 feet square; and that, when located as desired, involves considerable cost.

If well chosen, that presents no serious impediment to your wishes. Your purposes require *not the lower part of the building*. You can, therefore, rent that *well* for commercial uses (*stores*). Rentals on commerce in such thoroughfares are far more safe and certain than Art dependences. You require only the upper part of a building yourselves, the letting of which is the great drawback to Broadway property, *or even to know what to do with it*.

Dwell on that, you possess in it very—very peculiar *advantages*, which should not be lost sight of or neglected. The building you erect under such advantages should be so constructed as to earn enough to bear its entire interest, cost, and maintenance. The Institution should be left its apartments RENT *free*, which, after the first term or two, can doubtless be *accomplished*—though certainly not without some care or trouble—from which you have no right, under any circumstances, reasonably to expect to be exempted. You cannot, merely because you are artists, rest on a bed of clover.

Several years ago I reported to you in writing—now on your Minutes—the belief that the Institution could not look solely to its future Exhibitions or Art product alone, with safety, for sustainment.

From experience, it was evidently not to be expected that an Annual Exhibition would bear and sustain the cost of your increased wants, and greatly extended Institution; nor could it be looked for; and I see *no cause*, with greater consideration, to change that *opinion*. Yet, so long as the Academy provides, as it may, a highly interesting and meritorious exhibition of works of art annually, so long it will receive a reasonable amount of public support and revenue. But that public attention, with the increase of the city, will not be divided, or that other and more interesting Exhibitions in opposition will not spring up, to claim a share of the attention, is not to be expected.

Annual Exhibitions are not, either to artist or public, what they were twenty years ago. The present Exhibition, and the comments thereon, fully confirm that opinion—the "*general excellence*," as it is called; but want of prominent pictures is universally stated and believed.

That is so; and how does it arise? Simply from the fact that, years ago, the Artist had no place, no matter *what* the extent or merit of his picture, in which to exhibit it, but at the Annual Exhibition. Now, if the work is of any size or merit, private enterprise is ready to claim and receive it, exhibit it, engrave and publish it, obtain subscribers, and return the artist profit, freed of trouble. Is it to be wondered at that the Exhibition should be wanting in such works?

Depend upon it, hereafter works of such merit as will command a support at private exhibition, will not come to the Annual display.

A few words on your legislation and laws, with which you have tampered so much.

During the many years I have served the Institution, deserved complaints have been made against its constitutional requirements; yet seldom, with justice, to an extent that required alteration. Artists are not good legislators; yet it is not often I have met with a more disinterested body, or a more justly disposed administration. If error be committed, it is from impulse—on which they generally act—not matured intention. I speak aside from their Art works, or of the hanging thereof in the Annual display (on which most, if not all, seem extremely sensitive—I may say, peculiarly, unnecessarily so); so far, that I do not think I will ever be instrumental in hanging another picture.

In Art bodies, it seems to be generally admitted that there is but little *business* capacity (that is concededly so in the Academy); between the Studio and outer world there is little in common. Of the truth of that I am satisfied.

I have conducted your pecuniary affairs for, now, near 36 years, and have been with you in poverty, in moderate circumstances, and to your present wealth; during that period, I have alone, or in connection with others, built for you five times; though never the whole building, or uncontrolled by others' interests and views, and with little thanks, I believe, or general satisfaction to any in the construction *of lights*, or wall for the purposes of exhibition; indeed, I doubt its accomplishment.

It is not a month ago I read a statement in an English periodical, that there was not a well-constructed Gallery in *Europe*. Nevertheless, gentlemen, I will not desert the *financial post*.

My greatest wish is to see you firmly located in a building of your OWN, reasonably adapted to your wants and interests; and for the accomplishment of that object, aside from artistic arrangement of lights, wall, and "color" thereof, I am willing to work.

The exceptions I have named you must take on your own younger shoulders and dictation. The time for feeling the interest I once had in such matters has passed. I am now a *non*-Exhibiter, but so far as your business management is concerned—so far as standing between you and the business world is at stake, I am at your disposal to conduct your affairs.

One more remark, and I have done. Charles M. Leupp is no more; yet not a word, a remark, or resolution passed by our body. That is discreditable; and it reflects severely on us. I trust the evening will not pass without its being remedied.

Respectfully,

THOMAS S. CUMMINGS.

Which, with the regular Financial Report, was accepted.

The total receipts of the year were $7,323.84; the disbursements, $7,313.31; balance, $10.53.

Mr. Jonathan Sturges, the only surviving Trustee, not an Academician, was present; and Mr. Morse favored the meeting with his attendance.

Mr. A. B. Durand was elected President; Charles C. Ingham, Vice-President; J. B. Stearns, Recording Secretary; T. Addison Richards, Corresponding Secretary; Thomas S. Cummings, Treasurer.

Gray, Huntington, Baker, Cassilear, Edmonds, and Stone were elected Members of Council.

A. H. Wenzler, E. Leutze, A. Bierstadt, J. W. Ehninger, and Eastman Johnson, were elected Academicians.

At that stage of the proceedings, Mr. Cummings was "sent for—a *ruse*"—by one of the members. During his absence, Mr. Edmonds offered the following preamble and resolution, as a testimony of appreciation of his long, efficient, and faithful services to the Institution:

PREAMBLE AND RESOLUTION.

WHEREAS, Thomas S. Cummings has for many years past devoted a large portion of his time to the service of the Academy, and has, by his careful management of the monetary affairs, brought them to a sound and healthy condition; whereas, by his unwearied efforts, the real estate has been so nursed and managed that it is now about to yield a large profit on its original cost: Therefore,

Resolved, That the sum of one thousand dollars be presented to Mr. Cummings out of the proceeds of the sale of the real estate of the Academy; and that the Trustees are hereby authorized and directed to carry the same into effect.

Which was unanimously carried.

As Mr. Cummings did not ascertain that evening that anything in particular had been done—though he could certainly see that something mysterious had been going on—he was not enabled to make any acknowledgments on the subject. It was afterwards done.

The Academicians adjourned at 7 o'clock, to partake of the legally demanded "Annual Dinner," which was prepared and held in the building. After a few of the usual toasts, and speeches from the President and some of the older members, they were entertained by Mr. Sturges, who read a paper on "Art in the Days of Cole"—Mr. Morse giving some very interesting accounts of the early struggles of the "Electric Telegraph."

The members enjoyed themselves until rather a late hour, and departed highly delighted. A more harmonious Annual Meeting had never been witnessed, and was one of the largest assemblages the body ever had.

May 16. The following resolution was offered:

"*Resolved,* That a vote of thanks be presented to Mr. Jonathan Sturges, 'the best friend of the Academy,' for the extremely disinterested and liberal manner in which he has aided the Academy at various times, thereby enabling it to enjoy that state of prosperity which it this day presents."

Carried.

After the sale of the Academy property, and on June 11th, the Trustees made a statement of their trust and doings, and a full and final financial report; from which it may be found that the *cash* balance on hand, after discharging every indebtedness, was $3,290. That the incoming bonds having part, to the whole of the year to run, which bonds were secured by a mortgage on the property, was $60,000; the total availabilities, $63,290.

Stearns and Cummings were appointed to audit the accounts. Mr. C. suggested, that as he had kept the accounts and "made the report," it would be highly improper that he should act, and requested that some one else should be put in his place, and named Mr. Durand; which was adopted.

The Committee, after a thorough investigation of the accounts and vouchers, and having destroyed the canceled "Bonds," reported the accounts, vouchers, and books true. Whereupon it was "*Resolved,* That the said Trust, and the

several estates of the members thereof, be released and discharged from all and every liability or accountability to the National Academy of Design."
There terminated *Trust No. 2.*

The affairs and financial management then passed, under a previously executed Trust Deed, into the hands of the same persons, or the survivors of them, with one or more additions; and the Trust became Messrs. Sturges, Cummings, Edmonds, and Durand, who were, by such third Trust Deed, authorized and empowered to receive the funds from the previous Trust, and with it to "purchase a site, and erect a building thereon, for the National Academy of Design," &c., &c. Mr. Cummings acting as Financial Manager, Secretary, and Treasurer.

June 10. The Exhibition of the Academy was on the eve of closing, indeed, had closed, when the Japanese Embassy arrived in the city. On the suggestion of the Vice-President, Mr. Ingham, it was determined to hold the works on the walls, and delay distribution until it could be ascertained if the Embassadors were desirous of viewing the collection, by invitation, in a strictly private manner; and, by order of the President, such an invitation was forwarded—viz. :

MR. CUMMINGS TO CAPTAIN DUPONT.

To the Japanese Embassy :

The Council of the National Academy of Design respectfully solicit the pleasure of the Embassy's attendance at a private view of the Thirty-fourth Annual Exhibition of the National Academy of Design, expressly held together for that purpose, at such time during the day or morrow as may be the pleasure of the Embassy to designate.

CAPTAIN DUPONT'S REPLY.

To Thomas S. Cummings, Esq. .

SIR :—I have to acknowledge the receipt of both your notes of yesterday, inviting the Japanese Embassy to attend the Annual Exhibition of the National Academy of Design.

While I appreciate fully the kind consideration which prompted the invitation, I deem it but proper to state, that they take very little interest in viewing works of art. Their engagements, moreover, are such as to preclude their attendance at your Institution. &c., &c.

Their Royal Highnesses had no desire to see works of art. Rather a *princely failing.*

The Trustees, on the purchase of a site and the erection of a building, proceeded at once to the execution of their task; and on the 15th of June the following, extracted from their Minutes, was forwarded to the Academy :

"*Resolved*, That Mr. Cummings ascertain the wishes of the Council as to the location, and general plan of building desired by the National Academy of Design, and that he procure slight or outline plans thereof, and also a general estimate of the cost; and further, that he ascertain how far the present assets and funds of the Academy can be made available for said purposes, and report the same to the Trust at his earliest convenience."

June 19th. A Special Meeting of the Council was called, to receive the communication from the Trust on the subject of a proper site for a building. The N. W. corner of Twenty-third Street and Fourth Avenue was designated.

Mr. Ludlow, then present, informed the Board that it could be had for $50,000. Whereupon the Council expressed themselves to the effect, "that the Trustees should take the matter into consideration, *as a site* that will meet the interests of the Body."

Two of the Council voting in the negative; but merely as to the special location chosen—not as to the matter.

June 26. Another Special Meeting of the Council was called, for the purpose of receiving a communication from the Trustees, and for the examining the plans, and more fully determining on a site, for the building for the National Academy of Design.

The following communication was submitted by Mr. Cummings, together with two carefully-drawn plans for a building:

To the National Academy of Design:

Gentlemen :—You have imposed upon your Trustees "the selection of a site, and the erection of a building thereon, for the uses of the National Academy of Design."

The creation of the Trust, and the consenting of the gentlemen to serve as such, were, to my own knowledge, designed to be strictly beneficial to your interests. It is therefore not a supposable case that they would proceed in the work without consulting your wishes—you, the body for whose uses and occupation it is intended, and to whom it is to belong.

It is for these reasons they again refer to you; and your determination on both the important particulars they esteem a necessary preliminary to any proceedings on their part.

It should be well understood that the mere ownership of a building will of itself, although well sounding to the ear, confer no benefit to the Institution, unless there be carried with it positive pecuniary advantages or art accommodation; and these two points, particularly the first, must and will be well weighed by the Trustees before proceeding in the undertaking.

It has become an established fact, that you cannot now rely upon the receipts of your Annual Exhibition for giving you more than from three thousand five hundred to four thousand dollars per annum; and that amount, even with great economy, will be required to defray the necessary yearly expenses of the art department, exclusive of any charge of rent, and not including any additions to the Library, or other incidental appropriations which may be made during the year by the Council or general body of the Academy.

That you may not be so circumscribed in your income, and that you may have at least a liberal and proper support, it becomes, under that calculation, an actual necessity that you should receive, or be capable of receiving, if requisite, a part, at least, of the income derivable on the amount of your own money, invested in your building, &c., &c. ; or, in other words, the building must to that extent be a commercially paying one, or no benefit will be derived to you by its ownership.

There are two plans for a building herewith submitted to you, and your careful consideration is solicited.

Respectfully,

T. S. CUMMINGS.

Whereupon, it was

"*Resolved*, That of the two plans submitted, the one by Mr. Cummings, marked B, has decidedly the advantage and preference of the members present."

That plan contained a full line of stores on Fourth Avenue. Subsequently, those were stricken out. Without such, there existed no excuse for attachment to the chosen location. The building, entirely devoted to Art purposes, should have gone to Murray Hill and Fifth Avenue. The stores, however, in the writer's estimation, should not have been *stricken out*, and may in future require to be recalled.

Some very trifling alterations in the different sizes of the rooms were suggested, as also the consideration of "substituting sky-lights for the lantern-lights."

These were left open, for future consideration; and the plan was then otherwise *fully endorsed*, as the approved interior.

It was then desired, by some present, that they yet should be allowed to call on another artist for a "*sketch of a front.*"

That request was acceded to, and the two gentlemen desiring it were requested to procure it. That brought matters to the 26th of June; and, as it then appeared, the FRONTS only were undecided. The Summer had come, and tempted the artists to the country, which no persuasion could induce them to forego. No further action or quorum was had until October.

The Treasurer, however, with the Architect, had been actively at work in perfecting the details of the interior adopted, in every requisite that had been suggested, or could be thought of.

July —. In view of the intended visit to this country of the Prince of Wales, and for cogent reasons hereinafter set forth, which were supposed sufficient to arouse the *esprit du corps* of the artists, the writer endeavored to make a fine "REVIEW" Exhibition, and to allow it remain open until such time as the Prince should arrive in New-York, provided that should be embraced in his programme; and thereby display to him and suite the most favorable specimens of American Art; and issued to the artists then in town the following, for their signatures and concurrence:

To the Members of the National Academy of Design:

WHEREAS, We have heard that the past, the Thirty-fifth Annual Exhibition of the National Academy of Design, has proved less productive, in a pecuniary point of view, than the one preceding it; and that the receipts therefrom will not be sufficient to meet the expenses of the Institution for the current year. And as there are probably no other resources with which to meet said expenses, excepting, perhaps, by trespassing on the fund destined for the purchase of a site, and erection of a building for the National Academy of Design; and which, if practicable, is not desirable: Therefore,

Resolved, That, to meet this contingency, we, the undersigned, tender to the Institution the loan of ——— pictures, for the purpose of holding a "Review Exhibition" in the coming Fall; thereby to endeavor to raise the necessary funds to meet the anticipated deficiency.

Said Exhibition to open to the public in the Galleries in Tenth Street, on or about the 15th of September, or between that and the 1st of October. To continue open from four to six weeks. To consist only of a selection by each party exhibiter of works previously exhibited at the Annual Exhibitions, or such other works as, by reason of any cause, may be ineligible thereunto.

The arrangements and "hanging" thereof to be made by any three of the Academicians who may be in town.

To the obtainment of this object, we will give our support, and loan of works, as specified in the accompanying formula.

Respectfully,

T. S. CUMMINGS.

An agent was employed to call on the artists to ascertain their views.

It was unsuccessful.

Some declined exhibiting at all in the *old rooms;* some preferred that such an Exhibition should inaugurate the new building; some thought it too early—some too late; and, in fact, few or none who were seen were in its favor.

After two days' incessant labor, the matter was dropped. It was undoubtedly an unfavorable time to make the attempt; but had there been any encouragement, it could have been accomplished; and doubtless would have been successful in paying off some indebtedness—which was desirable—if of no other benefit.

August 17. Died, Victor G. Audubon, Academician, son of the distinguished Ornithologist. He was an artist of much merit—a devotionist to his father's fame and works, which he continued to retouch and publish until his death.

September 18. Death again; which deprived the Institution of its Honorary Member, Joshua Shaw—one of the oldest artists of Philadelphia.

OBITUARY.

"Joshua Shaw, the celebrated landscape painter, died at Burlington, N. J., on the 8th inst., at the advanced age of 83. He was born in Bellingbroke, Lincolnshire, England. Early left an orphan, he was successively a farmer-boy, post-boy, and apprentice to a country sign-painter. Young Shaw found this last occupation the most congenial, as he had greater opportunities to indulge his taste for painting, and by persistent effort he succeeded in bringing his name before the public, through the excellence of his landscapes. He brought over with him the great picture which West executed and presented to the Pennsylvania Hospital—"Christ Healing the Sick." Mr. Shaw was distinguished as well for his inventive as his artistic talent. Improvements which he made in gun-locks were adopted by our Government, and according to statistics preserved in the Department at Washington, he was entitled to commissions amounting to $170,000. For many years he petitioned Congress for some substantial reward, and in 1848 an act was passed granting $25,000, provided that the Secretary of War considered the award equitable and just; $18,000 was allowed by the Secretary, and handed over to Mr. Shaw. The balance, $7,000, still remains unpaid, although Secretary Floyd has since decided the said balance to be justly due. The Secretary of the Treasury, however, declines payment, upon the ground that it has reverted to the surplus fund. The Emperor of Russia also awarded a premium to Mr. Shaw for improvements in naval warfare, and also promised a commission on his patents, which are extensively used throughout that Empire. It is said that Mr. Shaw's heirs are to bring a suit to recover this commission.

"Some years since, in experimenting upon a new invention in gunnery, Mr. Shaw lost the use of an arm. For seven years previous to his death he was afflicted with paralysis, and for the last twenty-four months was confined to his bed. He retained his faculties, however, to the last."

September 20. Art attracted the special notice of the French Prince—an Academician the recipient.

"Yesterday morning his Imperial Highness the Prince took a carriage at the hotel, and, accompanied by Monsieur Mercier, Colonel Rajon, and Mr. Sands, went aboard his yacht, lying off the Battery. In the afternoon the Prince took another drive before dinner, as did also the Princess, accompanied by the Duchess De Abrantes.

"His Royal Highness, attended by M. Montholon and four gentlemen of his suite, also visited the studio of R. Gignoux, in Tenth Street. The Prince expressed himself greatly pleased with the artist's last work, 'The Indian Summer,' which he hoped would find its way to the next Annual Exhibition."

In Paris probably meant! October 6. Died, Rembrandt Peale, Honorary Member, aged 83 years—probably the oldest artist in the country. Mr. Peale was an Academician in 1826, and removed to the list of Honorary Members in 1827, in consequence of removal from the city.

OBITUARY.

"DEATH OF REMBRANDT PEALE.—The decease of this venerable artist, which occurred at his residence in Philadelphia on the morning of the 4th inst., will create more sorrow than surprise. Mr. Peale had already passed the allotted term of human life, having reached his eighty-third year on the twenty-second of last February. A few months ago he met with a serious accident while in Connecticut, and was obliged to remain for some time in Stonington,

HISTORIC ANNALS OF THE

where, by kind attention, he recovered sufficiently to return home. He was taken ill last Tuesday night, and died at half-past six o'clock Thursday morning.

"Mr. Peale belonged to a family of artists, and was the son of Charles Wilson Peale, of the old Peale's Museum of Philadelphia, a branch of which occupied a building on Broadway, opposite the Park. The large collection of portraits now in Barnum's establishment was formed by Mr. Charles W. Peale. The building in Philadelphia—near the site of the Continental Hotel—was burned down several years since, and the principal contents of Peale's Museum of this city were long ago transferred to Mr. Barnum.

"Rembrandt Peale was born at the time when Washington was at Valley Forge, and learned his profession in his father's studio at Philadelphia; for Peale *père* was a painter as well as a showman, and had painted several portraits of Washington, who, in 1795, sat three times to the son Rembrandt, then but seventeen years old. The young artist was much frightened, but the study of Washington's head he then made served as the basis for his future portraits of this subject. He subsequently painted therefrom a picture which, in 1832, was purchased for two thousand dollars by the Government, and placed in the United States Senate Chamber. Peale continued almost to the time of his death to paint pictures of various kinds—portraits, landscapes, and compositions. One of the most remarkable is his "Court of Death," a large allegory on canvas, which has been extensively copied in engravings, and was recently exhibited in this country, Mr. Colton, the exhibiter, having, it is said, paid the artist twenty thousand dollars for it. Some two years ago, when Mr. Peale was eighty years of age, he made a copy of his Washington portrait, and this, we believe, was his last artistic labor. Quite recently he delivered in Philadelphia a lecture upon the various portraits, by Stuart and others, of Washington.

"Mr. Peale's early acquaintance with the leading men at the Seat of Government made him widely known, and insured for his artistic ability a large patronage and remuneration. He enjoyed here a position as similar to that of a 'court painter' abroad as could exist under our form of government. He loved his art, but found time to devote some attention to literature, and in 1839 published the 'Portfolio of an Artist,' consisting of selections from various authors in art matters. He also wrote some fair poetry. His later life was passed in unusual quietude, surrounded by numerous personal friends and a large family. He was twice married, and leaves a widow, children and grandchildren."

And on October 6 still another loss—Charles Fraser—whose death is thus noticed in a Charleston paper:

"Mr. Fraser was a resident of Charleston, S. C. He was a lawyer by profession, and was engaged in his practice at the bar for eleven or twelve years. He was a literary man, contributing largely to the *Southern Quarterly Review*, and delivered discourses on many important and interesting occasions.

"His productions were exhibited, under the title of 'The Fraser Gallery,' in Charleston, 1857, and contained no less than 313 miniatures by his hand, and 139 landscapes and fancy pieces."

October 7. The Life and Antique Schools were opened for the season in their previous temporary accommodations, (Cummings's Studio Building,) under the directorship of Professor Cummings, as heretofore. The class of draughtsmen who entered were of decided ability; *very* many of the older students, and some of the members, for many years absent, attending.

October 13. At that date the artists of the Tenth Street Studio made a collection in their Gallery of their works, and through the Mayor as master of ceremonies, invited the Prince of Wales, then in the city, to view them. The invitation being of a private character—under a perhaps very proper general rule, adopted by the youth's older advisers—was not, for that reason, formally accepted by or for him; though it was definitely understood by the Committee from the Mayor, that if there were none to be present at the exhibition but the artists, the Prince would be present, and a time was appointed. The artist exhibiters assembled at the appointed hour, and waited in the Gallery until late in the night—but no Prince or suite appeared. The exhibition was minus the distinguished guest, and the artists were disappointed.

It is much to be regretted that New-York should be the only city in the Union through which he passed that Art did not make a part of the quota of his amusement. The collection of American works hastily gathered together by Messrs. Williams & Stevens, with which to decarate his rooms in the Fifth Avenue Hotel, being the only collective Art representation New-York afforded him; and of course that was a very limited one.

October 15. Mr. Cummings reported on the state of the negotiations on a site, and the purchase of Broadway lots —viz.: "That he saw difficulties in the way—undividable mortgages on the property, which could NOT be satisfactorily arranged."

Whereupon, it was

"*Resolved*, That the proposed purchase of the property on the corner of Thirty-fourth Street and Broadway be abandoned, and that the Council recommend the purchase on the corner of Twenty-third Street and Fourth Avenue to the Trustees, as a desirable site."

Carried. Mr. Cummings only voting in the negative; and in that, simply as to locality.

After struggling to the last to keep them off the East side, the writer had to submit to the will of the majority; and the corner of Twenty-third Street and Fourth Avenue was directed to be purchased.

October 15. Mr. Leeds held one of his "Annual Native and Foreign Production Sales" in the Galleries of the Academy.

As his annual sale of paintings had become an institution in the community, it assumed an interest that it otherwise had not. The following very pleasing account of the rise and progress of these sales, so far as Mr. Leeds is concerned, will, it is thought, prove interesting:

NEW-YORK, *November* 16, 1860.

To Professor T. S. Cummings:

DEAR SIR:—Agreeably to your request, we give you a synopsis of our connection, for the past sixteen years, with the Art sales. You can cull from the particulars such facts as may be useful to compile the work you propose to publish.

Sixteen years ago we commenced the fancy auction business, and connected with it the sale of pictures. We have had regular sales every week since that period, with few exceptions. At the commencement of these sales, we seldom had pictures of very great value; purchasers generally were unwilling to pay more than from 25 cents to $2.50 for a picture. Gradually the taste improved, as well as prices. The highest price at which we sold a single picture during the first five years, was a large one by Correggio; that picture had been exhibited, and we sold it at private sale for $2,100.

The sale of pictures gradually increased in amount and frequency, until it has now assumed an imposing amount.

About five years since, we determined to have ANNUAL SALES, or, more properly speaking, trade sales, and they have been continued by us ever since, with great success. These annual sales now amount to from $20,000 to $30,000.

At the present time there appears to be hardly any limit to the price persons will pay, if the quality of the painting will warrant the price. We sold twelve months since a picture by Winterhalter for $3,250, and had several bidders for it. We have sold pictures by call for $750; Verboekhoven for from $600 to $900 each, &c.

These annual sales are now attracting attention even in Europe, and we are getting large consignments of costly pictures from the first artists as contributions to these sales. It has now become a settled institution, the same as the trade book sales. At these annual sales we generally have from 400 to 600 pictures, and could increase the number, if desirable.

Formerly we had two evenings' sales; then three; and the last sale, four evenings. It would not surprise us if it increased to such an extent as to require a week or ten days to make one of these sales hereafter, and not very remote either.

I have given you these scattering particulars, from which you can select such facts as you may require, and any further information we will give you that you may require.

Very truly yours,

HENRY H. LEEDS.

October 25th. The Building Committee of the Trustees made the following report to the Council:

NEW-YORK, *October* 25, 1860.

To the Council of the National Academy of Design:

GENTLEMEN:—We beg leave to report, that in accordance with the request of the Academicians, the Trustees have made an agreement with Mr. Niblo for the purchase of the property owned by him on the northwest corner of Fourth Avenue and Twenty-third Street, and that the Committee are prepared to proceed with the erection of a building thereon, on the basis of the plan submitted to the Council on the 26th June last, which was then pronounced as having "the decided advantage and preference" over all others. The FRONTS were not decided upon at that time, because drawings of fronts were promised. These have not been sent in, and, to prevent loss of *interest* and delay in the execution of the work, the Committee beg leave respectfully to request, that if the Council have any sketches of fronts, or propositions to offer, or any suggestions to make on any point, that they will be pleased to hand them in to the Committee in writing on or before the 15th day of November next, that the same may receive the consideration of the Committee prior to the adjustment of the specifications and final awarding of the work on the estimates.

An early answer is respectfully urged.

THOMAS S. CUMMINGS,
F. W. EDMONDS,
Committee of Trustees on Building N. A. D.

November 12. Mr. Cummings presented the agreement for the purchase of the corner of Twenty-third Street and Fourth Avenue, as duly executed by the parties. Whereupon, it was

"*Resolved,* That the same meets the approval of the Council; and so far as relates to the execution of the Bond, and the joining in the mortgage, as related therein, that the same be, and they are hereby adopted as the acts of this body. And further, that the said agreement be, and it is hereby directed to be engrossed in full upon the Minutes."

The latter part of the communication made by the Building Committee of the Trustees, as is seen, solicited from the Council sketches or suggestions for the fronts. That was perhaps illy advised.

In the Council, a Committee was appointed to consult with Architects, and the Chairman of the Committee reported that the terms exacted by such "were, superintendence of the building, as recompense for the plans;" and the following was offered:

WHEREAS, *The plans for the interior* of the Academy Building *having been adopted:* Therefore,

Resolved, That a Committee of three be appointed *to procure* three plans for the EXTERIOR, at an expense not exceeding $100 each: Provided the Trustees approve and agree to pay for the same.

On motion,

Resolved, That the Building Committee be requested to extend the time of receiving the plans for the Academy from the 15th of November to the 1st of December.

Adopted.

Mr. Cummings, as one of the Trustees, undertaking to say that they will comply with the request as to payment.

And the meeting adjourned.

After which, the Building Committee requested an extension of time for receiving plans from the 15th of November to the 1st of December. Already had the period from June to that date been consumed. Yet, as the object was especially to gratify those the building was intended for, it was granted by the Trustees.

On the 3d of December, three days after the expiration of the extended term, it was further directed that the Architects be informed that the designs for the Academy fronts *must be in* on or before the THIRTY-FIRST of December; and it was subsequently extended to the 14th of January; and no action was taken in Council until the 21st of that month.

The Exhibition of 1860 appears to have been marked by misfortune. *Vide* the following advertisement:

"Two HUNDRED AND FIFTY DOLLARS REWARD.—The paintings numbered on the Catalogue 34 (a Miniature) and 310 ("Maidenhood") having been stolen from the Thirty-fifth Annual Exhibition of the National Academy of Design, the Academy hereby offers a reward of $50 each for their recovery, and $250 for such information and testimony as shall procure the conviction of the thief or thieves.

"By order.

"T. ADDISON RICHARDS,

"*Corresponding Secretary.*"

The miniature was returned, through one of the Express Companies, to T. S. Cummings's address, and was restored immediately to the owner. It purported to have come from Philadelphia; and on reference to the books of the Philadelphia office, it was seen to have been there received. The painting had evidently been removed from its frame, and appeared to have gone through the Photographing process. No further inquiry was made.

The other picture never came to hand, and was paid for by the Academy.

The circumstances were the more remarkable, as extra precautions had been taken for the preservation of the works on exhibition.

The abstractionists were evidently adroit performers— certainly not acting without risk. True lovers of art, per- haps—though with defective title to the works. Their prac- tice perhaps better observed in the breach than the observ- ance.

The many separate Exhibitions open in the city outnum- bering all former years—an absolute plethora.   "The Bay of New-York"—the "Dana," by Wirtmuller, exhibited in the city some forty years ago, and quite captivated the youthful Inman, then preparing to study with Jarvis—"Cinderella" —"Adam and Eve"—"The Dusseldorf and Jervis Collec- tion"—"Mr. Hardinge"—the third annual "French School" —"The American and Foreign Gallery"—Page, "Moses on Mount Horeb " — Thorp's " Niagara " — Rossitter's "Miriam," "Noah," "Jeremiah"—the Galleries of Wil- liams & Stevens—Weston—Wilmart—Snedecor—&c.

January 10. Died, Charles W. Hackley, Honorary Member. A graduate and Professor of Mathematics at 1861. West Point Academy; afterwards a clergyman of the Protestant Episcopal Church; and subsequently President of Jefferson College, Mississippi. At his death he filled the chair of Mathematics in Columbia College. He was a lover of art and of art society—a member of the original or *old* Sketch Club.

January 21. The Council was especially called together for the determination of *one* from the *many* designs offered for FRONTS for the proposed building for the National Academy of Design. Their decision, it was agreed, should be made by ballot; and they balloted many times, "reconsidered," and finally determined "That TWO DRAWINGS be sent to the Trustees, as those preferred by the Council, among all the plans submitted to them."

Which was succeeded by the following:

"*Resolved*, That the vote referring designs of ——— and ————— be declared unanimous, and that they be *equally* recommended for the choice of the Trustees."

Which, however, was not carried.

That was all altered; and on the 28th of January it was then

"*Resolved*, That the resolution on the designs of ——— and ———, recommended to the Trustees at the last meeting of the Council, be, and it is hereby rescinded."

And it was unanimously

"*Resolved*, That the drawing submitted by ————— be, and is hereby fully approved by the Council, and recommended to the Trustees."

At the last meeting, the writer was the presiding officer, and did not vote. There was evidently a very great preponderance of the profession—in and out of the Academy—in favor of the design chosen.

The drawing or design was at once forwarded to the Board of Trustees, of which the writer was one.

And the following answer was returned:

To the Council of the National Academy of Design:

GENTLEMEN:—The duty devolves on me of informing you that, at a meeting of the Trustees held on the 1st inst., they were reluctantly constrained to dissent from the Council in the adoption of the fronts for a building submitted to them, on the ground of the *too great expensiveness thereof*.

The Trustees, feeling fully satisfied that the erection of such would extend the cost of the building beyond anything they have money to meet, and very far beyond fifty thousand dollars, the amount, as far as possible, to which they wish to confine the contracts for the building. Under these considerations, it becomes not alone a matter of choice, but one of an actual necessity.

THOMAS S. CUMMINGS,

Treasurer and Acting Sec'y of Board.

March 4.   It was

"*Resolved*, That the bill to be presented to the Legislature, asking the exemption of the Academy buildings from taxation, be so changed as to ask to be relieved from assessments, ORDINARY and EXTRAORDINARY."

Mr. Cummings opposed the amendment, as being likely to prevent the obtainment of anything, by asking too much.

Secretary Richards communicated a vote of thanks from the Artists' Fund Society for the use of rooms of the Academy for their first Exhibition and sale.

February 16.   Died, Samuel Waldo, aged seventy-eight years—one of the oldest artists in the country—a portrait painter in the City of New-York for over fifty-three years.

Whereupon, it was

"*Resolved*, That whereas we have heard with feelings of sorrow of the decease of Mr. Samuel Waldo, a resident, for over half a century, of this city—a distinguished artist, and member of this Institution: Therefore,

"*Resolved*, That as a token of respect for the deceased, we wear the usual badge of mourning for thirty days; and that a copy of this resolution be transmitted to the relatives of the deceased, with the expression of our deepfelt sympathy with them in the bereavement which they have recently sustained."

Early in March, the Council were verbally informed that estimates had been taken on the FRONTS presented to the Trustees, and it was found that the adoption of such designs would "*extend*" the cost of the building 20 to 25,000 dollars.

A second communication was received from the Council, with a design similar, but not quite so elaborated as the first, with the following resolution:

"WHEREAS, It is supposed that the second design for a building, submitted by the Council, can be carried out at an expense not exceeding $50,000: Therefore,

"*Resolved*, That the Trustees be requested to consider it."

To which, on the 16th of March, the Trustees recommunicated:

To the Council of the National Academy of Design:

GENTLEMEN:—Herewith please find a copy of a resolution passed by the Trustees on the 15th inst.—viz.:

"WHEREAS, The Trustees have, after submitting the same to reliable *builders*, come to the conclusion that the *second* plan, by ————————, *is too expensive;* and have therefore unanimously adopted one of the plans originally submitted to the Council, marked ——, as being, in their opinion, one within the means of the Academy to erect, and one which they believe, when finished, will receive general approbation.

"But, while they do not wish to dictate to the Council, or insist upon any plan, they beg to remind them, that so much time has been already lost, that longer delay will, in all probability, defeat the erection of the building for the year."

Respectfully,

T. S. CUMMINGS,

Trustee and Secretary of Board.

March 16.   Which was answered by the following:

"*Resolved*, That the Council hereby refer back to the Trustees the matter of obtaining a building—as it originally stood—to be carried on according to their judgment."

March 28.   Mr. Durand tendered his resignation as President:

NEW-YORK, *March* 28, 1861.

T. ADDISON RICHARDS, Esq.,

Secretary National Academy of Design:

DEAR SIR:—Having satisfied myself that I can no longer discharge the duties of the offices of President of the Academy and that of Trustee of its building fund, I have resolved to resign these offices into the hands of the Academy. Please lay before the Council my resignation herewith, as President of the National Academy of Design, and of Trustee of its building fund; both to take effect immediately.

Respectfully yours,

A. B. DURAND.

It appeared, and it was hoped, that the difficulty attendant on the fronts had exhausted itself. At a meeting of the Trustees held on the 22d of March, after the resolution of the 16th had been received, there appeared a most decided earnestness to proceed at once with the work. Mr. Cummings was ordered to complete all arrangements as to obtaining the working plans, and to procure estimates from mechanics, without delay, for the proposed building. They were brought in, and submitted to the Trustees—opened—canvassed, and found to be within the amount of the Trust limit; and the writer was requested to confer with the

Architect on the same, and to report "*complete*" on the 18th of April.

In the mean time, civil war had broken out, and when the 18th arrived, there was no action. A panic appeared to have seized on everybody and everything; and a call was made by the Trust for a conference with the body of the Academicians, for the 24th of May.

The writer called a meeting of the Trustees on the 22d, and endeavored to avert so unfavorable a REFERENCE—but without effect.

At the meeting to be on the 24th, it was proposed to urge the payment of $20,000 on the land, and "to ask the discharge of the Trustees from all liability."

That would have *divided* the means at the disposal of the Trustees, and the prospect of obtaining money to build on a second mortgage highly improbable; and would have virtually defeated the accomplishment of the Trust—viz., "The purchase of the ground, and the putting up a building thereon," which the Trust was directed to do, and which, in good faith, they had so far proceeded with.

At the meeting of the 24th of the Academicians, Mr. Cummings intentionally absented himself.

"The proposition" was warmly urged, and Mr. Cummings was *sent for* to reply to the arguments. A spirited and severe debate ensued. The claims for a releasement of the Trustees was pressed, and responded to by Mr. Cummings, on the ground of the *utter destruction* to the Academy's obtaining a building, if the matter was so disposed of. The reasoning of Mr. C. prevailed, and a vote almost unanimous was obtained.

The Academy rejected the proposition; and "it was ordered that the Trustees go on with the building."

The Academician and Trustee who had urged the proposition stated that he only wanted the decision of the Academy on the matter; and he retired, apparently satisfied to proceed.

Yet, at a meeting of the Trustees on the 9th of July, it was resolved to pay Mr. ———— $20,000, and relieve the Trust.

Remonstrance was vain—it had apparently been previously determined on. Yet the writer so far succeeded as to compel the taking of counsel before enforcing the resolution.

Singularly, a second resolution had been made in Council, and transmitted to the Trustees—viz.:

"WHEREAS, The Trustees having solicited the Council to express their views of the kind of building to be erected by them for the Academy; and agreeably thereto, the Council having adopted a design, first for the interior arrangement by one architect, and then for the fronts by another, and known as the production of ——; which design the Trustees did not accept, alleging therefor as a reason, want of funds, but referred the matter back to the Council, with their approbation of another design by ——; and this design not being approved by the Council, as suitable, in their opinion, for the requirements of the Academy: Therefore,

"*Resolved*, That the Council hereby refer the whole matter again to the Trustees, as it stood before they solicited '*our*' advice; distinctly disclaiming any expression of approbation or disapprobation, of sanction or protest, of desire or opinion, as to the movements of the Trustees—expecting them to proceed in the Trust precisely as if they had not consulted '*us.*' The whole power having been originally granted them by the Academy—not resulting in any manner from the subsequent motions of this Council."

Mr. Cummings was requested to draft another petition to the Legislature, asking exemption from taxation of the Academy's property, and to procure the draft of a law there for immediate presentation.

Which was done, numerously signed, and forwarded:

To the Honorable the Members of the Legislature of the
State of New-York, in Senate and Assembly assembled:

GENTLEMEN:

The undersigned, members of the National Academy of Design of the City of New-York, an Institution chartered by your Honorable Body, in 1828, for the "cultivation and extension of the Arts of Design." "Its funds to be employed in promoting that object."

Beg leave respectfully to represent: That, unaided by any but their own exertions, they have faithfully pursued their course under their Charter for thirty-three years, and, as they hope, to the benefit of Art, and the students thereof; and that, by untiring industry and rigid economy, they have now accumulated a sufficient sum wherewith to erect a building for their use; and by the liberality of their townsman, Mr. William Niblo, who sells them the lot of ground on the corner of Twenty-third Street and Fourth Avenue, the whole of the purchase money to remain for years on mortgage, they are now prepared to erect, and will at once proceed to erect, a building thereon suitable for their purposes; and from which, after paying expenses, no very important income may be expected to be derived therefrom to Art support.

Under these circumstances, your petitioners respectfully ask that the aid of the State may be so far extended towards them as to exempt their property, lot, and buildings from taxation; thereby thus far sympathizing with them in the object they have in view—objects, as artists, which they hold professionally dear, and to which they hope the people of the State of New-York will render cheerful aid, to the extent asked by your petitioners; and for which they will ever pray.

Respectfully, your obedient servant,

THOMAS S. CUMMINGS.

The above paper was signed by the members of the Academy, as well as by many distinguished citizens of the City of New-York.

Which, together with a draft of a bill to be submitted to the Legislature, as per order, was forwarded.

The necessity of giving up the lease of the Tenth Street Galleries, to prevent paying a whole year's rent ($3,000) for the short period of an Exhibition, with the probability of a new building within the ensuing year, induced the proposition by the writer to open the Exhibition at a much earlier date than usual (20th March), closing the 25th of April, in time for the return of the works prior to May 1st, the appointed time for the surrender of the premises.

It was opened to the public on the 20th of March, and as it closed on the 25th of April—making but twenty-eight working days—and received $2,596.50; average $92.60 per day; 577 works—IT may justly be termed the "Exhibition of the Year of the Rebellion;" of course not meeting anything like its expenses.

It had been proposed to preface the Exhibition with a "Dress Reception," ladies, music, &c.; but, at the eleventh hour, that arrangement was changed. Ladies were excluded—the members, exhibiters, and press alone received. Punch, sandwiches, cigars, substituted for ladies and full dress. As Prince Metternich would say, in his non-committalism, "Some preferred it—some did not."

After the commencement of the Exhibition, (finding the Galleries would not be occupied, and could be had by the month,) it was proposed to extend the Exhibition to the usual time, and to engage the rooms therefor. The whole of that arrangement was frustrated by CIVIL WAR. On the 19th of April the receipts were reduced to the actual daily expenses; and a day or two after, very much below that point, and it became economy to stop it; and it was closed on the 25th.

WORTHY OF NOTE.

On the 22d of April was passed a resolution awarding an amount for the purchase of *arms* for the Door-keeper—a worthy man—not for the defence of the Galleries—but the Capitol. He was called as a citizen soldier of the State for the "*defence of Washington;*" and it was to aid him in preparing for that sudden emergency. Like a good citizen, he left his wife and children to the mercy of friends, and went forth to his country's defence. The writer is happy to say he returned, after a year's service, unharmed.

A Committee was appointed, consisting of Messrs. Huntington and Gray, to "open communications with the Secretary of State of the United States (unfortunately, no longer united,) in regard to sending American Art produc-

tions to the proposed International Exhibition in London."
Much enthusiasm prevailed on the subject. Large prospects of works were entertained, and great benefit to American Art prospectively promised, through the Academy's supervision and interest. The Exhibition to take place in the Fall of 1862.

No report appears to have been made. It was probably lost sight of in the Summer vacation.

May 8. Was held the Annual Meeting, and were present 34 Academicians.

MR. INGHAM'S REPORT.

GENTLEMEN:

In consequence of the unexpected and much to be regretted resignation of our worthy President, Mr. Durand, the task of making a report devolves upon me. If I do not perform it to your satisfaction, I beg of you to place the failure to the want of ability, rather than to a deficiency of inclination.

I cannot congratulate the Academy on the present state of the Fine Arts. The great Rebellion has startled society from its propriety, and war and politics now occupy every mind. No one thinks of the Arts. Even among the Artists, patriotism has superseded painting, and many have laid by the palette and pencil, to shoulder the musket. "Union for the Country" is the word on every lip, and the feeling in every heart.

Let us not, however, in our love of country, forget our love of art, nor forget that if union is good in the nation, it is also good among the artists; and as unity in a nation is absolutely necessary to command the respect of mankind, so a united body of artists is equally necessary to obtain the respect of society.

The arrangements reported on the sale of the property 663 Broadway have so far been complied with and fulfilled.

The Trustees' Report will give you particulars.

I beg leave to call the attention of the Academy to that part of the Treasurer's last year's Report which refers to obtaining some *memento* of our lamented friend, Charles M. Leupp, and regret that it has not been accomplished.

I congratulate the Academy on the flourishing state of that essential part of our Institution, *the Schools*. The discipline therein is admirable; the numbers gratifying; there being 28 in the Life, and 50 in the Antique. This success is entirely due to the care and attention of the teacher, our worthy *Treasurer;* and it rescues the Academy from the charge of being a mere Trades' Union.

In this ever-changing community, where ambition has unlimited scope, and Young America treads on the heels of Old America, and essays to push her from her stool, the Academy has maintained a calm position, and in thirty-six years has had but two Presidents.

As one of the remaining founders of the Institution, and one of the oldest men in the Academy, I think I may state, without wounding the self-love of any other member, that I have claims upon the Presidency. These, however, I forego, and sink my own ambition into the desire to see once more at the head of the Institution the man who brought the unconnected artists together, and perhaps more than any other person may be considered the founder of the Academy. To Mr. Morse is justly due the compliment that he should be the President that shall introduce the Academy into the building they are about to erect, and which it is expected our excellent Trustees will in a short time have completed.

It is to be wished that in all things we could be as unanimous as I am sure we will be in our vote of thanks to our late President for his long and faithful services.

I remain, Gentlemen,

Your most ob't serv't,

CHS. C. INGHAM,

Vice-President.

From the Treasurer's Report it appears that the total receipts were $4,742.94; the total disbursements, $4,893.89: the Treasurer being in advance $150.95.

May 7. Mr. Ingham was in ill health, did not desire or feel able to attend to the office, and had, with the sincere interest of the Institution at heart, solicited Mr. Morse to allow his name to be used as President once more, even though but for a short time. To which Mr. Morse replied:

To Messrs. Durand, Ingham, and others,
Members of the National Academy of Design:

GENTLEMEN:

Your flattering request that I would allow my name to be used for a candidate for the Presidency of the Academy at the ensuing election has just been handed to me.

There are many reasons, of mainly a personal nature, which make me unfeignedly reluctant to accede to your request. I have been so long out of the traces of Art, that I am conscious of inability to fulfill the duties of the position either to my own or your satisfaction; and the great pressure of other duties demanding my time and attendance add to my reluctance. Yet it has been so strongly represented to me that the vital interests of the Academy are to a great extent involved in my yea or nay, that in this view of the case, the feeling of paternity is strongly moved in my heart, and I cannot forget the early travail with my honored associates, which brought into existence the National Academy of Design.

The request of so many members, given with such sincerity, cannot be slightly regarded by me, and I yield my inclinations and doubts at their bidding.

I make one condition, however, to wit: that one term only of the Presidency must be considered as the utmost limit of my acceptance.

With sincere respect,

Your obedient servant,

SAMUEL F. B. MORSE.

Mr. Durand's resignation, or now rather declination, was accepted. A vote of thanks was tendered to him.

Samuel F. B. Morse was elected President; Henry Peters Gray, Vice-President (defeating Ingham on the fourth balloting); T. Addison Richards, Corresponding Secretary; J. B. Stearns, Recording Secretary; Thomas S. Cummings, Treasurer; A. E. White, J. F. Kensett, R. W. Hubbard,

D. Huntington, W. Hart, J. W. Cassilear, Members of Council.

Twelve Academicians and sixteen Associate Members were elected.

On the 20th of July died, Miss Sarah C. Frothingham, Associate Member, daughter of James Frothingham, Academician, aged forty years.

The Summer stampede of artists having occurred, there is little left to be enumerated during those months.

In the early Fall (September) appeared the appointment of "National Commissioners to the Exhibition of the Industry of all Nations."

October 15. Died, in Paris, P. P. Duggan, Academician. The following, from Paris papers, may, and is, in fact, perhaps the only notice had of this artist's decease:

DEATH OF PAUL DUGGAN, THE ARTIST.

[Correspondence of the *Evening Post*.]

PARIS, *October* 18, 1861.

The artists of New-York, and the numerous friends of Mr. P. Paul Duggan, will hear with sorrow that he died at Paris on the evening of October 15th.

It is, I believe, well known that he had been for more than ten years an invalid, being subject to hemorrhage of the lungs. Finding the climate of America unfavorable to his complaint, he left New-York, and has resided in London or the neighborhood of that city for some years, near his sister and two brothers. By careful attention to his physical system, he was so fortunate as to enjoy better health than his friends had anticipated, and to pursue his artistic and literary labors, with an occasional return of his old malady. Last May he decided to come to Paris. He had been here some years before, and now found so much to attract him in the climate, the mode of life, and the numerous works of art in this city, that he determined to make a long sojourn here. But he had not been here many weeks when his attacks of hemorrhage returned with unusual frequency. With remarkable vitality, he struggled against disease and despondency, until, about six weeks ago, it was thought necessary that his sister should come on from London, to be with him and take care of him. But from some cause, whether the climate, or the food, or over-exertion of bodily strength, he latterly became much worse, until about a fortnight since, when he was attacked by an inflammation of the lungs. His brother, Joseph L. Duggan, the eminent musical composer, was sent for, and came to him. To the very last they hoped he would gain strength enough to return with them to England. But all hopes proved vain. He grew weaker and weaker, until about eight o'clock on Tuesday evening of the 15th he breathed his last, calmly, without a struggle, and still apparently unconscious how ill he was. To the last he was full of plans for future labors and studies.

Those who know Duggan will not need to be reminded how rare and gifted a mind and how warm and true a heart were his. As an artist he is well known in New-York, his old adopted home. He had the soundest and broadest views of art, and that thorough knowledge of anatomy and drawing which qualified him, at a very early age, for his professorship in the New-York Free Academy. But he was no less remarkable for his clear, deep, and original intellect in matters of science. And during the last months of his life, when his breath would not permit him to talk, draw, read or write, except very spar-

ingly, he was accustomed to beguile his long hours of tedious illness by re-
volving some deep or abstruse subject of philosophy. The books I usually
found on his table were all of this character.

He had a rich vein of humor running through his most serious talk, and a
faculty of expressing himself on all subjects that made him an unusually interesting companion in conversation.

Music, too, in its principles and in its practice, was an element in which he
lived and had his being. Not only did he cherish the most elevated views of
this branch of art, in its spiritual and æsthetic relations, but he was gifted
with a remarkable musical genius, and an ear so delicate that, though self-
taught, he would reproduce at the piano whole pages of delicious harmony
and melody which he had chiefly caught by ear.

As a friend, pure, noble, warm-heated, sympathetic, disinterested. "None
knew him but to love him; none named him but to praise." All selfishness
seemed left out of his composition; and if he ever repined at the long years
of ill-health, it was that he could not devote himself to the works to which his
genius called him.

His remains were yesterday interred in the Cemetery of Montmartre.

October 30. Died, Eugene H. Latilla, Honorary Member
of the National Academy of Design, at his residence, Chap-
paqua, Westchester, New-York, aged fifty-one years.

November 4. The Life and Antique Schools opened
for the season, closing on the 4th of March, and, as before,
under the charge of Professor Cummings. In time of war
or rebellion, it could not be expected that the Fine Arts
should receive much attention; and the knowledge of the
many absent at the seat of war, either as soldier, or in the
Art Corps illustrative, it was thought the Schools would
not be well attended, or even, perhaps, called for. It was
quite the reverse. The entries were about fifty in the Antique, and twenty-five in the Life. The average attendance better than usual. The order perfect. The School
never looked better, or evinced a livelier interest. The
students presented a formula of thanks for the kind treatment, attention, and advantages they had received. Models were scarce.

November 13. Died, in Philadelphia, Bass Otis, one of
the oldest artists in the country, eighty-four years of age.
He was well known in Philadelphia, and, as an artist, of
merit.

December 16. Mr. Cummings was directed to entertain
negotiations for an Exhibition on a plan submitted—viz.:
The parties to take charge of the Exhibition after the pictures offering were arranged, paying all the expenses, and
giving the Academy half the net proceeds.

That would have made the Institution the borrower of
the pictures, and which, by such an arrangement, they
would have placed from under their control, &c., &c.

To the Council of the National Academy of Design:

Gentlemen :—In compliance with your instructions, as passed at last meeting of the Council, I have prepared a "form" of an agreement, as you therein required. I have not made a transcript of it, or obtained legal aid in reference to it, which I do not deem necessary; nor do I propose to do so, until after such time as its points shall have been examined, approved, and adjusted by you; and, among other reasons, for the following—viz. :

An examination of the subject necessary to enable me to project a form of agreement, forces me to the conclusion that the *whole plan* is one which should be viewed with distrust; nay, more, *wholly avoided.*

With the above, I have prepared a "form," embodying the idea entertained, under a reciprocal inversion of the parties ; and, although not materially different, removes many of the objectionable features. It is not without objections, and probably would not be accepted by any party outside the Institution. The plans are herewith submitted.

Respectfully, your very ob't serv't,

THOMAS S. CUMMINGS.

January 19. 1862. Died, Mosley J. Danforth, Honorary Member, an engraver of eminence, and one of the American Bank Note Company Association. A student of the old Drawing Association, and one of the original founders of the Academy. He was removed from Academicianship, in consequence of non-residence, to the Honorary Membership list. Resolutions were passed expressive of the high sense the deceased was held in the Academy, and crape was worn in token of respect to his memory.

February 3. It was resolved to press the application to the Legislature for exemption from taxation of the Academy property, and the writer was again dispatched to Albany for the purpose of forwarding that object, with but one opinion—that of its being an extremely unpropitious time to press such an application. Under the favorable entertainment of Mr. White, it obtained a first reading in the Senate, and by the exertions of Mr. Benedict it was passed to a third reading in the Assembly, when an unexpected opposition was suddenly sprung upon it. It was too late in the session to hope for a change of opinion, (being within a few hours of its close,) and the matter there ended for the year.

February 21. Died, at his residence, Audubon Park, 155th Street, John Woodhouse Audubon, in the fiftieth year of his age. Associate Member of the Academy, brother of the late Victor B., Academician, and son of the celebrated naturalist, John J. Audubon. Resolutions of condolence were passed in Council, and the usual mourning was worn.

March 3. A Biography of the late Paul P. Duggan,

Academician, was ordered to be prepared for the Academy and publication, and Mr. Falconer was appointed to that duty. It has not, it is believed, yet appeared.

March 18. Death again entered the ranks. The veteran Charles B. King, Honorary Member, was taken at the advanced age of seventy-six years. A native of Rhode Island, though for some forty years preceding his death, a resident of Washington City. He enjoyed a fair reputation as a painter, and was particularly marked for his Indian portraits, of which he had made a large collection, having painted all the Delegates of the Chiefs to Washington during nearly half a century. Mr. King had amassed a property by his professional industry, and by his will gave a large portion of his estate to public and charitable institutions. His remains are interred in his native place, Newport.

April 4. An amusing scene—"a Salmon piece a Sign" in Court. An action was brought by the plaintiff to recover the value of an oil painting—a fish, a salmon—alleged to have been confided to his use by the defendant. It was claimed that the painting "was an original," by a celebrated German artist, and the best living delineator of fish, "and that it had been placed in the window of the hook, line, bob and sinker store, No. 48 Maiden Lane, as an ornament, and that it was worth some $4,000.

" The defendant denied title in the plaintiff, and claimed that the painting was owned by his firm, and that the conversion, if any, was the act of his firm, and not his individual act. It was urged that the other members of the firm should have been made co-defendants. To show title, the defendant proved that his firm purchased the stock of fishing tackle in the store in Maiden Lane, together with the *fixtures* of the store ; and the counsel argued that as this painting of a fish was one of the ' signs ' of the business, having been long used as such, it was a *fixture*, and was passed to his firm with the other fixtures conveyed by the sale.

" The Court held that there were no decisions in the annals of the Court of Appeals that would warrant the determination that an oil painting, shown to be of such value, could or should be classed with shelves, desks, and other ' fixtures' of a fishing-tackle business. The Court also held that a claim for damages for conversion can be assigned, and that the assignee can sue thereon without a new demand. (McKee *vs.* Judd, 2 Kernan.) Judgment for the plaintiff for $250.

"Rufus J. Bell for plaintiff; Samuel Owen for defendant."

April 12. Was the private demonstration to the 37th Annual Exhibition. No ladies invited. The artists, exhibiters, members of the press, &c., &c., met, and had a "good time generally."

The east room of the Galleries—the Derby—received no light, other than from the front windows on Broadway. That was well known on the taking of the Galleries, and equally understood as undesirable for the exposition of paintings. That room the Committee unaccountably determined should be used for the exhibition of works of art, and likewise that the windows should be *closed*, and that it should be kept constantly lighted with gas.

The writer admonished them that it was impracticable, and if for no other cause, its great cost; and that there were other reasons, viz.: the great contrast in the color of the light as compared with the day-lighted Galleries, the too great heat, &c., &c., which was disregarded. The latter soon showed itself, and gained the ascendency. It was an oven—an unbearable oven—and arrangements were at once made, even to working all night, to change the unfortunate determination.

The following were among the remarks made on the subject by the Press:

"Whatever could be done to create artificial distinctions between the works of the exhibiters and to depress merit, while undue prominence has been given to pictures remarkable for the absence of it, has been accomplished. By converting into a sort of oven the front gallery, from which the light of day is but imperfectly excluded, and which consequently struggles for ascendency with that of the gas-burners, a *locus penitentia* has been provided, to which we need not say all those who do not find favor in the eyes of privileged mediocrity are remorselessly consigned."

April 14. The Exhibition opened to the public at the Derby Art Gallery, 625 Broadway—closing on the 23d of June. Receipts, $4,315 70. Open sixty-one working days, and averaged $70 75 per day. 555 the highest catalogue number.

During the Exhibition a novel mode of advertising was proposed, and received favor. It was tried, at a very considerable *cost*, but the success, if any, was not apparent.

May 14. Was held the Annual Meeting. Thirty-eight Academicians present.

Mr. Cummings sent an excuse for his *first* absence.

Mr. Morse made a verbal report, and declined a re-election, which had been previously understood by letter. The Treasurer's accounts showed the total receipts for the year $2,598 97—the disbursements the same amount. That

308   HISTORIC ANNALS OF THE

represented but a part of the year's accounts. After that amount *all* the expenses of the Institution—the bonds issued for rent of Tenth Street Galleries, appropriations (ordinary and extraordinary) made by Council—indeed, all outstanding indebtedness, had been discharged by the "Trust," and are to be found in their accounts.

Daniel Huntington was elected President; Henry Peters Gray, Vice-President; T. Addison Richards, Corresponding Secretary; J. B. Stearns, Recording Secretary; Thos. S. Cummings, Treasurer; and the usual number of six Academicians to form the Council.

Wm. H. Beard, Samuel Coleman, Jr., and Launt Thompson, were made Academicians. Ten Associates, and four Honorary Members. Among the latter, Henry R. Cummings, son of the writer.

May 13. It was rather singularly *Resolved*, That the *interpretation* of the term "publicly exhibited" in the CONSTITUTION be left to the discretion of the Council.

A vote of thanks was passed to S. F. B. Morse for his kindness in consenting to occupy the Chair during the past year, and expressive of the high regard for him as founder of the Institution—"one who, by his acknowledged talents, reflects honor on the profession and country."

There appeared to have been no further meetings of the Council until November. Nearly six months dormancy—half a year's administration unprovided for.

June 4. Louis R. Minot, Academician, made a sale of his works by the Art Auctioneer, Leeds, producing, as was publicly announced, over five thousand dollars. It was preparatory to his going abroad. He sailed on the 26th in the leviathan, the "Great Eastern," from Flushing Bay, where Her Majestyship was anchored.

July 23. Died, Dr. Andrew Hammersley, M. D., Honorary Member of the Academy. He was highly distinguished in his profession, and had lectured on Anatomy before the students.

August 17. Died, John Wesley Paradise, Associate Member, aged 53. An engraver of merit, and son of the late respectable artist portrait painter of the city, John Paradise.

Likewise died, Rev. John Hunter, Honorary Member, "an eloquent man, of remarkably fine appearance, and keen appreciation of the Fine Arts." He frequently attended the meetings of the Academy. He is especially regarded for some remarks of peculiar beauty and sympathy made at a meeting held shortly after Inman's death, and equally felicitously alluded to by Jonathan Sturges,

Esq., in his remarks at the late Annual Meeting dinner of the Academy.

October 1. The Schools, Life and Antique, opened under the charge of Professor Cummings, and closed on the 16th March. Everything well except the attendance, which had been limited—51 students only entering, 28 to the "Antique," 23 to the "Life." War and patriotism had taken its share away, and the immense " *Corps Artistic* " at the "*front*," seeking material for the illustration of publications, deprived the schools of yet many more.

October 10. Splendid generosity—handsome donation. Rossitter, Academician, presented the Sanitary Commission with his fine picture of " Washington at Valley Forge," and a highly interesting correspondence was had between him and the Mayor of the city. See *Times* of October 10th, '62.

It is amusing to observe the idiosyncrasies of fashion in art, as in everything else, if equally closely observed— such as the culmination of one quality or idea, and the sudden and consequent reaction to the furthest and opposite extreme.

Panoramas were the rage, size an object, and, as a recommendation, advertised to be " three miles long ! ! ! " Flowers and fruits in extreme *small* follow immediately on its heels, and obtain high favor, and culminate in " effects " in color of not more than an inch or so square—some twenty or more on a sheet. The giant and the dwarf side by side. What becomes of quality under such *fashion* circumstances ? A very good anecdote is remembered in Clark's *Knickerbocker* on the subject of *time* in the execution of works of art, similarly brought out—such as a merit that it was done in ten minutes, three shakes of the brush to the second, or, as a still greater merit, in no time. Ridiculous extremes ! What next ?

October 24. The writer is happy to be able to chronicle that Art commands attention, and high prices obtained, notwithstanding the unfortunate and unsettled condition of the country. A few are always fortunate. The object here, however, is only to name the art prices—a matter of general historic interest. The *Herald* says, " Gignoux has just sold his Indian Summer to M. O. Roberts for $5,000, and is finishing a picture to order for Count De Paris for a similar amount." Sometimes errors occur, however. The papers chronicled the purchase of a beautiful small full-length statue in marble of Napoleon the First, pronounced by Canova, and good enough to be by any one, by T. S. Cummings, the writer. *Not quite so fast*, Mr. Editor. Such was the case, but justice must add, it was not for himself, but for a friend, Mr. James M. Fuller, a gentleman of wealth, taste and refinement, who fully appreciates the merit of the work he has obtained. It was further noted that an English gentleman had purchased Story's statue of Cleopatra for $3,000, and the African Sybil for a similar or larger amount. The obtainment of such prices is creditable to American art and artists.

Fine art items may certainly now include photography. The Messrs. Anthony are said to have added those of the Empress Eugenie and the Prince Imperial to their collection. Certain it is that history and historic portraiture, and indeed every branch of history, will receive an extraordinary and impartial, and never-before-obtained recorder by photography. Think of instantaneous, reliable, non-influenced records by that art, and their incalculable advantages to the world one thousand years hence. What would be given, what the advantages of a peep at *ancient* history through such a source! Had photography existed two thousand years ago, it might, perhaps, have destroyed half the controversial matter of the world, saved much bloodshed, and millions of lives.

"The oil paintings and other artistic works, the property of the late Rembrandt Peale, to be sold at auction on Thursday next, the 18th inst., at the Pennsylvania Academy of Fine Arts, in Philadelphia. The catalogue includes the duplicate copy of Peale's original portrait of Washington, painted in 1795; also, copies of the Washington portraits by other distinguished artists. At the same time other pictures of interest, as may be seen by referring to the advertisement."

The disturbance to all financial matters by the Rebellion, the first effect of which was a reduction in the value of property of some fifty per cent., caused a new doubt to arise in the Trust as to the management of its finances. The amounts promised and due on the Academy sale had not been received, and, for reasons given, there was no security for future payments. Foreclosure was in no case to be thought of, unless the parties desired the return of the property—there were no purchasers in the market. The property was not wanted back, however profitable that might have eventuated. There was, therefore, no alternative but patience; and the more particularly so, that the main building, Mozart Hall, had been destroyed by fire, and no revenue could be derived therefrom.

In the latter part of 1862, matters assumed a better aspect. Purchasers began to appear for property on Broadway at the *reduced prices*, and it was thought a favorable opportunity to bring matters to a conclusion.

November 3. A Committee was appointed to request of the Trustees a "definite statement of the condition of the affairs of the Academy under their charge," which was served on the Trust on the 17th November. Mr. Cummings, on behalf of the Trust, made the following statement:

To the Council of the National Academy of Design:

GENTLEMEN:—In reply to your questions made to me as Trustee, please find the following answer, though not in concurrence or in consultation with the other Trustees:

First, I beg leave to refer you to a report of the Trustees made to you May —, 1860, (as per your Minutes,) in which you will find your gross receipts placed at $73,333.09; including a judgment against ——————— for $10,042.96.

Since that date, the Trustees have, by your order, become petitioning creditors that said ——————— ——————— be discharged from his indebtedness. Said judgment will not, therefore, further be continued as assets, available or otherwise.

Exclusive of that amount, the assets may be stated at $63,290.13.

Since which time, $5,630.48 have been discharged and paid by the Trust, outside of the said accounts proper, in liquidation of indebtednesses of the Institution, by the Institution's order.

That would have seriously reduced the amount of assets; but that economical care has been exercised, and the expenses kept within the interest receivable account.

Since said report, the relations with Mr. —— have been somewhat changed. Twenty thousand dollars have been paid on account of the purchase, and the Institution has become possessed of the fee of the lots purchased. Said twenty thousand dollars, however, are, by especial agreement, been made returnable to the Institution, in furtherance of the erection of the building, as per terms of agreement—provided the same be claimed within three years from date of the said agreement, viz., November 1, 1861. It will therefore be counted in the available assets of the *Building Fund.*

The present assets, therefore, are as follows:

Returnable by Mr. ——, as per agreement	$20,000 00
Mortgage due on property 663 Broadway, and capable of foreclosure at any time	31,930 80
Deposit in the New-York Life Insurance and Trust Company	5,000 00
Interest due to 1st November	1,163 36
Balance on hand	333 22
	$58,427 38

It may be restated that the mortgage on the old property is due, and yet unpaid.

The Trustees did not proceed in a foreclosure, simply because, in the depreciated state of property on Broadway, they feared, by so doing, it might revert to the Academy—a matter strenuously to be avoided, in the present position.

They have not proceeded with the building, for the reason that they did not possess or have satisfactory assurance of the coming in of means wherewith to carry it to completion. To have commenced might have been fatal to your interest.

The Trustees are as anxious, or even more so than yourselves, to proceed with the building, to the end that they be enabled to complete their trust, and be relieved from the responsibilities; but have so far, with due regard to your interest, been prevented. Any means you may furnish to relieve the impediment will, I may add, be truly acceptable to the Trust, and receive their consideration.

Respectfully,

T. S. CUMMINGS.

December 2.   A sale by auction of a collection of paintings and sketches, the works of Mr. Richard M. Staigg, Academician, to the number of 73, including an original miniature, from the life of Daniel Webster. This method of disposing of artists' accumulative studio productions is becoming general and profitable. The sale of Mr. Staigg's works is said to have produced between four and five thousand dollars.

December 18.   The famous collection of pictures known as the "Dusseldorf Gallery," originally collected by the late Mr. Boker, and exhibited in this city for many years, was this day offered at sale at public auction, at the Gallery, 548 Broadway, where they had reposed for some two or three years. The largest picture of all, "The Martyrdom of Huss," by Lessig, had been previously removed, and a few others had been disposed of at private sale.

The auction was largely attended by artists and well-known connoisseurs. The occasion was indeed one well calculated to call together a large representation of these classes, as the collection was probably one of the finest and most valuable ever offered for sale; and had, during its exhibition here, contributed a great deal to advance a more just appreciation of the fine arts.

The sale began in the early forenoon, the catalogue showing a list of 107 pictures from Hildebrandt, Kohler, Camphausen, Volkhatt, Bower, Plumot, Simmler, Verheyden, Roser, Van Ostade, Rosenboom, and other German and Dutch artists. American art represented by a few landscapes of Sontag and Johnson, and the domestic scenes of Lilly Spencer.

The collection is said to have brought at private and public sale about $45,000.

Thus ended the most successful of all the experiments made in the city for the establishment of a permanent Exhibition. It was generally pointed to, and indeed claimed by all to be a *decided success*. The writer never believed it. On the contrary, he supposed it upheld itself as a private mart for the sale of foreign works, and by the commission on the sales, rather than by exhibition. Be that as it may, it run out.

For the prices obtained, if desired, see *Evening Post* 19th.

There was yet another attempt at a permanent Gallery—viz., "The International Art Union"—"The Foreign Artists' Experiment." The writer had supposed that institution long since closed. It appears that about November, 1861, many of the pictures were sold at private sale. Like all other attempts, it had failed and closed up. It was located on the corner of Fourth Street and Broadway, and made a fine display. The Institute of Art, Broadway, Cincinnati, &c., found the same fate, notwithstanding the Art Union principle attached thereto.

Thus, again and again, the permanent exhibition system seemed to fail in this city; for that it had ceased to be profitable, although sustained by capital and foreign influence, is certain. Had it been otherwise, there could have been no doubt of its continuance.

All these the Academy has outlived; and must continue to survive all others of a similar character, as well as the many free expositions, now so numerous, which must have their day and doom. That is New-York taste, and love of change—unlike, perhaps, all older sections of the globe. Such the Academy must be prepared to meet, and by commercial combination and revenue to be derived therefrom in its building, be prepared to "weather," or its future success cannot be counted on as a certainty.

January 5. A letter was submitted from Mr. Alexander J. Davis, offering the records of "The American **1863.** Academy of Fine Arts" for deposit in the archives of the National Academy of Design. Historically it was important. Messrs. Cummings, Baker, and Gray were appointed a Committee to wait on Mr. Davis, who expressed his desire and his expectation to give the "*Records*" to the National Academy "as soon as that Institution should provide a suitable place for their safe keeping, (fire proof,) and make a regular official application for them." It was a little difficult to see how the Academy could make an official application—having no right over them. If it was wished to give them, it could have been done, and there end the matter. It was not, however, so determined.

In January it was proposed to establish "A Fellowship" to the Academy, for the purpose of raising funds for the greater embellishment of the proposed building, and the following circular was issued ;

"FELLOWSHIP FUND OF THE NATIONAL ACADEMY OF DESIGN."

The interests of the City of New-York require that the Fine Arts should be provided for on more solid foundations. Other cities of the Union have Art Institutions firmly established and endowed, with spacious buildings, galleries and collections of casts from the Antique, &c., while in this city, though we have our Academy of Design, it has no permanent Edifice, and therefore lacks completeness and energy.

Here is the largest number of Artists, and a wide circle to appreciate their works, yet we are in want of the means to concentrate their talents, as well as the public taste and admiration, in one noble Institution, which shall be a suitable Home for the Arts.

Our beautiful city should no longer be wanting in such a central School of Art, on a scale commensurate with our growing wealth and importance. A spacious artistic building, with a Library of Art, thoroughly conducted Schools for study, and galleries sufficient both for the Annual Exhibitions and permanent Collections, would add greatly to the charm of life in this city, and attract numerous visitors and residents.

It has been found in Europe that a thorough training among the students of the Fine Arts not only raises the standard of excellence in the higher departments, but is diffused through all the branches of the Mechanic Arts, and adds beauty and value to designs for manufacture, to furniture, to fabrics of every kind, and objects of use as well as ornament; thus proving a source both of wealth and refinement to the citizens.

The National Academy of Design has been in existence nearly forty years, and for a long time kept pace with the advance of our city in wealth and taste. For the last few years, for the want of a suitable building, the Academy has not fulfilled the hopes of the public.

The property of the Institution, under the direction of the Trustees, has increased from $8,000 in 1847, to $60,000. A site has been purchased, but the funds are not sufficient for the erection of an appropriate building. There is enough of talent and zeal among the Artists, but the want of a central rallying-point scatters their forces and dampens their ardor.

We need, and we must have, a Building. Should one be erected of striking and beautiful Architecture, the various Societies of Art would cluster around it, and the schools of design and collections of models might be so amply provided as to stimulate the zeal of students, and tend to raise American Art to the highest excellence.

To accomplish the above purpose, the undersigned, Members of the National Academy of Design, pledge themselves to renewed efforts for the completion of a building, and do hereby form themselves into an Association auxiliary to the Academy, for the purpose of establishing a Fund, to be devoted to perfecting the building, and generally advancing the interests of the Academy.

The Fund of the Association shall be formed by subscriptions of money, proceeds of pictures, and other works of Art presented, and by grants of Fellowship, (the Academy consenting thereto,) as follows:

PROPOSED AMENDMENTS TO THE CONSTITUTION.

ARTICLE XII.

Sec. 1. There shall be established a Special Fund, separate from the ordinary Treasury of the Academy, and called *The Fellowship Fund*, to be formed by subscriptions of money, the proceeds of pictures or other works of Art presented, and by grants of Fellowship; and this Fund shall be devoted to perfecting the building, sustaining the schools, and generally advancing the interests of the Academy.

Sec. 2. A subscriber of $100 to the Fellowship Fund shall be presented with a Diploma, constituting him a Fellow of the National Academy of Design for Life, and entitling him to ten season tickets to the Exhibition, annually, access to the Library and Reading Rooms, and invitations to all the Conversations held by the Academy; also, to nominate two students, annually, who, on passing the usual examination, shall be admitted to the schools of the Academy, free of charge.

Sec. 3. A subscriber of $500 to the Fund shall receive a Diploma entitling him to all the privileges of a Life Fellowship in perpetuity, and be entitled to convey his Fellowship to an heir or assignee, and the holder of the Diploma shall enjoy the privileges of the original subscriber.

Sec. 4. The Fellowship Fund and its affairs shall be controlled by a Standing Committee of seven Academicians, to be selected in the first instance immediately after the passage of this Law, and thereafter, annually, at the Annual Meeting of the Academy. They shall choose their own officers, viz.: a Chairman, Treasurer and Secretary, and make a full report of their finances and proceedings to the Academy, at the Annual Meeting of the body.

Sec. 5. The funds of the Committee shall be deposited in one or more of the Trust Companies of the City of New-York; and should the whole amount collected exceed $20,000, one-half of such excess shall be invested in stocks of the State of New-York, or of the United States, to be held as a Reserved Fund, the interest thereof to be applied to maintaining the building, the schools, and general objects of the Academy.

Which, on the 14th of January, were unanimously adopted, and from thence became Law.

The writer was unavoidably detained from the meeting; and at which the following was passed :

"WHEREAS, We have been informed that a majority of the Trustees are desirous of reconveying their trust to the Academy, as soon as the funds of the Institution are in a state to make such a step safe and judicious; and

"WHEREAS, To insure perfect harmony and unity, it is desirable that the building proposed to be erected, should be erected by the Council : Therefore,

"*Resolved*, That the Trustees be requested to reconvey their trust to the Academy, as soon as they shall deem it safe and practicable."

And at a subsequent special " Council Meeting," on the same evening, was reported back to the body the following, as the first Standing Committee for the Fellowship Fund : viz., Messrs. Gray, Suydam, Cassilear, Hicks, Huntington, and Baker. Mr. Gray was made Chairman, Mr. Suydam Treasurer, and Mr. Hicks Secretary.

It is scarcely necessary to say that the Fellowship Fund proved an immense, a wonderful success.

January 12. Died, James Renwick, LL.D., Honorary Member, in the 71st year of his age. Funeral services at Grace Church on the 16th.

January 17. Died, Horace Vernet, Honorary Member, aged 74 years. "Born in the atmosphere of a Court, and inheriting wealth as well as fame, Horace Vernet had to struggle against none of the traditional difficulties which usually beset the way of young artists. He was early taken into the favor of Napoleon I., and was specially patronized by Marie Louise. He painted portraits and composition pieces in vast numbers, always commanding the most liberal prices. On the downfall of Napoleon, he, of course, lost the Court favor, and, disgusted with France because his pictures representing the victories of Napoleon were excluded from the Louvre, he went to Italy, where he lived for many years. At length, however, Vernet was forgiven by Charles X., and called to his Court. Vernet's admiration for Napoleon did not prevent him from painting frescoes on the Louvre in honor of the Bourbon king, who rewarded the facile painter with the appointment of Director of the French Art School at Rome. When Louis Philippe was made king, the lucky Vernet was again called to Paris, and, among other works there painted, with his own unaided brush, were the numerous pictures of scenes in the French wars in Africa, which cover the walls of the Constantine Gallery, at Versailles. Louis Philippe was so much pleased with this feat that he offered to make Vernet a peer of France; but the artist, like his grandfather, who had declined a similar honor from Louis XV., preferred to remain a simple citizen.

February 9. Mr. Cummings announced to the Council the death, on the 7th, of Francis W. Edmonds, Academician, and offered the following:

Whereupon, it was

"*Resolved*, That whereas it has pleased our Almighty Father, in His all-wise providence, to remove from us our early friend and member, Francis W. Edmonds. And while we bow in submission to the will of that Providence which ruleth all things, we cannot but deeply lament that, by his sudden and unexpected death, we have been deprived of a member and friend, whose counsel, in the ripeness of his age and experience, was ever of value to the Institution, and to the younger members of the profession, of which he was so bright an ornament.

"*Resolved*, That in token]of our respect for the deceased, we wear the usual badge of mourning (crape on the left arm) for thirty days. That the Academicians, Associates, Honorary Members and Students of the National Academy of Design, attend the funeral of the deceased as a body.

"*Resolved*, That Mr. Cummings be, and is, requested to prepare a biographical remembrance of the deceased for the Academy, and publication; and that a copy of these resolutions be transmitted to the family of the deceased. That a copy of the same, draped in black, be framed, and placed, as a memento of the deceased, in the Council Room."

To the Council of the National Academy of Design:

GENTLEMEN:—In compliance with your request, as per resolution passed in Council, I submit a brief biographical notice of our deceased brother Artist, Academician, Officer, and Trustee.

FRANCIS W. EDMONDS.

Francis W. Edmonds was, by his election as an Academician of this Institution—*vide* its By-Laws—declared to be a "professional artist;" and truly in excellence he deserved the title, as well as in the fact, "a necessary qualification," that he sold his pictures, and in the regular order of a commercial transaction, received money therefor. Yet, without injustice, it may be said that he was essentially an Amateur Artist, and probably so considered himself. Banking was his ostensible profession, and doubtless his living; Art an accessory.

For the greater portion of the facts contained in this notice the writer is indebted to Judge Edmonds, brother of the deceased.

General Samuel Edmonds, the father of our artist, was born in the City of New-York, and after serving through the whole of the Revolutionary War, and on the dissolution of Washington's army at Newburg, settled on the banks of the Hudson River, at the landing which afterwards became the City of Hudson; living there until his death, which occurred in 1826.

Francis W.'s mother was of the family of the Worths, who originally emigrated from Devonshire, in England, and settled on the Island of Nantucket.

Two of the Worth brothers, Thomas and Shirbael, were of those who founded the City of Hudson.

Francis W., the son of Samuel Edmonds, and the subject of our memoir, was born in the City of Hudson, State of New-York, on the 22d of November, 1806.

Francis W., it is said, was in early childhood of a grave and sedate temperament; this, in after years, in art practice particularly, ripened into that deep pathos, quiet humor, and pithy wit, which was so frequently to be remarked in his works.

When quite young, he evinced a striking tendency for art. His first attempts were made almost as soon as he had learned to use a slate and pencil; and so marked was this tendency in him, that his father took some steps towards binding him as an apprentice to a distinguished firm of engravers, then flourishing in Philadelphia. Before that arrangement was consummated, he was offered by his uncle, the late G. A. Worth, a clerkship in the Tradesmen's Bank in New-York, which was accepted; and Francis, at the age of eighteen, was transferred to the City of New-York, which henceforth, excepting a short interval, became his future home. He remained in various positions in that Bank until 1830, when, arrived at the age of twenty-four, he was called to the Cashiership of the Hudson River Bank in his native place. While Cashier at Hudson, he married Miss Norman, a lady of that place, and by whom he had two children, a son and a daughter: the latter survives him; but his son, who displayed as strong, if not stronger, ability for the Arts than even his father, died at the early age of eighteen. He was a pupil of the writer, who can professionally bear testimony to the accuracy of the Judge's remarks on this point.

Francis W. Edmonds continued in Hudson only until 1832, when he was appointed Cashier to the Leather Manufacturers' Bank in the City of New-York.

He continued his connection with that Bank until 1839, when he was appointed Cashier of the Mechanics' Bank, in which post he continued until the 26th of July, 1855, when he retired from that Bank, and from the banking business.

During his career, Mr. Edmonds ranked high among the bankers of the city, and his opinions were much respected; his ready mastery of the details of accounts, and the soundness of his judgment on money matters, were well-established facts, and fully appreciated. He was one of the first to point out the advantages of a "Clearing House," and was recognized as a leader in that measure; the reputation he enjoyed enabled him to do more, perhaps, than any other towards harmonizing the many differences of opinion existing thereon, and to adjust the delicate details of that organization. He was appointed Chairman of the first Clearing House Committee, and he was twice elected to the responsible office of Chamberlain of the City of New-York.

To return to his art practice, it may be remarked, that it was not until his qualifications as a Banker were fully established and admitted, that he ventured to exhibit his productions under his own name. He had frequently exhibited under a *nom de plume;* and this, perhaps, may explain the mystery and oft cause of astonishment expressed at the excellence of the Banker Artist Edmonds's *first* works in art.

They were not his first works; he had painted for years, and as he had often expressed to the writer, when drawing by his side in the early meetings of the "Academy School," that he in reality devoted as many hours per day to art as the generality of professional artists—viz., as he stated, from 4 to 9 in the morning, and 4 to 10 in the evening.

After leaving the Mechanics' Bank, Mr. Edmonds, with others, established a Bank Note Engraving Company, which afterwards became absorbed in, and formed a part of, the "American Bank Note Engraving Company," now the largest and most complete establishment of the kind in the world. He became its Secretary, and was one of the Directors when he died. Many of his pictures were used as models in that establishment. "The Barn-Yard," "The Sewing-Girl," "The Mechanic," and "Grinding the Scythe," were among the many which therein attracted attention and use.

His early education was no more than that which was afforded by a tolerably good village school; but during his clerkship he studied hard to make up the deficiency, and frequently contributed to the light literature of the day;* though "it was only occasionally, and after dark, that he was thus occupied with his pen;" almost, if not all, his leisure was devoted to painting, and to improving himself in art practice. His performances soon attracted notice; and though he loved the art with his whole soul, he never permitted it to interfere with his "business." (Here the Judge evidently takes the same view of his profession as indicated by the writer.) He, however, gave himself up to it, to the exclusion of all those enjoyments which are ordinarily so powerfully attractive in youth.

In 1836, he brought out one of his pictures at the Annual Exhibition of the Academy of Design—"Sammy the Tailor"—not Hudibras, as the Judge supposes. Fearing that his inexperience and innocent practice in art; his choice of amusement in place of "fast horses" and prodigal expenditure, might jeopard his reputation as a fiscal agent,—which the latter, from precedent, it is presumed, would not,—he entered it in the Catalogue to the benefit of "E. F. Williams;" and under that title he exhibited for several years. He was, however, discovered, and elected an Associate of the Academy, and some years afterwards an Academician; and he was ever after received among the artists of the country as their "fellow." He appears in the records of 1845 as the Recording Secretary of the National Academy of Design, and many times as one of the Council.

The only opportunity he ever had of studying art, "beyond the leisure of his business as a banker," was afforded him on a brief visit to Italy—on the occasion of his breaking down in health under the pressure of his labors in the examination of the accounts of the Manhattan Bank, which he undertook in addition to his regular business as Cashier of the Mechanics' Bank.

F. W. Edmonds was likewise a Director in the Harlem Railroad Company, a Director in the American Art Union, was one of the original or old "Sketch

* The Biography of F. Agate is among the number of his productions.

Club," was one of the founders of the "Century Club," and was, with Cummings, Sturges, and Leupp, Trustee of the property of the National Academy of Design, when it was so placed in trust; and although in that capacity he acted merely advisory, (Mr. Cummings having been placed in the entire care of the trust,) yet his advice was always valuable; and he may therefore be considered as entitled to his share in the making of $60,000 therein, which formed the nucleus of the Academy property, and the means of building, though since so greatly enlarged by public munificence.

Mr. Edmonds was of a warm and affectionate nature, but by no means demonstrative of his feelings. He was very sensitive, and very shy of showing that he was so. He was strong in his prejudices, and equally so in his friendships; was intimately known to but few, but by that few he was very highly esteemed.

Mr. Edmonds died as suddenly as unexpected, at his country residence at Bronxville, on the 7th of February, 1863, in the fifty-seventh year of his age, most likely of disease of the heart. He had arisen very early in the morning, as is presumed to visit the room of his children, who had been sick. Feeling probably suddenly unwell, he had taken a seat in an easy-chair near his own bed—in that position, *dead*, he was shortly found by his wife, who arose, in consequence of his prolonged absence, to inquire the cause. That lady, his second wife, was Miss Lord, daughter of Mr. Joseph Lord, of this city, by whom he had six children, who survive. His two youngest are sons, now only eight and six years of age; and they are both said to display remarkable talent; the eldest as a musician, and the younger as an artist.

The following happy allusion to the talents and memory of Edmonds is extracted from the report of D. Huntington, Esq., President of the National Academy of Design, in his *exposé* to the Academy of May 13th, 1863:

" He first exhibited, in 1836, a small picture called ' Sammy the Tailor,' attributed in the Catalogue to E. F. Williams. It was so admirably painted as to excite the attention of the artists; and on inquiry, it was discovered that it was painted by a bank clerk by the name of Edmonds. He exhibited for two or three years under the name of Williams, partly to avoid the suspicion of neglecting his bank duties, and partly to test his powers of winning a reputation. In 1838 he was elected an Associate, and ever after exhibited under his own name, and ranked as a distinguished artist of the country.

" His talents were certainly great, and had he been willing to relinquish the engrossing duties of a Bank Cashier, he might have attained the highest excellence in the department of humorous and familiar subjects, which, notwithstanding the counter-claims of a business life, he cultivated with much eminent success. His masculine mind gave great value to his counsel in the Academy, whose interests he faithfully studied; and his estimable character as a man will long endear him to those who were privileged to enjoy his intimate friendship. Resolutions highly complimentary to the deceased were passed by the Harlem Railroad Company, by the Century Club, and by other societies of which he was a member.

" Thus has passed to the grave one of the brightest ornaments of Art of our city. His funeral was numerously attended by the artists and other distinguished residents of the city."

He was buried in the village of Bronxville.
His exhibited works are:

    1836. " Sammy the Tailor."
    1837. " The Skinner"—" Dominie Sampson."
    1837. " Ichabob Crane Teaching Katrina Van Tassell Psalmody."
    1837. " Comforts of Old Age." All under the title of E. F. Williams.
    1839. He exhibited, under his own name, " The Penny Paper" and
         " Commodore Trunnion."
    1840. " The City and Country Beaux"—" Sparking."
    1841. Nothing.

1842. "Italian Mendicants"—"The Bashful Cousin."
1843. "Stealing Milk."
1844. "Beggar's Petition"—"Image Peddler"—"Sam Weller."
1844. "Vesuvius"—"Aqueducts at Rome"—"Florence."
1845. "Facing the Enemy"—"The New Scholar."
1846. "Lord Glenallan and Elspeth Macklebackit."
1846. "Spleepy Student"—"Wood Scene."
1847. "The Orphan's Funeral."
1848. "First Earnings"—"Trial of Patience."
1849. Nothing.
1850. "The Two Culprits"—"Courtship in New Amsterdam."
1851. "What can a Young Lassie do wi' an Auld Man?"
1852. "The Speculator."
1853. "Passage from Burns."
1854. "Taking the Census."
1855. Nothing.
1856. "The Thirsty Drover"—"All Talk and No Work."
1857. "Time to Go."
1858. "The Windmill"—"The Pan of Milk"—"Bargaining."
1859. "The New Bonnet."
1860. ⎫
1861. ⎬
1862. ⎭

February 14. Died, Alvan Fisher, Honorary Member, at his residence in Dedham, Mass. A landscape painter of merit. Whereupon it was

"*Resolved*, That the Academy hear with deep regret of the death of their late Honorary Member, Alvan Fisher, of Boston, who, by his numerous pictures of rural life, gave the first impulse to that department, and contributed much to the advancement of American Art in its earliest history.

"*Resolved*, That we sincerely sympathize with the large circle of his friends and relatives in the loss of this amiable gentleman, and that the Secretary be requested to communicate these resolutions to the family of the deceased."

The number of works of art on exhibition during the winter, the auction sales, and almost fabulous prices obtained thereat, surpassed all previous years.

The paintings of the International Institute were not all sold at the time, as previously written. Some remained over undisposed of, and it was only finally closed this winter.

February 20. T. Addison Richards, Academician, made a sale by auction of his pictures, studies and sketches, numbering some 141 productions, netting the artist handsome and remunerating prices. The product of the sale was some $4,000.

February 23. On motion of Mr. Cummings, a special meeting of the Academicians was called to receive the resignation of the Trustees, and the BOOKS, PAPERS, ACCOUNTS, MONEY, &c., under their charge. The accounts had been audited by the Trustees and by the Council, and were ready to be presented to the Academicians at the General Meeting.

At the same meeting of the Council it was

"*Resolved*, That it is expedient we build on the lots we now own at the corner of Twenty-third Street and Broadway, and that a Building Committee of five be appointed, to report to the Council at its earliest convenience."

And Messrs. Cummings, Gray, Baker, and Kensett were chosen. Mr. Huntington, President, was added as Chairman of said Committee.

March 9. Was held the Special Meeting, to receive the report of the Trustees, which was as follows:

Jonathan Sturges, Thomas S. Cummings, and Asher B. Durand, surviving Trustees of Jonathan Sturges, Charles M. Leupp, Thomas S. Cummings, Francis W. Edmonds and Asher B. Durand,

To the National Academy of Design:

Report:

That said Trustees received from the previous Trust—A balance, left after the final settlement of accounts, of $3,290.13; and that they have received on account of the sale of the property 663 Broadway, $50,000; for rental of lots on Twenty-third Street, $215; interest receivable, $8,872.77; and from sundries, $54.60. Making a total of $62,432.50.

And that they have paid and disbursed as follows:—To Mr. William Niblo, on account of the purchase of the land, $20,000; Interest, taxes, assessments, and general expenses, $8,492.02; Indebtednesses of the Academy, outside the Trust accounts, $5,630.48; Sundries, $2.50. Making a total of $34,372.50; and leaving a cash balance on hand, herewith handed in, of $28.060.

The further assets are, $10,000 derivable from the mortgage yet unpaid on 663 Broadway.

The $20,000 paid is made returnable from Mr. Niblo, to assist in the erection of the building, as per his contract, on file. Making the available building assets $58,060.

Respectfully,

THOMAS S. CUMMINGS,

Treasurer and Trustee.

Whereupon, on motion, it was *Resolved*, That

"WHEREAS, The Trustees of the National Academy of Design have submitted their resignation of their Trust; and

"WHEREAS, The accounts of said Trust have been audited by Mr. Sturges, Trustee, and are therefore satisfactory to the Council: Therefore,

"*Resolved*, That the resignation of said Trust, and the resignation of said Trustees, be, and is hereby accepted by the Academy; and the said Trustees are hereby fully and honorably discharged therefrom; and the President and Secretary of the National Academy of Design are by this authorized and directed to execute, deliver, and attach the Corporate Seal of the Academy to all papers necessary to fully discharge the said Trustees, and each of them, from all liabilities, of whatsoever name or nature, growing out of, or by reason of said Trust, and their and each of their acts or doings as said Trustees."

The papers had been submitted by the Academy to Mr. Tracy for his opinion, which proved satisfactory, and a full satisfaction piece was executed to the Trustees, discharging them forever; and a vote of thanks was tendered to Jonathan Sturges, Esq., for his long and faithful services as Trustee; and it was

"*Resolved,* That Mr. Sturges be requested to sit to any one of the Academicians he may select, for a portrait, to be preserved in the Gallery of the Academy, as a lasting testimony of our respect for his character, and gratitude for his services."

Which was transmitted, and the following answer returned:

T. ADDISON RICHARDS, Esq.,
          Corresponding Secretary N. A. D.:
      DEAR SIR:—I should be glad to convey through you to the Academy, in suitable words, the gratification its resolution of the 9th, which you inclose to me, has afforded me. But this I cannot do. I think the Academicians will understand my feelings better than I can express them. I cannot consent that the Academy should feel under any obligations to me. I have been doubly compensated for all I have done by the pleasant intercourse I have so long been permitted to enjoy with so many of its members. I can truly say that my connection with art and artists has been a source of great profit to myself and family, in the refining influences it has had upon us all for many, many years.
      I am getting to be amongst the seniors of your friends, and I must congratulate you that such a host of new ones are coming forward to aid you in completing what I trust the exertions of your late Trustees have been somewhat instrumental in laying the foundation for. I should have preferred that the Academy had named an artist to paint a portrait of myself, which it has so kindly asked me to sit for; but since the choice is left to me, it seems most fitting, from my long association with your late excellent President, A. B. Durand, Esq., that the portrait should be painted by him. If he is willing to undertake it, I shall be happy to sit to him, at his convenience.
      With my best wishes for the Academy and its individual members,
                    I am, dear Sir,
                    Most truly yours,
                              JONATHAN STURGES.

March 16.   The Schools closed for the season.   The attendance had been good, the order perfect—no premiums. A pleasing remembrancer was awarded by the Students to Professor Cummings.

March 16.   A resolution was passed that —— dollars be appropriated to procure a portrait of the late Charles M. Leupp, Esq., Trustee, and Mr. Gray was appointed to paint it. The work was admirably executed. The Council, in token of their appreciation of the faithfulness of the task performed, voted Mr. Gray the thanks of the meeting. The preservation of the semblance of that faithful friend of the artists and the Institution must ever prove a boon to all.

March 16.   The former Building Committee appear to

have been superseded, and it was *Resolved*, That a Committee of three be appointed to recommend an architect and a plan for a building, both front and interior, and to report to the Council at the next meeting.

Messrs. Gray, Baker, and Kensett were appointed said Committee, which Committee, on the 23d, unanimously reported on Mr. Peter B. Wight; and Mr. Wight was then appointed Architect.

More doubt arose as to the desired extent of the purchase on 23d Street and 4th Avenue; and Messrs. Huntington and Cummings were appointed a Committee to negotiate with Mr. ——— for the purchase of the two adjoining lots to the property on 4th Avenue. They reported that he asked $18,000 each for the lots and building improvements, and was unwilling to sell at any price.

The report was accepted, but the purchase was not entertained.

March 23. There appeared further doubt on the building location, and Messrs. Gignoux and Cummings were appointed a Committee to negotiate the sale of the property of the Academy on the corner of 23d Street and 4th Avenue. The Committee reported, on the 15th April, That the parties who had appeared the most anxious to purchase the property had declined it; and although the auctioneer was sanguine of a sale, the Committee felt constrained to report "that there appeared no prospect of an immediate sale at a price consistent with the views of the Academy," and begged to be discharged. They were so discharged, and the subject dropped.

April 6. It was *Resolved*, That further delay in the matter of the Academy building is *inexpedient*, and the Special Committee on *sale* and purchase of property be instructed, and are hereby directed, to report definitely to the Council on Tuesday evening next. The subject to be made the special object of the meeting.

April 8. The price of the Exhibition Catalogue, in consequence of the increase of price in paper and labor, attendant on the war, was raised from 12 to 15 cents.

April 14. Was opened to the public the 38th Annual Exhibition, 625 Broadway, closing on the 24th June—62 working days, averaging $83.93 per day—471 productions.

April 18. An actual commencement was made towards the building corner of 23d Street and Broadway. A contract had been signed for digging the foundation, and on the morning of the 20th, at 6 A. M., actually entry was made in the earth, by Daniel Huntington, Esq., President, lifting the first shovel-full. On the 13th June estimates

were handed \in and signed, and on the 27th June Mr.
Huntington again commenced the work by laying the first
stone, assisted by Mr. Coddington, the mason for the
building.

During the winter was sold, at the Derby Gallery, the
copies of "Cole's Voyage of Life," Stearn's Series, and
other works. The sale was considered a successful one.
The Washington Series (four pictures) brought $3,250—
probably one-third more than given for them on the original purchase. The Voyage of Life—that is, the copies
—$2,350.

The collection of paintings of a Philadelphia gentleman
were sold at auction, and said to have realized $45,000.

Exhibition and sale of pictures seemed to be in high
ascendency and favor.

Mr. Cummings reported having received the final payment of $10,000 on the Mozart Hall property, and the
conclusion of that sale.

April 29.

REPORT OF BUILDING COMMITTEE.

The Building Committee, which now offers its report to the Council, would
respectfully beg their attention to a few preliminary remarks.

Early in the Winter, when the "Fellowship Fund" was instituted, its direct design on the part of its originators was, that this Fund should be devoted
to the perfecting of the building.

It was not contemplated by any one that the whole Fund was to be used in
erecting a building; and more especially as they doubted the possibility of
raising so large a sum as we now have subscribed.

It was supposed that 30 or 40 thousand dollars was as high as they dared to
hope for; and we mention this to show that they expected to assist the Trustees
to the amount of 25 or 30 thousand dollars to build, instead of a plain brick
building, one suitable to the public needs and our own tastes as a piece of
architecture.

This was the height of our ambition to be reached; if the Fund failed, by
still greater exertions and sacrifices. But the Fund proving an eminent success, established us at once in the fact that we were certain to be able to erect
such a front as we needed; predicated, however, on our former ideas as to
cost, extent, elaboration, &c.

These ideas, in short, until this Committee was formed, had ever been, that
about 30,000 dollars, in addition to the cost proposed to be spent by the Trustees, would effect our object.

The Architect whom you have selected also gave his written estimate that
about 80,000 dollars would cover the expense.

In selecting a plan, therefore, we have deemed it our duty to take this sum as
a limit, especially as you must reflect that we shall have many expenditures
not enumerated by the Trustees for their plan at 50,000 dollars; for instance,
about 20 per cent. on the amount of our expenditures.

The engine and apparatus for heating;

The furniture and fittings;

The high cost for digging the ground, and the probable necessity for driv-
ing piles for a foundation, &c., &c., which cannot be less than —————
dollars.

We beg, therefore, to impress on you the absolute necessity, even with all the means we have, and can reasonably expect to get, of cutting our new coat according to our cloth; and to add, that it seems clear to us that we are abundantly able to erect a building in every respect superior to the ideas entertained by any of us previous to the rather elevating "sweep of the Fund."

In the minds of the Committee, there has been little, if any, variation from the first, that the plan which we would offer for your adoption should be—all these things duly considered. That known among us as Mr. Wight's second plan—modified in respect to the ornament over the cornice, the height of the entrance, and the openings in the first story.

We cannot but feel, while expressing the greatest obligations to Mr. Wight for his interest in furnishing a third plan, which in some respects is superior to the others, in our judgment, that in order to compass this one, we should have either to expend considerably more, or leave off some of the ornaments which recommend it; while, with the second plan, we have the great satisfaction of a very general approval by our members and the public, and a conviction that it can be built as it is drawn within the limit of our means.

The ornament of the third plan can be substituted over the cornice of the second. The entrance can be raised by raising the whole story one or two feet. The door and long window of the first story can easily be reconciled to the different uses assigned to that story.

With these alterations, we very respectfully submit Plan No. 2.

Your obedient servants,

HENRY PETERS GRAY,
J. F. KENSETT,
GEO. A. BAKER,
Building Committee.

Thus, from June, 1860, to April, 1863, was consumed in the consideration of fronts—viz., nearly three years—costing interest on the purchase money on the land, $10,000, and payment for plans of some $500 more.

May —. The extraordinary high price obtained at the numerous sales of paintings during the Winter had naturally excited explanation as to the cause—which was generally attributed to the inflation of the currency—" Greenbacks."

That would not appear to be the only cause for the unprecedented rise. Witness the following, where " Greenbacks" are not in favor—where gold yet reigns—cut from an English paper:

A REMARKABLE SALE OF PICTURES.

Mr. Bicknell's Collection sold in London for nearly $300,000.

A remarkable auction sale of English pictures and sculpture, forming the collection of Mr. Elhanan Bicknell. The prices obtained for these home productions of British artists far exceeded anything of the kind before known in England. The *Morning Star* says that Mr. Bicknell was a private Englishman, a man of comparatively obscure position, engaged at one time in mere trade, not even pretending to resemble a Genoese or Florentine merchant prince, but simply and absolutely a Londoner of the middle class, actively occupied in business, who, nevertheless, had brought together a picture gallery which would have done no discredit to Lorenzo the Magnificent.

Nearly ninety thousand dollars were given at this sale for pictures by Turner, some of which had been obtained by the late owner direct from the hand of the artist himself, and some of which had never been exhibited before. Devon, Cumberland, and Northumbrian scenery were among the subjects of his pencil, put up at this sale, with his Venetian scenes and glimpses of Dutch towns, and his "Rock of Ehrenbreitstein." The last named picture brought 1,800 guineas; the "Port Ruysdael" (the ninth picture of Turner's Dutch series exhibited at the Royal Academy in 1827, and bought by Mr. Bicknell,) sold for 1,900 guineas; Turner's "Palestrina," a magnificent gallery picture, (also bought by Mr. Bicknell in 1830,) for 1,900 guineas; and his "Antwerp," for 2,510 guineas.

Several pictures by Landseer, some of which were painted expressly for Mr. Bicknell, were also sold at large prices. "The Prize Calf" brought 1,800 guineas; the "Two Dogs," 2,300; the "Highland Shepherd with two Dogs," (painted for Mr. Bicknell in 1850,) for 2,230 guineas.

Clarkson Stanfield's "Lago di Garda," painted for Mr. Bicknell in 1838, brought 820 guineas; and his "Beilstem on the Moselle," first exhibited at the Royal Academy in 1837, 1,500 guineas.

A picture by Roberts was sold for 505 guineas; illustrations by Stothard of Boccaccio's "Decameron" sold for 245 guineas; Roberts's "Tyre and Sidon" for 710 guineas; and Leslie's celebrated picture, "The Heiress," sold for 1,260 guineas.

In all, one hundred and forty-five lots were sold, yielding the enormous amount of £58,600 ($293,000), by far the largest ever produced in England from a like number of pictures. This sale was to be followed immediately by another, comprising a splendid collection of drawings in water-colors, also formed by Mr. Bicknell.

May 13. Was held the Annual Meeting; yet in the temporary accommodations, Cummings's Studios in Thirteenth Street; 37 Academicians present.

D. Huntington, Esq., the President, read his

ANNUAL REPORT.

The past year has been marked by decisive events in the history of the Academy. At the first meeting of the Council the subject of the building was revived, and it was apparent that, to proceed with the plans of the Trustees, the building must be very plain. The Trustees declined to proceed unless the Council approved; and the Council refused to sanction a plain building, being desirous of adopting a beautiful design some time since selected by them. We were at a dead lock. The discussion of this subject led to the idea of raising a fund for the building, and resulted in the "Fellowship Fund."

This project, formed simultaneously in the minds of several members, was considered at a caucus held at the "Century Club." A rough draft was drawn up; the founders of the Academy were advised with. Invaluable suggestions were made by Professors Morse and Cummings—suggestions which guarded the rights of the Academicians to the sovereign control of the Institution, avoided the danger of individual liability, and more carefully defined the privileges of the subscribers. The plan was remodeled and perfected at successive meetings, and resulted in a statement and agreement, which was presented to the Academicians for their approval, and signed by nearly all the members in December last. This paper is preserved in the records of the Fellowship Fund Committee, and I will only recall to your recollection that by it subscribers of $100 were to be entitled to 15 season tickets, instead of 5, as afterwards determined.

That $300 was to entitle to perpetual Fellowship, instead of $500, as at present; and that the following modest paragraph was appended:
"It is also agreed that subscriptions shall not be payable unless the aggregate amount of $10,000 is subscribed before the 1st January, 1864."

While this matter was in progress, another subject came up, which ought to be explained. In conversation with the Trustees, it was discovered that a majority of them were desirous of relinquishing their trust, if it could be done with safety to the finances of the Academy. This proposal came first from our late member and Trustee, Mr. Edmonds, was seconded by Messrs. Sturges and Durand, and acceded to by Mr. Cummings, after deliberately weighing the consequences. Thus the Trustees unanimously resigned. This act, voluntarily performed, to insure harmony in the prosecution of our plans for building, naturally called forth marked expressions of gratitude to the Trustees for their many years of faithful labor. As nearly all of them were our fellow-members, this expression took gracefully the form of a vote of thanks to Mr. Sturges, and a resolution to procure his portrait. An appropriation was also made to procure the portrait of that generous man and friend, the late Charles M. Leupp. Compliments to the other Trustees, who are of our own body—as it were, in the family—ended in a pithy speech from the Vice-President; and I may add, confidentially, in a bottle or two of Champagne, drank to the health of the retiring Trustees.

    *   *   *   *   *   *   *

You are well aware of the laws we passed for the conduct of the Fellowship Fund, and of the earnest manner in which the Committee have labored, seconded by many others in and out of the Academy.

The name of Robert Hoe, for $1,000, obtained by Mr. Kensett, stands at the head of the list. Others rapidly followed for the same amount; among the earliest of which was the honored name of our founder, Professor Morse. The full report of the Fellowship Fund Committee will be read to you by its Chairman. Yet I will not dismiss the subject without saying that you owe a lasting debt of gratitude to that Committee for their indefatigable labors. Having been a member of it, I ought not to speak of their devotion to your interests; of the zeal with which they have hunted the men of taste and fortune from their homes to Wall Street, and from Wall Street again to their homes, till they pinned them to a Fellowship; or the calm audacity with which they held the restless Clubman by the button till he enrolled; or the effrontery with which they invaded even the sacred privacy of the evening domestic circle, and pressed a man's wife and daughters to inveigle him to a signature. Propriety forbids my enlarging; but I will say, you cannot too highly esteem the services of the officers of that Committee.

Whether it be the vigor, promptness and enthusiasm of the Chairman, the inexhaustible energies of the Secretary, overloaded with endless lists, letters, circulars and records, or the exact and faithful labors of the Treasurer, whose quiet studies among the moonlight bays have been deserted for ceaseless visits to the banks, with his pockets crammed with checks and certificates of the Treasury.

The Council have chosen Mr. Wight as architect of the building, and he is now engaged in slightly modifying the design—the third he has made—which they have mainly approved.

The work is begun, and it may be hoped that before another Annual Meeting your long-cherished dreams will stand out in the sunlight a beautiful and solid reality.

    *   *   *   *   *   *   *   *

Finally, gentlemen, permit me to urge upon you to continue your zealous efforts to carry on to perfection the work so well begun for our building; to devise means to establish a thorough, complete system in our Academic schools, and to stand firmly to those principles on which this Institution has been founded, and on which, by God's blessing, I trust it will stand, with honor and usefulness, to the latest generations.

D. HUNTINGTON,
Pres't National Academy.

A debt referred to in the purchase and proposed building, and which the Council were not willing to adopt, ($50,000,) may be thus explained:

The Trustees, by the deed of trust, were ordered "to purchase a site and erect a building"—two objects combined. The means at their disposal, prospectively and otherwise, after paying off the indebtedness of the Institution, was about $60,000. That, it was clear, would not enable them to pay cash for both. They therefore purchased the ground at $50,000, all on credit, on mortgages of ten years, and proposed to erect the building within the cash means left them. The object in the design of the building was, first, for the internal conveniences of the Institution. That received the utmost and unanimous commendation of the Academy—(galleries same as now). The next—stability and security to visitors, extent, &c.—for such no expense was spared; and the only place left on which economy could be exercised without injury, was the exterior. That, therefore, they made of plain, simple, though elegant proportioned brick and brown stone trimmed work.

The ascent on 23d St. being much the same as now, except as to carving, and the whole upper part exclusively devoted to Art. To meet the future maintenance of the Institution, they placed a line of stores on Fourth Avenue, which it was supposed would bring in $5,000 per annum, pay the interest on the mortgage, and leave something for assistance towards the support of the Art department.

That plan of interest and support the Trustees rigidly adhered to. Hence the difficulties.

The plainness of the fronts—the difference, and the only difference, that existed, or ever had existed, between the Academy and the Trustees.

REPORT BY THE *FELLOWSHIP FUND COMMITTEE* TO THE
ACADEMY.

GENTLEMEN:

When we consider the success of the Committee in raising the proposed sum of one hundred thousand dollars, its inception and earlier efforts will appear to you very modestly proportioned.

We beg you, nevertheless, to look back for a few weeks only to the proper birthday of the scheme, with which its progenitors had quietly labored till it was nearly ready to be brought forward.

The Academy amended its Constitution to make the provisions of the Fellowship Fund a part of its laws, on the 14th of January, 1863. The Council elected your Committee on the same day, and on the 9th of February (twenty-five days) we had $39,100 subscribed. If we could present to you, even remotely, a faithful diary of our proceedings—the humble aspirations towards fifteen or twenty thousand dollars, and the confessed fears of reaching even that modest sum—the occasional enthusiasm which held out fifty thousand as a possibility; and the flattering joke, with which we allowed ourselves to be cajoled, that we might want and might get seventy-five thousand—it would be not a little amusing to find that they finally resulted in a formal resolution to raise one hundred thousand dollars.

Gentlemen, we confess ourselves the most astonished parties in the matter, when we announce to you "*that we have done it.*" The subscription-lists this day promise that amount, at your disposal, through this Committee; and they have only to add that, in their opinion, the virgin and generous soil they have turned in such luxurious furrows is by no means exhausted. We believe the capacity of the yield of our fertile citizens, so far from being measured by this success, that it is only inferred.

We do not doubt that there are yet one thousand persons who stand ready, on proper application, to furnish one hundred dollars each for our object. Are there not fifty of us who can get twenty names each, and thus accomplish a work so fairly opened?

If your Committee, which has so devoted its time, energies and money with perhaps as great a sacrifice as could be expected, feel this—if they believe that only themselves are exhausted, may they not ask co-operation and stimulus from your exertions, which will renew their vigor and make our victory complete?

For the Committee.

HENRY PETERS GRAY,

Chairman.

Mr. Cummings read his Annual Report as Treasurer.

The Treasury appeared to have been short during the year; for it opens with a loan, and subsequent payment to the Treasurer.

The total amount received into the Treasury under the different heads named in the Report, including that from Trustees, and final payment on the Mozart Hall sale.. $67,946 00

The offset consists in a deposit in the Life and Trust Company of $28,000; a payment on the mortgage on the property in fee on Twenty-third Street, of $24,000; general expenses, &c., of the year, of $5,606.66; and a balance of $10,340.34....... $67,946 00

THOMAS S. CUMMINGS.

The Treasurer of the Fellowship Fund Committee read his Report, which was as follows:

That from the 31st of January, 1863, to date, he had received from various members of the Fund the sum of 54,800 dollars.

That he had invested, under the order of the Committee, in the Sub-Treasury of the United States, as a temporary loan, at 5 per cent., 50,000 dollars.

Leaving a balance in the Bank of 4,800 dollars.

JAMES A. SUYDAM,

Treasurer.

Mr. Daniel Huntington was elected President; Henry Peters Gray, Vice-President; T. Addison Richards, Corresponding Secretary; Junius B. Stearns, Recording Secretary; Thomas S. Cummings, Treasurer.

Messrs. Kensett, Hicks, Suydam, Thompson, Whitteridge, and Baker, who, with the officers, form the Council for the next year.

Thomas Le Clerc, J. Q. A. Ward, J. B. Brevoort, W. J. Hennessy, J. G. Brown, W. P. W. Dana, John Rogers, were elected Academicians; and George H. Hall, Eugene Benson, John La Farge, A. H. Ritchie, Victor Nehlig, Herman Feuchsel, A. H. Warren, Eliu Vedder, Associates.

J. Q. A. Ward and George H. Yewell, Associate Members, on the Hanging Committee.

May 18. Mr. Rockwood, the distinguished photographer, offered, through one of the Board of Council, to photograph the Academicians, quarto size, to form an art portrait volume, and to present a copy to the Academy, provided the members would give him the opportunity.

The generous offer was accepted, and arrangements were made to induce the Academicians to give sittings to the artist.

Here, certainly, is one of the wonderful effects—one of the advantages of the art. Instantaneous portraiture, &c., &c.—by it may be handed down to futurity, in compact and undeniable truthfulness, the portraits of all. The battlefields—nay, almost the battles—have been given by Brady; and the very doings in the streets, by Anthony's instantaneous views—everything that may be interesting to future generations.

May 18. At a meeting of the Council, "the Minutes of the Annual Meeting were read and approved."

Rather a novelty in legislation.

And on June the 1st, the following resolution was offered:

" WHEREAS, It has become obvious to our subscribers, as well as to ourselves, that the ground now owned by the Academy is too contracted—if not for our immediate convenience, certainly for future developments of our usefulness:

"It is moved, that a Committee of three (3) be, and hereby is, appointed—who are instructed to arrange the preliminaries for the purchase of the two adjoining lots, north of our property, (on Fourth Avenue,) at a price not exceeding 25,000 dollars, and to report as soon as possible to the Council."

It *was not* carried.

June 10. A grand reception was given to E. Leutze, Academician, at Dusseldorf, by the Artists of that city. As the guest, he was received at the "Garden gate" by a band of music, and escorted in a triumphal manner until he arrived at the spot where "the Artists were standing to receive him." For a full description of this enthusiastic reception the reader is referred to the *New - York Illustrated News* of July 1, 1863.

June 15. Cummings and Gray were appointed a Superintending Building Committee.

June 18. The Council adjourned *sine die*, and did not reassemble until October.

August 21. The *Evening Post* records one of the results of the war as follows:

"DRAWING—DRAFT.

"Among the persons drafted yesterday in the Fifteenth Ward were TEN ARTISTS, as follows: W. P. W. Dana, W. J. Hennessy, Daniel Huntington, William Hart, John O. B. Inman, John Pope, A. Bierstadt, J. E. Griffith, George H. Hall, Theodore Pine."

The following note of the death of Lord Lyndhurst, son of Copley, the Artist, may possess interest:

"This aged peer died on the 12th instant, in his ninety-second year. He was of American birth; one of a number which must be now very small, born in Massachusetts while that was a British colony. His father was John S. Copley, a painter of note, who is best known by his 'Death of Lord Chatham,' which is now in one of the great public galleries of London. The painter was drawn to England by a desire to prosecute his art. His son, who was born May 21st, 1772, sailed for England with his mother and sisters, May 27th, 1775, when he was just three years old.

"Young Copley was educated at Trinity College, Cambridge, and was called to the Bar in 1804. Before this year he had visited the United States, and used the occasion to pay a visit to General Washington. Some time after his return he entered political life, under Tory auspices, though he had, earlier, manifested liberal tendencies. His promotion was rapid. He was made Sergeant-at-Law in 1813; became Chief Justice of Chester in 1818; was Solicitor-General from 1819 to 1823; Attorney-General, 1823 to 1826; and Master of the Rolls from 1826 to 1827. On the retirement of the Earl of Eldon in 1827 he was constituted Lord Chancellor of the Empire, when he attained his peerage by patent (under the title of Baron Lyndhurst) dated April 27, 1827. He resigned the Chancellorship in 1830 to resume it in December, 1834, for a short period. For the third time he was appointed to this post in September, 1841, from which he finally retired in July, 1846. During the interval after his first withdrawal (1830) he held the place of Lord Chief Baron of the Exchequer."

The *London* "*Times*" thus refers to the Royal Academy of London, after which, to a great degree, the National Academy was fashioned:

"The Royal Commission appointed to consider the best means of improving the Royal Academy has presented its report. It recommends that the forty Academicians should be raised to sixty, among whom should be eight Architects and ten Laymen; that the Associates should be increased by thirty, and have a vote in the governing body; that the President should be elected by the governing body, and be assisted by a Council of eleven; that an honorary class should be added of Artists from all countries; and that another should be formed of Art-workmen of distinguished eminence. The Academicians, moreover, are to exhibit only four pictures instead of eight, and the Academy should either have the whole of the National Gallery or migrate to Burlington House."

Are they, too, getting Democratic? Mechanics to be put on a footing with Royal Academicians! Soon, indeed, will the poetry of Art be of the past; and this, too, to emanate from England, the stronghold of Art Aristocracy! *Que.* Is it not all a joke?

October 12. At the first meeting of the Council held after the vacation, it was *Resolved* to have a public demonstration on the occasion of laying the corner-stone of the new building of the Academy.

Cummings, Gray, Hicks, Baker, and Richards were appointed a Committee to carry it into effect; and the following notice was issued:

"THE NEW ACADEMY EDIFICE, CORNER OF TWENTY-THIRD STREET AND FOURTH AVENUE.

"The Academicians, Associates, Fellows, Honorary Members, and Students of the National Academy of Design, Members of the Press, and the Artists of the city generally, are hereby invited (*without other notice*) to assist in the Celebration of the Laying of the CORNER-STONE of the New Academy Edifice; and are requested to meet the COUNCIL at two o'clock, in the afternoon of Wednesday, the 21st inst., at the 'Century Club,' 45 East 15th Street, between Union Square and Irving Place—to proceed thence in a body to the Academy grounds, at the corner of 23d Street and Fourth Avenue, where the Exercises will commence at 3 o'clock, P. M.

"Should the weather be stormy, the ceremony will take place at the same hour, and in the same order, on the first fair day thereafter.

"By order.

"T. ADDISON RICHARDS,

"*Cor. Secretary N. A.*"

National Academy of Design.

MDCCCLXIII.

ORDER OF EXERCISES,

AT THE CEREMONY OF THE

Laying of the Corner-Stone

OF THE

NEW ACADEMY EDIFICE,

At the corner of Twenty-Third Street and Fourth Avenue

(*At 3 o'clock, P. M., Wednesday, October 21st.*)

INVOCATION, by the Rev. FRANCIS VINTON, D. D.

MUSIC.

INTRODUCTORY REMARKS, by the PRESIDENT of the Academy.

ADDRESS, by PARKE GODWIN, Esq.

MUSIC.

REMARKS, by Professor S. F. B. MORSE, Ex-President of the Academy.

MUSIC.

ADDRESS, by WILLIAM CULLEN BRYANT, Esq.

MUSIC.

ADDRESS, by Hon. GEORGE BANCROFT.

MUSIC.

ADDRESS, by the Rev. H. W. BELLOWS, D. D.

MUSIC.

The Laying of the Corner-Stone,

Preceded by the offering of a SILVER TROWEL to the President of the Academy, by the Builders, through the Architect,

P. B. WIGHT, Esq.

MUSIC.

ADDRESS, by Rev. E. H. CHAPIN, D. D.

MUSIC.

VOLUNTARY ADDRESSES.

Committee of Arrangements.

THOMAS S. CUMMINGS,	HENRY PETERS GRAY,
THOMAS HICKS,	GEORGE A. BAKER,

T. ADDISON RICHARDS.

The writer had collected the material for this entry; but the more perfectly-arranged description, speeches, &c., &c., collated by T. Addison Richards, the Secretary, as published for the Academy, and for which he received their vote of thanks, render its use undesirable; and he avails himself of the much more perfect copy of his friend, who has his acknowledgments.

The tender allusion therein to one who, but a short moment after, was no more, is used, to insert the little memento published to his memory by the writer; and which closes this record.

CEREMONY

OF THE

LAYING OF THE CORNER-STONE

OF THE NEW EDIFICE

OF THE

NATIONAL ACADEMY OF DESIGN,

Twenty-Third Street and Fourth Avenue, New-York,

WEDNESDAY, OCTOBER 21, 1863.

PREPARED BY T. ADDISON RICHARDS,

Corresponding Secretary of the Academy.

THE site of the beautiful edifice now being erected for the National Academy of Design was purchased in the Autumn of 1860, from Mr. William Niblo, at a cost of fifty thousand dollars.

Numerous designs were about that time, and at the solicitation of the Academy, submitted by most of the leading architects of the city, among which was the admirable plan of P. B. Wight, Esq., which is now, with some modifications, being so successfully executed.

At the time of the presentation of Mr. Wight's design, the Council, though most cordially and unanimously approving of it, were yet unable to adopt it definitely, from the want of sufficient means for the construction of so costly an edifice; and for a long time it was an earnest question whether they should erect only the plain building which they could then safely compass, or devise measures for the enlargement of their funds to meet a greater expenditure. Happily, the latter alternative was accepted, in view of the great importance to the profession and to the city of an Academic Home, which should be at the same time in every way suitable in its interior arrangements, and artistically worthy in its exterior aspect.

To meet the emergency, it was resolved to call upon the well-known and ample sympathy of the large body of connoisseurs and lovers of art outside of the Academy, although it had been the boast of the Society heretofore, in all its long and varied existence, of nearly forty years, to have lived and prospered without any exterior aid whatever. It was, indeed, this most honorable, and, we believe, unexampled fact, which persuaded the Academy, in this important crisis of its history, to call with confidence for assistance upon their fellow-citizens at large.

As an efficient means both of accomplishing the immediate object in view, and of perpetuating the public interest in the labors and fortunes of the Academy, it was, at the suggestion of the President, cordially approved by the Council, determined to submit to the Society the project of establishing a new class of members, who should receive the honorary degree of Fellows of the Academy; such members paying into the treasury certain sums of money, from which should be formed a fund, to be known as the Fellowship Fund, and to be employed in the construction of the new edifice, and in the maintenance of the Institution.

The Committee commenced its labors at once with such ability and zeal, and our citizens of means and taste responded with such generous liberality, that after a very few weeks only the Council felt fully assured of being able to realize their cherished plans in the amplest manner. Many gentlemen, indeed, with a munificence quite unexpected, contributed not merely the sums required by the terms of the Fund, but in large excess thereof; while the Committee is still so actively engaged, and the public is yet so liberally responding, as to leave no doubt of the successful completion of the new edifice in the highest style of the art, and also of the endowment of the Academy in such a manner as to enable it for all future time to worthily achieve its important ends, and to ever increase its beneficent influence.

On the 18th day of April, 1863, three months after the passage of the amendments establishing the Fellowship Fund of the Academy, the contracts had been made and the ground was first broken for the erection of the new edifice, in accordance with the design submitted by Mr. Wight in January, 1861.

Such progress was made in the work, that by the middle of October following the builders were prepared to lower the corner-stone of the edifice into its place, which part of their labors was deemed by the Council to be of such memorable interest that it was ordered to be done publicly, and with all fitting ceremonies; and Messrs. Thomas S. Cummings, Thomas Hicks, Henry Peters Gray, George A. Baker, and T. Addison Richards, Academicians, were appointed a Committee to make and carry into effect arrangements necessary for the occasion.

The Committee of Arrangements gave prompt and effective attention to their duties, and published a programme for the occasion. They were most fortunate in the cordial co-operation they received from the distinguished gentlemen whom they solicited to assist as speakers at the ceremony, as they were also in all the other details of their labors from beginning to end.

The day chosen for the celebration, Wednesday, October 21st, 1863, was one of unwonted beauty—with skies so sunny, and airs so balmy, as to make the necessary out-of-door exercises as convenient and agreeable, even at that late Autumn season of the year, as they would have been in the early Summer. So auspicious, indeed, was the weather, in all respects, that it could have been felt as nothing less than a happy omen by all the large and distinguished audience who had the pleasure to assist on the interesting occasion.

The spacious reception-rooms of the Century Club, in East 15th Street, near Union Square, and not far from the Academy grounds, having been most kindly offered to the Committee as a place of rendezvous, the Members of the Academy and other guests of the day were invited to assemble there, in order to proceed in a body to the scene of the coming celebration.

At two o'clock in the afternoon, a large concourse of artists, authors, and other distinguished citizens were gathered in the rooms of the "Century," and half an hour later they took up their line of march for the Academy grounds, at the corner of Twenty-third Street and Fourth Avenue, in the following order: Mr. Isaac H. Brown acting on the occasion as

JANITOR,

Bearing the large Copper Box, in which had been previously deposited, in presence of the Council of the Academy, the various articles which were to be placed in the Corner-Stone.

The Reverend Clergy, Accompanied by the President of the Academy.

The Orators of the Day, Accompanied by the Council of the Academy.

The Academicians.

The Associates of the Academy.

The Fellows of the Academy.

The Honorary Members.

The Students of the Academy.

Artists generally.

Editors and Authors.

Other Distinguished Guests.

Citizens generally.

The procession, soon after starting, entered Union Square, where a slight *détour* from the direct route to Twenty-third Street was made, in order to pass around the equestrian statue of Washington, which adorns that locality, every head being uncovered in token of reverence for the memory of the illustrious Father of his Country. To add to the pleasant interest of this impromptu digression, was the fact that Mr. H. K. Brown, the sculptor of that fine work of art, was present at the moment in his place among the Academicians.

Arriving at the site of the new edifice, the procession was greeted by the welcoming strains of the excellent Band, secured for the occasion, and which continued to discourse agreeably, while the guests were taking their places on and around the platform which had been erected on the Twenty-third Street front.

As the music ceased, the assembly was called to order by the President, D. Huntington, Esq., when the following Invocation was offered by the Rev. Francis Vinton, D.D. :

INVOCATION—By Rev. Dr. Vinton.

(Preceded by the Reading of the Lord's Prayer.)

ALMIGHTY GOD, without whom all our purposes are ineffectual, and all our efforts vain, grant Thy presence and blessing to Thy humble servants assembled together to lay, with all solemnity, the corner-stone of an edifice to be devoted to Thy honor and the benefit of Thy creatures, and to the beautiful in nature. Nature is the art of God. Thou, Lord, hast made all things beautiful. Inspire our hearts with an humbling sense of our dependence upon Thee, at all times and in all undertakings. May the foundation of this Institution rest upon Thy favor. Open the hearts and hands of Thy people to give of their abundance for carrying the design into effect. Prosper every effort for its advancement, and every person engaged in its erection and support. May its blessings be enjoyed by many, and conveyed to the remotest generation. Above all, may it be an effectual, though humble, means of advancing Thy name and praise among this people. All which we ask through the merits and for the sake of Thy Son Jesus Christ our Lord. *Amen.*

At the close of the Invocation, the President introduced Mr. Henry Peters Gray, Vice-President of the Academy, and Chairman of the Committee of the Fellowship Fund, as follows :

"*Ladies and Gentlemen*—You are well aware that we are chiefly indebted to the efforts of the Fellowship Fund Committee, generously seconded by our munificent citizens, for the means to erect the building, to lay the corner-stone of which we have to-day assembled. Mr. Gray, the Chairman of that Committee, has labored with untiring energy to promote its interests, is intimately acquainted with the history of the Institution, and will now address you."

ADDRESS OF HENRY PETERS GRAY, ESQ.

"*Ladies and Gentlemen, and Members of the Academy*—You have been invited to participate in the ceremony of the laying of the corner-stone of the National Academy of Design. It is my privilege to welcome you to a spectacle which I hope may be as interesting as it certainly is novel, and briefly as possible to detain you from the favorite speakers who have kindly consented to address you on this occasion, while I say a few words about the Institution which, with your approbation, we are now to inaugurate on this solid foundation. The National Academy of Design was instituted in 1825. I quote from memory, from a synopsis of the history of the Academy, nearly completed, by our

Treasurer, Thomas S. Cummings, Esq., one of the original founders, five only of whom now remain. It held its first Exhibition in a room twenty-five by fifty feet, on the corner of Reade Street and Broadway, in 1826. This Exhibition was open in the evenings, and advertised as brilliantly lighted by gas from six burners It is interesting to note that this was the first time gas was ever used for an exhibition of pictures. The pecuniary result of the Exhibition was unsuccessful, leaving a deficiency which was supplied by the subscribers. The next Exhibition Rooms were in Chambers Street, over Stoppani's Baths—a locality since become distinguished by various public occupants—at the annual rent of $300. The next rooms were in Clinton Hall, in 1830, at $500 per year. The next, in 1840, in Broadway, corner of Leonard Street, over the Society Library Rooms, at $1,000 per year. These were occupied ten years most successfully, until 1850, when the Academy bought the " Brower's Stables,'' 663 Broadway, opposite Bond Street, which was then the up-town limit of travel of this line of the Broadway omnibuses. The whole property of the Academy was then less than $10,000. After using these rooms a few years they were sold, and since that time the Academy has hired various places for its Exhibitions while waiting for the building we have now started. The sale of the property in Broadway, under the management and through the noble generosity of Messrs. Jonathan Sturges and Charles M. Leupp, Trustees, assisted by Thomas S. Cummings, Esq., Trustee, whose able services these gentlemen have often acknowledged, produced for the Institution a clear profit of $60,000. And with this sum, increased nearly three-fold by the success of the Fellowship Fund last Winter, we have bought and so far built this property as a permanent abode. We have existed heretofore, we are told, in spirit. We are now to have a material form—such an one, I hope, as shall manifest our unity, peace and concord, and increase our prosperity and usefulness. I said this was certainly a novel spectacle. Is it not ?—when we reflect that this is the first Academy of the Fine Arts this side of the Atlantic—the first instance of the building of an Academy of Design, not only in the United States, but on this continent, governed and directed entirely by the artists, carried on strictly under Academic regulations, and dependent heretofore wholly on our own resources. And now, strongly wedded to public sympathy by a new order of members—its ' Fellows'—their subscriptions will enable the Institution to appear before you in a form of elegant architecture, which, we trust, will be a characteristic feature of this locality, and an ornament to the metropolis. In conclusion, may I not plead, while we have our shoulders at the wheel of this enterprise, that our friends and subscribers will seriously entertain a proposition, which, if carried into effect, will pay the whole cost of it, including a fund for its maintenance ? I propose that, recognizing the importance of ennobling our city by establishing a permanent Gallery and Academy of the Fine Arts, we will each of us endeavor to obtain a subscription to the Fellowship Fund of the National Academy of Design of equal amount to our own.''

At the close of Mr. Gray's remarks, and after the usual musical interlude, the President introduced Parke Godwin, Esq., Fellow of the Academy, who addressed the assembly as follows :

MR. GODWIN'S ADDRESS.

"It is an event in the history of any city or nation, when its leading citizens come together to lay the foundations of a superb structure to be devoted exclusively to Art. It marks a double rise in the genial currents of our civilization ; the existence, in the first place, of a demand for other satisfactions and other enjoyments than those of material nature ; and, in the second place, of a class competent by their genius and skill to supply the exigencies of that superior interest.

" We assemble, under the soft splendor of these autumnal skies, and amid the misty, many-colored glories of this second Summer of the year, to begin the record, in a durable and effective form, of this substantial progress. Impelled by no debasing lust of gain, with no vanity or shallow pomp, under the promptings of a high and almost holy sentiment of reverence, we propose to rear an altar to the Beautiful, where the active ministers in her service may yearly bring their richest offerings, and the broad brotherhood of her faith may come up to perform their profoundest worship.

" Here let me observe that, strange as it may seem, I cannot but think you have chosen both an appropriate and a propitious time for this inauguration. Strange, indeed, it must seem, that I should connect this hour of a desperate war, in any favorable sense, with the serene and gentle arts of peace. We are in the midst of a stupendous national convulsion, when the earth heaves as with the birth of earthquakes, and the wild air sobs with the shouts and wails of conflict. Borne on every southern breeze comes the flash of crossing arms and the deep thunder of the cannon ; and even while I speak, perhaps, many a brave heart sinks, many a manly form goes down, as the angel of death sweeps by, in undiscriminating wrath.

" But you that have before heard me discourse to artists know it is a favorite theory of mine, that the mighty struggles in which nations are put to their noblest strain are but the tempestuous spring-time and seed-time of a glorious summer of intellectual growths. In these crises, or supreme moments of life, when the soul of a people is called to exert the heroic virtues—when all that is strong and grand in human resolve, and all that is enduring and Godlike in human patience, is summoned to trial; when whole communities are led to cast out of their consciousness whatever is low, and groveling, and selfish, to make room therein for an influx of the divine and generous sentiment of self-sacrifice ; when the universal mind is fused, as by a spark of Heaven's lightning, into a unity of disinterested and irresistible emotions, whether it be of patriotism or religion, then the soul of the people is lifted into the true creative sphere ; its thoughts and feelings glow with spontaneous activity ; and the higher spirits of the time, catching its subtlest essences and finer electricities, blossom into wonderful forms of loveliness and power. And then, too, come the eras which are the culminating points in social destiny.

" It has often been remarked, that there have been certain periods in history which mark the efflorescence of the arts—when they seem to attain their most brilliant development ; and these, hastily enumerated, may be described in general terms as the age of Pericles in Greece, or of Augustus in Rome, of the Troubadours in early Europe, of Lorenzi di Medici in Italy, of Louis the Fourteenth in France, of Elizabeth in England, and the nineteenth century in more modern times. Now, why were these ages so distinguished? Was it because of the patronage which kings and princes are supposed to have lavished in munificent gifts upon artists and academies? As well ascribe to that source the stars which glitter in the skies, the gleam of sunsets, or the awful music of the winds in the woods. Patronage may foster what is already born, but the breath of the Lord alone gives it life. No ; those ages were great, because the spirit of the people, raised by the mighty events in which they participated to celestial heights of enthusiasm, energy and unity, could but overflow in all the appropriate intellectual manifestations.

" Greece, in the age of Pericles, had just emerged from the gigantic wrestle with Persia, in which her spirit, sublimated into unexampled vigor by unexampled efforts, bloomed and bourgeoned into Æschylus and Phidias, and Plato and Demosthenes. From the internecine conflicts of the civil wars in Rome sprang the silver splendors of the literature which illuminated the reign of the First Emperor. When Europe, impelled by a universal outburst of religious enthusiasm, flung herself in countless hosts upon Asia for the rescue of the Holy Sepulchre, then first arose, like a forest of tapering shafts and pointed arches, the mighty Gothic cathedrals, while the lays of the Troubadours and the tales of the Trouveres broke forth like a twittering chorus of birds in the mornings of Spring. No Medicean grace, but the fiery conflicts of the Italian Republics, aroused the genius of Italy to its almost superhuman strength, and crowned her laureled head with the eternal masterpieces of Da Vinci, and Michael Angelo, and Raphael. The religious and civil wars of France, not the luxurious but effeminating protection of Louis Quatorze, inspired the finest models of French style,—while the passions and strivings of the Reformation—the grand tournaments of the mind—the daring spirit of maritime adventure and scientific discovery, the new enterprise and freedom and aspiration, the almost universal ferment of thought which followed the release of society, and especially of England, from the despotism of the Middle Age, wrought the brain of mankind into the glow and energy necessary to produce the magnificent personality of Shakespeare. Thus, too, not to pursue the line of proof tediously, may we not hope that out of the throes and convulsions of our darkened and strenuous Present may be born a Future of grandeur and radiance? Nay, may we not discern on the very smoke-wreaths of battle the same glorious Bow of Promise which the Divine Benignity paints on the storm-clouds when the tempest is overpast?

" But, to attain that lofty consummation, our artists and our public must learn to estimate Art in its true dignity and character; not as a frivolous pastime, like the antics of Harlequin; not as a minister to ostentation, like a fashionable upholsterer—not even as a better sort of schoolmaster teaching a finer selfishness—but, as indeed it truly is, the purest and best efforts of the purest and best minds in their purest and best hours. Art amuses us, it is true, like many meaner things, but it elevates while it amuses; it delights us, but it ennobles us through that delight; it instructs us, but it informs us, or forms us inwardly, while it instructs. The genuine products of a mysterious fusion, which blends the Sense that sees all beauty with the Wisdom that perceives all truth and the Love that sympathizes with all life, it has no other function and no other sphere than to speak to the whole of man's higher nature—to his most exquisite sensibility, his shaping imagination, his penetrative reason, and his vivifying soul.

" Let me, then, in closing this simple overture or prelude to the richer strains which are to follow, exhort the artists who are actively engaged in this work of building a new Academy, to conduct it in the most lofty and serious intents, and resolve to make it, not a mere market-house for the barter of commodities in shoddy, nor a museum where dead monsters and withered specimens of abnormal forms are to be exhibited to the curious, nor an inquisition which shall cramp the free movements of the æsthetic soul into a killing uniformity of faith and practice, nor even a theatre for the display of lively imitations of buried ages, but a real and majestic Temple of Art; where all may come to indulge a divine communion, because it shall be filled and hallowed with the very presence of the God."

Following the speech of Mr. Godwin, it was hoped that Professor Morse would be able to address the assembly, and it was so set down in the programme. In explanation of Professor Morse's absence, it should be said, that the time for preparation was too limited to give him sufficient notice of the occasion to enable him to reach the city from his country-seat in time. The Committee of Arrangements trusted to being able to inform him in season of the part assigned to him in the exercises of the day. They took the liberty to thus include him in their arrangements, without conferring with him, on the sufficient grounds of their assurance of his entire sympathy with them, from the fact of his having been one of the chief founders, if not the father of the Academy; of his having filled its Presidential Chair, from the time of the establishment of the Society through a score of laborious years—resigning it, indeed, only when the pressure of other duties in the great field of science forbade his occupying it any longer—and from the unabated interest which he has ever, and upon all occasions, manifested in the fortunes of the Institution. The regrets since expressed by Professor Morse, in letters and otherwise, to members of the Academy, that he was not advised in season to permit him the pleasure of assisting at the celebration, as the Committee desired, fully excuse the liberty which was so familiarly taken in using his name, even without his previous consent.

Professor Morse being unavoidably absent, as has thus been explained, the President next introduced William Cullen Bryant, Esq., Honorary Member and Fellow of the Academy, who spoke as follows:

MR. BRYANT'S ADDRESS.

"I regret much that the absence of Professor Morse, to whom the cause of Art in this country, and the cause of Science throughout the world, owes so much, is not here to address you in a more impressive manner than I have the ability to do.

"I well recollect the time when, rallying the artists of the city under one standard, he led them to the encounter with the old Academy of Fine Arts—a useful Institution enough in its day, but no longer suited to the time. I recollect how, after a few Exhibitions of this Academy of ours, to which such artists as himself, and Durand, and Ingham, and Inman, sent their paintings, the old Institution quietly expired, and left the field open to its younger and more vigorous rival.

"For my own part, as an early friend of the Academy, I, too, have some title to say a word or two on an occasion like this. I was a witness of its birth, nearly forty years since. I lent its founders such an aid as a daily press could give, and its pupils accepted from me a short course of lectures on the Mythology of the Ancients. I congratulate its members, and I congratulate the public, who will be equally the gainers, on the favorable turn which its fortunes are now taking. In the history of certain races of mankind it is related, that in the Éarlier stages of their civilization they led a wandering life, dwelling in tents, migrating from place to place, and pasturing their herds wherever the glitter of cool waters or the verdure of fresh grass attracted them. As they made one advance after another in the arts of life, and grew numerous from year to year, they began to dwell in fixed habitations, to parcel out the soil in metes and bounds, to gather themselves into villages and to build cities. So it has been with this Academy. For more than a third of a century it had a nomadic existence, pitching its tent, now here and now there, as convenience might dictate, but never possessing a permanent seat. It is at last enabled, through the munificence of the citizens of New-York—a munificence worthy of the greatness of our capital, and most honorable to the character of those who inhabit it—to erect a building suitable for its purposes, and in some degree commensurate with the greatness of its objects. It no longer leads a precarious life; the generosity of its friends insures it an existence which will endure as long as this city shall remain the seat of a mighty commerce.

"When this Institution came into existence I could count the eminent artists of the country on my fingers. Now, what man among us is able to enumerate all the clever men in the United States who have devoted the efforts of their genius to the Fine Arts? For a taste so widely diffused we must have edifices of ample dimensions and imposing architecture, dedicated to that purpose alone; and one such we shall possess, hereafter, in the Temple of Art whose corner-stone we are this day assembled to lay."

After a further interval of music by the Band, Mr. Bryant was followed by the Hon. George Bancroft, Fellow of the Academy. Mr. Bancroft thus addressed his attentive and interested audience:

ADDRESS OF HON. GEORGE BANCROFT.

"The occasion on which we meet is full of earnestness and promise. The artist rightfully takes his place among those who specially devote themselves to the study of the Good, the Beautiful, and the True; and his creations open to us glimpses into the ideal world. It is time that this edifice should rise.

Our artists have already filled the earth with their fame. In sculpture and in painting their names are already world-renowned, and nowhere to-day would a gallery of art be esteemed perfect if it did not include productions of American hands and American minds. I have a favorite belief that in this nation, beyond any other, art is destined to thrive and attain its highest result. The reason is obvious. All genuine art appeals to that which is universal and unchanging. Whenever art has languidly flourished under the protection of aristocracy or princes, it has been compelled, in some measure, to cater to the tastes of those princes or that aristocracy. Here, art must appeal to universal sympathy. Here, art must appeal to that sentiment of the beautiful which lies deep in the human soul, which constitutes one of those great endowments that make man an immortal being, transcending all things around him. It is in that appeal to the universal sense of the beautiful that, in a Republic, art can attain its sublimest success. If you look through the line of ages, you will find that there have been but few epochs when art has in this manner carried out the highest conceptions of which human genius is capable, and it has been always either in connection with religion or in connection with liberty. Here is a nation distinguished above all other nations for religiosity and for freedom; and, therefore, here, above all other nations, is art destined to achieve its greatest triumph. Our artists give us the most earnest guarantee for the purity and elevation of their purpose in the time which they have chosen for founding this edifice—the work is begun in the midst of civil war, in the midst of our trials, in the midst of the most wonderful display of disinterested love of country, and of the loftiest attachment to the best interests of mankind. I respond, entirely, in that connection, to the remarks of Mr. Godwin; and I have nothing to add to them, except the hope that the gleam of light which shines on us to-day, from the undoubting patriotism of our artists, may be like the wing of the halcyon on the stormy wave, the harbinger of joy, and life, and triumph, and peace."

The Rev. Henry W. Bellows, D. D., Fellow and Honorary Member of the Academy, was the next speaker presented to the assembly. He spoke eloquently and at length, as follows:

SPEECH OF REV. DR. BELLOWS.

"It can hardly be necessary to add anything to the eloquent words which have already been spoken. All the *ideas* that should animate an occasion like this, have been furnished by Mr. Godwin in his opening speech; he has left the rest of us nothing to say except in the purely practical direction. Not that ideas are not the most practical of all things in their results; but they work out of sight, and I wish to say a few words about matters that can be put plainly in view. Let me first say, that the final cause of the failure of memory in our venerated and illustrious poet (Mr. Bryant), who preceded me, was to enable me to say, that however he himself might forget what he had written, nobody else ever could.

"I agree fully with the distinguished historian who has just taken his seat, that this country is finally to be the principal seat of the Fine Arts, because it is to be the home of everything great and good in the gradual unfolding of our common humanity. My faith in this rests upon no partiality for our particular race, or age, or place, but simply on the fact that more of human nature is to be developed here, and in a riper form, because of the universal spread of education among our people. And when I say education, I mean equally that which is derived from participation in affairs, from active and inspiring pursuit of a career open here to all, and that which is derived from what is technically called schooling. We have these united in an unexampled degree. As I must believe that Providence has scattered with an impartial hand the seeds of all possible excellency, of all arts and sciences, in our nature—the region in which that nature receives its largest and widest culture, will bring forth the best and broadest harvest. Whatever talents our countrymen possess will not sleep in their bosom for want of opportunity. Just as I believe that political, social, domestic, religious interests will flourish here as they never flourished elsewhere, so I believe the Fine Arts will. Indeed, you cannot have any of these things flourishing separately from the others, except in a temporary and exotic way. The true, the good, the beautiful, are each the side of a solid cube, which, let it present which face it will, implies the presence and potency of the other dimensions. You cannot have true Freedom without true Religion and true Art; nor true Religion without true Art and true Liberty; nor true Art without true Liberty and true Religion. These things go together, or else not at all. The universal popular education of America, with its equal institutions, opportunities, and incitements, for the first time secures a state of society equally favorable to each of the fundamental interests of our nature, and therefore one promising the greatest success for each and all. But I did not intend to generalize, but to speak on practical matters.

"It is essential to the just pride and dignity of a metropolis like this, that Art should have her visible and sightly home in it. She has been a houseless wanderer, a tenant-at-will, a first-of-May mover quite long enough for her own dignity, and quite long enough for our reproach. Henceforth, on this corner-stone, is to stand an edifice worthy to represent the Temple of the Fine Arts, and where gradually may be accumulated, I trust, the best products of our native genius, to attract the steps of art-pilgrims from all corners of the land. Were it not a matter of pride and of feeling, it could easily be established to be a matter of municipal interest. A conspicuous home of Art—a central depot of the works of American genius—an annual exhibition of the yield of the year in the immortal fields of Painting and Sculpture in a place worthy of their appearing, would draw to this community, and hold here, an extra population making itself abundantly felt in the added wealth and income of our city. The subtle, yet real connection between the elevation and gratification of the higher tastes of a population, and its economic and material prosperity, is best understood by philosophic observers. I found, for instance, only yesterday, in visiting Mr. Lawrence's beautiful carriage factory in Broadway, that the creation of the Central Park had affected the whole livery interest and the construction of vehicles of every kind to an enormous extent. Nobody accustomed to reflection ought to be surprised to hear that the enormous outlay on the Central Park had added twenty times as much to the wealth of this city, by the increasing value it has put upon our real astate; and twenty times as much to the income of the industrious classes, as it had added taxes. Has anybody ever considered what the influence of the honor and dignity paid to the Fine Arts repays a community, in the gradual effect it produces upon the whole style of architecture, house-building, furniture, costume patterns and decorations of every kind, gradually creeping down into the humblest ramifications of life? I have sometimes thought that if I had a half million of dollars to give away, I would establish—not a hospital, nor a school, nor a church—but a band of music, of the highest and purest character, whose sole function should be to play in the Central Park a certain number of hours of every day in the year! What should I expect from such an endowment? I should expect to draw thousands who now never breathe the free air in purity, and amid scenes of beauty and order, into that lovely retreat; to break up a disastrous devotion to business; to bring the rich and the poor together; and to breathe, by the subtile power of music, a spirit of harmony and of peace, and of innocent and elevated enjoyment, through this vast metropolis. I should expect to raise beneficently the feeling of civic attachment, and to increase the pride of local feeling.

"In like manner, I say, we cannot, as sagacious and prudent citizens, as tax-payers and lovers of peace and order, do too much to naturalize Art, in all its forms, among us. I consider every print-shop window a public teacher, and a guarantee for civic order. I believe the crowd that walks down past Washington's Statue, and looks in at Goupil's and Williams & Stevens's windows, is a better and more truly civilized, patriotic, and refined crowd than it could be without them. This building, in its beauty and stateliness, dedicated to Art, and year after ,year gathering new, and richer, and more fragrant associations from the hours of admiring and instructive pleasure passed in its galleries, will enrich and adorn, and cast a healing and protecting shadow over this avenue, one of the chief entrances to the city! The depots of locomotion above, the Medical College on yonder corner, the churches along its side, the great hotels at its corners, the vista ending in Washington's Statue below, and in the subterranean tunnel through which ebbs and flows the great human tide that morning and evening fills and drains our population—these public structures will have no more significant edifice among them all, than this that speaks of the aromatic, imponderable interest of Beauty—that subtle, exquisite element that refines even Religion itself—a power which the tasteless and most stupid cannot wholly escape, and which increases in its dominion and benignant sway in precise proportion to the culture, elevation, and breadth of its subjects.

"I rejoice to see these works of luxury, of peace, and of beauty going on in a time of civil war. They show the inherent productive, industrial, and pacific spirit of our people and our institutions—the irrepressible nature of our civilization. At this very moment, as all through the war, the most costly of our recent public buildings, the United States Treasury, has been lifting its costly monoliths around the very rooms in which were going on the manifold operations by which we create a currency that feeds with a thousand millions the sinews of war. As I have seen those monstrous stones poised in the air before swinging to their unshakable places, I have seemed to see the very pillars of the Union and the State in the balance of civil war, swinging perilously in the air of destiny, but all the while held by a gigantic Providence over their proper places, and slowly, steadily settling anew upon their everlasting foundations.

"A few weeks hence, the City of Boston, the home of so much refinement, artistic taste, public spirit, and patriotism, will call her æsthetic population together to witness the opening of an organ, so far transcending all other organs in this country as to make comparisons absurd—an organ which has cost $100,000—whose bellows are worked by steam power, and yet so exquisitely poised in its machinery, as to be more manageable at its keys than our ordinary organs. Perhaps not more than three or four instruments in the world exceed it in the number of its stops, and the majestic size of its larger pipes, of thirty-seven feet length, up and down which a man may easily pass. And this is a product of a time of war! 'The piping times of peace' do not give over because the trumpet and drum fill the streets. Boston Capital knows that now is the time to bid for the patronage of the lovers of Music, Art, and Beauty; and wisely do her merchant princes invest their gains in this wondrous giant and king of instruments.

"May I not congratulate this assembly upon the enlightened liberality with which, in a time when millions are expending here to equip and forward thousands of armed men to the defence of our country, over a hundred thousand dollars is reserved and given for raising of the structure, to be dedicated to peace, beauty, and the universal language of art—that tongue that speaks in color and form, and addresses by one set of symbols, and merges in one nationality our German, Italian, French and American populations? May I not suggest the importance of seizing the very time when the National heart is most generously open, the hand of wealth most relaxed—when great deeds and great thoughts, great liberality and impersonal services are most rife—to complete what has been so nobly begun?—to carry this subscription up to an adequate amount to place the Academy upon an easy and dignified basis? Certainly another hundred thousand dollars are richly due to this cause, and ought not to strain in the least the resources of our metropolis.

"Gentlemen, no city is great whose wealth has not crystallized into beauty; no materialism supportable which has not blossomed into the rich clusters of art. On visiting the Capital of the Nation a few days ago, and lifting my eyes to that magnificent iron dome, which did not cease to feel the peaceful throb of the workman's hammer, even when there barracked in the Senate Chamber and slept in the Speaker's chair the armed men that rushed to the defence of the Sacred City of our Freedom—I saw the staging erected that was to crown all with the last work of one of our chief and most honored American artists. Art must finish what artisans began. The symbolic statue of Liberty, cut by Crawford's dying fingers, must surmount the dome of the Capital; and Art must occupy the last and highest place in the temple that enshrines our Constitution and our Nationality. That Art may have that place in the honor and reverence of this community, and that she may always represent and hallow the image of Liberty, is the hope and the prayer with which we lay this corner-stone. May it rest here forever!"

When Dr. Bellows had concluded his address, and it had been followed by inspiriting strains from the Band, the next portion of the exercises was the more immediate ceremony of the laying of the corner-stone.

At this interesting point the Architect, P. B. Wight, Esq., appeared before the audience to present to the President of the Academy, on the part of the builders, a beautiful SILVER TROWEL, with which to lay the corner-stone of the new edifice. Mr. Wight thus addressed the President:

REMARKS OF THE ARCHITECT, P. B. WIGHT, ESQ.,

On offering a Silver Trowel to the President.

" MR. PRESIDENT—It becomes my duty, on the part of the builders, to present to you the implement with which to lay the corner-stone of this building. Thus far we have proceeded with the work, but we this day suspend our labor, and request you, as the President of the National Academy of Design, to lay this chief corner-stone which we have prepared.

" We congratulate you upon the success that has thus far crowned your undertaking, and on the prospect that this Association, after an existence of forty years, has now found a permanent habitation.

" Please accept this Trowel, and when you spread the mortar under the stone, fear not to injure it, as it is made for a practical purpose. When in after years it is preserved as a memento of this event, its stains and scratches will be of far greater value than the metal of which it is made."

Upon receiving the Trowel, Mr. Huntington, the President, addressed the Architect as follows:

MR. HUNTINGTON'S REMARKS.

" In the name of the Artists, and more especially of the Members of the Academy whom I have the honor to represent, I thank you, Sir, and through you, those who have united with you, for this beautiful and appropriate present.

" I am glad that it is a *Trowel*, and that it is of *Silver*. I remember that distinguished American artist, the late Charles R. Leslie, once saying, ' We hear a great deal about the "golden glow," but give me in preference the delicate lustre of silver, which, by its purity and refinement, far better suggests the subtle and modest tints which form the greatest beauty of coloring.'

" I am glad, too, it is a *Trowel*, the ancient form of the palette, on which the colors can be spread; and not unlike the chisel, which will please the sculptors, but chiefly as it is the implement of that industry which patiently works out such mighty and triumphant results; fitly reminding us of the skill and faithfulness which the craftsmen of this building have already shown, and will, I am sure, continue to show till a perfect work shall crown their efforts.

" So it is that human art emulates the divine; for is not God a Builder, and hath He not through ages silently and wondrously built the world? Let us, then, humbly tread in His sacred footsteps!

" I am glad, too, Sir, that you are the honored Architect of our building; that you are a son of our dear old City of Manhatta, and a graduate of her Free Academy; and I doubt not that what you have designed so beautifully you will finish thoroughly, and present us with a worthy home for the Arts of our country.

" Once more I heartily thank you, and now let me proceed to lay the foundation-stone."

At the conclusion of the address, the President and the Architect descended from the platform to the southwest angle of the building at the corner of Twenty-third Street and Fourth Avenue, and proceeded to lay the corner-stone, silently and earnestly watched by the audience. As the box with the mementoes of the day was put into its place, and as the upper stone was being gently lowered upon it, the President, using his Silver Trowel, spread the mortar thereon, saying, as the ceremony ended:

" Thus we lay the foundation-stone of the National Academy of Design, and solemnly dedicate the same to the Fine Arts, in the name of the Father, and of the Son, and of the Holy Ghost. *Amen.*"

The box, (a copper case about eighteen inches long, twelve wide, and eight deep,) which was buried in the corner-stone, contained the following articles, which had been previously deposited, in presence of the Council:

A copy of the Constitution and By-Laws of the National Academy of Design.

A copy of the Exhibition Catalogue of the Academy for the year 1863.

A copy of the List of the Statuary of the National Academy of Design.

The Letters of Abraham Lincoln, President of the United States.

Historical Record of the National Academy of Design, by Thomas S. Cummings, Treasurer.

Officers of the Academy of 1863–64; names of the Architect and Builders.

List to date of the Fellows of the National Academy of Design.

Postal currency of the United States below the sum of one dollar.

Copies of the daily papers—*Herald, Times, Tribune, Post,* and *Commercial Advertiser—Army and Navy Journal,* and *Harper's Weekly.*

Catalogue of the Columbia College Law School.

Columbia College Annual Report.

Coin of the United States—1c., 3c., 5c., 10c., 25c., 50c., $1 gold.

Medal of Samuel F. B. Morse, ex-President, by C. Müller.

Medal of Asher B. Durand, ex-President, by C. Müller.

Head of Liberty, bronze medal, by C. Müller.

New-York Firemen, by C. Müller.

Minstrel's Curse, by C. Müller.

Medal of the Union League, Philadelphia, July, 1776 and 1863.

The completion of the work of securing the corner-stone in its place was greeted by hearty plaudits from the multitude, and by the spirited performance of popular National airs by the Band.

When the attention of the assembly was regained after this especial portion of the ceremonies of the day, it was again, and for the last time, most eloquently addressed by the Rev. E. H. Chapin, D. D., Honorary Member of the Academy.

ADDRESS OF REV. DR. CHAPIN.

" *Ladies and Gentlemen*—I am quite of the opinion that the corner-stone of this edifice, dedicated to the purposes of Art, ought to be laid in strict accordance with artistic rules—with the rules of harmony and proportion. Under this impression, and considering, moreover, this animated picture around me, framed by this glorious autumnal day ; considering also the figures that have been made prominent in the scene, I might expect that I should be suffered to fall into the background, and remain there undisturbed, because, really, I am coming in after everything—after the silver trowel, and indeed after several silver and golden trowels of ' words fitly spoken.' I am coming in at the last of the feast, and if, in defiance of the rules of perspective, I am thrust into the foreground, I fear that I shall make a speech that will be much foreshortened ! After all, I can only repeat what has been already well said. What are the claims of this Institution upon New-York and upon this country ? I do not suppose there are many here who are disposed to ask this question, but there may be a few who think that art is merely synonymous with ornament; who think that it plays only the decorating part in a nation's character and career. It is only to such that I need say that art springs out of the deepest life of the nation ; it expresses that life ; it helps create that life ! It is essential to the individual that he should be l fted above the plane of mere sense, of mere animal existence ; that he should be elevated to something above himself and of himself ; it is essential also to states and to nations that they should be lifted above themselves and out of themselves—out of whatever is narrow, selfish and groveling, to the ideal. Art is one of the instruments of the good, the beautiful and the true, which have been spoken of here to-day. In fact, Art is the most subtle and effective expression of the good, the beautiful, and the true, and as such an expression, exerts an incalculable influence. We call this ' a *refining* influence ;' and sometimes this is said with a sneer, as if there were no strength, no virtue, no inspiration in *refinement.* Art *does* refine us. Thank God, that power by which in all ages men have been civilized, has gone side by side with every noble and brave effort to refine men, to turn their eyes towards the beauty of the world, to clarify their vision to look through the thick veil of sense to that which is highest and holiest in existence, and thus leading them to nobler conditions of life. Thank God, then, for an Institution like this, that is at once with every good and true work. And no better time for its erection could have been selected than this time. The nation is a greater nation to-day, a richer nation, a nation with nobler aspirations, than it ever had before. The mother who weeps over her unshrouded boy, the father who has made his heart's last sacrifice, the mechanic who has borne heavy burdens for his country's sake, and every drop of blood which has fallen, have enriched the country. The entire people have become richer in themselves, and see with finer vision ; they take hold with nobler sympathies of religion, duty, and everything incumbent upon the nation. We were living a life too low and too limited, thinking too much of material good and material acquisition. The stroke that has smitten us and made us bleed, has opened deeper and better fountains within us, and we welcome religion, we welcome truth, we welcome goodness, with an appreciation that we never had before. Two great elements constitute the sources of noble art—those elements are Nature and Humanity. We know how lavishly our country is endowed by the former. We know what subjects have inspired the pencils of men whose names are known all over this continent, and who may confidently challenge their compeers in Art in the Old World as well as in the New. I repeat, we know how nature has inspired the pencil of the American artist. But now Art is doubly endowed by its association with humanity. Every spot where a brave man has fallen—every field where liberty has been vindicated—every furrow that has received the noble dead, or been torn by the battle-shock for liberty and the right, has made nature more humanly expressive, and nature and humanity to-day hand to Art their combined traditions to be commemorated forever.   It would be presumption for me to repeat what others have said ; and I will merely close with my heartfelt benediction upon these services.   Let us welcome this Institution.   May it stand here in the City of New-York, so rich in noble edifices and works.   Amid these rolling wheels of traffic, these currents of human life, these green islands of charity that rise out of the lagoons of misery and suffering, amid these churches that point to heaven, let this Institution rise.   It *does* rise to-day to our sympathies and hopes, as the fabled city of old arose to the strains of music.   Let it rise and stand, its walls tapestried with glorious objects of nature, transfigured with the ideals of beauty, and burnished with consummate expression of goodness and truth—a Pantheon of heroic deeds and grand achievements, a source of perpetual influences, that shall appear in the strength, the virtue and the refinement of the Nation.''

At the conclusion of Dr. Chapin's address the Benediction was pronounced by the Rev. Dr. Vinton, when the exercises of the day were closed.

A DESCRIPTION OF THE NEW EDIFICE

OF THE

NATIONAL ACADEMY OF DESIGN.

THE new building for the National Academy of Design occupies the whole of a lot situated at the northwest corner of Fourth Avenue and Twenty-third Street, eighty feet wide on the street, and ninety-eight feet nine inches long on the avenue. It will be three stories high besides the cellar. The lower part, or basement story, contains—*First*, the Janitor's apartments, the floor of which is raised one step above the sidewalk, occupying the whole end on Twenty-third Street. *Second*, the rooms of the School of Design, the floor of which is four feet lower than that of the Janitor's rooms; thus giving a ceiling sixteen feet high, and which occupy three-fourths of the whole basement story. The accommodations for the School are ample. It will occupy three Studios or alcoves on Fourth Avenue, lighted by large windows, and a hall for casts and models, the whole covering a space of forty-seven by sixty-eight feet. The Life School will occupy a hall, in the north side of the building, twenty-seven by fifty-four feet, and partially lighted from a court-yard. The entrance to all the rooms in this story is by a door in the southern end of the Fourth Avenue side.

The principal story is reached by a double flight of steps on the Twenty-third Street end, and is entered by a large door-way, from which a hall, eighteen feet wide, runs nearly the whole length of the building. The whole Fourth Avenue side is occupied by a suite of four rooms; the most southerly is the Reception-Room, twenty-two by twenty-six feet; the next two, each the same side as the Reception-Room, are for the Library. The most northerly is the Council-Room, which is twenty-two by forty-five feet. To the west of the Central Hall are ladies' and gentlemen's Dressing-Rooms; and a Lecture-Room, which is immediately above, and the same size as the Life School Room, in the story below.

The upper story is for the Exhibition Galleries. In the centre is a hall thirty-four by forty feet, divided by a double arcade, supported on columns of polished marble. In this hall will be hung the works of Art which belong to the National Academy. Around this are the Galleries, all opening out of it: one thirty by seventy-six feet; one twenty-two by forty-six; one twenty by forty; one twenty-one by thirty—all lighted by sky-lights; also, a Gallery for Sculpture, twenty-one feet square, lighted both from the roof and the side.

Visitors to the Galleries will enter at the main entrance in the first story. On the left of a person so entering, is the ticket office; on the right, the umbrella depository. Passing through the vestibule, the visitor enters the Great Hall; in front are the stairs leading up to the Galleries above; four steps, the whole width of the hall, lead to a platform, where he gives up his ticket and buys his Catalogue; from this a double flight leads to another platform, from which a single flight reaches the level of the Gallery floor.

These stairs, together with all the doors, door and window trimmings, mantels, &c., are to be of oak and walnut combined, oiled and polished. The vestibules will be floored with mosaic of tiles.

On the exterior, the walls of the basement story will be of Westchester County gray marble, with bands of North River graywacke. The walls of the first story of white marble, with similar bands; and of the third story, of white and gray marble, in small oblong blocks, forming a pattern of chequer-work. The building will be surmounted by a rich arcaded cornice of white marble.

The School of Design, in the basement, will be lighted by wide double windows, with segmental arches, each pair of arches supported in the middle on a clustered column, with a rich carved capital and base, and resting, on each side, on a carved corbel. All the other windows in the building will have pointed arches, and those of the first story will have their archivolts decorated by voussoirs of alternately white and gray marble. There will be no windows in the upper story upon the street, but circular openings for ventilation, filled with elaborate plate-tracery. The principal entrance will be very high. A broad archivolt, enriched with sculpture and varied by voussoirs, alternately white and gray, springs from columns, two on each side, of red Vermont marble, with white marble capitals and bases. Under this, the tympanum above the door will be filled with an elaborate pattern, in mosaic, of small tiles. The double flight of steps, leading to this door, will be an important feature of the building, being entirely of marble, having, under the platform, a triple arcade, inclosing a drinking fountain, and being richly decorated with sculpture.

As will be inferred from the above description, the style of architecture is that revived Gothic now the dominant style in England, which combines those features of the different schools of architecture of the Middle Ages, which are most appropriate to our nineteenth-century buildings. The style has resulted from the efforts of many architects working together, to produce buildings which shall combine, harmoniously, convenience and beauty; and the success of their enterprise has shown that truly decorative architecture, or the art of making buildings beautiful, by the addition to them of color and sculpture, is not among the "lost arts," but is still to be cultivated by those who desire to surround themselves with beautiful things. If a name for the style be demanded, it can only be said that the name of no past style of Architecture is altogether appropriate to it: as the revived Gothic goes on towards more perfect success, it will find a name for itself.

All the carving is carefully studied from natural forms. The flowers and leaves of our woods and fields have furnished the models for all the sculpture which has been designed, under the direction of the Architect, by the stone-carvers who have done the work. For this purpose, a special appropriation was made; the carving was not included in the contract, but paid for by the day, as it was done.

The builders of the Academy have seized upon the opportunity afforded them, by the erection of their costly building, to show, by actual example, the proper and only possible way of making a building rich in sculptured ornament. The stone-carvers have cut these capitals and archivolts with the feeling and purpose of sculptors executing independent and original works of art. The result, thus far attained, has shown that the only difference between a carver of good leaf capitals, and the producer of heroic human sculpture, is in the amount of his knowledge and power.

HISTORICAL MEMORANDA*

OF THE

ACADEMY AND ITS EXHIBITIONS.

(DEPOSITED IN THE CORNER-STONE.)

In the early part of the Autumn of 1825, there was formed, in the City of New-York, a "Drawing Association," for art-study and social intercourse, which embraced among its members the greater portion of the artists then in the city. This Association prospered in such a degree, that it soon became necessary to extend its field of operations. The attempt to effect this object resulted in the foundation, on the 19th day of February, 1826, of the present National Academy of Design. The "Drawing Association," thus remodeled and renamed, adopted a Constitution and By-Laws, and elected Samuel F. B. Morse President, Henry Inman Vice-President, John L. Morton Secretary, and Thomas S. Cummings Treasurer.

The new Academy was chartered by the Legislature of New-York on the 5th day of April, 1828.

Of the twenty-five original founders of the Institution, only five are now living: Messrs. Morse, Cummings, Ingham,† Durand and Evers.

The Society, having no apartments of its own, held its meetings in rooms generously loaned to them by the Historical and Philosophical Societies, which were then established in the old Alms-House Building in the Park fronting Chambers Street, which is now (in 1863) the site of the new City Hall.

The first Annual Exhibition of the Academy was held in the year 1826, on the second story of a building at the southwest corner of Broadway and Reade Street. One room only was occupied, and that a small one, being but fifty feet long and twenty-five feet wide. It was lighted in the evening by six ordinary gas-burners, which fact was advertised as a notable attraction! It was really notable as being the first instance on record of a public exhibition of pictures at night. This first Exhibition failed to pay expenses, and the members were assessed to make up the loss.

The second Exhibition (1827) was held in a room on the third story of the Arcade Baths in Chambers Street, about midway between Broadway and Centre Street, a building which afterwards became Burton's Theatre, and which is now the United States Marshal's office. It was leased to the Academy by D. E. Tylee for three years, at three hundred dollars per annum. The third, fourth, and fifth Exhibitions (1828, 1829, and 1830) were held at this place.

---

* Compiled by Thomas S. Cummings, N. A., from his work now in press, entitled "Historic Annals of the National Academy of Design, New-York Drawing Association, etc., etc., with Occasional Dottings by the Way-Side," from 1825 to the present time (1863).

† Charles C Ingham, N A., died in New-York on the 10th of December, 1863, leaving but four of the founders of the Academy now among the living. His last public act, in the profession, was to assist at the laying of the corner-stone of the new building.

For the sixth Exhibition (1831) greatly increased accommodations were obtained in a suite of rooms on the third floor of the Mercantile Library in Clinton Hall, then at the corner of Nassau and Beekman Streets. These apartments were leased by the Academy for ten years, at an annual rent of five hundred dollars; and here the exhibitions from the sixth to the fifteenth inclusive (1831 to 1840) were held.

In 1840, at the expiration of the Clinton Hall lease, the Academy again removed, and this time went up town, settling for another decade on the upper floor of the Society Library Building, at the corner of Broadway and Leonard Street. These galleries were larger and more commodious than any yet occupied by the Society. The annual rent at the Society Library was increased to one thousand dollars. These Exhibitions from the sixteenth to the twenty-fourth inclusive (1841 to 1849) were held here.

In 1850, the Institution moved yet further up town, having purchased the property on Mercer Street, in the rear of Broadway, with the lease of a lot on the latter street as an entrance. This site had been occupied by Brower's Stables, and was the up-town terminus of the Broadway line of stages. A suite of six fine galleries was erected here, with a total length of one hundred and sixty-four feet, and a breadth of fifty feet. The whole of this property was placed in the hands of Messrs Sturges, Leupp, Edmonds and Cummings, as Trustees of the Academy, and was so ably managed by them, under the charge of Mr. Cummings, that after years of patient labor, it produced the first means of any amount ever in the possession of the Academy. After five years of occupancy, this property was sold for about one hundred and twenty thousand dollars, netting the Institution a clear return of sixty-nine thousand dollars, and leaving, after the payment of all outstanding indebtedness, a balance of nearly sixty thousand dollars. All honor to Messrs. Sturges and Leupp, through whose purse and friendly aid such happy results were obtained.

The Exhibitions of 1850 to 1854 (twenty-fifth to twenty-ninth) inclusive, were held in these Galleries.

After the sale of the property at 663 Broadway, it became necessary to find other accommodations for the Exhibitions, and temporary quarters were secured in the gallery over the entrance to the Rev. Dr. Chapin's Church, at 548 Broadway. Here we held the thirtieth and thirty-first Annual Exhibitions, in 1855 and 1856.

For the thirty-second Exhibition, in 1857, the old rooms, 663 Broadway (remaining then unchanged), were rented by the Society.

In 1858 a suite of galleries was fitted up by the Academy on the upper floor of the buildings erected by Maltby G. Lane in Tenth Street, on the corner of Fourth Avenue. The thirty-third, thirty-fourth, thirty-fifth and thirty-sixth Exhibitions, 1858-59-60 and 61, were held at this place. The rent here, of three thousand dollars per annum, proved to be too heavy, and the lease was relinquished.

The thirty-seventh and the thirty-eighth Exhibitions, 1862 and 1863, were held in the galleries of the building known as the Institute of Art,* No. 625 Broadway, under a temporary arrangement with the proprietor, Mr. Derby.

---

* It is proposed to hold the ensuing Exhibition of 1864, the thirty-ninth, in these galleries ; and for the next in order, the fortieth, in the Spring of 1865, it is expected that the noble edifice now being erected for the Academy, will be fully ready.

BUILDERS OF THE ACADEMY EDIFICE.

P. B. WIGHT, Esq., Architect.

ALEX. MAXWELL & CO., the Marble and the Carving.
GEORGE T. CODDINGTON, Jr., the Masonry.
JOHN H. CUSHIER, the Carpenter's Work.
S. B. ALTHOUSE & CO., the Iron Work.
FISHER & BIRD, and } the Columns and Ornamental Tiles, &c.
CASONI & CO.,
J. PHILBIN, the Gas Fittings and Fixtures.
JOHN McEWAN, the Plumbing.
WARNER & CO., the Heating Apparatus.

THE LATE MR. INGHAM.

Charles C. Ingham, N. A., long a distinguished portrait painter in our city, whose death was announced in the *Evening Post* last Friday, was born in Dublin in 1796, and was a descendant of a gentleman who went to Ireland as an officer in Cromwell's army. At the age of thirteen he was placed under the charge of one of the first artists in Dublin, to study the art of portraiture, and with this accomplished artist he studied for four years. During this period the youthful student received a premium from the Dublin Academy for a composition in oil-colors, representing the "Death of Cleopatra."

In 1816 Mr. Ingham's father's family emigrated to New-York, the young artist with the rest. His "Cleopatra" was exhibited in the Gallery of the American Academy of Fine Arts, at their first Exhibition. The work attracted attention, and soon brought the artist full employment. He afterwards continued in full and successful practice, working at his easel, as long as daylight hours permitted him to do so, until within a few days of his death.

On the formation of the National Academy of Design, Mr. Ingham enrolled himself on the side of the artists; was one of the original founders of the Institution, and one of the few remaining with us until this time. The number is now reduced to Morse, Durand, and Cummings. Mr. Ingham was a valuable member of the Institution, was frequently placed on its "Council," and was for many years its Vice-President. Among his prominent works may be mentioned his "Girl Laughing," "White Plume" (a composition from Byron's "Don Juan"), his "Flower-Girl," and his portraits of many ladies of this city, well remembered. All his works were of the most exquisite beauty of finish and delicacy, and stamped him as the leading "lady portrait painter," a reputation he enjoyed to the last.

Mr. Ingham was one of the originators of the old "Sketch Club," and its President. He was likewise a member of the "Century Club." He was never married. He was exemplary in the highest degree as a man, a son, and a brother; and his doings with all were just, exact, and honorable. In manners he was what may be classed as the old-school gentleman; warm in disposition and frank in manner, and always a pleasant companion. His virtues endeared him to his many friends. He was, as Dunlap very justly remarked, "one among a large class of our present artists who are looked up to, and sought for in the most enlightened society."

THOMAS S. CUMMINGS.

APPENDIX.

OFFICERS OF THE ACADEMY,

From the Adoption of the Constitution in

1827.

Presidents.

Samuel F. B. Morse.	1827 to 1845
A. B. Durand	1845 to 1861
Samuel F. B. Morse	1861 to 1862
Daniel Huntington	1862 to 1865

Vice-Presidents.

Henry Inman	1827 to 1831
William Dunlap	1831 to 1838
Henry Inman	1838 to 1844
A. B. Durand	1844 to 1845
C. C. Ingham	1845 to 1850
Thomas S. Cummings	1850 to 1859

Treasurers.

Thomas S. Cummings	1827 to 1865
Francis W. Edmonds (nominally, during Mr. Cummings's occupancy of the Vice-Presidency,)...—	1850 to 1859

Recording and Corresponding Secretaries.

John L. Mortón	1827 to 1844
A. B. Durand	1832 to 1838
James Whitehorne	1838
James Frothingham	1844 to 1845
John G. Chapman	1844 to 1848
Francis W. Edmonds	1844 to 1848
J. H. Shegogue	1848 to 1850
T. Addison Richards	1850 to 1865
J. B. Stearns	1850 to 1865

The Annual Exhibitions, Dates, and the Receipts from 1826 to 1863.

1st,	1826,	May 14 to July 16 (no record), estimated at............$	300 00
2nd,	1827,	May 6 to July 16, Arcade Baths, Chambers Street ...	532 00
3d,	1828,	May 6 to July 10, " " ...	812 83
4th,	1829,	May 11 to July 13, " " ...	1,053 86
5th,	1830,	May 1 to July 5, " " ...	1,031 29
6th,	1831,	April 28 to July 9, Clinton Hall...............	1,115 84
7th,	1832,	May 21 to July 8 (Cholera).	862 00
8th,	1833,	May 8 to July 6...................	1,387 00
9th,	1834,	April 25 to July 5...................	1,215 00
10th,	1835,	May 5 to July 4...................	2,381 75
11th,	1836,	April 27 to July 9...................	3,758 50
12th,	1837,	April 21 to July 4...................	4,587 00
13th,	1838,	April 23 to July 7...................	4,699 23
14th,	1839,	April 24 to July 6...................	3.944 40
15th,	1840,	April 27 to July 8...................	3,259 00
16th,	1841,	May 3 to July 5, Leonard Street and Broadway........	4,902 00
17th,	1842,	April 27 to July 9, " "	3,949 00
18th,	1843,	April 27 to July 4, " "	4,631 00
19th,	1844,	April 24 to July 6, " "	4,964 86
20th,	1845,	April 17 to July 5, " "	5,163 24
21st,	1846,	April 16 to July 4, " "	5,665 18
22d,	1847,	April 2 to July 3, " "	6,278 22
23d,	1848,	April 3 to July 8, " "	4,446 91
24th,	1849,	April 3 to July 7, " "	2,753 47
25th,	1850,	April 15 to July 6, 663 Broadway........	3,066 61
26th,	1851,	April 8 to July 5, "	2,918 17
27th,	1852,	April 13 to July 7, "	2,849 45
28th,	1853,	April 19 to July 9, "	2,306 58
29th,	1854,	March 22 to April 25, "	2,584 87
30th,	1855,	March 12 to May 10, 548 Broadway........	2,550 75
31st,	1856,	March 14 to May 10, "	2,711 25
32d,	1857,	May 18 to June 20, 663 Broadway........	3,861 75
33d,	1858,	April 13 to June 30, 10th Street........	4,297 25
34th,	1859,	April 13 to June 25, "	5,888 92
35th,	1860,	April 14 to June 16, "	4,144 07
36th,	1861,	March 20 to April 25, "	2,596 50
37th,	1862,	April 14 to June 23, Derby Gallery........	4,315 70
38th,	1863,	April 14 to June 24, "	5,203 85

Schools, Number of Students attending, and the Years Fees were taken, from 1825 to 1861.

1825.	....	26 Students, at	......	$5.	....
1826.	....	17 "	......	5.	Premiums.
1827.	....	29 "	......	5.	"
1828.	....	36 "	......	5.	"
1829.	....	24 "	......	5.	"
1830.	....	31 "	......	5.	"
1831.	....	44 "	......	5.	"
1832.	....	21 "	......	5.	"
1833.	....	No charge.	......		No Premiums.

1834.	....	22 Students, at ...... $5.	Premiums.
1835.	....	37 " ...... 5.	"
1836.	....	38 " ...... 5.	"
1837.	....	41 " ...... 5.	"
1838.	....	No charge.	"
1839.	....	"	"
1840.	....	"	"
1841.	....	"	"
1842.	....	"	No Premiums.
1843.	....	"	"
1844.	....	"	"
1845.	....	"	"
1846.	....	"	"
1847.	....	"	"
1848.	.. ..	"	"
1849.	....	No School.	"
1850.	....	"	....
1851.	....	"	....
1852.	....	14 Students, at ...... $5.	No Premiums.
1853.	....	....	....
1854.	....	....	
1855.	....	11 Students, at ...... $5.	No Premiums.
1856.*	....	75 " No charge.	"
1857.	....	91 " "	"
1858.	....	83 " "	"
1859.	....	91 " "	"
1860.	....	91 " "	"

* Under the charge of the Vice-President, T. S. Cummings.

And was so continued, until the removal from the 13th Street Studios to the new building, May, 1865.

INDEX.

364	INDEX.